THE ENTRENCHMENT OF DEMOCRACY

This volume of essays brings together a group of leading political scientists, legal scholars, and political theorists to describe and analyze the body of constitutional law and practice within and upon democratic institutions, in particular examining how constitutional law shapes electoral democracy. Constitutional law and practice on this question are complex and varied. This volume therefore takes a thematic and regional approach: it selects a range of key theoretical questions related to democratic constitutional design and offers a series of chapters featuring a diverse range of voices, as well as a blend of theory, qualitative studies, and quantitative methods. Readers will gain a multifaceted understanding of a phenomenon of growing importance. The volume will also be useful to students of comparative constitutionalism, who will gain a rich array of empirical evidence to stimulate further work. This title is also available as Open Access on Cambridge Core.

TOM GINSBURG is Leo Spitz Distinguished Service Professor of International Law at the University of Chicago and a research scholar at the American Bar Foundation.

AZIZ Z. HUQ is the Frank and Bernice J. Greenberg Professor of Law at the University of Chicago; his most recent book is *The Rule of Law: A Very Short Introduction*.

TARUNABH KHAITAN is the Professor (Chair) of Public Law at the London School of Economics and Political Science and an honorary professorial fellow at Melbourne Law School. Previously, he was Professor of Public Law & Legal Theory at the University of Oxford.

COMPARATIVE CONSTITUTIONAL LAW AND POLICY

Series Editors

Tom Ginsburg *University of Chicago*
Zachary Elkins *University of Texas at Austin*
Ran Hirschl *University of Toronto*

Comparative constitutional law is an intellectually vibrant field that encompasses an increasingly broad array of approaches and methodologies. This series collects analytically innovative and empirically grounded work from scholars of comparative constitutionalism across academic disciplines. Books in the series include theoretically informed studies of single constitutional jurisdictions, comparative studies of constitutional law and institutions, and edited collections of original essays that respond to challenging theoretical and empirical questions in the field.

Books in the Series

The Entrenchment of Democracy: The Comparative Constitutional Design of Elections, Parties, and Voting Tom Ginsburg, Aziz Z. Huq, and Tarunabh Khaitan

Deciphering the Genome of Constitutionalism: The Foundations and Future of Constitutional Identity Ran Hirschl and Yaniv Roznai

Courts that Matter: Activists, Judges, and the Politics of Rights Enforcement Sandra Botero

The Story of Constitutions: Discovering the We in Us Wim Voermans

Democracy Under God: Constitutions, Islam and Human Rights in the Muslim World Dawood Ahmed and Muhammad Zubair Abbasi

Buddhism and Comparative Constitutional Law Edited by Tom Ginsburg and Ben Schonthal

Amending America's Unwritten Constitution Edited by Richard Albert, Ryan C. Williams, and Yaniv Roznai

Constitutionalism and a Right to Effective Government? Edited by Vicki C. Jackson and Yasmin Dawood

The Fall of the Arab Spring: Democracy's Challenges and Efforts to Reconstitute the Middle East Tofigh Maboudi

Filtering Populist Claims to Fight Populism: The Italian Case in a Comparative Perspective Giuseppe Martinico

Constitutionalism in Context David S. Law

The New Fourth Branch: Institutions for Protecting Constitutional Democracy Mark Tushnet

The Veil of Participation: Citizens and Political Parties in Constitution-Making Processes Alexander Hudson

Towering Judges: A Comparative Study of Constitutional Judges Edited by Rehan Abeyratne and Iddo Porat

The Constitution of Arbitration Victor Ferreres Comella

Redrafting Constitutions in Democratic Orders: Theoretical and Comparative Perspectives Edited by Gabriel L. Negretto

From Parchment to Practice: Implementing New Constitutions Edited by Tom Ginsburg and Aziz Z. Huq

The Failure of Popular Constitution Making in Turkey: Regressing Towards Constitutional Autocracy Edited by Felix Petersen and Zeynep Yanaşmayan

A Qualified Hope: The Indian Supreme Court and Progressive Social Change Edited by Gerald N. Rosenberg, Sudhir Krishnaswamy, and Shishir Bail

Reconstructing Rights: Courts, Parties, and Equality Rights in India, South Africa, and the United States Stephan Stohler

Constitutions in Times of Financial Crisis Edited by Tom Ginsburg, Mark D. Rosen, and Georg Vanberg

Hybrid Constitutionalism: The Politics of Constitutional Review in the Chinese Special Administrative Regions Eric C. Ip

Constitution-Making and Transnational Legal Order Edited by Tom Ginsburg, Terence C. Halliday, and Gregory Shaffer

The Invisible Constitution in Comparative Perspective Edited by Rosalind Dixon and Adrienne Stone

The Politico-Legal Dynamics of Judicial Review: A Comparative Analysis Theunis Roux

Constitutional Courts in Asia: A Comparative Perspective Edited by Albert H. Y. Chen and Andrew Harding

Judicial Review in Norway: A Bicentennial Debate Anine Kierulf

Constituent Assemblies Edited by Jon Elster, Roberto Gargarella, Vatsal Naresh, and Bjorn Erik Rasch

The DNA of Constitutional Justice in Latin America: Politics, Governance, and Judicial Design Daniel M. Brinks and Abby Blass

The Adventures of the Constituent Power: Beyond Revolutions? Andrew Arato

Canada in the World: Comparative Perspectives on the Canadian Constitution Edited by Richard Albert and David R. Cameron

Constitutions, Religion and Politics in Asia: Indonesia, Malaysia and Sri Lanka Dian A. H. Shah

Courts and Democracies in Asia Po Jen Yap

Proportionality: New Frontiers, New Challenges Edited by Vicki C. Jackson and Mark Tushnet

Constituents before Assembly: Participation, Deliberation, and Representation in the Crafting of New Constitutions Todd A. Eisenstadt, A. Carl LeVan, and Tofigh Maboudi

Assessing Constitutional Performance Edited by Tom Ginsburg and Aziz Z. Huq

Buddhism, Politics and the Limits of Law: The Pyrrhic Constitutionalism of Sri Lanka Benjamin Schonthal

Engaging with Social Rights: Procedure, Participation and Democracy in South Africa's Second Wave Brian Ray

Constitutional Courts as Mediators: Armed Conflict, Civil-Military Relations, and the Rule of Law in Latin America Julio Ríos-Figueroa

Perils of Judicial Self-Government in Transitional Societies David Kosař

Making We the People: Democratic Constitutional Founding in Postwar Japan and South Korea Chaihark Hahm and Sung Ho Kim

Radical Deprivation on Trial: The Impact of Judicial Activism on Socioeconomic Rights in the Global South César Rodríguez-Garavito and Diana Rodríguez-Franco

Unstable Constitutionalism: Law and Politics in South Asia Edited by Mark Tushnet and Madhav Khosla

Magna Carta and Its Modern Legacy Edited by Robert Hazell and James Melton

Constitutions and Religious Freedom Frank B. Cross

International Courts and the Performance of International Agreements: A General Theory with Evidence from the European Union Clifford J. Carrubba and Matthew J. Gabel

Reputation and Judicial Tactics: A Theory of National and International Courts Shai Dothan

Social Difference and Constitutionalism in Pan-Asia Edited by Susan H. Williams

Constitutionalism in Asia in the Early Twenty-First Century Edited by Albert H. Y. Chen

Constitutions in Authoritarian Regimes Edited by Tom Ginsburg and Alberto Simpser

Presidential Legislation in India: The Law and Practice of Ordinances Shubhankar Dam

Social and Political Foundations of Constitutions Edited by Denis J. Galligan and Mila Versteeg

Consequential Courts: Judicial Roles in Global Perspective Edited by Diana Kapiszewski, Gordon Silverstein, and Robert A. Kagan

Comparative Constitutional Design Edited by Tom Ginsburg

The Entrenchment of Democracy

THE COMPARATIVE CONSTITUTIONAL DESIGN OF ELECTIONS, PARTIES, AND VOTING

Edited by

TOM GINSBURG
University of Chicago

AZIZ Z. HUQ
University of Chicago

TARUNABH KHAITAN
London School of Economics and Political Science

CAMBRIDGE
UNIVERSITY PRESS

CAMBRIDGE
UNIVERSITY PRESS

Shaftesbury Road, Cambridge CB2 8EA, United Kingdom

One Liberty Plaza, 20th Floor, New York, NY 10006, USA

477 Williamstown Road, Port Melbourne, VIC 3207, Australia

314–321, 3rd Floor, Plot 3, Splendor Forum, Jasola District Centre, New Delhi – 110025, India

103 Penang Road, #05–06/07, Visioncrest Commercial, Singapore 238467

Cambridge University Press is part of Cambridge University Press & Assessment, a department of the University of Cambridge.

We share the University's mission to contribute to society through the pursuit of education, learning and research at the highest international levels of excellence.

www.cambridge.org
Information on this title: www.cambridge.org/9781009447737

DOI: 10.1017/9781009447713

First published 2024

A catalogue record for this publication is available from the British Library.

A Cataloging-in-Publication data record for this book is available from the Library of Congress

ISBN 978-1-009-44773-7 Hardback

Contents

Illustrations

FIGURES

TABLES

Contributors

Adem Kassie Abebe is Senior Advisor at the Constitution Building Programme of International IDEA and Extraordinary Lecturer at the Centre for Human Rights, University of Pretoria, South Africa.

Tom Gerald Daly is Professor at Melbourne Law School and Director of the global online research platform Demoptimism (www.demoptimism.org).

Yasmin Dawood is Professor of Law and Canada Research Chair in Democracy, Constitutionalism, and Electoral Law at the University of Toronto.

Rosalind Dixon is Scientia Professor of Law and ARC Future Fellow at the University of New South Wales.

Stephen Gardbaum is Stephen Yeazell Endowed Chair in Law at UCLA Law School.

Tom Ginsburg is Leo Spitz Distinguished Professor of International Law, Ludwig and Hilde Wolfe Research Scholar, and Faculty Director of the Malyi Center for the Study of Institutional and Legal Integrity at the University of Chicago Law School.

Aziz Z. Huq is Frank and Bernice J. Greenberg Professor of Law at the University of Chicago Law School.

Samuel Issacharoff is Bonnie and Richard Reiss Professor of Constitutional Law at NYU Law School.

Brian Christopher Jones is a senior lecturer in law at the University of Liverpool School of Law and Social Justice.

Tarunabh Khaitan is Professor (Chair) of Public Law at the London School of Economics and Political Science.

David Landau is Mason Ladd Professor and Associate Dean for International Programs at Florida State University.

Richard H. Pildes is Sudler Family Professor of Constitutional Law at NYU Law School.

Elizabeth H. Reese is Assistant Professor of Law at Stanford Law School.

Silvia Suteu is Associate Professor of Law at the University College London.

Yvonne Tew is Anne Fleming Research Professor, Professor of Law, and Faculty Director of the Center for Transnational Legal Studies at Georgetown Law Center.

Mila Versteeg is Henry L. and Grace Doherty Charitable Foundation Professor of Law and Director of the Human Rights Program at the University of Virginia Law School.

Acknowledgments

Thank you to Dean Thomas Miles of the University of Chicago Law School, as well as the Russell Baker Scholars Fund and Malyi Center for Institutional and Legal Integrity for supporting the project. We are also grateful to all participants and discussants at the workshop held at the Chicago Law School in 2022 to workshop many of the chapters in this volume.

For research assistance, we thank Marin Murdock. Thanks to Kile McVey of the Malyi Center for help with finalizing the volume.

1

Introduction

Tom Ginsburg, Aziz Z. Huq, and Tarunabh Khaitan

A central function of a written constitution is to set forth "rules about rules," otherwise known as *metarules*, that create a structure for political life. Constitutions do so by providing clear institutional pathways, instructions and limits that guide the subsequent creation of ordinary law and regulations, as well as by shaping the exercise of official discretion. Because these metarules are durable, they do not need to be recreated repeatedly – hence enabling democratic choice over the many policy questions of ordinary quotidian politics. In a democratic society, among the most important constitutional metarules are those that concern the principal offices of state, typically specifying the "who," the "how." and the "when" of selection of their occupants. Because of the centrality of elections to modern democratic practice, the constitution's core task of institutional specification, at least in the context of a democratic order, almost always entails close attention to how electoral contestation will unfold, what spatial units of representation will be used, how preferences will be translated into outcomes, the duration of office-holding, and the terms or conditions concerning when and how transfer of power will (or must) occur.[1]

In modern accounts of how democracies work and thrive, these who, how, and when questions are considered in light of the ambition to create durable democratic rotation through broad popular participation in meaningfully competitive elections. The practical operation of elections, in turn, usually depend upon the existence of political parties.[2] The latter typically (albeit not inevitably) play a central role in providing legible choices and hence lowering information costs for voters (which, Tarunabh Khaitan in Chapter 4 argues, is one of four key democracy-related costs that parties reduce). The party label conveys information and allows voters to both punish incumbent regimes and meaningfully anticipate the effects of voting for a neophyte candidate. In their contest over the possession of representative political

[1] Modern democracy is realized through elections, with sortition being infrequently deployed. Perhaps this is a mistake. But we stick here to that modal observed institutional choice.

[2] There are nonpartisan elections, for instance, in the context of judicial selection in some US states, too.

offices, political parties hence critically provide an epistemic structure for political life that endures over time and between different elements of government. They give electoral politics temporal and geographic cohesion and,. as Khaitan puts it, "grease the wheels of representative democracy."[3]

It is not just that parties are central to the functioning of constitutions. The choice of constitutional arrangements conversely shapes parties in vital ways. That is, a constitution's design creates and distributes the incentives for party formation and organization. Parties emerge endogenously within a particular constitutional order. Hence, they tend to be tailored to those regimes (although this does not necessarily mean that their incentives align with the goal of regime preservation). When designing offices and electoral institutions, then, constitution-makers are also calibrating the incentive structures of political life. By shaping the rules of politics, they are crafting its core players.

Less frequently noted, but no less important, is the role that political parties play in promoting a constitution's endurance. Parties emerge in ways that are adapted to specific constitutional arrangements. A change to those arrangements can be costly for a party, inducing a sort of Burkean orientation toward institutional rules. Relatedly, a party's collective leadership typically has a longer time horizon than a particular leader. Because the party (if not the leader) often has an investment in the endurance of the constitution's metarules as such, it may act to check a potential strongman or -woman. This offers a subtle friction against a leader's aggrandizing aspirations toward one-person rule. Further, a constitution's stable metarules for democratic competition ideally offer losing parties grounds to anticipate that they could have a shot again at political power through the ballot box, so that they need not resort to short-term violence. Parties hence have good reasons to keep in place constitutional protections (such as free speech rights) for opposition actors. This effect may be especially acute in federalized regimes, where a party might be both in power and in opposition at different levels of government.

Despite political parties' important constitutional functions, the burgeoning literature in comparative constitutional studies contains relatively few contributions that systematically address parties' constitutional functions, or that explore systematically the constitutional law of electoral design more generally. Writing of the British constitutional order, Vernon Bogdanor once noted that "it is perhaps because the law has been so late in recognizing political parties that constitutional lawyers and other writers on the constitution have taken insufficient note of the fact that parties are so central to our constitutional arrangements."[4] The same can be said more generally of comparative constitutional scholarship across the globe.

[3] See Chapter 4.

[4] Vernon Bogdanor, "The Constitution and the Party System in the Twentieth Century," *Parliamentary Affairs* 57(4): 718–733 (2004), cited in Ingrid Van Biezen, "Constitutionalizing Party Democracy: The Constitutive Codification of Political Parties in Post-war Europe," *British Journal of Political Science* 42(1): 187–212 (2012), at 189.

To be sure, some of these questions have received attention in the political science literature. Of particular importance is work on the ways in which constitutional design and the embedded choice of electoral systems shape party formation. Much of this work turns on a dichotomous distinction between first-past-the-post district elections and proportional representation, charting the effect of this binary choice on party systems[5] and the consequent quality of democratic rule.[6] Further, a debate dating back several decades has fleshed out in illuminating detail the relative merits of presidential, semi-presidential, parliamentary, and – more recently – semi-parliamentary systems.[7] Yet much of this scholarly discussion has proceeded at a fairly high level of generality. It offers judgments on stark, binary choices based on analyses of acontextual big-N datasets. It is often penned by political scientists, who are not focused on the granular legal details of the constitutional metarules. While a useful starting point, this literature leaves unaddressed many questions of singular importance: What kinds of details of election and party system–design should be addressed in constitutions? When, in contrast, should those questions be left to the democratic process itself through statutes or regulation? When should rules be nationally uniform, and when can they be left to local or substate actors? How can the constitutional design of election systems (and hence of party systems) facilitate the larger ends of democratic rotation and endurance? What trade-offs exist in the design of electoral systems? How do choices concerning electoral systems and legislative-executive relations interact with choices in the design of central government or vertical choices of federalism? Are there independent, nonpartisan, judicial and "fourth branch" guarantor institutions (such as boundary commissions and electoral commissions) that should be assigned or allowed a place in electoral system design? If so, what is their role? Has the recent era of democratic backsliding, which has seen the employment of novel, subtler, and more incremental tools to undermine democracy, changed the answers to these questions? Finally, and most foundationally, is a transhistorical or historically durable, albeit modest, constitutional "theory" of elections and parties wise or possible? Or are those constitutional questions irredeemably anchored in contingent, local, and temporally situated dynamics?

5 Maurice Duverger, *Political Parties: Their Organization and Activity in the Modern State*. John Wiley & Sons, 1954; Arend Lijphart, "The Political Consequences of Electoral Laws, 1945–85," *American Political Science Review* 84(2): 481–496 (1990); Michael Gallagher and Paul Mitchell, eds. *The Politics of Electoral Systems*. Oxford University Press, 2005.

6 Larry Diamond and Marc F. Plattner, eds. *Electoral Systems and Democracy*. Johns Hopkins University Press, 2006.

7 Torsten Persson and Guido Tabellini, *The Economic Effects of Constitutions*. MIT Press, 2003; see also Steffen Ganghof, *Beyond Presidentialism and Parliamentarism: Democratic Design and the Separation of Powers*. Oxford University Press, 2022); Tarunabh Khaitan, "Balancing Accountability and Effectiveness: A Case for Moderated Parliamentarism," *Canadian Journal of Comparative & Contemporary Law* 7: 81 (2021).

This volume is an effort to address some of these, and related, puzzles. Its chapters examine the constitutional treatment of parties and elections both as a matter of theory and from the perspective of nationally and regionally specific historical and contemporary practice. To this end, it draws together a series of contributions from a diverse range of scholars working in distinct disciplines. This approach aims to take advantage of the perspectives distinctive to each discipline. Political scientists tend to treat political parties as their key object of study, while comparative constitutional lawyers have largely ignored them, preferring to focus on other institutional questions. What follows brings each perspective into conversation with the other. The characteristic disciplinary positivism of political scientists and the typical normative optimism of constitutional lawyers, we hope, create the dialectic necessary for significant intellectual progress on the topic.

This introduction frames the conceptual challenges of constitutional design that all the contributors to this volume grapple with, as well as providing some more general context. It canvasses, in particular, various models of constitutional treatment of elections and parties before introducing the contributions that follow.

1.1 CONSTITUTIONS TO FACILITATE POLITICS

Like any competitive game, democratic contestation requires certain ground rules. One needs to know, at the most basic level, which offices of state that candidates can vie for; what qualifications are required to run and to vote for such offices; when elections are to be held; who and how votes are to be counted, and in what geographic units; and how potential disputes about eligibility and accuracy will be resolved. This list, to be sure, is illustrative, not exclusive. Yet with increasing frequency, many of these questions are resolved in constitutional text because of a sense among constitutional scholars and designers that a core constitutional function is to provide an enduring structure for democratic politics.

As a technology of specifically democratic governance, written constitutions are attractive because of two typical characteristics: their supremacy and their entrenchment. Constitutions are not just normatively superior to statutes, regulations, or executive actions. In many jurisdictions, they are the *highest* legal norm, superseding even international law. While most constitutions generate norms that are legal in character, not all constitutional rules are enforceable in a court. This quality of "non-justiciability," as it is known in the technical literature, does not mean those rules cannot be both efficacious and also fundamental to the governance of the state.[8] Rather, constitutionalization endows a normative legitimation to certain rules that may give them force even without a judicial sanction. To that end, appeals are often made to the hypothetical authority of a *pouvoir constituent*. In the political

[8] Tarunabh Khaitan, "Constitutional Directives: Morally-Committed Political Constitutionalism," *Modern Law Review* 82: 603–632 (2019).

theology of democratic constitutions, the "people" have chosen this particular set of metarules. Supremacy facilitates legitimacy. Alternatively, constitutional supremacy can be defended on the ground that its abandonment would quickly give way to Hobbesian anarchy. On this view, supremacy is a response to the brute demands of realpolitik.

Entrenchment is the idea that constitutional norms are typically harder to amend than ordinary law. An organic document can hence take certain issues off the table or make some elements of the status quo ante more difficult to change.[9] Removing issues from ordinary politics is useful when participants in a democracy believe that their core interests are at stake and such that leaving questions open to democratic revision creates intolerable uncertainty. This logic often underwrites the creation of constitutional rights. Alternatively, there may be a fear that leaving a question to change by simple legislative majorities will create perilous instability.[10]

Even where norms are not entrenched legally, political practice can engender de facto entrenchment by inducing beliefs and attitudes in key political actors. Consider here the Australian convention that the Governor General must assent to every Bill duly passed by both Houses of Parliament. This norm persists despite clear text to the contrary in section 58 of the Constitution, which leaves the matter to her discretion.[11] Such rules are politically entrenched in the sense that changing them would typically attract considerable public resistance and so demand the expenditure of significant political capital. As a result of this grip on political elites' collective imagination, they can also provide a stable basis for political life.[12] Judicially-enforced constitutional norms are therefore not the sole means of stabilizing democratic constitutions.

At the same time, the idea of entrenchment should not be taken too literally or too far. It is easy to assume, especially in a field dominated by the study of US practice, that entrenchment in constitutional text will induce insurmountable difficulties in amending the constitution. The actual practice of constitutionalism around the world is quite different. The American model of rigid entrenchment is a distinct outlier. In general, constitutional entrenchment makes change difficult but not politically impossible. Its modal mechanism, as Adem Abebe (Chapter 6) explores, is one that frustrates the ruling party's ability to make a constitutional change unilaterally, while allowing for constitutional change that enjoys broader political consensus from the ruling party as well as from sections of the opposition.

[9] Stephen Holmes, *Passions and Constraint*. University of Chicago Press, 1995; Cass Sunstein, *Designing Democracy: What Constitutions Do*. Oxford University Press, 2001.

[10] Kenneth J. Arrow, "A Difficulty in the Concept of Social Welfare," *Journal of Political Economy* 58: 328–346 (1950); Stephen Holmes, "Gag Rules or the Politics of Omission," *Constitutionalism and Democracy* 19–58 (1988).

[11] It is unclear whether the convention permits an exception where the assent is refused on the advice of ministers (yet not a matter of the Governor General's discretion). See Anne Twomey, "The Refusal or Deferral of Royal Assent," *Public Law*: 580–602 (2006).

[12] Nicholas Barber, *The United Kingdom Constitution*. Oxford University Press, 2021, ch. 6.

On the other hand, in many jurisdictions there are likely to be many sub-constitutional arrangements that are not legally or constitutionally entrenched but are nonetheless very difficult or de facto impossible to change because of widely shared beliefs or attitudes.

Even without supremacy or an extreme form of entrenchment, constitutional texts can facilitate democratic politics by providing simple rules for coordination. Without some designation of who holds legislative power, for how long, and to what ends, citizens and residents cannot answer the basic question of what is valid law. Without knowing how a head of state is chosen, conflict over who has the role might be destabilizing. And without rules for the timing and composition for a first session of parliament, as well as other "first period" solutions,[13] a polity might be trapped in an infinite regress trying to determine how to open official proceedings. Simple coordination on the names, nature, and timing of offices, as well as how office-holders are selected, is essential for any durable system of collective decision-making.

One might think that the basic democratic design of the political system should always be entrenched beyond revision through ordinary democratic processes. A government that can use its transient turn in power to completely change the rules of political competition would be sorely tempted to make its temporary grip on power more durable, even permanent. This creates worries in terms of both moral hazard and a related dynamic of adverse selection. Moral hazard occurs when sitting politicians try to change the rules to retain their office and insulate themselves from electoral challenge. The very possibility of such a move creates in turn the problem of adverse selection: In effect, the electoral system would create greater payoffs for anti-democrats than democrats, drawing bad actors into the system and squeezing out those who would rather compete on fair terms. Constitutionalizing basic elements of electoral choice beyond easy change helps tamp down on these complementary risks.

All this is to say that some choices need to be entrenched in a constitution to enable democratic politics. But which ones, to what extent, and in how much detail? The entrenchment frame suggests that constitutions might want to be very comprehensive in detailing the rules of political competition. A constitutional designer may think that the risk of leaving any metarules to the whims of self-interested politicians is simply not worth the candle.

Yet there are countervailing considerations, even setting aside the dubious idea that we can distinguish selfless constitutional designers and self-serving politicos. For one thing, we might not be sure we have the right answer at the time of constitution-making to some specific design question – say, the most desirable spatial dimensions of representational units. The "optimal" geographic units, or voting rules, might also

[13] See generally Tom Ginsburg and Aziz Z. Huq, eds., *From Parchment to Practice: The First Period Problem of Constitutional Implementation*. Cambridge University Press, 2020.

change over time (say, as the polity enlarges to include groups previously denied recognition as full citizens, or as technological change leads to different patterns of economic activity). Entrenchment may make intuitive sense when it comes to fundamental rights on the theory that these embody enduring moral interests for which we think there are always limited justifications for infringement. But the same is rarely thought to be so when it comes to the design of political institutions. There may be no obviously decisive normative case for having, say, 200 or 300 members of the legislature, or holding elections on the Saturday of the third or fourth week of May. Nor have political scientists identified a universal "correct" answer to the choice between majoritarian, district-based elections, and multimember, proportional representation systems. Even the well-debated issue of whether presidentialism, parliamentarism, semi-presidentialism, or semi-parliamentarism is better remains up for grabs.[14]

For many of these questions, the "optimal" choice is likely to turn on some mix of the durable feature of the polity (say, geography, demography, history or education) and some of its more transient features. Even if there was an obvious normatively preferable option for a given context, it is possible that political constraints and path dependencies require a constitution's framers to settle for sub-par alternatives. Or new circumstances – say the emergence of digital social media platforms – can render design choices that were normatively optimal in the past perverse or ineffective. As technological, social, or economic conditions change, the *demos* can (and, often, should) decide to modify its view, either through its elected representatives or by acting directly (through, say, a referendum) or in concert with its representatives. This counsels for a more limited extent of constitutionalization or a general open and viable route to constitutional amendment.

This is not the only possible pathway. A constitution can also create "variable speeds" of amendment difficulty. It can assign issues where less certainty obtains to a "lower" level of entrenchment than (say) fundamental rights.[15] There are many design possibilities. But the core point here is that that maximal entrenchment is not always desirable. There is some unavoidable trade-off between the need for rigidity and flexibility in constitutional design.

One might also assume that only the very important issues ought to be put into the constitution. But again this is not obviously desirable. Very trivial issues, such as the choice of the first or the second Sunday of December for an election, might also be constitutionalized precisely because there is no strong reason for a particular choice. Further, the gains from the coordination enabled by a durable settlement (and the absence of conflict or opportunities for gamesmanship) may be greater than

[14] Jose Cheibub, *Presidentialism, Parliamentarism and Democracy*. Cambridge University Press, 2006.

[15] Rosalind Dixon and David Landau, "Tiered Constitutional Design," *The George Washington Law Review* 86: 438–512 (2018).

the risk of spending scarce political energy on it later on. As Louis Brandeis put it, sometimes it is more important that an issue be settled than it be settled correctly.[16] By deciding a divisive issue once and for all, a constitutional designer preserves political attention for more important tasks down the road. To use a metaphor introduced by Hannah Arendt, constitutions set the furniture that we can then use to engage in democratic debate and decision.[17]

Very important issues, on the other hand, should be put into the constitution precisely because not doing so risks overwhelming and distorting ordinary politics. If each incoming government could completely overhaul critical elements of the political system unilaterally, this would create the aforementioned moral-hazard and adverse-selection problems. When the stakes of political competition are too high, there is little incentive to give up power upon electoral loss, such that electoral rotation is undermined. By lowering the political stakes, constitutionalization can help mitigate this problem, making democracy more durable. Of course, the status quo preserved by this strategy may well be sufficiently morally objectionable, such that any pro-democracy gain seems insufficient. The antebellum American experience with slavery exemplifies this possibility. Constitutional rigidity is only as valuable as the substantive merit of the system thereby preserved.

An intermediate path between constitutional silence and comprehensive constitutionalization of the metarules is to direct the legislature to adopt rules within a broad constitutionally prescribed framework without fully specifying their content. In this vein, so-called by-law clauses are frequently used for issues related to the political system and election.[18] A constitution may use by-law clauses to establish a broad framework for elections and political parties, while leaving regulatory details to be determined by a specific (sub-constitutional) statute, which the legislature must enact post-ratification.[19] Roughly one in ten constitutions in force, for example, leave the question of the immunity of legislators from either civil or criminal process to ordinary law. Similarly, 15 percent of constitutions in force explicitly leave to ordinary law the process for replacing individual legislators who are no longer able to serve. A further 14 percent leave legislator salaries to ordinary law.[20] Virtually every democratic country has a sub-constitutional electoral law that provides for the details of election management. And the enactment of these laws is often directed by the constitution itself. Kenya's 2010 constitution includes a long list of provisions about parties, requiring that they have a national, non-ethnic character,

16 *Burnet v. Coronado Oil & Gas Co.*, 285 U.S. 393 (1932); see also David Strauss, "Common Law, Common Ground, and Jefferson's Principle," *Yale Law Journal* 122: 1731–1735 (2003).

17 For discussion of Arendt's metaphor, see Jeremy Waldron, *Political Political Theory: Essays on Institutions*. Harvard University Press, 2016.

18 Rosalind Dixon and Tom Ginsburg, "Deciding Not to Decide," *International Journal of Constitutional Law* 9: 636–672 (2010).

19 See, e.g., Const. Cape Verde (1980), Art. 127 ("Political parties may only be barred by judicial decision and in cases established by law.").

20 Data on file with authors.

and that they be internally democratic and refrain from violence. It then requires an electoral law to be passed by parliament within a year and that a code of conduct for political parties be produced by the Independent Electoral and Boundaries Commission.[21]

As a matter of observed practice, constitutional designers are increasingly choosing to weigh in on these questions. As Ginsburg and Versteeg show in Chapter 5, constitutional texts now say more and more about parties and elections, including by providing for new electoral institutions such as commissions and electoral management bodies as part of the "fourth branch" of regulatory ("guarantor") institutions.[22] Constitutions have also consolidated parties' positions as central actors in the democratic process, even as their actual role as agents of representation is weakening in many democracies.[23] Even when using by-law clauses, constitutions increasingly limit the discretion of ordinary legislators by allowing judicial review of whether the legislature has created (say) an electoral commission with the constitutionally mandated degree of independence.[24] This paradox of greater substantive regulation in an era in which democracies overall have experienced a decline in performance reflects a core challenge of our moment.

1.2 CHALLENGES

In his classic book, *Party Government*, the American political scientist E. E. Schattschneider wrote that "political parties created democracy and ... modern democracy is unthinkable save in terms of parties."[25] Elections, by definition, create winners and losers. A losing party must have some incentive to return to the fray rather than overturn the chessboard with protests or violence. It should be incentivized instead to jettison unpopular leaders and policies or to restrain figures that might be tempted to remain beyond their elected term. So nudged, well-functioning parties make an enduring system of representation possible, not least by creating a

[21] Const. Kenya, Art. 88 (IEBC); Art. 91 (character of parties); Art. 92 (legislation).

[22] Mark Tushnet, *The New Fourth Branch*. Cambridge University Press, 2021. Tarunabh Khaitan, "Guarantor Institutions," *Asian Journal of Comparative Law* 16: S40–S59 (2021); Tarunabh Khaitan, "Guarantor (or 'Fourth Branch') Institutions" in *Cambridge Handbook of Constitutional Theory* ed. Jeff King and Richard Bellamy. Cambridge University Press, 2024; Heinz Klug, "Transformative Constitutions and the Role of Integrity Institutions in Tempering Power: The Case of Resistance to State Capture in Post-Apartheid South Africa," *Buffalo Law Review* 67: 701 (2019).

[23] Van Biezen, "Constitutionalizing Party Democracy."

[24] See Glenister cases from South Africa; also *APDH v. Côte D'Ivoire*, African Court on Human and Peoples' Rights (2016), www.african-court.org/en/images/Cases/Judgment/JUDGMENT_APPLICATION%20001%202014%20_%20APDH%20V.%20THE%20REPUBLIC%20OF%20COTE%20DIVOIRE.pdf.

[25] E. E. Schattschneider, *Party Government*. Routledge, 1942.

vehicle for carrying forward the interests of defeated politicians over the horizon of electoral loss.[26]

In recent decades, however, some democracies have been suffering from what some have called a "crisis of representation," involving a sharp decline in the strength of relationships between a party's rank-and-file and its leaders. The classic account of such a decline of parties is the late Peter Mair's analysis of European politics. Mair showed how Europe's political elites remodeled themselves as a homogeneous professional class, withdrawing into state institutions that offered relative stability against fickle voters' preferences. At the same time, non-democratic agencies and practices proliferated and gained credibility – not least among them the European Union itself.[27] Other accounts suggest that globalization has given us an economy with a mobile cosmopolitan elite pitted against a larger, far less wealthy group that is locally bound and economically precarious.[28] Under such conditions, traditional parties are no longer able or willing to screen out anti-institutionalist autocrats; nor are they able to provide effective representation. This has led to calls, by Frances McCall Rosenbluth and Ian Shapiro most prominently, for a concerted effort to revitalize parties.[29] Kim Lane Scheppele argues that "The Party's Over," at least the traditional mainstream ones, in that such parties are in decline as social and representative institutions even as they remain necessary for a healthy democracy.[30] She claims that the main reason for the collapse of mainstream parties is that the traditional left-right economic axis of politics has been superimposed by a cross-cutting cosmopolitan-nativist axis, but parties have not yet managed to reorganize themselves sufficiently along the new axes. In the terms Khaitan uses in Chapter 4, this development leaves salient voter types without a partisan home, thus breaching the "party system optimization principle" (one of four principles he argues constitutions should account for in relation to party systems).

A crisis of parties (or, better, of party *systems*) has metastasized in many countries into a more pluralist and less containable crisis of constitutional democracy. Instead of facilitating the predictable ebb and flow of representation that makes democracy possible, some parties have themselves become a vehicle of democratic

[26] Bernard Manin, *The Principles of Representative Government.* Cambridge University Press, 1997.

[27] Peter Mair, *Ruling the Void: The Hollowing of Western Democracy.* Verso Books, 2013. For a different diagnosis from a more easterly longitude, see Stephen Holmes and Ivan Krastev. *The Light That Failed.* Simon and Schuster, 2020.

[28] David Goodhart, *The Road to Somewhere: The Populist Revolt and the Future of Politics.* Oxford University Press, 2017. For an important challenge to this view, see Marc Stears, *Out of the Ordinary: How Everyday Life Inspired a Nation and How It Can Again.* Belknap Press, 2021.

[29] Frances McCall Rosenbluth and Ian Shapiro, *Responsible Parties: Saving Democracy from Itself.* Yale University Press, 2018.

[30] Kim Lane Scheppele, "The Party's Over," in *Constitutional Democracy in Crisis?* ed. Mark Graber, Sanford Levinson, and Mark Tushnet. Oxford University Press 2018, 495–515.

backsliding.[31] In some cases, they have repudiated the principle of rotation in office, leading to what some of us have called partisan degradation of democracy.[32] Such parties aim to replace the constitutional entrenchment of uncertainty with the certainty of partisan entrenchment.

Party-led degradation can unfold in a couple of different ways. In some instances, an insurgent party takes advantage of a capsizing system of previously hegemonic actors to stake out a new claim and lock up political office. In other cases, a formerly mainstream party can be hijacked by demagogic populists, who then seek to fuse it with institutions of the state. We observe examples of both phenomena around the world today. In the first category, Jair Bolsonaro's Social Liberal party in Brazil had won less than 1 percent of votes in the legislative contest prior to his successful presidential run. The Philippines' Rodrigo Duterte rode to power in 2016 under the banner of the Partido Demokratiko Pilipino–Lakas ng Bayan (PDP-Laban), which held only one legislative seat at the time of his nomination. Examples of the second category include Donald Trump's ascent within the Republican Party in the United States and (arguably) Narendra Modi's rise in India's BJP.[33] In Chapter 2, Richard Pildes and Samuel Issacharoff explicate how it is that minorities or individuals within parties can execute a take-over, facilitated by a series of poor regulatory choices.

In either of these scenarios, the ultimate result is that parties cannot restrain their anti-democratic leaders. The direction of representation is reversed. The party is either founded as, or becomes a vehicle of, concentrated personal power, rather than as a vehicle of deliberation and coordinated group action. Such dynamics are common in weak democracies generally.[34] But they are a relatively new feature in more established democracies. Once an autocratic leader personalizes the party, and hence makes contests over political office a matter of personality rather than policy, elections can take on an all-or-nothing quality. They can be framed as existential contests that can undermine the fabric of society itself. Democratic continuity will then be at stake.

31 Tom Gerald Daly and Brian Christopher Jones, "Parties versus Democracy: Addressing Today's Political Party Threats to Democratic Rule," *International Journal of Constitutional Law* 18: 509–538 (2020); Tarunabh Khaitan, "Killing a Constitution with a Thousand Cuts: Executive Aggrandizement and Party-State Fusion," *India' Law and Ethics of Human Rights* 14: 49–95 (2020).

32 Aziz Huq and Tom Ginsburg, *How to Save a Constitutional Democracy*. University of Chicago Press, 2018.

33 Of course, note that both examples are controversial: Modi and Trump can also be seen as the manifestations of anti-democratic psychological trends already latent in the Bharatiya Janata Party and the Republican Party respectively. Obviously, we take no position on that debate here.

34 Mouli Banerjee, "Here, There, and Everywhere: Locating the Political Party in Democratic Transitions and Backslides," in *Democratic Consolidation and Constitutional Endurance: Comparing Uneven Pathways in Asia and Africa* ed. Tom Gerald Daly and Dinesha Samararatne. Oxford University Press, 2023, 81–98.

How a constitutional order should respond to threats from political parties is therefore one of the difficult normative questions of our time. Answering it requires attention to the contributions of both positive social science and normative political theory. Even if one cannot get to an "ought" from an "is," the real-world plausibility of adopting normative solutions should inform discussion. Addressing these challenges, it is inevitable that we seek to unearth lessons from existing models of democratic politics. It is to these models that we now turn.

1.3 MODELS OF CONSTITUTIONALIZING ELECTIONS AND PARTIES

Over time, two different constitutional models have emerged for regulating politics with an eye to preserving its democratic cast. These could be called respectively first-order and second-order regulation. By "model," we here mean a configuration of several institutional features that tend to co-occur, either by convention or by internal logic. These models can provide a template for jurisdictions to develop bespoke institutional designs.

A *first-order* – or command-and-control – regulatory model seeks to identify rogue parties that threaten democracy in order to ban or punish them. *Second-order* regulatory models, on the other hand, emphasize the importance of "background competitive structures" that shape decision-making, instead of seeking to police behavior directly through first-order commands directed at political actors.[35] A constitution organized along these lines seeks to craft these background competitive structures so as to make it difficult for anti-democratic parties to acquire or wield political power. These two models are not necessarily alternatives. Rather, they can exist simultaneously in the same jurisdiction.

First-order regulatory models can take one of two forms: (i) substantive regulation to protect democratic competition and democratic values and (ii) non-substantive regulation to ensure partisan non-domination. The most well-known model of substantively regulating anti-democratic parties is that of so-called *militant democracy*, developed by Karl Loewenstein in the 1930s.[36] Loewenstein was addressing the immediate problem of European fascist parties that had taken power through legal and democratic means during the interwar period. A modern encapsulation of their approach to democracy is the phrase "one man, one vote, one time." To inoculate political systems against such threats, Lowenstein recommended prima facie undemocratic measures. These included bans of political parties with antidemocratic programs; hate speech restrictions; and "eternity clauses," such as those

[35] Samuel Issacharoff and Richard H. Pildes, "Politics as Markets: Partisan Lockups of the Democratic Process," *Stanford Law Review*: 643–717 (1998), at 647.

[36] Karl Loewenstein, "Militant Democracy and Fundamental Rights I," *American Political Science Review* 31(3): 417–432 (1937); Karl Loewenstein, "Militant Democracy and Fundamental Rights II," *American Political Science Review* 31(4): 638–658 (1937).

discussed by Silvia Suteu in Chapter 12. All of these instruments are supposed to be deployed to protect the democratic basis of the state from constitutional amendments; and limits on political speech. (Some authors include term limits for high executive offices under the "militant democracy" rubric too.)[37] Several of Loewenstein's ideas were adopted in Germany's 1949 Basic Law as guarantees of a "free democratic order."[38]

The literature on militant democracy is large and growing, as is the popularity of its institutional recommendations.[39] Ginsburg and Versteeg, in Chapter 5, document the expansion of these clauses in constitutional texts. As a result of militant democracy's diffusion, roughly 30 percent of constitutions in force either prohibit a specific party or a type of party program. In Africa, several countries ban parties of an ethnic or regional character.[40] Poland's constitution bans parties "whose programs are based upon totalitarian methods and activities of Nazism, fascism and communism."[41] Militant democracy is not restricted to schemes in which it is subject to explicit constitutional embrace . Some constitutional courts have gotten into the action through the invention of the doctrine of "unconstitutional constitutional amendments."[42] Such judicial moves can be facilitated by eternity clauses, but their deployment frequently goes well beyond constitutional texts.[43] This phenomenon highlights a technocratic implication of militant democracy: *some* institution – typically the apex court – must be put in position to evaluate who can participate in democratic politics.

Militant democracy provisions have their advocates. But in recent years, the risks associated with their adoption have also come increasingly to the fore.[44] Militant democracy tools are attractive to prevent the rise of undemocratic parties. But once

37 Zachary Elkins, "Militant Democracy and the Pre-emptive Constitution: From Party Bans to Hardened Term Limits," *Democratization* 29(1): 174–198 (2022).

38 Basic Law of Federal Republic of Germany, Art. 21.

39 See, e.g., Jan-Werner Müller, "Militant Democracy," in *The Oxford Handbook of Comparative Constitutional Law* ed. Michel Rosenfeld and Andras Sajó. Oxford University Press, 2012, 1253–1269; Alexander Kirshner, A *Theory of Militant Democracy: The Ethics of Combating Political Extremism*. Yale University Press, 2014; Anthoula Malkopoulou and Ludvig Norman, "Three Models of Democratic Self-defence: Militant Democracy and Its Alternatives," *Political Studies* 66(2): 442–458 (2018); Andras Sajo, "Militant Democracy and Emotional Politics," *Constellations: An International Journal of Critical and Democratic Theory* 19 (4): 562–574 (2012); also Giovanni Capoccia, *Defending Democracy: Reactions to Extremism in Interwar Europe*. John Hopkins University Press, 2007, 203–220; Giovanni Capoccia, "Militant Democracy: The Institutional Bases of Democratic Self-Preservation," *Annual Review of Law and Social Science* 9: 207–226 (2013). For an extension to the social media platform context, see Aziz Z. Huq, "Militant Democracy Comes to the Metaverse," *Emory Law Journal* 72: 1105–1141 (2023).

40 E.g., Const. Niger Art. 9 ("political parties with an ethnic regionalist or religious character are prohibited").

41 Const. Poland Art. 13.

42 Yaniv Roznai. *Unconstitutional Constitutional Amendments*. Oxford University Press, 2016.

43 Silvia Suteu, *Eternity Clauses in Democratic Constitutionalism*. Oxford University Press, 2021.

44 Rune Møller Stopp and Benjamin Ask Popp-Madsen, "Defending Democracy: Militant and Popular Models of Democratic Self-defense," *Constellations* 29: 310–328 (2022).

such a party has taken power, the tools of militant democracy can be used against those they were designed to protect. The Hun Sen regime in Cambodia, for example, has used hate speech and anti-terrorism laws to harass and ban political opposition. A concern with the "abusive" use of party-bans to undermine rather than uphold democracy is particularly important in an era of democratic backsliding.

One variant has been put forward by Jan-Werner Müller called "soft militant democracy." This does not rely on the heavy-handed tool of party ban. Instead, it limits undemocratic parties' effective reach by making "life for the party difficult."[45] He offers the example of Israel, which does not ban racist parties, or those that deny the State's "Jewish and Democratic" character. Rather, Israel prohibits such groups from registering for Knesset elections. India also does not allow certain kinds of speech appealing to religion and ethnicity during election campaigns, even though it is generally legal at other times.[46] (Of course, it might be questioned whether either Israeli or Indian law have been successful in excluding anti-system parties from political office.) Denying parties access to public financing or broadcasting time is another option. Application of anti-discrimination norms to political parties is yet another such "soft" substantive intervention. In Germany, in a recent case concerning the National Democratic Party, a far-right group with an anti-democratic program, the Constitutional Court refused to ban the party but permitted some less dramatic measures to be taken against it.[47] In this way, a democratic system allows undemocratic speech, and so avoids the risks and potential blowback of censorship, while penalizing politicians who refuse to moderate their appeals in conformity with inclusive democratic norms.

It could also be argued that intraparty democracy helps to protect democratic governance more broadly. Some constitutions, like Germany's, require that political parties maintain internally democratic processes for leadership and candidate selection.[48] The argument is that internal democracy is a device for discouraging personalism or other autocratic forms of organization. It could also ensure epistemic openness, so parties change policy positions as their ordinary members change their minds. At the same time, it is unclear as an empirical matter whether a substantive

[45] Jan-Werner Müller, "Protecting Popular Self-government from the People? New Normative Perspectives on Militant Democracy," *Annual Review of Political Science* 19: 249–265 (2016), at 259.

[46] However, the Supreme Court has held that "Hindutva" (politico-cultural ideology based on the Hindu identity) is a "way of life," distinct from Hinduism, and therefore carved out an exception for campaigning for majoritarian ethos: *Prabhoo v. Kunte*, 1996 AIR 1113.

[47] BVerfG, Judgment of the Second Senate of 17 January 2017 – 2 BvB 1/1, paras. 1–1010, www.bverfg.de/e/bs20170117_2bvb000113en.html.

[48] See, e.g., Const. Kenya, Art. 92 ("Every political party shall . . . have a democratically elected governing body; promote and uphold national unity; [and] abide by the democratic principles of good governance, promote and practise democracy through regular, fair and free elections within the party . . ."); Edwin Babeiya, "Internal Party Democracy in Tanzania: A Reflection on Three Decades of Multiparty Politics," in *Democracy, Elections, and Constitutionalism in Africa* ed. Charles Fombad and Nico Steytler. Oxford University Press, 2021.

legal requirement of intraparty democracy is indeed causally related to the creation of a more democratic polity. One could even postulate, instead, that stringent intra-democracy rules within parties may damage the quality of a democracy. More extreme base voters who tend to vote in intraparty elections are often more likely to prefer extremist candidates than the party establishment, driving a party toward anti-democratic stances.[49] The effectiveness of a legal requirement of intraparty democracy as an effective tool of soft militant democracy is therefore yet to be established.

All militant democracy models of constitutionalizing power ultimately depend on the availability of "neutral" observers to identify and discipline undemocratic parties. This has given rise to critique of militant democracy as elitist.[50] Stopp and Popp-Madsen argue that militant democratic tools rest upon a "depoliticizing, elitist, and exclusionary understanding of politics, relying on handing power to unelected and potentially unaccountable technocrats or jurists."[51] This critique has special force in an era of populism. Technocratic and elite institutions are suspect. The use of tools viewed as elitist to discipline popular movements risks adding fuel to the fire of antidemocratic populism. Theorizing in this vein, Tom Daly and Brian Christopher Jones in Chapter 7 argue that party bans can sometimes be counterproductive and potentially make the banned party even more appealing, since the party can style itself a martyr or can reincarnate itself with a new label, offering a brand of politics that they call "far-right lite."

Could we avoid or reduce the danger parties pose to democracy without requiring a (typically unelected) body to reach controversial judgments about which party and which candidate is sufficiently democratic? This is what the non-substantive first-order regulation seeks to achieve by focusing on securing partisan non-domination – that is, a system in which no party or parties have systemic or structural advantages that allow them to dominate other parties. Although there is considerable debate on the definition of what constitutes a dominant party or a dominant party system, the literature tends to reserve the term for a party that wins a (sufficiently large) threshold number of seats/votes (usually a majority or a supermajority of seats and a plurality or majority of votes), over a sufficiently long and unbroken period of time (such as three continuous election cycles), with a divided, dispersed, or negligible opposition.[52] Systems in which one or more parties dominate others may be classified based on (i) the number of dominant parties, (ii) the extent of their domination over the political system, and (iii) the mode of political domination.

49 For exploration of this complex question in one jurisdiction, see Stephen Gardbaum and Richard H. Pildes, "Populism and Institutional Design: Methods of Selecting Candidates for Chief Executive," *NYU Law Review* 93: 647 (2018).

50 Malkopoulou and Norman, "Models of Democratic Self-defence."

51 Stopp and Popp-Madsen, "Defending Democracy."

52 For an overview of the literature, see Matthijs Bogaards, "Counting Parties and Identifying Dominant Party Systems in Africa," *European Journal of Political Research* 43: 173–197 (2004).

Along the first dimension, depending on the number of dominant parties, a system may be a monopoly (i.e., dominated by one party), a duopoly (a domination of two parties over all others), or an oligopoly (domination of a few parties over all others). Along the second dimension, systems can vary based on the degree to which they permit or enable partisan domination. Indeed, the most extreme degree of domination is a total prohibition on the existence of opposition parties (i.e., a de facto and also de jure one-party system). Even when this is not the case, a lesser degree of domination can be achieved if law or official institutions sufficiently favor the dominant party, whether directly or indirectly. This may be done, for example, by affording some parties better or sole access to state or corporate funds,[53] facilitating or tolerating its use of civil or criminal regulation against political rivals for partisan reasons, partisan capture of unelected offices of the state, and so on. Cutting across these possibilities is a third dimension – that is, the modalities of domination. This concerns whether hegemonic parties secure their domination by de jure and de facto means (where the domination is baked into the laws of the country and coercively enforced in practice) or only de facto tools (where the domination exists in practice but is not required by the law).[54]

A de jure (and de facto) monopoly arises where only one party is allowed to exist. This is the most extreme form of partisan domination. In other monopolies, smaller allied parties may be allowed to operate but not allowed to hold or compete for effective political power. The People's Republic of China, for example, has eight parties. But the "leading role" of the Communist Party is constitutionalized and has always been beyond question. Today, only five countries, all communist, retain a formally one-party or hegemonic party model. The favored "vanguard" parties are the Worker's Party of Korea, the Lao People's Revolutionary Party, and the Communist Parties of China, Cuba, and Vietnam. Historically, the single-party model is not uncommon. It is found in fifty-two other historical constitutions, or roughly 8 percent of all texts ever written. Typically, the favored party is a national liberation front that led the struggle for independence from colonialism or civil war.[55]

Sometimes a single-party monopoly arises because of a breakdown in the initial transition to democracy. This is common when a national liberation movement itself becomes the new dominant party. The ZANU-PF in Zimbabwe, and to a lesser extent the African National Congress in South Africa, became dominant forces that locked up politics over time. Both eventually became corrupt. Sujit Choudhry has identified

[53] See the fully anonymized electoral bonds issued by the Indian state under the Modi government, which have overwhelmingly generated funds for the ruling Bharatiya Janata Party, making it the richest political party in the country by a huge margin!

[54] See generally, Zim Nwokora and Riccardo Pelizzo, "Sartori Reconsidered: Toward a New Predominant Party System," *Political Studies* 62(4): 824–842 (2014), at 833.

[55] See, e.g., Const. Seychelles (1979), Art. 5 (Seychelles People's Progressive Front); Const Guinea-Bissau (1984), Art. 4.1 (African Party for the Independence of Guinea and Cabo Verde) Const. Gabon (1975), Art. 4 (Gabonese Democratic Party).

some characteristic tendencies of such systems.[56] These include the use of public resources to distort electoral competition, attempts to fragment opposition parties to minimize credible alternatives, and the subordination of parliamentary members to extra-parliamentary leadership. He argues that courts in such conditions should actively seek to constrain such tendencies . In the US context, Richard Pildes and Samuel Issacharoff have characterized the United States as an effective duopoly. The two dominant parties have created de jure structural barriers that prevent the successful emergence of third parties.[57] Of course, what one makes of a monopoly or a duopoly turns on the degree of intraparty democratic fluidity, among other matters.

To address partisan domination, non-substantive first-order regulation often focuses on preventing what Issacharoff and Pildes call "partisan lock-ups."[58] This directs attention to the architecture of democratic competition, not the substantive content of political programs or political speech. Such machinery must be insulated from party influence – not as a means to institutionalize substantive choices about who can compete but rather to prevent capture. A common way of ensuring non-domination is an independent electoral commission that can guarantee free and fair elections.[59] Another alternative, explored by Aziz Huq in Chapter 11, is the exercise of judicial review over election laws and election results. Huq's chapter examines the choice between courts and fourth-branch bodies as supervisors of the democratic process.

Concern over partisan capture can also motivate rules about campaign finance and advertising. For example, the Israeli Supreme Court struck down an amendment to the country's election law that reduced advertising time for all parties, while increasing it for incumbent Knesset members, on the ground that the change advantaged those parties that had already succeeded in securing seats.[60] Similarly, the Indian constitution was amended to make floor-crossing by legislators difficult, by requiring party-switching by a minimum threshold of one-third of a party members for it to be legitimate, in the face of experience with financially dominant parties simply bribing opposition members to change affiliation, so as to make up any shortfall in the dominant group's legislative majority.[61]

56 Sujit Choudhry, "'He Had a Mandate': The South African Constitutional Court and the African National Congress in a Dominant Party Democracy," *Constitutional Court Review* 2: 1–86 (2009).

57 Issacharoff and Pildes, "Politics as Markets."

58 Issacharoff and Pildes, "Politics as Markets."

59 Tarunabh Khaitan, "Guarantor Institutions," *Asian Journal of Comparative Law* 16: S40–S59 (2021); Michael Pal, "The Fractured Right to Vote: Democracy, Discretion, and Designing Electoral Districts," *McGill Law Journal* 61(2): 231–274 (2015).

60 *Agudat Derech Eretz v. Broadcasting Authority* [1981].

61 Aradhya Sethia, "Where's the Party? Towards a Constitutional Biography of Political Parties," *Indian Law Review* 3(1): 1–32 (2019). The amendment may have had a perverse effect inasmuch it encouraged even more legislators being bribed to meet the constitutional threshold.

Just because constitutions do not substantively regulate parties directly does not necessarily mean they are indifferent to the role of parties in upholding and threatening democracy. For instance, *second-order* regulatory models do not seek to constrain behavior of parties by direct command-and-control methods. Rather, they seek to organize the institutional ecosystem of politics to reward or facilitate good behavior while punishing or frustrating undesirable conduct. Of course, many of the institutional choices embedded in a constitution shape the subsequent behavior of political actors. A representative democracy must choose *some* kind of electoral system. Its constitution cannot realistically be wholly agnostic on the matter. Yet, as we have noted, the distinctive features of any system necessarily shape the behavior of politicians differently. Even a system that wants to adopt direct (rather than representative) democracy will need to make institutional choices concerning selection of the executive, the mode of decision-making, and so on.[62] All of these institutional design choices influence the nature of the party system that comes about. The question is not so much whether to have second-order regulation but what type of second-order regulation is likely to encourage a party system conducive to a durable democratic order.

The US constitution is an early example of attempted second-order regulation of the party system. The American founders had a "keen terror" of parties, as interests that were partial rather than concerned with the country as a whole.[63] Madison saw the institution of representative (as opposed to direct) democracy in a large but federated country as the key means of preventing a "faction" emerging that would be "adverse to the rights of other citizens, or to the permanent and aggregate interests of the community."[64] He claimed that, first, the principle of representation would ensure that "if a faction consists of less than a majority, relief is supplied by the republican principle, which enables the majority to defeat its sinister views by regular vote."[65] Second, he reasoned, the process of representation itself would reduce the risk of factionalism inherent in a direct or "pure democracy [that is] . . . a society consisting of a small number of citizens, who assemble and administer the government in person, can admit of no cure for the mischiefs of faction."[66] In a representative democracy in a large enough country, Madison reasoned, "it will be more difficult for unworthy candidates to practice with success the vicious arts by which elections are too often carried; and the suffrages of the people being more

62 Leah Trueblood, "Are Referendums Directly Democratic?," *Oxford Journal of Legal Studies* 40: 425–448 (2020).

63 Richard Hofstadter, *The Idea of a Party System: The Rise of Legitimate Opposiution in the United States* 1780–1840. University of California Press, 1960, at 69. See generally David Ragazzoni, "Parties, Democracy, and the Ideal of Anti-Factionalism: Past Anxieties and Present Challenges," *Ethics & International Affairs* 36(4): 475–486 (2022).

64 Federalist No. 10. On the difficult of this definition, see Robert A. Dahl. A *Preface to Democratic Theory*. University of Chicago Press, 1956.

65 Federalist No. 10.

66 Federalist No. 10.

free, will be more likely to centre in men who possess the most attractive merit and the most diffusive and established characters."[67] For Madison, the mechanisms of selecting representatives for the national government, coupled with the diluting effect of the large geographic scope of the new United States, offered second-order regulatory mechanisms that disarmed prophylactically "factions," or anti-system parties.

Madison admitted that there were faults in this system. He noted that the large size of the country might "render the representatives too little acquainted with all their local circumstances and lesser interests." But this cost could be mitigated by a federal structure, he contended, such that "the great and aggregate interests being referred to the national, the local and particular to the State legislatures."[68]

Drafters' imaginations are inevitably limited. The Madisonian hope that mere representative government in a large country would suffice to prevent the emergence of antisystemic factions has plainly not materialized in the United States. American elections are managed at the state level, and the federal courts have been historically reluctant to constitutionalize them.[69] Only in the 1960s did the national government and the federal (i.e., national) courts move to address minority voter suppression in Southern states, and much of that work has been undone by the US Supreme Court in recent years through its reading down of the Voting Rights Act of 1965.[70] Partisan gerrymandering remains widespread and judicially tolerated.[71] In effect, Madison's dream of candidate filtration through careful institutional design has collapsed as a consequence of partisan workarounds.

Yet Madison's was a relatively simplistic second-order regulatory model. Far more sophisticated tools have since been experimented with or proposed in other jurisdictions. These include:

- compulsory voting rules, including in primaries, to ensure that parties are forced to account for the interests of those voters least likely to vote;[72]

67 Federalist No. 10.

68 Federalist No. 10.

69 With the notable exception of a few cases like *Baker v. Carr*, 369 U.S. 186 (1962), which held that redistricting questions were justiciable under the Fourteenth Amendment to the US Constitution, and *Reynolds v. Sims*, 377 U.S. 533 (1964), which held that districts had to be of roughly equal size.

70 Examples include *Brnovich v. Democratic National Committee*, 141 S. Ct. 2321 (2021); *Rucho v. Common Cause*, 588 U.S. __ (2019); *Shelby County v. Holder*, 570 U.S. 529 (2013); *Crawford v. Marion County Election Board*, 553 U.S. 181 (2008).

71 *Vieth v. Jubelirer*, 541 U.S. 267, 158 2d 546 (2004); *Gill v. Whitford*, 201 L. Ed. 2d 313, 138 S. Ct. 1916 (2018).

72 Lisa Hill, "Increasing Turnout Using Compulsory Voting," *Politics* 31: 27 (2011).

- ranked-choice or preferential voting systems that incentivize parties to build broad-based coalitions in order to win enough second-ranked votes to win elections,[73] combined at times with multimember districting;[74]
- independent nonpartisan election management bodies and boundary commissions;[75]
- bicameralism to reduce ruling-party domination (along with anti-deadlock rules);[76]
- federalism to ensure multiple centers of partisan power;[77]
- parliamentarism or semi-parliamentarism, which tend to empower parties relative to their leaders, rather than presidentialism, in which parties tend to be weaker;[78]
- staggered elections to mitigate the impact of partisan "waves";[79]
- a regime of opposition rights and powers that resists winner-take-all dynamics;[80] and
- effective campaign finance rules to reduce the impact of the monetary might of the ruling party.[81]

This list, while long and no doubt controversial, is just illustrative rather than exhaustive. These and other second-order regulatory models are informed by the belief that party-systems and institutional design are mutually constitutive. Even as parties scramble institutional rules, institutional arrangements (along with political culture, context, and path dependencies) influence the arc of a party system, as well as the number and nature of its parties.

[73] Donald L. Horowitz, *Ethnic Groups in Conflict*. University of California Press, 1985; Benjamin Reilly, "Centripetalism and Electoral Moderation in Established Democracies," *Nationalism & Ethnic Politics* 24(2): 201 (2018); Khaitan, "Balancing Accountability and Effectiveness."

[74] Lee Drutman and Aziz Huq, "Winning without the Courts," *Democracy Journal* 63: 6–17 (Winter 2022).

[75] Rosalind Dixon and Mark Tushnet, "Constitutional Democracy and Electoral Commissions: A Reflection from Asia," *Asian Journal of Comparative Law* 16: S1–S9 (December 2021); Michael Pal, "Constitutional Design of Electoral Governance in Federal States," *Asian Journal of Comparative Law* 16: S23 (2021); Tarunabh Khaitan, "Guarantor Institutions," Asian Journal of Comparative Law 16: S40 (2021).

[76] Ganghof, *Beyond Presidentialism and Parliamentarism*; Khaitan, "Balancing Accountability and Effectiveness"; Stephen Gardbaum (Chapter 9).

[77] Heather K. Gerken, "Federalism 3.0," *California Law Review* 105: 1695 (2017).

[78] David J. Samuels, "Presidentialized Parties: The Separation of Powers and Party Organization and Behavior," *Comparative Political Studies* 35(4): 461–483 (2002); Ganghof, *Beyond Presidentialism and Parliamentarism*.

[79] Khaitan, "Balancing Accountability and Effectiveness."

[80] Waldron, *Political Political Theory*, ch. 5; Grégoire Webber, "Loyal Opposition and the Political Constitution," *Oxford Journal of Legal Studies* 37: 357–382 (2016); David Fontana, "Government in Opposition," *Yale Law Journal* 119: 548–623 (2009–2010).

[81] Eugene D. Mazo and Timothy K. Kuhner, eds., *Democracy by the People: Reforming Campaign Finance in America*. Cambridge University Press, 2018.

Before we end this discussion on the two models for regulating parties, it is worth noting the emergence of yet another approach to the problem that parties pose to democracy. Unlike the two regulatory models discussed above, this "direct democracy" approach takes parties to be an irredeemable threat to democratic order. It seeks to bypass them, either for a set of crucial decisions or for all political decisions. This back-to-the-people agenda has found some influential scholarly backers in recent years.[82] They envisage a party-less utopia characterized by direct political participation of citizens via mechanisms such as sortition, referendums, citizens' assemblies, and virtual voting. While these approaches recognize the dangers that current parties can pose to democracy, they often ignore the irreplaceable service political associations provide in facilitating democracy under conditions of imperfect information and limited resources.[83] It is possible, as Madison feared, that the anti-democratic risks are greater, rather than lesser, in a direct democracy, were such a thing even possible and sustainable over time in any reasonably large state.

***

The chapters in this volume address these challenges in myriad ways. The volume begins with consideration of constitutional theory writ large. Fragmented and concentrated power is the theme of Chapter 2 by Samuel Issacharoff and Richard Pildes, which revisits some of the terrain of their important 1998 article "Politics as Markets."[84] Democracy, on their view, requires a strategy to avoid either of these tail outcomes. Starting with a history of recent electoral regulations in the United States, they show how reforms and court decisions have weakened party leadership. The result is a fragmented party landscape in which minority candidates can with some regularity triumph in general elections. They pithily label this phenomenon the "tyranny of the minority over the majority" and explain why and how it became a central threat to democratic legitimacy. They canvass and assess some recent proposals to improve the situation, including ranked-choice voting, and repealing

82 Lawrence Lessig, *They Don't Represent Us: Reclaiming our Democracy*. HarperCollins, 2019; Mark Tushnet, *Taking Back the Constitution: Activist Judges and the Next Age of American Law*. Yale University Press, 2020; James S. Fishkin, *Democracy When the People Are Thinking: Revitalizing Our Politics through Public Deliberation*. Oxford University Press, 2018; Hélène Landemore, *Democratic Reason: Politics, Collective Intelligence, and the Rule of the Many*. Princeton University Press, 2012; Hélène Landemore, *Open Democracy: Reinventing Popular Rule for the Twenty-First Century*. Princeton University Press, 2020; Cf. Ming-Sung Kuo, "Against Instantaneous Democracy," *International Journal of Constitutional Law* 17: 554–575 (2019); J. Vrydagh, "The Minipublic Bubble: How the Contributions of Minipublics Are Conceived in Belgium (2001–2021)," *European Political Science Review*: 1–16 (2023).

83 Nancy Rosenblum, *On the Side of Angels: An Appreciation of Parities and Partisanship*. Princeton University Press, 2008; Jonathan While and Lea Ypi, *The Meaning of Partisanship*. Oxford University Press, 2016; Barber, *The United Kingdom Constitution*, ch. 6.

84 Issacharoff and Pildes, "Politics as Markets," 643–717.

"sore-loser" laws that empower more extreme primary electorates to screen out more centrist potential winners.

In Chapter 3, Rosalind Dixon and David Landau draw on their previous, influential scholarship concerning the concept of "abusive constitutional borrowing," Here, they catalog a whole range of constitutional provisions such as voting rights, electoral quota, and establishment of dedicated electoral machinery, among others. They further examine the discourse and practice of election monitoring. In each case, they demonstrate how pro-democratic norms and practices can be repurposed toward the undermining of democracy. Canvassing the causes of abusive practices, they go on to propose a series of solutions to reinforce constitutional democracy.

In Chapter 4, Khaitan lays out his own specifically *constitutional* theory of parties. Drawing on what he calls the Janus-faced character of parties as entities that mediate the public-private divide in complex ways, he shows how well-functioning parties can reduce information costs for voters and facilitate politics. He then draws upon this ideal type to provide a framework for thinking about pathological parties. He derives from this four principles of constitutional design. Constitutions, on his view, should provide maximum autonomy for parties within constraints necessitated by the exercise of state power; they should seek to structure a party system that represents major groups of voters; they should separate party and state; and they should discourage factionalization of parties.

The volume then turns to empirical inquiries into the same issues. Tom Ginsburg and Mila Versteeg (Chapter 5) document a massive increase in the propensity of written constitutions to regulate elections, voting, and parties, along with instruments of direct democracy, over the course of the twentieth century. The steepest increase has been in provisions associated with parties. Employing statistical analysis, they show that at least some of these provisions are *negatively* associated with democracy. Pairing two recent case studies in Kenya and Thailand, moreover, they show how constitutionalization can be a double-edged sword. In Kenya, regulatory provisions were adopted to empower democratic politics and prevent lock-ups. But under Thailand's authoritarian-drafted document, militant democracy provisions were weaponized to undermine new parties.

The volume then turns to a series of investigations into more specific legal or constitutional means of safeguarding democratic stability. A number of these chapters offer case studies from generally under-examined regions. Focusing on Africa, for example, Adem Abebe (Chapter 6) surveys the continent's approaches to regulation electoral systems and political parties, with a focus on how they have performed during the recent era of democratic backsliding. He develops the critical role of opposition parties in a democracy and the importance of constitutions in protecting their ability to function as a prophylactic against the winner-take-all politics that dominate the region, by drawing upon a rich set of examples that are not usually accounted for in the literature.

Tom Gerald Daly and Brian Jones (Chapter 7) look closely at political parties as *threats* to liberal democracies. While political parties are central to democracy, their very importance can therefore easily pose a threat to such a system given their unique positions, making it ever more important that they are properly governed. Usefully taxonomizing traditional approaches to dealing with unconstitutional parties as being legal, constitutional, or political, the authors explain how they are all inadequate to the current threat. They go on to consider novel approaches that leverage multiple branches of government, including quasi-judicial entities, to ensure the decision-making power over political parties does not fall to one sole person or entity. They also examine emerging international mechanisms and stronger controls on electoral manipulation, concluding that more international involvement and cooperation will be necessary to make use of these options.

In Chapter 8, Yasmin Dawood examines the value of a constitutionalized right to vote. She demonstrates that this right is best understood as a multidimensional and complex one, involving plural constitutional and legal elements. Yet these aspects are also dependent on a broader institutional infrastructure. While recent literature has suggested that the right to vote is not, on average, efficacious in the sense of leading to greater implementation, Dawood argues that it is normatively valuable nonetheless. At a minimum, the right has an expressive function. Even if this can sometimes be abused by autocrats, the right to vote remains a core feature of constitutional democracy.

In Chapter 9, Stephen Gardbaum examines the role of different types of political systems in addressing another set of trade-offs. He begins by stipulating democracies' need for effective, responsive, stable, and accountable government, as well as legislative bodies that are both representative and deliberative. He argues that not all of these values can be maximized at the same time. Regime types in the form of presidential, parliamentary, and semi-presidential systems provide different balances, conditioned by the operation of party systems. Here, he looks not just at the number of parties but whether they suffer the pathologies of being "polarized, hyper-partisan, and/or fragmented." Such pathologies undermine the ability to achieve the core values. He also considers recent proposals for "semi-parliamentarism" as a solution to the problems, arguing that its core "solution" of modified bicameralism is more generally feasible than proponents have suggested. By introducing some of these design features into presidential and semi-presidential forms of government, Gaudbaum suggests, constitutional design might begin to ameliorate some of the pathologies of contemporary government associated with both fragmented and concentrated power.

Turning to specific institutions used to safeguard the quality of the democratic process, Aziz Huq (Chapter 10) analyzes the role that courts can play in maintaining or undermining the democratic character of a regime. He canvasses the different roles that apex courts in particular (as opposed to the wider array of judicial bodies lower down in a hierarchy of adjudicative instruments) have been called upon to play in the constitutional law of elections and parties with increasing regularity.

He considers further whether other nonpartisan bodies, such as election commissions, can play the same function at lesser costs. Comparing the emergence of fourth-branch bodies to the possibilities of judicial review to preserve democratic stability, he expresses some skepticism about the temptation to favor either courts or fourth-branch as a categorical matter, as opposed to making more situated, contextually dependent judgments.

In Chapter 11, Elizabeth Reese offers case studies from Native American tribal nations in the United States. Their constitutional governance has evolved from a complex mix of traditional institutions, federally incentivized formal documents and more recent rounds of reforms and amendments driven by the tribes themselves. In the case of the Cherokee Nation, for example, contestation over who holds power has led to more than one constitutional crisis, but constitutional design has interestingly led to an escape from political gridlock. In the case of the Citizen Potawatomi tribe, the adoption of at-large voting by those outside the physical state of Oklahoma led to a change in dynamics. In both cases, constitutional institutions have managed to support continuity of political identify in conditions of ongoing colonial confrontation but also to resolve specific institutional challenges of governance that recur in other settings. Reese's chapter also makes a general case for a more central role for Native American constitutions in the field of comparative constitutional law.

In Chapter 12, Silvia Suteu takes up a quite different mechanism that is often the focus of democratic preservation, namely unamendable "eternity" clauses that stipulate the permanence of the core commitments of the constitution. She examines how these devices can shape the field of electoral competition, using two examples: party bans and the protection of parliamentary mandates. In her view, a normative evaluation of those tools is inseparable from the political context in which decisions are being made. Questions of the party system, the electoral balance of power, and the availability of courts and other institutions are critical for any normative assessment. This nuanced approach is a helpful corrective to the literature, which tends to be generally optimistic about eternity clauses.

In Chapter 13, on this theme of specific institutional choice, Yvonne Tew examines another "neutral" institution that has an effect on political competition: the constitutional monarchy of Malaysia. Although the crown is nominally above politics, there have been recent moments in which the monarch has played a decisive role in government formation and in both undergirding and undermining democratic structure. The role of neutral third parties has been underexplored in the literature to date in reference to courts and fourth-branch bodies. Tew's intervention usefully opens up a vista of fresh possibilities.

1.4 CONCLUSION

Together, the chapters in this volume offer a comprehensive, interdisciplinary account of the challenges of constitutional regulation of parties and elections. Any constitutional system contains a whole series of metarules that structure politics, most directly the rules regulating parties and their activities, and the electoral system which indirectly shapes the party system. In addition, there is also a structure of third-party decision-makers to draw boundaries, administer voting and resolve disputes, and a set of rights that express values and condition mobilization. The very complexity of the interaction of all these elements makes it difficult to draw conclusions strong predictive judgments about the effects of any particular institutional feature on its own. There are often too many moving parts to be confident of what one marginal change will do.

Further, the enduring analytic and conceptual challenges raised by Madison and his colleagues two centuries ago remain as pressing as ever. Self-interested political actors will endeavor to manipulate rules to their advantage, and so an enduring constitutional settlement requires not only some attention to deep structures but also to new institutional innovations that address the ever-changing challenges of democratic societies. This volume, we hope, goes some way toward showing how recent experience and theory can help us understand, and perhaps try to meet, those challenges at a moment when democracies around the globe are under particular strain.

PART I

Understanding the Crisis

2

Majoritarianism and Minoritarianism in the Law of Democracy

Samuel Issacharoff and Richard H. Pildes

2.1 FROM ELECTORAL MAJORITIES TO MINORITY RIGHTS

Democracies grapple with the tension between the principle of majority rule and ensuring respect for the interest of political minorities, however those might be defined in different societies and different circumstances. As an initial matter, constitutional designers confront this tension in the original architecture of a democratic system. Should the system be a strongly majoritarian parliamentary one? Should there be distinct, geographic-based representation in one chamber of a bicameral legislature of certain units, such as counties, states, provinces, and the like? Should there be explicit representational guarantees for identified minority groups, as in consociational democracies? If majorities have too much concentrated power, the risk is a form of majoritarian domination. If minorities are given too much power, the risk is a minority veto over government.

But the balance struck between majorities and minorities is not exclusively settled through the original constitutional design. In the United States, at least, legal doctrine and statutory enactments have also been centrally engaged in an ongoing fashion with this fundamental tension. Nor are the dominant concerns in one era necessarily those of another; solutions that appear best for a particular period of time are not necessarily appropriate as circumstances continue to evolve over time. At certain moments, the democratic system might be judged to be too strongly majoritarian, with the interests of political minorities being excessively subordinated. At other moments, the system might turn out to grant too much power to political minorities, with the ultimate risk being minority capture or paralyzed government.

The difficulty begins with the fundamental question of how much is due to those that triumph electorally. At its irreducible core, democracy turns on elections. Elections separate those able to muster popular support from those unable to inspire sufficiently. Elections provide the major mechanism for accountability of the governors to the governed and, through rotation in office, forestall the emergence of an alien governing elite. Elections reward institutions that wed effective campaigning to subsequent performance in office. When functioning well, democratic elections provide what Jonathan Rauch terms "dynamic stability,"[1] a process by which parties and programs are tested and retested, but within a relatively stable set of institutional arrangements.

Twenty-five years ago, we turned our attention to the potential distortion resulting from the ability of incumbent powers to improperly lock up the capacity for change, borrowing the concept of a "lock up" from corporate law and the competition for control of a firm. In the "Politics as Markets"[2] approach, the natural predilection of incumbents for stability compromised the dynamism of the political system and permitted an agency-cost gulf between the governors and the governed. Drawing from diverse sources, most notably John Hart Ely and Joseph Schumpeter, we examined whether barriers to entry and other anticompetitive encumbrances thwarted the normal processes by which choice generates development through competition, much as the antitrust laws look to keep open the processes of creative destruction by which new entrants test the continued market dominance of the old.

Much has happened in the intervening quarter century, and today we look a bit more skeptically at the outputs of democratic processes, rather than focus almost primarily on the inputs. At the time of publishing "Politics as Markets," we were worried about majority parties and incumbents entrenching themselves through various control points in the political process; now we worry as much about minorities entrenching themselves within the parties and cutting off accountability to majoritarian preferences . As we have written about extensively, the fragmentation of political authority across the established democratic world[3] and the rise of populism[4] have yielded an all-or-nothing cataclysmic quality to elections, now increasingly shorn of the institutional moorings that defined the period of democratic ascendency. A good part of our attention turns to the current predicament of increasingly illiberal democracies gravitating toward executive command and legislative failure. This has forced a broad refocus to core questions of what ails democracy.

In this essay, our attention is directed to a reassessment of one of the persistent tensions in the law of democracy. We can think broadly of democratic stability as necessitating the avoidance of the twin shoals of excess power to the current majority

1 *The Constitution of Knowledge: A Defense of Truth* (Brookings Institution Press, 2021), 79 (phrasing the difficulty of enshrining an institution that maintains both continuity and innovation as the problem of maintaining "dynamic stability").

2 Samuel Issacharoff and Richard Pildes, "Politics as Markets: Partisan Lockups of the Democratic Process," *Stanford Law Journal* 50: 643 (1998).

3 Richard Pildes, "Political Fragmentation in Democracies of the West," *BYU Journal of Public Law* 37: 209 (2023). https://papers.ssrn.com/sol3/papers.cfm?abstract_id=4116648.

4 See Samuel Issacharoff, "Populism versus Democratic Governance," in *Constitutional Democracy in Crisis?* ed. Mark Graber, Sanford Levinson, and Mark Tushnet. Oxford University Press, 2018, 445.

and the risk of preemptive power flowing to factional forces. If these be the Scylla and Charybdis of democracy's journey, the problem is compounded in an era of weak institutions, first and foremost the political parties. Electoral arrangements that well served an expanding electorate in pushing open the centers of power now risk becoming instruments of democratic paralysis or even collapse.

As with "Politics as Markets," our inquiry can be rooted in the initial salvos of an assertive law of democracy in the period of *Baker v. Carr*[5] and *Reynolds v. Sims.*[6] Each case exposed the mechanisms by which institutional stasis could preserve an untouchable minority in power. As Chief Justice Warren noted at the end of his tenure on the Court, these groundbreaking opinions were intended to open political contestation over areas of American politics that had been laid relatively immune to an aroused militancy, even from a majority of potential voters . To this majoritarian commitment, we may add the initial thrust of the 1965 Voting Rights Act, which extended the ability to register and vote to excluded minority populations (in the South above all), designed to ensure elections would be responsive to the majority of all adult citizens.

It is common to think of judicial review as primarily protecting individual rights and vulnerable minorities. But many of the early law of democracy cases were actually in the service of majoritarianism, even if the indirect beneficiaries were expected to be discrete and insular minorities. Yet once the one-person, one-vote cases gave greater thrust toward majoritarianism, it soon became clear that this approach was insufficient to allow real access to effective political participation for America's persistently excluded minorities – particularly in the face of racially polarized voting patterns. Almost immediately, cases such as *Allen v. Board of Elections*[7] and *White v. Regester*[8] sharpened the institutional inquiry into the way in which majority-reinforcing institutions, such as at-large or multimember district elections, consistently frustrated minority electoral prospects. The entrenched politics of exclusion proved far more resilient than could be redressed by a simple expansion of the franchise or the requirement of equipopulous election districts.

Dubbed the second generation of voting rights claims, the battle for effective guarantees of minority representation, particularly after the 1982 amendments to the Voting Rights Act (VRA), transformed politics, especially in the South. Districted local government elections allowed different minorities to establish themselves, beyond the black constituencies that were the primary concern of the cases. In short order, partisan competition spread, the parties realigned across an increasingly racially driven axis, and the Southern Democratic hegemon was uprooted, together with its formal Jim Crow foundation.

5 *Baker v. Carr*, 369 U.S. 186 (1962).
6 *Reynolds v. Sims*, 377 U.S. 533 (1964).
7 *Allen v. State Board of Elections*, 393 U.S. 544 (1969).
8 *White v. Regester*, 412 U.S. 755 (1973).

But the logic of creating minority avenues to challenge encrusted power did not stop at formal barriers to black representation. The logic demanded greater minority footholds in all facets of the political process, including within political parties. Thus, in a series of ballot-access cases, the Court struck down excessively burdensome requirements for third parties or independent candidates to get on the general-election ballot. As the Court reasoned in one such case, overly restrictive ballot-access rules to those challenging the major parties were an unjustifiable entrenchment of the established parties:

> No discernible state interest justified the burdensome and complicated regulations that in effect made impractical any alternative to the major parties. Similarly, here, we perceive no sufficient state interest in conditioning ballot position for an independent candidate on his forming a new political party as long as the State is free to assure itself that the candidate is a serious contender, truly independent, and with a satisfactory level of community support.[9]

Indeed, this line of cases represented a growing distrust of majoritarianism as a stand-alone guarantor of democratic legitimacy. In *Gordon v. Lance*, a 1971 case expressing the same impulse toward restraining majorities, the Court upheld a West Virginia requirement of a 60 percent supermajority support for bond obligations:

> Certainly any departure from strict majority rule gives disproportionate power to the minority. But there is nothing in the language of the Constitution, our history, or our cases that requires that a majority always prevail on every issue. On the contrary, while we have recognized that state officials are normally chosen by a vote of the majority of the electorate, we have found no constitutional barrier to the selection of a Governor by a state legislature, after no candidate received a majority of the popular vote.[10]

Once popular majoritarianism was no longer the primary virtue courts sought to uphold in the political process, the issue of the measure of proper legitimacy surfaced fully. The background norm of proportionality always lurked as a possible template – certainly that was the language of much opposition to the 1982 VRA engagement with at-large elections – a ready measure of when historically vulnerable minorities had received their due share. But the use of single-member districts

9 *Storer v. Brown*, 415 U.S. 724, 746 (1974). *Storer* did, however, permit states to ban sore-loser candidacies – laws banning candidates from running as an independent if they had voted in the immediately preceding primary and had a registered affiliation with a qualified political party at any time within one year prior to the immediately preceding primary election.

10 *Gordon v. Lance*, 403 U.S. 1, 6 (1971). See also *Brady v. Ohman*, 105 F.3d 726 (10th Cir. 1998) (upholding requirement that a voter initiative must receive more than 50 percent of the number of votes cast in the last general election, which led to rejection of initiative that had received more than 50 percent support) Several states explicitly require a supermajority to pass a constitutional amendment or a voter-initiated statutory measure. See "Supermajority Vote Requirements," National Conference of State Legislatures, www.ncsl.org/research/elections-and-campaigns/supermajority-vote-requirements.aspx.

as the antidote to minority exclusion pushed forward a markedly inferior way to achieve proportional results unless districts were packed with so many voters of a certain description or inclination as to make the desired electoral result inevitable.

In a setting such as that presented in *Johnson v. DeGrandy*,[11] the claims for maximizing the protection of minorities reached the point of black constituencies and Hispanic groups fighting for super-proportional legislative representation as a matter of due, leaving the bare white majority with a presumed limitation to sub-proportional status. A unanimous Court rejected this result. Then, most notably, in a long series of cases starting with *Shaw v. Reno*,[12] and each turning on complicated factual assessments, the Court imposed an important, though ill-specified constitutional constraint on the level of deliberate minority guarantees that states could offer.

Rather than spark a turn to majoritarianism, the post-*Shaw* period channeled needs for minority representation into a broad current of efforts to claim the political parties as the terrain for capturing political power. A compressed form of a long and complicated story would focus on the McGovern-Fraser reforms in the Democratic Party (and corresponding developments in the Republican Party),[13] the financial strictures of McCain-Feingold,[14] and the rise of social media as a forum for candidate independence and private fundraising. Each had the effect of diminishing the power of the party leadership and giving rise to free agency within the formal boundaries of the party, or at least with the aim of battling for command in the increasingly decisive primary process.

The resulting picture of party fragmentation and the capture of electoral vehicles by the polar extremes is one that bedevils the entire democratic world. The ubiquity of the problem and the push toward illiberalism cautions any discussion that focuses on American legal and political developments as having unique consequences.[15] In democracy after democracy, we see "the external diffusion of political power away from the political parties as a whole and the internal diffusion of political power away from the party leadership to individual members" and, correspondingly, the "decline of parties as the locus of democratic politics and the rise of the individual-centered definition of politics."[16] Yet there is a clear domestic trajectory to the law of democracy since the 1960s, and we intend the following discussion to ground the

11 *Johnson v. De Grandy*, 512 U.S. 997 (1994).

12 *Shaw v. Reno*, 509 U.S. 630 (1993).

13 Stephen Gardbaum and Richard H. Pildes, "Populism and Institutional Design: Methods of Selecting Candidates for Chief Executive," *New York University Law Review* 93: 647–708 (2018).

14 Bipartisan Campaign Finance Reform Act of 2002, Pub. L. No. 107-155.

15 For fuller discussions of the breakdown of political authority in the face of illiberal populism, see Samuel Issacharoff, *Democracy Unmoored: Populism and the Corruption of Popular Sovereignty*. Oxford University Press, 2023; Richard H. Pildes, "The Neglected Value of Effective Government," 2023 University of Chicago Legal Forum, 185.

16 The quotes are taken from Issacharoff, *Democracy Unmoored*, n. 17.

problem of majoritarianism and minoritarianism in American law and politics. As the institutional centers of American politics lost command, the battle for the increasingly rudderless electoral vehicles empowered the further margins of each party.

One way of framing the inquiry is to go back to the key question posed by "Politics as Markets." As originally framed, we were concerned about legal obstacles to the accountability of the electoral system to the will of the voters and to those who had been historically excluded. There was both too much centralized party control and too little capacity for minorities to enter the fray. In discussing cases going back to the *White Primary Cases*, we tried to show that structural attention to the openness of competition could provide a mechanism for cohesive minorities to seek advantage within the domain of political inputs, with less reliance on difficult rights claims on what the ensuing political outputs should be. We were worried about majority parties entrenching themselves; now we worry as much about minorities entrenching themselves within the parties. As coined by William Galston, we face the threat of becoming a tyranny of a minority of the majority. Put another way, the law of democracy was born in the pursuit of majoritarianism. It soon shifted to attempting to ensure fair treatment of minority interests in the face of systematic conflict. But we now face the challenge of precluding extreme or factional minoritarian interests from capturing and controlling government.

2.2 RE-ESTABLISHING MAJORITARIANISMS

America's political parties are internally fragmented. Jumping ahead to the present, this is the most significant new challenge in American democracy.[17] Fragmentation has numerous ramifications for both elections and governance. In both primary and general elections, it has accentuated the risk that under plurality-voting rules, factional candidates with intense but minority support can capture a party's nomination and/or win the general election. In governance, the fragmentation of the parties means that even during periods of unified government, the parties are less able to cohere around the ability to deliver on a common platform of political objectives. In practice, this means that a minority faction in the party is able to exercise effective veto power over legislation.

In the second phase of the constitutional and statutory revolution in voting rights, the dominant concern was to ensure that racial and ethnic minorities would be fairly represented in representative institutions under circumstances in which majorities systematically declined to support candidates from those minority groups. The perceived problem to which law and policy responded was the risk that majorities would exercise a form of majoritarian tyranny, in which the interests of minorities

[17] Richard H. Pildes, "Democracy in the Age of Fragmentation," *California Law Review* 110(6): 2051–2068 (2022).

were systematically discounted. In our new era of extremism and fragmentation, instead, a major concern has become too great a compromise of the majoritarian thrust on which democratic systems ought ultimately to rest. Much of current institutional reform thought can best be understood as an effort to reassert the importance of majoritarian control over the outcome of elections.

2.2.1 *The Birth and Death of Majority Winners*

In early American democratic thought and practice, democracy was understood to rest on "the grand principle" of majority rule. Many state constitutions expressed this commitment in requirements that candidates could be elected to office only if they had won a "majority" of the votes cast in the election. Under these provisions, if no candidate received an absolute majority of the votes cast, the election was considered a failed election. No candidate was elected. These were called "no-choice elections" or "non-elections."[18]

This policy approach was consistent with certain democratic theory of the era, such as that reflected in the work of Condorcet (Madison and Jefferson were well aware of the work of Condorcet).[19] In his work on voting theory, Condorcet had argued that the ideal voting system was one in which the winner – whether a candidate or a policy – would defeat all other alternatives on the agenda in a series of pairwise comparisons.[20] The "Condorcet winner" was legitimately entitled to win because that candidate had received a majority of the vote against any of the other candidates. Voting systems should be designed to reveal the Condorcet winner (Condorcet recognized that, depending on the distribution of preferences, a Condorcet winner was not always possible.)

If an election failed, states employed one of two fallback mechanisms. One was to re-hold the election until one candidate did receive a majority of the cast votes. Alternatively, the power to fill the office fell to the legislature, which would then appoint someone to the office. The drawback of the first approach soon became obvious. In Massachusetts, for example, one office took twelve ballotings before a candidate was elected. At least one Massachusetts congressional seat remained vacant for an entire two-year term because voters repeatedly failed to make "an election." In Vermont, one congressional seat remained contested over the course

[18] The material in this and some of the following paragraphs is drawn from Richard H. Pildes and Michael G. Parsons, "The Legality of Ranked-Choice Voting," *California Law Review* 109: 1773 (2021).

[19] Iain McLean and Arnold B. Urken, "Did Jefferson and Madison Understand Condorcet's Theory of Social Choice," *Public Choice* 73: 445 (1992).

[20] For discussion of Condorcet's work on these issues, see Emma Rothchild, *Economic Sentiments: Adam Smith, Condorcet, and the Enlightenment*. Harvard University Press, 2002, 180–188.

of ten separate runoff elections – until one of the candidates died, a definitive if sub-optimal ultimate resolution.

The alternative fallback mechanism empowered legislatures to take over the choice from the voters, including for offices such as governor. The problems with this alternative, which remained in place in some states until late in the nineteenth century, were revealed in examples like the following, from Rhode Island: voters there went through four no-choice elections for governor in five years (1889–1893) due to the persistent presence of a third party (the Prohibition Party). In the gubernatorial elections of 1889, 1890, and 1891, the Democratic candidate received more votes than the Republican candidate but was only selected over his Republican opponent by the legislature once (1890). Then, following another no-choice election in 1893, the backup contingency failed as well, and no governor was selected after the Republican Senate and Democratic House reached an impasse. Instead, the governor elected in 1892 simply held over in office for the 1893 term.

As practical experience revealed that the "majority winner" rule could lead to repeated elections and vacant seats, and as voters came to reject the legitimacy of legislatures choosing officeholders for seats designed to be elective, nearly all state constitutions shifted to providing that the candidate receiving the "plurality" of the vote would be the winner. Only two states today still have majority-vote requirements in their state constitutions, Vermont and Mississippi. In Vermont, where the legislature still appoints if no candidate receives a majority of the vote, the legislature almost always appoints the plurality winner; yet in 1976, when a Democrat won the plurality but not majority of the vote for Lieutenant Governor, the Republican legislature appointed his Republican opponent. In Mississippi, the failure of any candidate to win a majority now triggers a run-off election (other states have similar run-off requirements via statute).

The rise of plurality-voting rules means that candidates who are not Condorcet winners can nonetheless be elected. If Al Gore had been pitted in a one-on-one matchup with George W. Bush in Florida in 2000, Gore might have defeated Bush; but with the presence of Ralph Nader on the ballot, Bush won the state's electoral votes with a plurality of the vote, 48.8 percent. In addition, strong factional candidates can also prevail.

France provides the most dramatic recent example. In the first round of the recent French presidential election, around 30 percent of the vote went to the two candidates on the extreme right, Marine LePen and Eric Zemmour. If France used a typical plurality voting system, it's not difficult to imagine that one such candidate could have been the plurality winner; Emmanuel Macron received 27.8 percent of the first-round vote (of course, the decisions of candidates and voters would have been affected had France used a single-round plurality-vote system). But when France abolished its electoral college and shifted to direct election of the president in the 1962 constitutional reforms that created the Fifth Republic, the system sought to ensure that only candidates supported by a majority could win. Thus, the system requires a second-round runoff between the top two first-round candidates if neither received a majority in that first round of the overall vote cast (the presidential election has required a second round run-off in every election since 1965 – and in the eleven elections held since then, three plurality winners in the first round have lost to a majority in the second round).[21] If a majority prefers an extremist candidate, the French system – and most democratic systems – cannot prevent that. But it can prevent a factional extremist candidate from taking over the country simply because a plurality-voting system is in use.

2.2.2 *Reforming Voting Rules to Re-establish Majority Winners*

As the French example reflects, one institutional mechanism to ensure only candidates with majority support in an election will prevail is through a second-round runoff election. In the United States, two states – Georgia and Louisiana – require a runoff in the general election if no candidate wins a majority in the initial election;[22] ten states require a runoff in primary elections.[23] But runoff elections in the United States have a tainted history, at least in some states, harkening to late nineteenth-century efforts to frustrate black electoral opportunity during Reconstruction. Of the ten states that have majority runoff requirements for primary elections, seven are in the South.

At the heart of the Jim Crow assault on the franchise, the 1890 disenfranchising constitution of Mississippi adopted the majority runoff election as part of the general effort to diminish the influence of black voters.[24] When voting is extremely polarized by race in majority-white jurisdictions, majority thresholds can create "a considerable obstacle to black, but not white, office holding" by providing an opportunity for "fragmented white voters [to] regroup behind the highest white vote getter and elect that person to office."[25] As would be gleaned from public choice theory, coherent minorities are less likely to fracture than diffuse majorities, meaning a self-identified minority can more readily leverage its political strength than a more differentiated majority.[26] A runoff gives the more diffuse majority a second opportunity to close ranks, as in effect happened in France with Macron.

A case from the North addressed the relationship of such majority vote requirements to concerns about minority vote dilution. To win the primary election for

21 The three plurality winners who have lost the runoff election are: Mitterrand in 1974, Giscard d'Estaing in 1981, and Jospin in 1995.

22 "Runoff Election," Ballotpedia, https://ballotpedia.org/Runoff_election.

23 "Primary Runoffs," Nat'l Conf. of State Legislatures, www.ncsl.org/research/elections-and-campaigns/primary-runoffs.aspx.

24 Laughlin McDonald, "The Majority Vote Requirement: Its Use and Abuse in the South," *Urban Lawyer* 17: 429 (1985).

25 Ibid. at 429.

26 Samuel Issacharoff, "Polarized Voting and the Political Process: The Transformation of Voting Rights Jurisprudence," *Michigan Law Review* 90: 1833 (1992).

three of the most significant city-wide offices in New York City (mayor, city council president, and comptroller), state law provided that if no candidate received at least 40 percent of the vote, a runoff between the top two candidates was required. In *Butts v. City of New York*, this requirement was challenged as both intentionally discriminatory against black and Hispanic candidates, and as a violation of the recently enacted "results" test of the VRA.[27] The Second Circuit first rejected the argument that such requirements were racially discriminatory in purpose on the ground that they were a justified means to ensure elections reflected the preferences of an ideological majority, not a racial one. The Court then rejected – correctly, in our view – the VRA claim on the basis that while the Act protects minorities against vote dilution in representative *bodies*, the concept of vote dilution has no application to elections for a single office. The VRA does not, in other words, preclude jurisdictions from choosing majority-winner voting rules rather than plurality ones, even if voting is racially polarized.[28] By creating a "single-officeholder" exception, *Butts* insulated majority requirements for executive office from the pressures for proportionality at the legislative level.

Runoff elections are one means to ensure majority winners. But there are two practical problems with this approach in the US context. Turnout in runoffs in the United States tends to fall below that in the general election, which weakens the basis for believing the runoff ensures that only candidates with broad, majoritarian support get elected. In the 2020 Georgia Senate elections, for example, Republican David Perdue received 2.4 million votes, but fell just below 50 percent of the vote, while in the runoff, his opponent Democrat Jon Ossoff won with two hundred thousand fewer votes than Perdue had received in the first round – 2.2 million votes – due to lower turnout . That dynamic stands in contrast to France, where turnout in the second round runoff of the presidential election is typically higher than in the first round.[29] Perhaps the difference is that French voters expect to vote in a second round, since every presidential election has required that since the current system was created. The runoff is also two weeks after the first round, unlike the considerably longer delays for most runoff elections in the United States. Second, the need to hold a second election after a primary or general election imposes significant costs on jurisdictions already strapped for election-administrative funding.

Ranked-choice voting (RCV) is best understood as a means to ensure majority winners without these practical problems. To be sure, there are a number of policy rationales that proponents of RCV offer, including that it encourages a less divisive form of campaigning, permits voters to express their sincere preferences without

27 *Butts v. City of New York*, 779 F.2d 141 (2d Cir. 1985), cert. denied, 478 U.S. 1021 (1986).

28 For criticism of *Butts*, see Pamela Karlan, "Undoing the Right Thing: Single-Member Offices and the Voting Rights Act," *Virgina Law Review* 77: 1 (1991).

29 "2017 French Presidential Election," Reuters: Reuters Graphics, http://fingfx.thomsonreuters.com/gfx/rngs/FRANCE-ELECTION/010031D933E/index.html.

feeling they are wasting their votes, and avoids candidates with similar policy commitments from fragmenting the vote between them and delivering the seat to a candidate with a conflicting policy agenda.[30] But at its core, the most important argument for RCV is that it denies victory to factional candidates and rewards those who demonstrate the broadest appeal to voters. Because it does this in one election, RCV avoids the cost of running a second election and the drop in turnout that often results. RCV can be seen as a modern way of recapturing the original ideal that democracy should mean that only candidates who gain support from a majority of voters should be elected. At the times states shifted to plurality-voting provisions to avoid the time and expense needed for further rounds of voting, for practical reasons, RCV was not recognized as an option. Now that it is, it can be viewed as a better alternative than plurality-voting for legitimately determining who voters want to represent them.

But RCV itself comes in different variations, and some versions do a better job of selecting for true majority winners – Condorcet winners – than others. The version of RCV that has been adopted thus far in the United States entails eliminating the candidate with the fewest first-choice votes, if no candidate receives a majority of first-choice votes. The second-choice preferences for the candidate who has been eliminated are then transferred to those candidates, and the process is repeated until one candidate crosses the majority threshold or there are no more votes left to be transferred. But as more analysis of RCV has emerged, it has become clear that this system does not ensure the Condorcet winner is elected and, indeed, can eliminate a Condorcet winner.[31] A different form of RCV that does a better job of identifying true majority winners is "Bottom Two" RCV; instead of eliminating the candidate last on first-choice ballots, this system engages in a pairwise comparison of the bottom two candidates and eliminates the one who loses in that comparison. But as Ned Foley has demonstrated, the form of RCV that comes closest to identifying the Condorcet winner is what he has dubbed "round-robin voting."[32] This approach uses the full array of information provided by ranked-choice ballots to perform pairwise comparisons between all the candidates; if a true Condorcet winner

30 See Lee Drutman and Maresa Stano. "Evaluating the Effects of Ranked-Choice Voting," *New America*, last updated on March 30, 2022, www.newamerica.org/political-reform/reports/evaluating-the-effects-of-ranked-choice-voting/.

31 Though RCV overwhelmingly elects Condorcet winners, there are two recent examples in which it did not – the 2009 Burlington mayoral election, in which Condorcet winner Andy Montroll was eliminated, and the 2022 Alaska Congressional election, in which Condorcet winner Nick Begich was eliminated. See Anand Sarwate, Stephen Checkoway, and Hovav Sacham, "Risk-limiting Audits and the Margin of Victory in Nonplurality Elections," *Statistics, Politics, & Policy* 4(1): 29, 48 (2013); Adam Gram-Squire and David McCune, "A Mathematical Analysis of the 2022 Alaska Special Election for US House," arXiv:2209.04764 (arXiv preprint 2022), https://arxiv.org/abs/2209.04764.

32 See Edward B. Foley, "Tournament Elections with Round-Robin Primaries," *Wisconsin Law Review* 2021(5): 1187 (2021); see also Edward B. Foley, "Requiring Majority Winners for Congressional Elections," *Lewis & Clark Law Review* 26: 365–404 (2022).

emerges, that candidate is elected, and the system has majoritarian-oriented default rules if no true Condorcet winner exists. Modern computing capacity allows the full set of comparisons to be run in no time. To be sure, the choice of the best RCV system would also have to take into account the likelihood of strategic voting and how different versions would fare in those circumstances, a matter beyond our scope here.

RCV is winning broader acceptance in states and cities, particularly in places where voters can directly adopt political reforms through ballot initiatives. But it is still novel and voters are reluctant to change familiar rules under which they have voted for years. Whether voters would be prepared to endorse any of these more sophisticated versions of RCV remains to be seen. But even the basic form of RCV currently in use does a better job than plurality voting in diminishing the prospects of factional candidates and enhancing the likelihood that candidates with majoritarian support will win – and decide to run, knowing that the system rewards such candidates.

2.2.3 *Reforming Voting Systems to Re-establish Majority Winners*

American elections are a two-stage process, with primary elections preceding a general election. But primaries can filter out potential candidates who would have the broadest appeal – who would receive a majority of the vote – when the candidates are put before the general electorate. When party leaders choose their nominees – as they do in many democracies and did in the United States before the advent of the direct primary in the early twentieth century – they have strong incentives to take "electability" into account. Party leaders want to be part of winning coalitions that control government or components of it, particularly if patronage or earmarks lubricate the returns to the victors. Primary voters might choose to take electability into account, but they do not have the same incentives as party leaders and can prefer candidates who more "purely" represent, in the view of primary voters, the party's commitments.

If primary voters prefer "purist" candidates over electable ones, they can block candidates from reaching the general election who would have the broadest support. If that happens, voters in the general election can be faced with a choice between two ideologically pure candidates, neither of whom is close to reflecting the preferences of the median voter. To return to the recent French presidential election, some have speculated that if France employed the US system of party primaries, Marine Le Pen would have ended up as President. She would have won the primary among candidates on the right, while Jean-Luc Mélenchon would have won the primary among candidates on the left, with Macron voters split between the two. In the ensuing general election, Le Pen would have beaten Mélenchon.

In the United States, voters in some states indeed perceive this dynamic to be taking place. Absent replacing primary elections with a different means of winnowing the field for the general election, the question is whether primaries can be reformed to reduce the risk of eliminating candidates with the broadest general election appeal. The most significant reform in this direction was recently adopted by Alaskan voters, who endorsed a ballot measure creating a "Top-4" primary election, with RCV to be used in the general election.[33]

The Top-4 primary lists all candidates on a single primary ballot but allows candidates to designate themselves with a party affiliation, or as nonpartisan, or as undeclared. All voters vote and the four candidates who receive the most votes go on to the general election. The winner in that election is determined through RCV. This system eliminates the party primaries altogether. But it retains a primary election as the means of filtering candidates for the general election. The theory behind Top-4, to be used for the first time in 2022, is that candidates who have broad appeal are likely to be among the top four vote-getters. Because the general election uses RCV, the candidate who wins is more likely to be a majority winner than a candidate chosen through the traditional mechanism of a party primary followed by a plurality-vote general election.[34]

"Sore-loser" laws, which exist in approximately forty-seven states, can be another barrier that precludes majority winners from being elected.[35] These laws accentuate the effect of traditional primaries. They bar candidates who compete and lose in a primary election from running in the general election as an independent candidate or nominee of another party. If states shifted to Top-4 primary structures, these laws would become irrelevant. But as long as we have traditional primaries, these laws enhance the way primaries can block candidates who might have broad appeal from reaching the general election. Indeed, in the last two decades, we have had two prominent examples of relatively more moderate incumbent Senate candidates who lost their primaries nonetheless go on to handily win the general election in states that did not have sore loser laws or permitted write-in candidacies of even those who had lost party primaries.[36]

33 Richard H. Pildes, "More Places Should Do What Alaska Did to Its Elections." *New York Times*, February 15, 2022, www.nytimes.com/2022/02/15/opinion/alaska-elections-ranked-choice .html.

34 The same effect was apparently not realized through Top-2 structures. See Edward B. Foley, "The Constitution and Condorcet: Democracy Protection Through Electoral Reform," *Drake Law Review* 70(3): 543, 554–556 (2023) (analyzing the Alaska senatorial election in these terms); Lindsay Nelson, "Ranked Choice Voting and Attitudes Toward Democracy in the United States: Results from a Survey Experiment," *Politics & Policy* 45(4): 535–570 (2017) (finding that voters are more willing to cross party lines in top-4 systems).

35 For a thorough analysis of these laws and an argument that they should be held unconstitutional, see Michael S. Kang, "Sore Loser Laws and Democratic Contestation," *Georgetown Law Journal* 99: 1013–1076 (2010). Half of the states with sore loser laws adopted them after 1976.

36 These are Senators Joe Lieberman and Lisa Murkowski. Lieberman, a Democrat, was defeated in a primary challenge by a candidate from the left; with no sore loser law in Connecticut, he could run as an independent in the general election and won. Murkowski, a Republican, was

When the Supreme Court upheld the constitutionality of these laws, it reasoned that the primary was designed to settle the choice between contending forces within a party and that the general election ballot was "not a forum for continuing intraparty feuds."[37] But the Court's decision occurred in the era before hyperpolarized parties had emerged, along with concerns that party primaries were vetoing candidates whom a majority would support in the general election. In addition, a risk of permitting sore losers to compete in the general election was that they would fragment the field and make more likely the election of candidates with less than majority support. But with RCV, that problem can be eliminated today. The repeal of sore-loser laws, combined with RCV general elections, could enhance the prospects of candidates who might face tough primaries but would be majority winners before the general electorate.

2.3 POLITICAL STRUCTURES

In Federalist 10, Madison famously wrote that the expanded size of the Republic would be an antidote to faction and the guarantor of broader deliberation in the service of the public interest. History proved him wrong on both counts. National political parties eventually formed and deliberation proved more effective across the party divide than among the unrepresented citizenry. The impetus for RCV begins at the local level, where party competition is typically nonexistent[38] and the ready capture by extremes is difficult to surmount.

Consider the 2021 Buffalo mayoral election as a cautionary note. The incumbent mayor, Byron Brown, stunningly lost to a declared socialist, India Walton, who drew support from national party progressives, such as Alexandria Ocasio-Cortez. Buffalo is a reliably one-party Democratic town, meaning the party primary typically is the only election, even though the primary draws few voters. In the primary, Walton received 11,000 of the 21,000 votes cast.[39] Brown was forced to run for re-election as a write-in candidate, appearing nowhere on the ballot – in fact, there were no other candidates on the ballot other than Walton. Brown managed to win almost 60 percent of the votes, despite not being on the ballot, in an election where over 64,000

defeated by a candidate from the right, and while primary losers in Alaska are barred from running as independents or nominees of another party, they are permitted to run as write-in candidates – Murkowski did so and won. For more on Lieberman, Murkowski, and similar examples in the sore-loser context, see Kang, "Sore Loser Laws and Democratic Contestation," 1046 n. 1, 1050; Foley, "The Constitution and Condorcet."

37 *Storer v. Brown*, 415 US 724, 735 (1974).

38 See David Schleicher, "Why Is There No Partisan Competition in City Council Elections?: The Role of Election Law," *Journal of Law & Politics* 23: 419–474 (2007).

39 See "Mayoral Election in Buffalo, New York (2021)," Ballotpedia, https://ballotpedia.org/Mayoral_election_in_Buffalo,_New_York_(2021)#June_22_Democratic_primary_and_after math; see also Luis Ferré-Sadurní, "How India Walton Pulled It Off in the Buffalo Mayoral Primary," *New York Times*, June 23, 2021, www.nytimes.com/2021/06/23/nyregion/india-walton-socialist-nyc-primary-buffalo.html (discussing Walton's victory in the low-turnout primary).

voters turned out.[40] With the weakness of the parties in terms of money and messaging, they too readily become subject to takeover by an activist minority, fueled by small donors or a few large benefactors, and reflecting the margins of electoral politics, rather than what the majority in a large-turnout election wants.

To be sure, the absence of majority vote requirements is but a subset of design defects that enshrine outsized minority control. The Senate, by virtue of the state-based distribution of population, enhances the power of national minorities, and the Electoral College can do so as well. It is possible to make the Electoral College more majoritarian, if all states, for example, would choose to allocate their electors in proportion to the popular vote in their state. But coordinating the states in that fashion, when Congress lacks the centralized power to impose a uniform approach on the states, is an unlikely prospect. Short of such options, these institutions are hardwired into the Constitution and cannot be made more majoritarian except by constitutional amendment.

But the excess factional control today pushes further to the core understandings of how democratic accountability should work. After all, following Goldwater and McGovern, the Republicans and Democratic parties veered to less ideological candidates and in short order could speak of Presidents Nixon and Carter. Partly, no doubt, the Democratic Party was exhausted by the Vietnam War and the Republican Party discredited by Watergate. More fundamentally, each party had the internal wherewithal to hew back to the center to reform an electoral foundation that could provide a governing coalition.

This pull toward electability identified by the median voter theorem might have been most realistic in an era in which party leaders had more control of both who the party nominated to run and of rank-and-file members once in office. Party leaders have the strongest incentive to internalize the need to form winning coalitions capable of giving the party strong control of a legislative chamber. Those incentives are not extinct – witness Sen. McConnell trying to play a more significant role in Republican Senate primaries after the disastrous 2012 cycle in which the party ended up saddled with unelectable nominees who destroyed the party's opportunity to gain control of the Senate, or Rahm Emmanuel's successful efforts as Chair of the Democratic Congressional Campaign Committee in the 2006 cycle to recruit conservative Democrats to run in competitive districts, which enabled Democrats to capture control of the House.[41]

[40] See Jesse McKinley, "India Walton Says She's Unlikely to Beat the Write-in Incumbent, Byron Brown, in the Buffalo Mayor's Race," *New York Times*. November 3, 2021, www.nytimes.com/2021/11/03/nyregion/byron-brown-buffalo-mayor.html (discussing Brown's dominant general election, write-in victory).

[41] Naftali Bendavid, "The House Rahm Built," *Chicago Tribune*, November 12, 2006, www.chicagotribune.com/politics/chi-0611120215nov12-story.html; Russell Berman, "Mitch McConnell's Nightmare," *The Atlantic*, April 25, 2022, www.theatlantic.com/politics/archive/2022/04/republicans-senate-midterm-elections/629657/.

Nonetheless, the inescapable fact is that party leaders now have much less control than decades ago in both determining who the party's nominees will be and corralling those in office to unify behind a party position. In the primaries, as politics has become hyperpolarized and more tribal, more voters are determined to vote for "purists" even if those candidates are widely viewed as less electable. With the emergence of social media, the rise of outside spending, the increasing prevalence of "safe" election districts, and the explosion of small-donor Internet-based fundraising, candidates and officeholders are now more capable of[42] existing as independent free agents.[43] They can reach a national constituency, through cable television and social media, without being dependent on high-ranking positions on major committees. They can fund their campaigns in the manner of start-ups without being as dependent on party resources. They do not need plum committee assignments for national visibility or fundraising power. As a result, party leaders have lost significant control over who gets nominated and have lost significant leverage over members once in office. This is why the parties are more internally fragmented and more difficult for party leaders to govern. Indeed, a major theme of John Boehner's recent memoir is his complete inability, as Speaker of the House, to control the extreme right flank of his party – what he called the "chaos caucus." All this means the median voter theorem might well not be applicable to the current structure of politics and political competition. In the absence of stronger party institutions, the polarizing effects of small donors, campaign activists, and social media come to dominate the political scene. The newly minted verb "to primary" is now the most important disciplining device in fidelity to the agenda of the poles of the parties. This is why devices such as RCV or majority run-off or top-four, which give the majority a chance to reclaim electoral results, have become more appealing.

In the early days of the law of democracy, the Court was able to strike a major blow for majoritarianism. Even if the Court had the will to do so today, though, it is not clear how much judicial decisions can bring about the structural reforms necessary under current conditions to enhance majoritarianism. These changes will more likely come through voter-initiated measures or legislation. Such mechanisms are necessary precisely because of the inability of the party to deliver majority-appealing candidates. Yet these same majority-reinforcing tools risk obviating the need for parties altogether, and compounding the problem that gave rise to their appeal. Reforms always risk entry into the world of the second best. Here the risk is

[42] For a discussion of the altered authority of party leadership, see Samuel Issacharoff, "Outsourcing Politics: The Hostile Takeover of Our Hollowed Out Political Parties," *Houston Law Review* 54(4): 845 (2017).

[43] See generally Richard H. Pildes, "Romanticizing Democracy, Political Fragmentation, and the Decline of American Government Feature," *Yale Law Journal* 124(3): 804–852 (2014).

that reinforcing the majoritarian strain of democracy may further erode the party structures, whose weaknesses are a major reason for the need for majoritarian protection at present. In the absence of meaningful bipartisan competition, however, whether at the local, statewide, or even national level, current tides might require redirection in favor of the majority at present. Persistent minoritarian capture threatens democratic legitimacy. The threatened tyranny of the minority of the majority now looms as a central challenge that democratic thought, policy, and doctrine must confront.

3

Constitutions and Abusive Electoral Regulation

Rosalind Dixon and David Landau

3.1 INTRODUCTION

Free and fair multiparty elections are essential to constitutional democracy. Without them, a constitutional system will, at best, be competitive authoritarian, and at worst, fully authoritarian in nature.[1] Both electoral freedom and fairness can also be undermined in a range of ways: voters may be legally or practically prevented from enrolling or turning out to vote at democratic elections. Or they may be allowed to cast a ballot but have their votes thrown out or diluted by illegal ballots. Electoral fairness can also be undermined through subtle forms of interference – including the intimidation and harassment of opposition candidates and voters and allocation of government benefits and programs to supporters of the government.

Democratic constitutions can play a vital role in constraining and deterring electoral abuse: they can entrench guarantees of electoral fairness and integrity and empower a range of independent institutions to enforce these guarantees. This includes constitutional courts, specialized electoral courts, and independent electoral monitoring and oversight commissions ("electoral integrity" bodies).[2] And as many of the contributions to this volume show, there are notable cases in which these institutions have served to protect and promote democratic commitments to electoral freedom and fairness.

Electoral integrity bodies have relied on these guarantees to postpone and set aside elections that cannot or have not been conducted freely and fairly and to exclude candidates and parties unwilling to comply with constitutional

The authors thank Vishal Karnamadakala for outstanding research assistance.

1 Mikael Wigell, "Mapping 'Hybrid Regimes': Regime Types and Concepts in Comparative Politics," *Democratization* 15: 230 (2008).

2 Mark Tushnet and Rosalind Dixon, "Weak-Form Review and Its Constitutional Relatives: An Asian Perspective," in *Comparative Constitutional Law in Asia* ed. Tom Ginsburg and Rosalind Dixon. Edward Elgar, 2014.

requirements. They have also relied on these guarantees to order the counting or discounting of certain votes and recount of electoral tallies.

This relationship – between electoral integrity bodies and democracy – however, is not one-way. Democratic constitutional norms can be used to protect electoral integrity but also to undermine it. For instance, electoral integrity bodies may begin life as independent bodies but gradually be captured or co-opted by the incumbent regime. They may then apply constitutional requirements in ways that restrict rather than advance electoral participation, or undermine the political opposition, rather than support it. This, we suggest, is an example of a broader phenomenon in contemporary constitutional discourse – the problem of "*abusive constitutional borrowing.*"[3]

There is growing knowledge worldwide of comparative constitutional norms and practices. This knowledge also extends to authoritarian and would-be authoritarian regimes, and would-be authoritarian actors are willing to use this knowledge both to *inform* and *justify* their actions. In some cases, this will involve the use of openly illiberal ideas and discourses to attack liberal democracy or liberal constitutionalism outright. But more often, it will involve the ostensible *adoption* of liberal democratic ideas, but in ways that are radically superficial, selective, acontextual or anti-purposive in nature, and which thus have antidemocratic effects.

In this chapter, we illustrate this problem of abusive constitutional borrowing in broad conceptual terms, but with a particular focus on its relevance to constitutional electoral regulation.

3.2 DEMOCRATIC CONSTITUTIONS, ELECTORAL REGULATION AND THE PROBLEM OF ABUSIVE BORROWING

Constitutional democracy arguably entails a range of *socio-cultural* commitments on the part of citizens and their elected representatives, including commitments to fair terms of political cooperation and norms of restraint among political parties.[4] But constitutional democracy also has an important institutional dimension: at minimum, it requires a commitment to regular, free and fair multiparty elections, and the political freedoms and institutions necessary to ensure this in practice. Previously, we have called this the idea of the "democratic minimum core" – that is, the core set of norms and institutions that almost all democratic theorists agree are essential to true democracy.[5] But we also note the degree to which constitutional

3 Rosalind Dixon and David Landau, *Abusive Constitutional Borrowing: Legal Globalization and the Subversion of Liberal Democracy*. Oxford University Press, 2021.

4 Steven Levitsky and Daniel Ziblatt, *How Democracies Die: What History Reveals about Our Future*. Broadway Books, 2018.

5 David Landau and Rosalind Dixon, "Abusive Judicial Review: Courts Against Democracy," *UC Davis Law Review* 53: 1313 (2020).

democracy can be understood to entail a range of thicker institutional commitments, to democratic deliberation and minority rights protection.[6]

Moreover, one of the functions of a democratic constitution is to *protect* this democratic minimum core from erosion by temporary political majorities and promote this broader set of deliberative and rights-protective norms. Constitutions can achieve this in a range of ways: They can provide principles governing the rights of voters and parties to participate in the electoral process. They can provide for, and encourage, norms of democratic deliberation. They can prohibit – or provide for legislation prohibiting – certain forms of electoral manipulation or interference or laws burdening minority rights. They can create electoral integrity bodies and empower them to ensure the fairness of elections. And finally, they can give special protection to these electoral integrity norms and institutions, by making it more difficult to amend the provisions creating them, compared to ordinary constitutional provisions.[7] In each case, the role of constitutional norms will be to advance commitments to democracy and especially the democratic minimum core.

Instead of being deployed to advance democratic aims, however, these same constitutional commitments can be used – or misused – to justify the erosion of electoral integrity and pluralism. This, we have argued, is the essence of "abusive borrowing" as a practice.

Instead of being used to ensure an equal playing field, electoral institutions and norms can instead be used to tilt the playing field in favor of incumbents, moving a regime toward competitive authoritarianism or outright authoritarianism. They can, for example, repress competition by using a wide range of mechanisms and give undue advantages to incumbents. Of course, abuse of the electoral machinery is not the only way in which this is done – recent scholarship has highlighted a number of tools, including control over the media, the judiciary, and civil society. But electoral norms and institutions have emerged as one key tool that is, unfortunately, often ripe for abuse.

3.3 ABUSIVE ELECTORAL REGULATION IN PRACTICE

Abusive borrowing can take numerous forms: for one, would-be authoritarian actors may seek to de-couple the form and substance of constitutional democracy in many different ways, including via radically superficial, selective, acontextual, and anti-purposive usages of liberal democratic norms and ideas.[8]

Superficial forms of borrowing involves the rhetorical invocation of liberal democratic norms, without any of their substance. Selective usages involve reliance on

[6] Ibid.

[7] David Landau and Rosalind Dixon, "Tiered Constitutional Design," *George Washington Law Review* 86: 438 (2018).

[8] Dixon and Landau, *Abusive Constitutional Borrowing*, at 43.

liberal democratic structures or institutions, without the accompanying protections or exceptions necessary to make those institutions truly democratic in function. Or they involve the partial and selective grant of democratic rights and privileges to some groups (i.e., government and party loyalists), when democracy is premised on the idea of self-government among citizens as free and *equal*. Acontextual borrowing involves the adoption of norms and structures that help promote democracy under certain conditions (e.g., institutional independence or democratic competition), in the clear absence of such conditions. And anti-purposive borrowing consists in the deliberate adoption of institutions or structures designed to promote one goal for the exact opposite purpose – for example, restricting instead of empowering civil society.

Abusive borrowing can likewise have different audiences: Competitive authoritarian or hybrid regimes, for example, may rely on abusive forms of justification in order to preserve support from voters committed to liberal democratic norms. More fully authoritarian regimes, in contrast, may rely on such tactics only with international audiences in mind: at home, they may rely on a mix of intimidation and coercion to diffuse the risk of political opposition, but abroad, they may rely on the abusive use of liberal democratic principles to mollify donors, lenders, and defense partners.[9] In some cases, the two audiences and sets of tactics may also overlap.

Abusive tactics can also be combined with explicitly illiberal tactics and discourses. As we note in prior work, one of the justifications for some of the recent anti-constitutional populist regimes is that they are "illiberal" but "democratic" in nature. Defenders of this model oscillate between emphasizing illiberal models and precedents (e.g., Russia, China, and Singapore) and democratic comparators (e.g., Germany and the United States), with the latter used abusively.[10] This is, in effect, a form of political gaslighting. But it seems to be relatively common: in the United States, for example, we have seen a turnover the last five years toward a more nativist, exclusionary discourse of who counts as the true "people" for democratic purposes.[11] Yet former President Trump and proponents of this "Make America Great Again" (MAGA) narrative maintain that they are seeking to uphold existing democratic constitutional traditions.[12]

3.3.1 *Voting Rights and Participation*

Take norms of equal participation, or equal access to the franchise. Norms of this kind are central to individual political rights and free and fair elections. They help

9 This seems to have been the case in Rwanda, for example. See notes 22–23 *infra*. It could likewise be seen to explain the actions of the Supreme Court in Cambodia. See note 32.

10 Rosalind Dixon and David Landau, "1989–2019: From Democratic to Abusive Constitutional Borrowing," *International Journal of Constitutional Law* 17(2): 489 (2019).

11 Michael Harriot, "'Patriots' Are Undermining American Democracy," *The Guardian* (December 30, 2021).

12 Ibid. See also sources notes 38–39.

ensure that all voters have equal political freedoms and that rival political parties compete on terms of substantive equality.

Practices that undermine rights of political participation, therefore, can have wide-ranging effects. Think of measures in the United States that increase hurdles to voter registration: these laws undermine the political equality of poorer or minority voters, and the electoral prospects of those parties and individuals they are most likely to vote for (i.e., Democrats).[13] The same is true of the citizenship laws passed in India in 2019, which effectively disenfranchised large numbers of potential Muslim voters and further undermined electoral support for the Congress party compared to the (Hindu-nationalist) BJP.[14]

By enshrining the right to vote, democratic constitutional norms aim to guard against these risks. Yet the right to vote can also be the target of abusive constitutional borrowing: Laws that expand access to the franchise can be passed not with a view to levelling the electoral playing field but, rather, to tilting it in favor of the incumbent political regime. Often, this will simply involve the *selective* expansion of voter rights, or rolls, in ways predicted to favor the government.

Laws passed in Hungary and Fiji illustrate the danger. In Hungary, after adopting a new constitution in 2011, the Hungarian Parliament passed legislation expanding access to citizenship for many people of Hungarian descent living outside of the country, including approximately one million people in neighboring countries in Eastern Europe.[15] At the same time, it made it more difficult for existing Hungarian expatriate citizens to vote. The logic was simple: Hungarians in neighboring countries were known to be more supportive of the government than the median voter within the country, whereas those in the West were seen be more critical than the average domestic voter.[16] And this prediction was borne out in increased electoral support for the incumbent Fidesz government at subsequent parliamentary and presidential elections.[17]

In Fiji, there has been a long-running battle for political control between rival factions and parties loosely allied to Indo-Fijian versus ethnic Fijian interests. There have also been a series of military coups, in 1987, 2000, and 2006. The most recent coup, in 2006, was led by Commodore Frank Bainimarama and led to the suspension of the 1997 Fijian democratic constitution. A key part of the rhetorical justification for the suspension of constitutional democracy by Bainimarama was a claim

[13] Brennan Center for Justice, "The Impact of Voter Suppression on Communities of Color," Fact Sheet (January 10, 2020), www.brennancenter.org/our-work/research-reports/impact-voter-suppression-communities-color.

[14] "Citizenship Amendment Bill: India's New 'Anti-Muslim' Law Explained," BBC News (December 11, 2019), www.bbc.com/news/world-asia-india-50670393.

[15] Dixon and Landau, *Abusive Constitutional Borrowing*, at 66.

[16] Ibid. at 67–68.

[17] Ibid.

that his post-coup regime was promoting greater political equality between indigenous and Indo-Fijians.[18]

3.3.2 *Electoral Equality and Quotas*

Another core democratic commitment is to ensure equal access to political office. This principle guarantees equality among citizens seeking high office and, even more important, equality among citizens in their ability to elect representatives able to represent their experiences and concerns. But, of course, in practice there are many obstacles to realizing this commitment, including voter prejudices and differential access to political networks and resources.

One common constitutional response is the creation of "reserved seats" or quotas within the legislature for disadvantaged groups. In India, for example, the Constitution provides that at least one-third of seats in "panchayats" or local councils are reserved for women as well as allowing for reserved seats (in proportion to population) for both "Scheduled castes" and tribes.[19] In Kenya, the 2010 Constitution likewise provides for reserved seats for a range of disadvantaged groups, including women, young people, and the disabled.[20] These provisions are seen to advance the goals of democratic participation and equality.

Electoral quotas, however, are also potential targets for abusive borrowing. That is, they can be used contextually and anti-purposively to advance the interests of incumbent political regimes, rather than ordinary voters.

Take gender quotas in Rwanda. Rwanda is widely celebrated internationally for achieving high levels of descriptive representation for women – in parliament and the judiciary. Indeed, Rwanda leads the world on most league tables for female representation in parliament.[21] And it has achieved this in part through ambitious gender quotas, which reserve 30 percent of seats in parliament for women.[22] The problem with these quotas, however, is that women are appointed rather than elected to these seats, in ways that further advance the electoral dominance of the ruling political party (the Rwandan Patriotic Front). In effect, they therefore advance the authoritarian, rather than democratic, nature of Rwandan politics.

[18] Ibid. at 69–71; Rosalind Dixon, "Constitutional Rights as Bribes," *Connecticut Law Review* 50: 767, 802–803 (2018).

[19] Constitution of India 1949 Art. 243D.

[20] Constitution of Kenya 2010 ss 97–98.

[21] "Proportion of Seats Held by Women in National Parliaments (%) – Rwanda," World Bank, Data, https://data.worldbank.org/indicator/SG.GEN.PARL.ZS?locations=RW; "Revisiting Rwanda Five Years after Record-Breaking Parliamentary Elections," UN Women (August 13, 2018), www.unwomen.org/en/news/stories/2018/8/feature-rwanda-women-in-parliament.

[22] "Revisiting Rwanda Five Years after Record-Breaking Parliamentary Elections."

3.3.3 *Electoral Integrity, Timing, and Oversight*

A third democratic principle is the principle of fair elections, or elections free from coercion or intimidation of voters, irregular voting, or the loss or destruction of votes cast for the political opposition.

Democratic constitutions advance this principle directly and indirectly. In some cases, they expressly regulate the fairness of elections. Section 81(e) of Kenya's Constitution, for instance, provides that the electoral system must ensure free and fair elections, which are: "(i) by secret ballot, (ii) free from violence, intimidation, improper influence or corruption, conducted by an independent body, (iv) transparent and (v) administered in an impartial, neutral, efficient, accurate and accountable manner."[23]

Many constitutions also indirectly regulate electoral fairness by providing for electoral oversight by independent electoral integrity bodies. Section 190 of the South African Constitution, for example, provides that the Electoral Commission must (a) manage elections of national, provincial, and municipal legislative bodies in accordance with national legislation; (b) ensure that those elections are free and fair; and (c) declare the results of those elections within a period that must be prescribed by national legislation and that is as short as reasonably possible.[24] More recent constitutions – including the Kenyan Constitution – have adopted similar provisions modeled on the South African approach.

Together with courts, these electoral integrity bodies have exercised their powers to uphold guarantees of electoral fairness. In Kenya, for example, there were credible suggestions in the 2017 presidential election of millions of votes being lost or discounted due to difficulties with electronic voting.[25] The Supreme Court invalidated the election and ordered the Electoral and Boundaries Commission to organize a new one.

The same machinery for upholding electoral fairness, however, can also be used – pretextually – to undermine it. Courts and electoral commissions can rely on the *language* of unfairness to undermine confidence in the results of a democratic election, or to indefinitely postpone fresh elections, in ways that create a form of de facto electoral dictatorship.

In Myanmar in 2020, for example, the Electoral Commission repeatedly canceled elections across the country, but especially in Rakhine state. As Renshaw and Lidauer note, these decisions "on election cancellations and postponements temporarily disenfranchised 1.2 to 1.3 million voters and left 22 seats in the Union parliament vacant. In Rakhine State, three quarters of all registered voters were

23 Constitution of Kenya 2010 s 81(e).

24 South African Constitution 1996.

25 Kimiko de Freytas-Tamura, "Kenya Supreme Court Nullifies Presidential Election," *New York Times* (September 1, 2017), www.nytimes.com/2017/09/01/world/africa/kenya-election-kenyatta-odinga.html.

disenfranchised by these measures."[26] The reason given was that the security environment did not allow free and fair elections, but the consequence was an ongoing and selective suspension of democracy.

Following a coup by the military junta in 2021, the new military-appointed government also appointed an eleven-member State Administration Council (SAC), headed by the Commander-in-Chief, which appointed new members to the Union Election Commission.[27] Shortly after the Commission announced that it had "begun its investigation on the voter fraud in the 2020 general elections."[28] On this basis, it also sought to discredit the prior democratic government, when most independent observers saw only minor rather than widespread irregularities.[29]

3.3.4 *Militant Democracy and Party Banning*

Following the important example of postwar Germany, a number of modern constitutions have instantiated militant democracy clauses that allow for anti-democratic or anti-constitutional parties to be banned. The basic idea of a militant democracy clause is that there are limits to the kinds of parties and movements that a liberal democratic order should tolerate and that some movements should be prohibited before they can become a threat to the democratic order itself. The rise of the Nazi party is often taken as an example of this kind of threat; and in the immediate aftermath of World War II, the new Constitutional Court in West Germany twice was used to ban political parties, first a neo-Nazi party and then, in a more difficult and longer decision, the Communist party.[30] Globally, work by Elkins and Ginsburg has found that the power to ban political parties is one of the most common "ancillary powers" of a constitutional court, with about one-third of courts having this power.[31]

But naturally, the extraordinary power to ban a political party is one that can be used to entrench authoritarianism rather than staving it off. Cambodia offers probably the most dramatic recent example. In the country's 2013 elections, in a shock result, the opposition Rescue party nearly won control of the Parliament, winning 55 of 125 seats in the national Parliament. The authoritarian regime in Cambodia, under the grip of the Cambodian People's Party (CPP), looked to be on the verge of democratizing.

[26] Catherine Renshaw and Michael Lidauer, "The Union Election Commission of Myanmar 2010–2020," *Asian Journal of Comparative Law* 16(1): 136 (2021).

[27] Ibid.

[28] "Global New Light of Myanmar," Announcement of the UEC, GNLM (February 5, 2021), www.gnlm.com.mm/announcement-of-union-election-commission-2/.

[29] Ibid.

[30] Samuel Issacharoff, *Fragile Democracies: Contested Power in the Era of Constitutional Courts*. Cambridge University Press, 2015.

[31] Tom Ginsburg and Zachary Elkins, "Ancillary Powers of Constitutional Courts," *Texas Law Review* 87: 1431 (2009).

But after initial negotiations failed, the CPP instead turned to the Cambodian Supreme Court, asking it to ban the Rescue Party. The Court, which was completely controlled by the regime, complied in 2017. It technically issued a default judgment against the Rescue Party, but it dove deeply into the merits and found the charges against the party to be substantiated.

The Court found that the party was under the control of a foreign power – in this case, the United States – by citing some of the speeches of its leadership. Most interestingly for our purposes, the decision sounded in the language of militant democracy, albeit abusively. The Court held that the Rescue Party itself was a threat to "multiparty democracy." It found support for this view in the fact that speeches and statements by party leaders used so-called color revolutions, such as those found in the post-Soviet world, as a model for what might lead to transition in Cambodia. Of course, these color revolutions were themselves generally attempts to democratize an authoritarian regime.

The result of this decision was quite dramatic. The Rescue party itself was dissolved: it lost all 55 seats in parliament and 100 of its party leaders were banned from politics for five years. In the next election, the CPP essentially ran an uncontested election, and won all 125 parliamentary seats. Rather than forming a "near miss" for a slide into authoritarianism, the Cambodian case perhaps situates the Supreme Court's decision as a "near miss" for democratization.[32]

The Cambodian case is not the only potential example of judicial use of militant democracy to undermine rather than support free and fair elections. Thailand offers what is in many respects a more ambiguous and difficult, but potentially interesting, example. Not long after the populist Thaksin Shinawatra won power in 2001, the judiciary began issuing decisions overturning his electoral victories and banning him and his allies from politics. Intermixed with a militant democracy cast was, as well, a kind of technical conception of the rule of law. The 2006 parliamentary elections, for instance, were annulled by the Supreme Court in their entirety on the grounds that the incumbent regime had breached several relatively technical aspects of national electoral law.

In 2007, Thaksin's party was banned by the Constitutional Court; in 2008, the Court also dissolved a successor party, and in 2014, it removed Thaksin's sister from the role of caretaker prime minister.[33] Between 2005 and 2014, the judiciary annulled the results of the 2006 election, removed three prime ministers, banned several incarnations of Thaksin's parties, and prevented much of its leadership from seeking political office.

[32] Tom Ginsburg and Aziz Huq, "Democracy's 'Near Misses.'" *Journal of Democracy* 29(4): 16 (2018).

[33] Hannah Beech, "A Political Party Banned in Thailand," *Time* (May 31, 2007), http://content.time.com/time/world/article/0,8599,1626711,00.html.

These actions occurred in a climate of increasing authoritarianism in Thailand. In 2006, the military carried out a coup and seized power in order to rewrite the constitution; a second coup in 2014 had more permanent effects, and the country has not had elections since. We have little doubt that the effects of the Thai decisions were negative for the democratic minimum core. What makes the case difficult, at any rate, are two features. The first is that, unusually, the actions were being taken against what was often the incumbent regime, not in favor of incumbents. In comparative terms, this is unusual. McCargo has argued that these actions were being taken by a diffuse set of actors labeled the Thai "network monarchy," a group including large parts of the judiciary and military, essentially a set of actors with ambivalent views toward democracy and who strongly disliked Thaksin.[34]

The second, more fundamental point is that Thaksin and his allies were, without question, themselves something of a threat to democracy, unlike (say) the Rescue Party in Cambodia. As a populist, Thaksin took steps to seek to consolidate power and undermine opposition groups. He undermined the independence of key checking institutions, including the Electoral Commission as well as other institutions like the Human Rights Commission. The Thai case thus may show how difficult the balance involving militant democracy can be in a new democracy, where anti-democratic threats may emerge from multiple sides.

3.3.5 *Electoral Commissions and Fraud to Stymie Democracy: Venezuela*

Venezuela offers a textbook example of the use of electoral commissions and courts as tools to undermine rather than support democracy. Over a long period of time during the Chavez and Maduro administrations, these institutions have been used to tilt (increasingly aggressively) the electoral playing field in favor of the regime, while making life increasingly difficult for political opponents.

After Chavez's death in 2013, Maduro won a close election. The Venezuelan constitution contains an unusual clause in comparative perspective, one that allows a recall of sitting presidents, although only within a fairly narrow period of time. Chavez famously faced (and easily won) such a contest in 2004, a survival that actually helped him consolidate power.

After the opposition won overwhelming control of the National Assembly (the unicameral legislature) in 2015, it sought to hold a recall vote in order to remove Maduro from power. Given the political context, one in which Maduro's allies had just been trounced despite an uneven playing field, there is a very good chance Maduro would have lost such a recall. But it was never allowed to go forward.

The recall process is multistage. After the opposition surpassed the first stage by gaining signatures from 1 percent of voters, the process moved to a second stage,

[34] Duncan McCargo, "Network Monarchy and Legitimacy Crises in Thailand," *Pacific Review* 18: 499 (2005).

requiring gathering of signatures of 20 percent of voters, a very onerous percentage to trigger the recall election itself. The National Electoral Commission (CNE) set what were essentially impossible conditions for the recall. On dubious textual grounds, it required that the 20 percent quota be met in every state, rather than merely nationally as in the 2004 recall election. More importantly, it provided an incredibly short time period for the signatures to be gathered – three days. Even with these impossible conditions, the CNE never allowed the second stage to go forward. Instead, it suspended the entire process based on rulings from lower courts that "fraud" had occurred in the gathering of signatures.

Similarly, accusations of electoral fraud were foundational to the regime's effort to nullify the power of the opposition-led National Assembly. The Electoral Chamber of the Supreme Court held that three electoral results in the 2015 election had been tainted by fraud. These three seats were important because they would have given the opposition a two-thirds supermajority. When the Assembly rejected the accusations and seated the three legislators anyway, the Supreme Court held the Assembly in contempt, beginning a long process through which the Court would essentially strip all power from the Assembly, leaving it unable to legislate, while transferring most of this power to Maduro.

This is a key point we shall return to in Section 3.4 – accusations of fraud, whether fictitious or just highly selective, seem to be key tools in an abusive discourse that uses electoral rules to undermine democracy.

3.4 ABUSIVE ELECTORAL INTEGRITY DISCOURSE

Another dimension to modern democratic governance is transnational in nature and involves the monitoring of electoral fairness by governmental and nongovernmental actors. These electoral monitors observe elections in new or at-risk democracies and hold governments to account by informing donors, allies, and international civil society about the fairness of the electoral process.

The Carter Center, established by former US President Jimmy Carter, is a good example. The Center has sent electoral monitors to observe 115 elections in 40 countries, and states the role of these observers as follows:[35]

> Election observation missions start long before election day, with experts and long-term observers analyzing election laws, assessing voter education and registration, evaluating fairness in campaigns, and monitoring the impact of social media. On election day, observers assess the casting and counting of ballots. In the days and weeks after the election, observers monitor the tabulation process, electoral dispute resolution, and the publication of final results. Before, during, and after an election, the Center's findings are reported through public statements.[36]

[35] The Carter Center, www.cartercenter.org/peace/democracy/index.html.
[36] Ibid.

Where voting irregularity is detected, the Center frequently calls these irregularities out, including in the international media. And this combination of electoral monitoring – and discourse about democratic fairness and integrity – has undoubtedly contributed to fairer elections. The discourse of electoral integrity, however, has also been the increasing target of abusive borrowing in the United States.

In the lead up to, and following, January 6, 2021, former President Trump and his supporters have consistently advanced the claim of electoral irregularities in the November 2020 presidential election. They use those claims to encourage supporters to undermine the minimum core of American democracy. They have drawn on pro-democratic arguments about electoral integrity to do so. In 2005, for instance, the Carter Center issued a report focused specifically on the dangers of fraud in postal voting.[37] Mail-in voting has been at the center of Trump's baseless claim that the election was stolen.

#Stopthesteal is therefore not just any anti-democratic discourse: it is a discourse that involves the abusive borrowing of commitments to electoral integrity to erode democratic commitments to alternation in office and the peaceful transfer of power.

Even before the 2020 election, Republicans used the claim of fraud as a tool to tilt the electoral playing field in their favor. In September 2020, for example, Senator Rick Scott introduced the federal "VOTER" Act, which would have made it more difficult for citizens to obtain and return mail-in ballots (despite the ongoing pandemic) and would have set an absurd, essentially impossible deadline for the counting of those ballots. Yet Scott defended the law as an effective expansion of the right to vote, emphasizing that the right to vote was "fundamental to our democracy" and "a sacred right that we must protect and cherish."[38] In effect, the proposal used the (essentially nonexistent) specter of fraud in federal U.S. elections to frame major voting restrictions as pro-democratic. The same discourse, of course, has animated a series of state-level Republican laws since the 2020 election, which (unlike Scott's federal bill) have passed and imposed new restrictions on mail-in voting and other topics.

As we discussed above, claims of fraud seem to be a particularly pervasive part of an abusive discourse that seeks to use electoral norms and institutions for anti-democratic ends. We discussed the example of Venezuela above; Varol – in a piece on "stealth authoritarianism" – has collected other examples.[39]

In Brazil, Jair Bolsonaro has also relied heavily on an electoral discourse that emphasizes voter fraud. Gearing up for a possible loss in 2022 to prior president Lula, Bolsonaro in 2021 launched a series of interviews and speeches alleging that the country's electronic voting system could well be rigged and that there would be no

[37] Amy Sherman, "Much Has Changed Since Jimmy Carter's Report on Fraud in Mail Voting," PolitiFact (September 22, 2021), www.politifact.com/article/2021/sep/22/much-has-changed-jimmy-carters-report-fraud-mail-v/.

[38] Dixon and Landau, *Abusive Constitutional Borrowing*, at 207.

[39] Ozan O. Varol, "Stealth Authoritarianism," *Iowa Law Review* 100: 1673 (2015).

way to know.[40] As in the United States, these claims fueled violent outbursts aimed at national institutions in the aftermath of Bolsonaro's loss.

3.5 HOW AND WHY ABUSIVE ELECTORAL DISCOURSE SUCCEEDS

An important question raised by these patterns is what underpins the success of abusive electoral tactics. One key factor is that in most democracies, electoral integrity depends on a series of honest and competent actions (e.g., ballot distribution and vote tallying) by a large number of decision-makers, none of whom are directly known to or visible to the public. This means that electoral integrity is a matter of elite institutional culture and competence, as well as public trust.

Trust can be eroded in a range of interconnected ways: first, governments may choose systematically to erode the independence, professionalism, and competence of relevant oversight institutions. Second, political elites may choose to make claims that exaggerate the magnitude or unusual nature of electoral misfeasance or misconduct, in ways that ordinary voters are poorly placed to assess. And third, populist movements may decide to target all forms of representative, trust-based models of decision-making, in ways that contribute to a narrative of distrust of voting systems and electoral processes.

As Muller explains, this plays into the argument of authoritarian populist leaders that they are the only legitimate representatives of the people. Thus, opponents can only win by cheating, and in turn accusations of cheating play into accepted narratives about the behavior of those opponents. This also explains why many narratives of voter fraud involve the "other" in populist narratives. Consider the frequency with which Trump and other Republican claims of fraud have involved baseless claims involving undocumented immigrants.[41]

The use of voter fraud as an abusive tactic is a case in point. Claims of fraud will often be especially powerful tools for abuse – in part because they have an emotional and democratic charge that technical violations of legal rules simply do not have. The requirement of a free and fair election is, after all, at the core of democracy, so an accusation that the opposition is not playing fair is a damning argument. It is not simply that the opposition has failed to comply with some technical requirement: they are cheaters.

Moreover, some claims of fraud may have at least a whiff or kernel of truth, even if the underlying claims that they swayed electoral results are completely baseless.

[40] Tom Phillips, "Brazil's Election Authority to Investigate Bolsonaro over Baseless Fraud Claims," *The Guardian* (August 4, 2021), www.theguardian.com/world/2021/aug/03/brazil-election-authority-bolsonaro-fraud-claims.

[41] Jazmine Ulloa, "G.O.P. Concocts Fake Threat: Voter Fraud by Undocumented Immigrants," *New York Times* (April 28, 2022), www.nytimes.com/2022/04/28/us/gop-vote-fraud-immigrants.html.

In some new or more fragile democracies, various forms of fraud are relatively common, and so captured courts and regime allies can point to plausible examples. But even in well-functioning democracies, there will generally be some examples of voting irregularities. What is critical for democratic functioning is that (a) these examples are few and far between and (b) examples of this kind often tend to be more or less random from the perspective of overall electoral outcomes.

In the United States, for example, academic and policy reports find fraud to be extremely rare. But it is not unheard of. Some voters actually do vote twice, as uncovered in media reports and highly uneven legal responses. And in extremely close elections, fraud may even place the outcome in doubt. In a 2018 congressional election in North Carolina, for example, an operative for the Republican candidate was accused of engineering an absentee ballot scheme involving several hundred absentee ballots, and the razor-thin election was ordered nullified and rerun by the state board of elections.[42] But in the vast majority of elections, minor voting irregularities have no impact on the overall result, and a small number of invalid votes are cast that benefit both major parties.

When in these circumstances political elites cite fraud to cast doubt on the result of a democratic election, they are engaging in a classic form of an abusive borrowing tactic: they are knowingly exaggerating both the magnitude of irregularities and the degree to which they are likely to benefit one side over another.[43] This is also the hallmark of abusive forms of selective, acontexutal discourse or "borrowing."[44]

3.6 CONCLUSION

What if anything can be done to counter these abusive tactics as tools for the erosion of democracy and the democratic minimum core? The problem is obviously complex and the range of potential solutions relatively few. Yet understanding the causes of the problem also helps point to some limited responses.

As other contributors note, the strength and independence of electoral oversight can be constitutionally guaranteed or entrenched via heightened super-majority or popular approval requirements for their repeal or amendment. Indeed, this accords with our argument elsewhere that aspects of the democratic minimum core should receive heightened protection under a "tiered" model of constitutional amendment and design.[45]

Further, constitutional democracies can do more to recognize the importance of repeat players to their health and functioning: long-run players generally have a

[42] Michael Graff and Nick Ochsner, "'This Smacks of Something Gone Awry': A True Tale of Absentee Vote Fraud," Politico (November 29, 2021) www.politico.com/news/magazine/2021/11/29/true-tale-absentee-voter-fraud-north-carolina-523238.

[43] Dixon and Landau, *Abusive Constitutional Borrowing*.

[44] Ibid.

[45] Landau and Dixon, *Tiered Constitutional Design*.

strong incentive to maintain *justified* public trust and confidence in the political system. Doing so increases the chance that the existing democratic system will survive and their individual position within it will be meaningful and respected.

"One-shot" players – that is, independents, third-party candidates, or mavericks (such as President Trump) engaged in a hostile take-over of an established party – in contrast, will have quite different incentives.[46] Their incentives will be to use rhetoric that can challenge the status quo and encourage their entry into the political system, even if it comes at the cost of a long-run loss of faith in the system as a whole. And while this does not mean that there is no role for such players in redirecting and revitalizing democratic politics, it does suggest that this role necessarily comes with risks. Political parties and their representatives are not immune from these incentives, but they have counterbalancing incentives to maintain faith in democratic electoral processes.

Finally, political incumbents could do more to adopt a mix of reforms and public rhetoric designed to increase public trust in democracy. One of the challenges for constitutional democracies is that public trust in the electoral process is essential to the preservation of democracy but that rebuilding trust is extremely complex. In the long run, measures such as stricter electoral monitoring, voter identification requirements, and integrity norms may help strengthen public trust in democracy.

But in the short run, their enactment may actively decrease public trust: minority voters may experience the decision to adopt measures, such as voter ID laws, as a deliberate attempts to disenfranchise or dilute their voting power, thus undermining trust in democracy as a system based on principles of equality. The challenge for defenders of democracy is to adopt measures that are helpful to promoting electoral integrity, without overplaying the necessity of such measures or the "broken" nature of the current electoral system.

Similarly, political incumbents could do more to educate citizens and voters about the residuum of "error" in ordinary constitutional politics. By itself, awareness may do little to increase trust in decision-making. In fact, it may increase distrust and cynicism. But if that awareness is accompanied by a repeated emphasis on the small-scale, insignificant nature of this error, the salutary benefits may be far greater. Instead of being blindsided by a claim of voter fraud and then being ready to discard a valid electoral outcome as a result, voters may be more willing to ask: How much fraud, when, where, and with what effect? In some cases, the answer may be too much for an electoral result to be accepted. But more often than not, in most consolidated democracies, the answer will be different: not enough to cast doubt on the result of a democratic election, or to buy in to abusive attempts to discredit it.

[46] Compare Marc Galanter, "Why the 'Haves' Come Out Ahead: Speculations on the Limits of Legal Change," *Law and Society Review* 9: 95 (1974). See also Rosalind Dixon and David Landau, "Constitutional End Games: Making Presidential Term Limits Stick," *Hastings Law Journal* 71: 359 (2020).

PART II

Constitutionalization

4

Political Parties in Constitutional Theory

Tarunabh Khaitan

4.1 INTRODUCTION

Political parties appear to be in crisis. Lazy clichés in popular culture routinely stereotype politicians and parties *as a group* to be self-serving, elitist, and corrupt. The recent wave of democratic deconsolidation in several established democracies has been accompanied – perhaps caused – by the collapse, authoritarian takeover, or external capture of mainstream political parties, the partisan capture of state institutions, and a rise in hyper-nationalistic and exclusionary partisan rhetoric.[1] This chapter forms part of a larger ongoing project in defence of parties, politicians, and politics, one that is examining relatively ignored non-judicial phenomena in constitutional scholarship, such as incremental party-state fusion,[2] rights and powers of opposition parties,[3] second chambers and semi-parliamentarism,[4] political directives

This chapter is a revised version of an article originally published in *Current Legal Problems* 73: 89–125 (2020). I am very grateful to dozens of colleagues who helped improve drafts in multiple workshops.

1 Richard Katz and Peter Mair, *Democracy and Cartelization of Political Parties*. Oxford University Press, 2018, 151–188; Tarunabh Khaitan, 'Executive Aggrandizement in Established Democracies: A Crisis of Liberal Democratic Constitutionalism', *International Journal of Constitutional Law* 17: 736 (2018); Peter Mair, *Ruling the Void: The Hollowing of Western Democracy*. Verso, 2009; Tarunabh Khaitan, 'Killing a Constitution with a Thousand Cuts: Executive Aggrandizement Party-State Fusion in India', *Law and Ethics of Human Rights* 14: 49 (2020); Mark A. Graber, Sanford Levinson and Mark V. Tushnet, eds., *Constitutional Democracy in Crisis?* Oxford University Press, 2018.

2 Khaitan, 'Killing a Constitution with a Thousand Cuts'.

3 Tarunabh Khaitan, Work-in-Progress paper on 'Elected, yet Disempowered: Opposition Rights and Powers'.

4 Tarunabh Khaitan, 'Balancing Accountability and Effectiveness: A Case for Moderated Parliamentarism', *Canadian Journal of Comparative and Contemporary Law* 7: 81 (2021).

as constitutional norms,[5] anti-plutocratic constitutional norms,[6] and the so-called fourth-branch guarantor institutions.[7]

Political parties and party systems have long been the central institution for analysis in political science. A significant part of the political science literature is taxonomical, based on relationship between parties, their leaders, their members, the electorate, the state, and electoral systems.[8] This literature has taught us about cadre and mass-based parties,[9] catch-all parties,[10] electoral professional parties,[11] cartel parties,[12] and market-oriented parties.[13] Some of this literature has also looked at the relationship between party systems and certain institutional arrangements – such as Duverger's law that a first-past-the-post system is likely to result in a two-party system,[14] and the correlation of strong and weak parties with parliamentary and presidential systems respectively.[15] The first set of scholarship shows just how dynamic, adaptable, and indispensable parties have been to numerous challenges democracy has thrown their way. The latter set shows – albeit at a very high degree of generality and typically in a monocausal fashion – how parties respond not only to

5 Tarunabh Khaitan, 'Constitutional Directives: Morally-Committed Political Constitutionalism', *Modern Law Review* 82(4): 603–632 (2019); Tarunabh Khaitan, 'Constitutional Directives and the Duty to Govern Well', in *Constitutionalism and the Right to Effective Government* ed. Vicki Jackson and Yasmin Dawood. Cambridge University Press, 2023.

6 Tarunabh Khaitan, 'Political Insurance for the (Relative) Poor: How Liberal Constitutionalism Could Resist Plutocracy', *Global Constitutionalism* 8(3): 536–570 (2019).

7 Tarunabh Khaitan, 'Guarantor Institutions', *Asian Journal of Comparative Law* 16(S1): S40–S59 (2021); Tarunabh Khaitan, 'Guarantor (or 'Fourth Branch') Institutions', in *Cambridge Handbook of Constitutional Theory* ed. Jeff King and Richard Bellamy. Cambridge University Press, 2024.

8 See Sartori's influential account classifying party systems based on number of parties and the ideological distance between them: Giovanni Sartori, *Parties and Party Systems: A Framework for Analysis*, vol 1 (Cambridge: Cambridge University Press, 1976). See also Robert Michel's classical characterisation of parties as oligarchies: Michels, R. (1962). Political parties: A sociological study of the oligarchic tendencies of modern democracy. New York: The Free Press.

9 Maurice Duverger, *Political Parties*, trans. Barbara North and Robert North. John Wiley & Sons, 1954.

10 Otto Kirchheimer, 'The Transformation of Western European Party Systems', in *Political Parties and Political Development* ed. J. LaPalombara and M. Weiner. Princeton University Press, 2006, 177–200.

11 Angelo Panebianco, *Political Parties: Organisation and Power*. Cambridge University Press, 1988.

12 Richard S. Katz and Peter Mair, 'The Cartel Party Thesis: A Restatement', *Perspectives on Politics* 7(4): 753–766 (2009).

13 J. Lees-Marshment, 'The Product, Sales and Market-oriented Party – How Labour Learnt to Market the Product, Not Just the Presentation', *European Journal of Marketing* 35(9/10): 1074–1084 (2001).

14 Duverger, *Political Parties*, 217f.

15 David J. Samuels and Matthew S. Shugart, *Presidents, Parties, and Prime Minister: How the Separation of Powers Affects Party Organization and Behaviour*. Cambridge University Press, 2010, 15.

the broader politico-social and economic developments but also to certain features of constitutional design. Other disciplines that have examined parties closely, although not to the same degree as political science, include political history[16] and political theory.[17]

While political parties have long been a central object of study in political science, Anglophone constitutional law and theory scholars have, until recently, largely ignored this key democratic institution.[18] The little attention constitutional scholars have given to parties either concern the jurisdictionally specific legal regulation of parties and elections[19] or (rarely) the impact of electoral or party systems on specific policy outcomes.[20] Comparative constitutional scholars and constitutional theorists have largely been silent due to the influence of the American and the British constitutional traditions on the field, which, unlike their European continental counterparts, are largely silent on political parties. This silence is mainly a feature of big-C constitutional codes in the Anglophone world. Small-c constitutional statutes, conventions, and judicial precedents in these states do, admittedly, engage extensively with political parties.[21] But the large-C textual silence is nonetheless indicative of the low level of salience this key constitutional institution has been given, both in constitutional practice and constitutional

[16] See, for example, Gary Cox's work on the evolution of the English party system in the mid-nineteenth century: Gary Cox, *The Efficient Secret: The Cabinet and the Development of Political Parties in Victorian England*. Cambridge University Press, 1987. See also Bruce Ackerman on the American founding and political parties in Bruce Ackerman, *The Failure of the Founding Fathers*. Belnap Press, 2007, ch. 1.

[17] Jonathan White and Lea Ypi, *The Meaning of Partisanship*. Oxford University Press, 2016; Nancy L. Rosenblum, *On the Side of Angels: An Appreciation of Parties and Partisanship*. Princeton University Press, 2010; Danny Rye, *Political Parties and the Concept of Power: A Theoretical Framework*. Palgrave Macmillan, 2014.

[18] Honourable exceptions, most of them cited in this chapter, do exist. Many of these insightful works focus on particular jurisdictions rather than general constitutional theory or on the relationship between electoral and party systems and particular policy outcomes rather than the fate of democracy itself. See, for example, Nicola Lacey, 'Political Systems and Criminal Justice: The Prisoners' Dilemma After the Coalition', *Current Legal Problems* 65: 203 (2012); Larry Kramer, 'Understanding Federalism', *Vanderbilt Law Review* 47: 1485 (1994), 1522f.

[19] See, for example, Jacob Rowbottom, 'Lies, Manipulation and Elections: Controlling False Campaign Statements', *Oxford Journal of Legal Studies* 32: 507 (2012); and Aradhya Sethia on Indian anti-defection laws, much of the literature on election law in various jurisdictions, German literature on militant democracy and party bans. Some scholars, however, have indeed examined the reverse relationship, i.e., the impact of law and policies on the nature, shape, and health of political parties: see, for example, Charles Fombad, 'Political Party Constitutionalisation in Africa: Trends and Prospects for Deepening Constitutionalism', in *Comparative Constitutional Law in Africa* ed. R. Dixon, T. Ginsburg, A. Abebe. Elgar 2022; Nicholas Stephanopoulas, 'The Impact of Partisan Gerrymandering on Political Parties', *Legislative Studies Quarterly* 45: 609 (2020).

[20] See Nicola Lacey, 'Political Systems and Criminal Justice: The Prisoners' Dilemma After the Coalition', *Current Legal Problems* 65: 203 (2012).

[21] On the big-C and small-c aspects of a constitution, see Anthony King, *The British Constitution*. Oxford University Press, 2007, 3.

scholarship. Madison, echoing Rousseau,[22] was famously hostile to the emergence of political parties as 'actuated by some common impulse of passion, or of interest, adverse to the rights of other citizens, or to the permanent and aggregate interests of the community'.[23] That he would go on to found one of the two first political parties in the United States is, of course, another matter.[24] Contrast Madison's ideological hostility to parties with Burke's more affirmative opinion that 'a party is a body of men united for promoting by their joint endeavours the national interest upon some particular principle in which they are all agreed'.[25] Sadly, this Burkean optimism about parties fails to inform constitutional theory despite the British influence on the field because structural features of the organic constitutional development in the United Kingdom never produced a big-C constitutional code.

Big-C codes typically design key state institutions in a democracy. Parcelling off considerations about political parties to small-c statutes and conventions has the effect that the shape of the party system becomes an afterthought, left to be regulated by small-c statutes while taking the design of key state institutions as a given. As this chapter argues, however, bringing parties to the forefront of the constitutional imagination has very important implications for how we ought to think of fundamental institutions and offices of the state. Furthermore, big-C constitutional change tends to require the buy-in of opposition parties, whereas small-c changes can usually be made by the ruling party/coalition alone. It is simply bad design to let one of the competing players unilaterally change the rules of the game. It is no surprise that continental big-C codes, led by Germany after the Second World War, are far more explicit in their attention to parties and their relationship with democracy. Even so, the Anglophone silence is mimicked in comparative constitutional studies scholarship, dominated as it is by American constitutional discourses, including the latter's attendant pathologies.[26] It is almost impossible to properly understand the functioning of different institutional arrangements without close attention to the party system in which they operate.[27] Constitutional scholarship that confines itself to institutional analysis alone, without understanding how they are conditioned by political parties, is looking at a seriously distorted picture of constitutional practice.

[22] Luc Bovens and Claus Beisbart, 'Factions in Rousseau's Du Contrat Social and Federal Representation', *Analysis* 67 (2007).

[23] *The Federalist* Number 10, [22 November] 1787.

[24] See generally, Noah Feldman, *The Three Lives of James Madison*. Penguin Random House, 2020, ch. 9.

[25] Edmund Burke, 'Thoughts on the cause of the present discontent' in *The Works of the Right Hon. Edmund Burke*, vol 1 (Holdsworth & Ball 1834) 124, 151.

[26] For an overview of the democratic pathologies in the American system, see Lawrence Lessig, *They Don't Represent Us*. HarperEnt, 2021.

[27] See generally, Cindy Skach, 'Political Parties and the Constitution' in *The Oxford Handbook of Comparative Constitutional Law* ed. Michael Rosenfield and András Sajó. Oxford University Press, 2012, 874.

To some extent, however, big-C constitutional silence on political parties is also explained by the serious conceptual and functional challenges they pose to (liberal democratic) constitutionalism. Conceptually, as the primary holders of real public power in most democracies (at least when in government), political parties should be apt for constitutional regulation. But, as the chief vehicle for organising democratic will, the level of autonomy that political parties enjoy is one of the markers of the health of a democracy. Like private clubs, their membership is voluntary and often informal. The control they have over their members is limited.[28] Their role as an intermediary between the state and its people make them insufficiently public to be burdened with the normal duties of state institutions, and inadequately private to be treated on par with rights-bearing citizens.[29] Functionally, parties organise popular will and thereby make democratic functioning possible. But as wielders of concentrated state power, they have also emerged as a key threat to liberal democracy (alongside the military and the very rich).[30] Constitutions therefore need to walk a fine line between preserving their ability to organise and channel popular will while reducing the threat they pose to democratic governance. Scheppele is right in exhorting constitutional democracies 'to find ways to support *and* regulate' parties, for – she says – 'the secret to democratic self-preservation may rest in the realization that the party isn't over yet'.[31]

In this chapter, Section 4.2 will first provide an idealised functional account of political parties and party systems. The idealised account presented in Section 4.2 clarifies what parties do when they function as they *should* function in a healthy party system of a representative democracy. As such, this is a conceptual and normative, rather than a historical, project. The normative account is acontextual, but the principles offered are pitched at a sufficiently high level of generality to be worth taking into consideration when making all-things-considered decisions in a wide variety of contexts, but not so high and abstract that anything goes. I will argue that parties are difficult to regulate constitutionally because of their Janus-faced public-private character. The key function they perform, when functioning as they ought to function, is to facilitate a mutually responsive relationship between public policy and popular opinion by acting as an intermediary between a state and its

[28] N. W. Barber, *The Principles of Constitutionalism*. Oxford University Press, 2018, 174–175.

[29] On the hybrid public-private character of parties, see Dieter Grimm, *Constitutionalism: Past, Present and Future*. Oxford University Press, 2016, 27–30. Acknowledging that they are conceptually distinct, in this chapter, I will use 'citizens' and 'people' more or less interchangeably, unless the context otherwise suggests.

[30] On the dangers of plutocratic capture, see Khaitan, 'Political Insurance for the (Relative) Poor'. On the possibility that militaries may sometimes play a democracy-protecting role, see Ozan O. Varol, 'The Military as the Guardian of Constitutional Democracy', *Columbia Journal of Transnational Law* 51: 547 (2013).

[31] Kim Lane Scheppele, 'The Party's Over', in *Constitutional Democracy in Crisis?* ed. Mark Graber, Sanford Levinson, and Mark V. Tushnet. Oxford University Press, 2018, 513 (emphasis added).

people. When they perform this function effectively, political parties significantly reduce four key information and transaction costs that would otherwise make democratic governance impossible: political participation costs, voters' information costs, policy packaging costs, and ally prediction costs. For critics of this methodological approach who might be worried that an idealised account is too far removed from how parties in fact function in the real world, the practical payoff is that it helps us identify pathological parties and party-systems and diagnose their particular ills. Even as pathological parties abound, especially in recent years, relatively healthy parties have existed and continue to exist around the world. Furthermore, if we started discounting norms simply because they may never be fully realised, our moral universe would become seriously impoverished indeed. I will therefore use this idealised account to ground four principles that can help diagnose the health of a party system and, consequently, principles that constitutions should seek to optimise in relation to political parties and party systems, with a view to avoiding, diagnosing, curing, or mitigating systemic pathologies.

Thus, I argue in Section 4.3 that democratic states (and their constitutions) should respect and optimise four distinct, and sometimes conflicting, political principles in relation to political parties:

i. They should guarantee maximum autonomy for the formation, organisation, and operation of political parties, moderated by the restrictions necessitated by their purpose of winning (a share in) state power (for fixed terms) in competitive elections by acting as intermediaries between the state and its people (the 'purposive autonomy principle').
ii. They should try to optimise the party system such that the total number of serious political parties is large enough to broadly represent every major 'voter type', but not so large that the information costs on judicious voters are too high (the 'party system optimality principle').
iii. They should ensure a separation of parties and the state (the 'party-state separation principle').
iv. They should discourage the factionalisation of political parties (the 'anti-faction principle').

These political principles are drawn from the value of democracy itself. They are likely to bring real world political parties and party systems closer to their idealised form as described in Section 4.2, thereby improving and deepening democratic governance. As such, they should – alongside other relevant political and constitutional norms – inform fundamental constitutional design choices. Retrofitting the regulation of parties through the small-c constitution after key design choices have already been made in the big-C code is, therefore, a mistake. Big-C constitutional silence on parties is as much a regulatory choice as any other and carries significant risks of unintended consequences. In other words, big-C constitutions – as the chief organisational tool for public power in democracies – simply do not have the option of remaining agnostic about the nature and functioning of political parties. The question is not so much whether to regulate parties but why and how.

Another important caveat – especially to the more lawyerly readers – is that not every desirable norm can be converted into law, nor should it be. Some of the implications of the arguments in this chapter are legal, many are matters of political morality. Saying that a norm is a matter of political, rather than legal, morality is not to suggest that there is nothing we can do about its enforceability. Constitutions can make it more likely that certain political norms will be complied with – these are also design choices, they simply transcend the law. In particular, different electoral systems, legislative design, and executive-legislative relations fare differently with respect to the principles defended in Section 4.3. These matters of constitutional architecture have serious implications for the health of a regime's parties and its party system and are largely settled outside the courts. The aims of this chapter are largely theoretical and conceptual. A more detailed account of what practical implications might follow if constitutions are to take these principles seriously have been canvassed in a different article.[32]

4.2 PARTIES: AN (IDEALISED) FUNCTIONAL ACCOUNT

In this section, I will argue that political parties, when they function as political parties ought to function, perform the key democratic function of acting as an *intermediary* between the state and its people in a representative democracy. Two particular features make this intermediary function of parties unique: the *bidirectionality* of their intermediation and the *plenary* character of political parties. A party system with healthy functional parties incurs lower levels of four key information and transaction costs: political participation costs, voters' information costs, policy packaging costs, and ally prediction costs. Keeping these costs low makes a representative democracy viable as a mode of governance. Clear recognition of these features of a healthy party system with functional parties allows us to distinguish them from pathological party systems and diseased parties.

4.2.1 *Parties as Intermediaries*

A democracy, by definition, requires the rule of (all) the people who constitute a polity. Systems that systemically engage in comprehensive exclusion or suppression of discrete groups of voters, therefore, are diseased democracies, or not democracies at all. If democracy was the only legitimacy criterion for a political regime, we would vest all decision-making powers directly in the people. But democracy is not the only value we care about. Most of us would consider a law requiring the enslavement or

[32] For the constitutional design implications of the normative arguments in this chapter, please see Khaitan, 'Balancing Accountability and Effectiveness'.

genocide of any group thoroughly illegitimate, howsoever democratic its pedigree might be. Less dramatically, rule of law (legality) values – such as fairness, consistency, efficiency, impartiality, non-retroactivity, and generality – invite us to distinguish between rule-*making* and rule-*application*.[33] We will put the enduring scholarly debates about the legitimacy, sharpness, and feasibility of the distinction aside for the purposes of this chapter, but note that constitutional practice in liberal democracies has, broadly, come to accept that while the rule-making aspect of political power must be *largely* vested in institutions that represent the people, rule-application is, on the whole, best left to experts of some description. With regard to rule-making, there are several ways of securing the normative ideal of a popular regime (i.e., a regime that is 'of the people' but not necessarily one that is all the rage with the electorate). Direct democracy usually imposes high transaction costs, especially in large and complex societies, although even simple democracies have need for at least some political offices (and committees) that can represent and act in the name of the people and procedures that determine how they may act validly.[34] Ancient Athenians used sortition – selection by lot – to fill political offices; in our times, election by universal franchise is the more common method. Political parties have emerged as the main – and arguably indispensable – vehicle for facilitating representative democratic elections in even moderately sized complex modern states.[35] What follows is an idealised functional account of political parties in a democracy. Real-world parties will no doubt fall short of these ideals, but the fact that we may never *fully* achieve an ideal is not a reason to give up on trying to realise them as far as possible.

The chief function of political parties is to act as intermediaries between the state and its people. This claim does not presuppose a specific type of party organisation: I use the term 'intermediary' in a loose sense here to be compatible with a varying range of intensity in the relationship between the party and the people.[36] What

[33] Joseph Raz, 'The Law's Own Virtue', *Oxford Journal of Legal Studies* 39: 1 (2019); Jeremy Waldron, *Political Political Theory: Essays on Institutions*. Harvard University Press, 2016, 45–72.

[34] Leah Trueblood, 'Are Referendums Directly Democratic?', *Oxford Journal of Legal Studies* 40: 425 (2020).

[35] Parties have often been identified as a problem for democracy. For a response to these criticisms, see Barber's claim that democratic politics is a team game rather than an individual sport: Barber, *The Principles of Constitutionalism*. Oxford University Press, 2018, 169; Nancy L. Rosenblum, *On the Side of Angels: An Appreciation of Parties and Partisanship*. Princeton University Press, 2010; Jonathan White and Lea Ypi, *The Meaning of Partisanship*. Oxford University Press, 2016.

[36] Thus, cadre-based parties, mass-parties, and parties that act as 'brokers' between the state and the people are all capable of acting as intermediaries. On these categories, see generally Richard Katz and Peter Mair, 'Changing Models of Party Organization and Party Democracy: The Emergence of the Cartel Party', *Party Politics* 1: 5 (1995). Katz and Mair's thesis concerning 'cartel parties', on the other hand, concerns the relationship between political parties and the state: as we will see later while discussing the party-state separation principle, cartelisation is an indication of a pathological party system.

matters is that parties have a threshold level of communicative relationship with the people. State officers and institutions are typically too removed from the people to access popular opinions directly, and ordinary civil society organisations are usually too removed from the state to influence state policies. Exceptions no doubt exist: in systems in which individual legislators represent sufficiently small constituencies, they can have a direct relationship with their constituents; similarly, many policy influencers, such as wealthy corporations, lobbyists, thinktanks, and powerful media houses, often have a significant influence on state policy. Yet political parties are a very special type of intermediary between the state and its people for two reasons: the *bidirectionality* and the *plenary character* of their intermediary function.

4.2.1.1 Bidirectionality of Parties

Mediation by parties is *bidirectional*, in as much as they simultaneously perform both functions of accessing popular opinion and shaping state policy. They are embedded in the structures and institutions of the state but also (at least ideally) have direct access to the people. This simultaneity is essential to the democratic legitimation that parties alone can provide to rule-making state institutions and offices. In general, the state functions through *offices* and *institutions*: these are modes of corporate action that are defined by a measure of *formalisation* of their processes, purposes, and modes of operation. This formalisation is typically necessary for satisfying various virtues (rightly) associated with the state: impartiality, rationality, fairness, legality, and so on. But formalisation imposes a cost – it reduces the ability of offices and institutions to (informally) connect with the people and build authentic interpersonal relationships of mutual understanding and dialogue. Healthy parties, on the other hand, despite their internal institutionalised structures, tend to retain the nimble flexibility and informality of civil society organisations – at least in their local units. This measure of informality allows them to perform their key coordinating function: to imbibe and influence popular opinion, on the one hand, and to formulate and justify their proposed policy package, on the other. The relationship between popular opinions and policy packages is mutually responsive – in a well-functioning democracy, they respond to each other and form a feedback loop. The central task of political parties is to facilitate this responsive relationship between popular opinion and policy.[37] Sometimes, they absorb popular opinions and translate them into policy proposals. At other times, they articulate policy proposals and mould public opinion to get behind them.

While Sartori accepts this dual function, 'grant[ing] that parties are a two-way communication channel', he insists that 'the conclusion does not follow that parties are a transmission channel downward *to the same extent* that they are a transmission

[37] See generally Nancy L. Rosenblum, 'Political Parties as Membership Group', *Columbia Law Review* 100: 813, 825–826 (2000).

belt upward'.[38] In part, his reluctance to idealise the bidirectional communicative purpose is based on his characterisation of what I have described as the *justification* of public policy to the people as 'manipulation' of popular opinion.[39] This pejorative characterisation under-appreciates the democratic need for the state to justify its policies to the people, including to those who disagree with the government, and the critical role that (healthy) parties play in demanding, articulating, and challenging such justification.

4.2.1.2 Plenary Character of Parties

The second special feature of the mediation role that well-functioning parties play between the state and its people is their *plenary character*. In heterogenous societies, the values as well as the interests of the people are likely to be diverse. Value pluralism as well as interest pluralism pose a huge challenge to the ability of the state to frame public policy that would be broadly acceptable to its people. The multitude of ways in which different values and interests may combine is so staggeringly large that any complex society faces the potential problem of being left with most of its population being perennially disgruntled. Parties (when they function well) perform a significant legitimation function for the state by coalescing around distinct families of values – often described as ideology – and aggregate the diverse interests of (all) the people of a state into a coherent policy package more-or-less compatible with their ideology. The policy package need not be internally coherent – it often involves the weighing of various interests, preferences, and values. It may entail a multitude of compromises that seek to bridge the gap between the ideal and the feasible and must frequently cater to logically opposed interests, values, and preferences.

The internal contradictions of the policy package of a well-functioning political party notwithstanding, the party can claim that its mediation has a plenary character in three distinct senses: first, it mimics the plenary nature of governance, which is at least potentially concerned with all issues affecting human flourishing (as well as interests of non-human beings). No state can decide to have a policy only on healthcare, for example. Even its silence or inaction on all other matters will amount to a policy decision, which it would be well-advised to adopt deliberately rather than inadvertently. As the drivers of governments-in-waiting, *governance* parties (that seek to capture high executive offices, as opposed to *influence* parties that primarily focus on policy impact) come up with policies on a wide range of issues, drawing upon their interaction with the people, and then seek to sell them

[38] Giovanni Sartori, *Parties and Party Systems: A Framework for Analysis*. Cambridge University Press, 1976, vol. I, p. 28 (emphasis in the original).

[39] Ibid.

politically to the people *as a package*. In doing so, they persuade their supporters to accede to certain compromises made with their own values, interests, and preferences so long as the overall policy package remains attractive to them. These policy platforms also make the opportunity costs of their policy packages transparent to voters, who are better able to prioritise their preferences in the context of resource constraint.

The policy package of a healthy party is also plenary in a second sense: it is one that is designed by putting the interests of *all the people* on the scales. I will shed further light on this feature when discussing the anti-faction principle. For now, it will suffice to note that a party need not – and cannot – commit itself to all the mutually incompatible values that the multitude of people in a state adhere to, nor can it sincerely claim to have aggregated the preferences of all the people in even a moderately diverse society. But what a non-factional party can – and should – do is to sincerely *seek* to aggregate the interests of all the people in its polity. No policy package can cater to all these interests equally, and some interests will of necessity be compromised or sacrificed for others. But parties should *consider* the well-being of all the people: any political group that a priori dismisses the interests of any section of the population as either irrelevant to its policy considerations or worse, meriting its hostility, is no longer committed to the rule of *all* the people and is basically a faction rather than a party.

Third, parties have a plenary character in as much as they are more likely than most other political actors in electoral democracies to have long-term horizons and therefore are likely to care more about the interests of the future people. Unlike the naturally limited lifespans of individual politicians, parties can – and usually seek to – endure over a long time. Sure, parties care about winning the next election, but that is not their only goal. It is sometimes rational for parties to prioritise ideological victories, organisation-building, performance in future elections, etc. over winning the next election only because parties have longer-term time horizons. As Rosenbluth and Shapiro correctly state, 'parties have reputations that outlive those of individual politicians, and to the extent that they must represent a wide view of societal interests, they are more capable of delivering desired outcomes than any amount of direct democracy, and more trustworthy than even the most appealing individual politician'.[40] Indeed, parties frequently outlast constitutions, even several constitutions. This endurance feature adds a temporal dimension to the inclusive plenary character of parties and makes healthy parties much more likely than parties dominated by single individuals to attend to issues such as climate change that will disproportionately affect non-voting children and future people.

[40] Frances McCall Rosenbluth and Ian Shapiro, *Responsible Parties: Saving Democracy from Itself*. Yale University Press, 2018, 230.

4.2.2 *Key Costs Reduced by Parties*

In providing this uniquely bidirectional and plenary mediation between the state and its people, political parties (in efficient multi-partisan systems)[41] reduce key information and transaction costs for both, making democracy possible. For Sartori, 'Parties make for a "system" . . . only when they are parts (in the plural); and a party system is precisely the *system of interactions* resulting from inter-party competition. That is, the system in question bears on the relatedness of parties to each other, on how each party is a function (in the mathematical sense) of the other parties and reacts, competitively or otherwise, to the other parties.'[42]

Parties are able to reduce the costs I am about to discuss mainly in well-functioning party systems. One-party 'systems', therefore, obviously fail to achieve a reduction in the costs that makes democracy possible. Multi-partisan systems – defined by the nature of the parties they have and the nature of the interaction between them – may be more or less efficient at reducing these costs. Other things being equal, constitutions will deepen democracy if they make their party systems and parties more efficient at reducing the following costs.

4.2.2.1 Political Participation Cost

First, healthy parties in efficient party systems reduce the transaction costs of political participation for citizens (*political participation costs*). Even in a smallish party-less democracy, an ordinary citizen acting on her own would almost certainly need to take up political engagement as a full-time occupation to have any hope of making a modicum of difference to state policy. Sooner or later, she will have to invent something that looks like a political party to enable some political engagement by citizens who do not wish to become full-time politicians. Parties also reduce the transaction costs of political participation for citizens – not only for partisans, but also for non-partisan citizens – who, in a well-functioning pluralistic democracy, are likely to find some party that reflects their values and priorities most closely and could therefore be their first port of call when raising a matter of political concern.[43]

High political participation costs can be debilitating for a democracy. Imagine a society without shoemakers. In such a society, one would have to make one's own shoes or do without them. By reducing the political participation costs, parties offer a similar service of specialisation to citizens – they can custom-build their own mode of political participation, but without parties this is going to be expensive, futile, or

41 A single party, in a one-party system, cannot reduce these costs.

42 Sartori, *Parties and Party Systems*, 39. Emphasis in the original.

43 Matteo Bonotti, *Partisanship and Political Liberalism in Diverse Societies*. Oxford University Press, 2017, 33–34. On the importance of parties for political participation, see generally *Benazir Bhutto v Pakistan* PLD 1988 SC 416 and *Benazir Bhutto v Pakistan* PLD 1989 SC 66.

both. One of the biggest limitations of recent innovations such as citizens' assemblies and other party-less sortition-based mechanisms aimed at enhancing political participation is that even as they facilitate political participation,[44] they are not likely to do so for most citizens *for the issues they care about* most. A person who is really interested in the question of climate change will not feel sufficiently included without any political party that incorporates the issue on its political agenda, even if this citizen is selected through sortition to participate in an assembly to determine whether abortion should be legalised.

Furthermore, because of their temporally plenary character, parties alone can provide a modicum of representation to future electorates, who are otherwise entirely unable to participate in a democracy. Note that, by definition, the political participation cost has to be affordable by *all* the people, if the regime is to count as a democracy. Any group that is permanently excluded from the political process because their participation cost is too high changes the very character of the regime. Thus, systems that systemically exclude or suppress voter types, gerrymander constituency boundaries to make their access to power very difficult, or permit political domination by the wealthy through inadequate regulation of campaign finance impose very high political participation costs. This is why, in a healthy party system, parties will be accessible to all persons without discrimination and have a fair chance of winning (subject to the principles explained in Section 4.3); if a salient voter-type finds itself without a political party representing it, the costs of creating a new party to provide such representation will also be relatively low in a healthy system.

4.2.2.2 Voters' Information Cost

Secondly, parties reduce information costs. In constituencies whose large size is typical of contemporary states, voters tend to lack personal knowledge of electoral candidates. Given modern population sizes and the predominance of *gesellschaft* relationships outside small kinship and friendship circles, it is usually not feasible to have constituencies so small that most voters are personally sufficiently acquainted with all candidates. Parties reduce the information costs for voters because party affiliations of different candidates provide them with a significant amount of broadly accurate proxy information about their political views and agendas, thereby reducing their *voters' information costs*. Party systems that get rid of individual candidates entirely and allow voters to vote directly for parties may be particularly efficient at keeping this cost low, assuming that the number of parties in the system is small enough and their policy platforms transparent enough for a reasonably diligent voter to make informed choices without too much effort. But voter education can be

[44] See generally, Hélène Landemore, *Open Democracy: Reinventing Popular Rule for the Twenty-First Century*. Princeton University Press, 2020.

difficult in closed list voting systems because it is not just parties that supply proxy information for their candidates; local candidates also educate voters about their parties. A system where both parties and local candidates (in single-member or multi-member constituencies) matter is likely to reduce voters' information costs to the greatest extent.

It is easy to take the lowering of voters' information cost by parties for granted, but in doing so we imperil democracy itself. When electing a government, the act of voting is not merely self-regarding but also other regarding. Given the serious implications my vote can have on the lives of others, it is reasonable to suppose that the right to vote also entails a (moral) duty to vote *judiciously*. Casting a vote is more like a judge deciding a case (albeit without the duty to give public reasons) than choosing what to eat from a restaurant menu. While a voter has a duty at least to discharge her democratic function with due diligence (if not also with an attitude of care towards her compatriots),[45] it is also incumbent upon the state to ensure that the diligence burden on a citizen trying to vote judiciously is not too onerous. One implication of this is that the voters' information costs should be kept relatively low.

4.2.2.3 Policy Packaging Cost

Third, parties also reduce information costs for democratic state institutions by revealing to them what combination of policies will be acceptable to what proportion of the people. All parties that campaign on policy packages provide this information to state institutions, whether they win or lose. And winning parties, in addition, inform state institutions about the particular policy packaging that a large proportion of – if not a majority of – the people are willing to at least tolerate. This information can be generated and revealed, and state policy be legitimised, only through the bidirectional and plenary character of the mediating function that parties perform. Let us label these information and transaction costs as *policy packaging costs*.

The importance of lowering the policy packaging costs for state institutions should be obvious. It allows them to be responsive to the people in a way that is likely to cause the least amount of disgruntlement among those who disagree with individual policy proposals. Bundling different proposals into a single policy platform, while also rejecting alternative policies, makes the opportunity costs of policies clear to voters. They know not only what they are getting but also what they cannot get if they choose a certain set of policies.[46] This is key to the legitimation of the state's policies to its people. The fact that the policy packages are themselves framed bidirectionally by political parties drawing upon their proximity to popular opinion,

45 On care generally, see Jennifer Nedelsky and Tom Malleson, *Part-Time for All: A Care Manifesto*. Oxford University Press, 2023.

46 Rosenbluth and Shapiro, *Responsible Parties*, 230–231.

and then justified to the people, buttresses the perceived as well as actual democratic legitimacy of partisan state institutions. Without parties, there is simply no efficient way for state institutions to gather this information: opinion polls can tell us the level of popular support for particular issues, but the unity that packaging brings to a stack of proposals is only possible through the iterative platform and the legitimising glue that only a political party can supply. In other words, in a party-less state, the regime-legitimising policy packaging costs are infinite.

4.2.2.4 Ally Prediction Cost

Finally, parties reduce information costs for other political parties as well as for state officers and institutions by indicating to them which office-holders are likely to be persuadable political allies, whose support can be taken for granted, and who are likely to oppose certain policy proposals. Moreover, when they are reasonably disciplined, parties permit the identification of key leaders whose support will likely translate into the support of a predictable number of legislators and what it might take to secure their support. By aggregating and publicising political leanings, parties reduce the information costs associated with discovering whether another political actor is a political friend or foe and the consequent transaction costs in making political decisions (*ally prediction costs*).

Ally prediction costs are also of considerable significance in a democracy. Without parties, any decision-maker will need to seek the individual consent of every representative. Because policy packaging will also be absent, the ensuing political bargains will need to be simultaneous, numerous, and mutually compatible. Every individual representative in such a system will have the incentive to maximise the concessions she can extract for her support, whereas the policy initiator must make these concessions until she has the necessary support – she will, after all, be working with little knowledge of potential allies given the high ally prediction costs. The number of possible veto-players will be too high, and thus, state policy will tend towards preserving the status quo. Democratic decision-making under such scenarios can become extremely difficult.

We can therefore see the important role parties can play in keeping these four key information and transaction costs low. Without them, these costs will be too high to permit the smooth functioning of a democracy . Recent proposals for directly democratic citizen's assemblies (especially when conceived as decision-making rather than advisory bodies) grossly underestimate – or ignore – the substantial hurdle that these costs pose and the role that political parties play in reducing them and making them affordable.[47] Parties are therefore the key vehicle for a responsive interaction between public opinion and public policy, the very essence of

[47] For one such proposal that gives a limited decision-making power to a citizen's assembly, see John P. McCormick, *Machiavellian Democracy*. Cambridge University Press, 2011, 170–188.

democratic governance. Apart from policy responsiveness, the intermediary role that parties play makes them ideal training grounds for tomorrow's leaders, for public education and debate on civics, and as a vehicle for social solidarity and camaraderie. The training role is often underestimated in our popular culture that does not appreciate that politics is a skilled profession, like every other, one that typically requires a politician to regularly meet political opponents who vehemently oppose and criticise them, to interact with a wide cross-section of society that includes people from backgrounds very different from their own, to be nimble with compromises to get things done, to be able to withstand the emotional burden of constant public scrutiny, to learn to speak pithily and engagingly, to respond quickly to changing circumstances. These virtues do not come easily to most of us; parties provide a forum for acquiring and honing these key political skills and a community for solidaristic support and mentoring from party colleagues that these difficult engagements often necessitate.

With respect to citizens, the acts of raising a concern with the local party representative, becoming a party member, campaigning in an election, or joining a political protest organised by her party transform a legal subject into a performative citizen. Healthy parties can translate an individual's grievances into common causes, allowing her to see, for example, that the absence of a girls' toilet in her daughter's school is a broader concern that implicates patriarchy and affects women and girls across the country.

In this section, we have seen that political parties are essential to the proper functioning of representative democracies in sufficiently large and complex polities. They act as intermediaries between the state and its people, on the one hand, transmitting popular opinion to state institutions that typically lack the ability to gauge it directly and, on the other hand, formulating state policies and justifying them to the people. This dual role gives them a Janus-faced public-private character – they need to operate as a private association proximate to the people in order to access popular opinions and justify state policies. They also simultaneously need to be embedded in (but not fused with) the institutional structures of the state to transmit popular opinions back to them and to help them formulate policies, which in turn they will help justify to the people.

Healthy parties in well-functioning party systems therefore grease the wheels of representative democracy by reducing the following information and transaction costs: the political participation costs and the voters' information costs for the people and the policy packaging costs and ally prediction costs for state institutions. This functional account of political parties has highlighted their indispensability to the effective functioning of a representative democracy. This alone should suffice to alert us that lazy dismissals such as 'all politicians are corrupt' and 'all parties play dirty' imperils democracy itself. While a discursive defence of the importance of parties in a democracy is crucial, the state and its constitution too can lend a helping hand. They can bolster the ability of individual parties to perform their important mediating function between the state and its people as well as structure the party system in ways that facilitate rather than hinder the ability of parties to deepen democracy. They are more likely to do this if they deliberately consider certain guiding principles in constitutional design.

4.3 CONSTITUTIONAL PRINCIPLES IN RELATION TO POLITICAL PARTIES

Section 4.2 offered an idealised account of what parties do in a well-functioning democratic system. This idealised account is helpful in distinguishing between parties and party systems that function reasonably well from those that are pathological. It also helps us diagnose the particular ailments that afflict a party or a party-system. It should be clear that parties that fail to perform their intermediary function appropriately and effectively are bad for democracy. A party system can tolerate a few malfunctioning parties and still be healthy, so long as most of the governance parties are sound. In this section, we will turn our attention to certain normative goals that constitutions ought to adopt in relation to parties that will make it more likely that parties and party systems are healthy or that – if there are diseased parties in the system – the system can still tolerate or mitigate their ill effects or even nurse them to better health. To do so, I will explain four principles that constitutions should adopt in relation to parties: *the purposive autonomy principle, the party system optimality principle, the party-state separation principle*, and *the anti-faction principle*. Readers should note that for reasons of space, this already ambitious chapter does not take the logical next step of outlining more concrete prescriptions that might follow from the adoption of these principles. Some of that discussion has been undertaken elsewhere.[48] In this section, I will argue that democratic states should, through their constitutions, consider and seek to optimise four distinct, and sometimes conflicting, political principles in relation to political parties:

i. They should guarantee maximum autonomy for the formation, organisation, and operation of political parties, moderated by the restrictions necessitated by their purpose of winning (a share in) state power (for fixed terms) in competitive elections by acting as intermediaries between the state and its people (the 'purposive autonomy principle').
ii. They should try to optimise the party system such that the total number of serious political parties is large enough to broadly represent every major 'voter type', but not so large that the information costs on judicious voters are too high (the 'party system optimality principle').

[48] For some institutional implications of these principles, see Khaitan, 'Balancing Accountability and Effectiveness'.

iii. They should ensure a separation of parties and the state (the 'party-state separation principle').
iv. They should discourage the factionalisation of political parties (the 'anti-faction principle').

As constitutional principles, they primarily address the state. However, because the ruling party/coalition, which typically holds the reins to state power, is unlikely to be particularly interested in respecting them – and may even have a strong self-interest in breaching some of them – these principles need to be constitutionalised as pre-commitments by the state. I hasten to add two caveats to this proposal: first, I do not take constitutionalisation to necessarily entail judicialisation.[49] In fact, sometimes it may be neither necessary nor desirable to express a constitutional principle as a constitutional norm directly regulating constitutional actors, let alone as a *legal* norm. Instead, establishing an institutional arrangement that is most likely to uphold that principle – what may be termed 'second order' regulation – may well be the most optimal design solution.[50]

Second, a norm can be 'constitutionalised' in multiple ways, its inclusion in a big-C constitutional code being only one of them. Other modes of constitutionalisation include judicial interpretation, quasi-constitutional statutes, and constitutional conventions. The proposed principles should ideally be reflected – at least at a broad level – in the big-C constitutional code so that the institutional arrangements of the state are framed *alongside* its party system rather than *ex ante*. The finer details will, obviously, need to be left to the small-c statutes, conventions, and caselaw. The key determinant in each context should, in the main, be feasibility and effectiveness in light of path dependencies and all-things-considered judgments. The following subsections will explain each of these principles in turn.

4.3.1 *The Purposive Autonomy Principle*

4.3.1.1 The Public Purpose of Private Parties

States and their constitutions must seek to support (existing and future) political parties in the performance of their bidirectional and plenary intermediary role between the state and its people, so that they are best placed to reduce the four key information and transaction costs that make democratic governance difficult. In order to do so, parties must remain simultaneously private as well as public – this duality is their unique strength and also the reason for the complexity in regulating them. Liberal constitutionalism has long adhered to a controversial public-private divide. This divide is premised on diametrically opposed default assumptions about

49 Waldron, *Political Political Theory*; Khaitan, 'Constitutional Directives'.
50 See discussion in Section 5.3.1.5.

the regulation of public and private actors. Private actors are granted the autonomy to do whatever they like, unless there are very good, and special, reasons for regulating their actions. Public actors, on the other hand, may not do anything at all unless they have good, and constitutionally permitted, reasons for doing something. This distinction has long been criticised, with some scholars calling for its abolition,[51] whereas others have argued that the distinction may be preserved while the line between the public and the private should be drawn differently.[52] In a previous work, I have argued that the distinction is best understood as a spectrum rather than two discrete boxes.[53] The spectrum is both actor-sensitive and action-sensitive and primarily tracks interpersonal power and other-regarding functions. At the public end of the spectrum stands the all-powerful state enacting a general criminal or tax statute in its legislature. At the other end, a natural individual person lost in deep thought in her bedroom is paradigmatically private. When she acts as the manager of a large firm the next morning, she has moved away from this private-most end and become more public. Some areas of law – such as discrimination law – have come to terms with the idea that the public-private divide is a spectrum.[54]

Constitutional law is yet to follow this trend. It continues, on the whole, to draw the line sharply, vesting private actors with constitutional rights and burdening public actors with constitutional duties.[55] This structural limitation is an important hurdle that must be overcome if constitutions are to properly regulate political parties without destroying their public-private duality. Treating them as just another state institution is likely to seriously compromise their ability to engage with the people directly. While constitutions must be careful about over-regulating political parties lest they destroy their private character, they should also worry about constitutional silences and under-regulation that fails to acknowledge their publicness. A fit-for-purpose constitutional scheme for political parties will pay attention to three dimensions: (i) subject to the principles discussed in this chapter, it will grant them maximum autonomy; (ii) it will vest in them the necessary rights, powers, and entitlements that will enable them to better discharge their functions; and (iii) it will impose only those duties on parties that are necessary to preserve their public character. Is there such a happy regulatory middle that would preserve their privateness while demanding that they be sufficiently public at the same time?

[51] See, e.g., Ruth Gavison, 'Feminism and the Public/Private Distinction', *Stanford Law Review* 45: 1 (1992); Catharine A. MacKinnon, *Toward a Feminist Theory of the State*. Harvard University Press, 1989.

[52] Julian Sempill, 'What Rendered Ancient Tyrants Detestable: The Rule of Law and the Constitution of Corporate Power', *Hague Journal on the Rule of Law* 10: 219 (2018).

[53] Tarunabh Khaitan, *A Theory of Discrimination Law*. Oxford University Press, 2015, 195–214.

[54] Ibid.

[55] Section 6 of the British Human Rights Act 1998 is a notable exception. So is the horizontal application of certain fundamental rights in some jurisdictions, such as South Africa, and the growing trend in other jurisdictions to expand the scope of constitutional duties to at least certain types of for-profit corporations.

To locate that regulatory middle, we need to point out with greater precision what precisely makes parties *public*. The private dimension of parties demands maximum autonomy for the formation and operation of political parties. But their public character demands a recognition of their *purposive* dimension: unlike natural individuals, political parties in a representative democracy cannot be allowed to choose their purpose with complete freedom. What makes them a political party in a democratic party system is their *public purpose* of participating in competitive elections – with other parties – in order to secure a measure of control of the levers of state power for fixed periods of time and to do so by acting as intermediaries between the state and the people. This purpose is definitional of what a political party in a democracy *is*. It is specified at a high level of generality, being compatible with an extremely wide range of more specific purposes that parties may have. But it is incompatible with certain purposes: such as instituting a single party state; making elections insufficiently competitive; barring or making it difficult for (other) parties to connect or communicate with the people; and so on.

4.3.1.2 The Autonomy of Parties

To respect their private dimension, constitutions should guarantee maximum autonomy for the formation (from scratch or by splitting an existing party), organisation, and operation of political parties, moderated by the restrictions necessitated by their public purpose of winning (a share in) state power (for fixed terms) in competitive elections by acting as intermediaries between the state and its people. Hence the *purposive autonomy principle*. Simply put, the principle permits significant autonomy to parties (and partisans) but seeks to ensure that they are committed to the purpose of being but one player in a multi-party democracy. The principle requires that parties should be relatively easy to form and disband and to enter or leave. The main barriers to their success should be political, not legal. New parties or opposition parties must not be locked out of political competition through high entry barriers.[56] High access barriers are not only bad for new parties but also for established parties – without an alternative political outlet, strong political forces that are excluded from partisan expression would eventually seek to capture an established party or upend the system itself. The autonomy of political parties is key to keeping the political participation costs in a democracy low.

Translating the need to protect their purposive autonomy into particular rights and duties requires further specification beyond the scope of this chapter. Full specification cannot, obviously, happen without catering to the peculiarities of a particular political context. In general, parties may need the whole suite of civil and

[56] For a catalogue of such barriers enacted against third parties in the United States, see Samuel Issacharoff and Richard H. Pildes, 'Politics as Markets: Partisan Lockups of the Democratic Process', *Stanford Law Review* 50: 643, 683 (1998).

political rights that citizens ordinarily have access to in a liberal democracy; sometimes they may even need special protections of their autonomy over and above what citizens are guaranteed. They are likely to need access to all the usual fundamental freedoms to enable them to be formed, to contact and connect with the people and mobilise them, to campaign and express political views, to contest elections, to raise funds, and so on. Without these freedoms, a political party may be woefully inept at reducing key democratic costs. Furthermore, a range of 'fourth branch' guarantor institutions that can effectively guarantee norms such as free and fair elections, probity, transparency, fair boundaries delimitation, campaign finance regulation, and a host of other norms that the ruling party/alliance may have reasons to want to undermine are usually necessitated by the purposive autonomy principle.[57] These constitutional protections of party autonomy are also necessary to insulate opposition parties from any self-interested targeting by the ruling party/coalition: not least because the autonomy of all (serious) parties matters, such that the principle of inter-party equity is embedded in the purposive autonomy principle.

4.3.1.3 Public Entitlements for *Serious* Parties

While their privateness demands the protection of their autonomy, their public purpose may entitle them to special privileges and powers, as well as make them fit for bearing special duties that are inapplicable to natural individuals. Public entitlements, such as (limited) state funding for political campaigns or immunity from defamation laws for political speeches, can help secure a level playing field between political parties and enable many of them to discharge their democratic functions effectively.[58] This would be especially useful for smaller parties in a hegemonic or a predominant party system.[59] Even if the predominant party is itself healthy, the party system isn't. Thus, any provision of state benefits has to avoid cartelisation. In order to reduce the political participation costs of all voters, a measure of state support to less powerful parties would usually be necessary. That said, it may be permissible to restrict these rewards to *serious* political parties. Seriousness is a measure of the party's intention to play the requisite intermediary role between the state and its people – a serious political party seeks a role in the governance of the state, or an influence in state policies, or both, primarily by winning elections and shaping political discourse. Note that both governance parties and influence parties are 'serious' in the sense I intend here. On the other hand, a party that doesn't campaign or put up candidates for elections hardly has a public dimension worth worrying

57 Khaitan, 'Guarantor Institutions'; Khaitan, 'Guarantor (or "Fourth Branch") Institutions'.

58 Article 40 of the Portuguese Constitution, for example, guarantees broadcasting time in public media to political parties. On party funding generally, see Keith Ewing, Jacob Rowbottom, and Joo-Cheong Tham, eds., *The Funding of Political Parties: Where Now?* Routledge 2012.

59 Zim Nwokora and Riccardo Pelizzo, 'Sartori Reconsidered: Toward a New Predominant Party System', *Political Studies* 62: 824 (2014).

about. Similarly, joke parties (such as the British Monster Raving Loony Party) and a number of single-issue parties (such as the Australian Help End Marijuana Prohibition Party) often don't even intend to win – and tend to be themselves surprised when they do win – even if their ability to focus the spotlight on an ignored issue can often be valuable for a polity. Such non-serious parties can largely be regulated as private clubs left to enjoy the autonomy that other political parties enjoy, but without the public benefits or burdens until they have proven their political seriousness.

While performance in past elections is a reasonable proxy of seriousness, it is generally a good idea to base it on aggregate performance in the three or four previous elections taken together, rather than the most recent election alone. For example, equitable state funding may be provided to every party that secured at least (say) 5 per cent of the popular vote share in any of the last three election cycles, or to every party that had a presence in the legislature in at least one of the last three elections. Where these seriousness thresholds are fixed is necessarily arbitrary and context-specific – any reasonably low threshold that has not been weaponised against particular parties and doesn't squeeze out smaller, but serious, parties should normally suffice (any such weaponisation would, we will see, breach the party-state separation principle). Admittedly, one problem with measuring seriousness (a forward-looking phenomenon) through past electoral performance is that it cannot distinguish between serious and non-serious *new* parties. Since the purposive autonomy principle applies not only to existing parties but also to future ones, any forward-looking public support may need to be extended to all new parties willing to accept the public duties imposed on serious parties, with exclusions kicking in after they have participated in (say) two election cycles.[60] Note also that while seriousness of a political party is a relevant consideration in determining public funding, it does not extend to calibrating the extent of funding proportionate to party size. If anything, the kind of distinction US law draws between *major* and *minor* parties in order to supply greater benefits to the major parties are likely to be inimical to the principle of equity embedded in the purposive autonomy principle (as well as the party-state separation principle).[61]

4.3.1.4 Public Duties of Parties

The public purpose of parties invites not only special entitlements but also some public duties. We will discuss some of them under the other principles to follow. But some duties flow directly from their role in reducing the political participation

[60] *Bergman v Minister of Finance and State Comptroller* (1969) HCJ 98/69 (the Israeli Supreme Court Sitting as the High Court of Justice). See also *Agudat Derech Eretz v Broadcasting Authority* HCJ 246/81 [1981].

[61] See www.fec.gov/introduction-campaign-finance/understanding-ways-support-federal-candidates/presidential-elections/public-funding-presidential-elections/.

costs and the policy packaging costs. Parties are likely to lower the political participation costs only if there is a fair measure of transparency surrounding their core value commitments, internal institutional structures, decision-making processes, financial affairs, and credible – even if internal – enforcement mechanisms of their institutional commitments. Serious parties should, therefore, have the duty to publicise these details, so that voters and partisans can rely on them and hold parties accountable. Likewise, parties are likely to lower the policy packaging costs (as well as the other three democratic costs) only if they offer a more-or-less comprehensive policy package in their election manifestos. Serious parties may, therefore, be mandated to adopt and publicise (at least broad) policy positions on a number of the key issues of governance of the day (such as taxation, foreign policy, education, health care, immigration, and so on) in their election manifestos, preferably published before a fixed period prior to elections to give them sufficient public airing.

On the whole, the purposive autonomy principle seeks to preserve the public-private duality of political parties that is essential to their role in facilitating democratic governance. Supporting parties requires guaranteeing considerable autonomy to all existing and future parties. At the same time, at least serious political parties need affirmative state support and protections that enhance their abilities to reduce the four democratic costs. The purposive autonomy principle also justifies the imposition of the duty to adopt transparent party constitutions and plenary policy manifestos on such serious parties. But all public *duties* imposed on parties need to be justified with reference to their public purpose of being but one player in a multiparty democracy. If we consider Article 21(1) of the German Basic Law, for example, it is broadly a recognition of the purposive autonomy principle:

> The political parties participate in the formation of the political will of the people. They may be freely established. Their internal organisation must conform to democratic principles. They must publicly account for their assets and of the sources and use of their funds as well as assets.[62]

'Broadly', because I am doubtful that inner-party democracy – mandated by the third clause above – can be justified by the purposive autonomy principle. It is by no means obvious that internally democratic parties are better at reducing the key democratic costs, not to mention the pragmatic difficulties in determining what suffices as an internally democratic party at an age of relatively loose and myriad ways of associating with a party.[63] If anything, base-voter-dominated party primaries have emerged as a key centrifugal force in US politics and the concomitant threat that force poses to democracy in the country.[64] Constitutions should be slow to

62 See also Article 51 of the Portuguese Constitution.

63 See generally, Kate O'Regan, 'Political Parties: The Missing Link in Our Constitution?' www.corruptionwatch.org.za/political-parties-the-missing-link-in-our-constitution/.

64 Barry Burden, 'The Polarizing Effects of Congressional Primaries' in *Congressional Primaries and the Poltics of Representation* ed. Peter Galderisi et al. Rowman & Littlefield, 2001, 95–115;

mandate inner-party democracy or regulate how parties discipline their members. Many courts have enforced fundamental rights claims by ordinary voters and party members against political parties and their leadership.[65] Doing so has clear, and often adverse and unintended, consequences for the purposive autonomy of political parties. The implication is not that parties should be allowed to treat their members in any manner they wish; it is rather that state regulation of the relationship between parties and their members should cross a high bar of purposive justification that takes their hybrid public-private character seriously.

4.3.1.5 Preference for Second-Order Regulation

The need to protect purposive autonomy of parties dictates not only a cautious approach to imposing duties on parties but also *how* any duties may be imposed. Duty-imposing norms should be crafted so as to not destroy the dual character of parties. In general, and subject to their effectiveness in a given context, three broad regulatory criteria should govern design possibilities for duty-imposing norms with respect to political parties:

- Political enforcement and self-regulation are better than judicial enforcement,[66]
- Nudges are better than command-and-control,[67] and
- Carrots are better than sticks.[68]

These criteria are partial to 'second-order regulation', which emphasise the importance of 'background competitive structures' that shape decision-making, rather than seeking to police behaviour directly through first-order commands.[69] Note that *all* background structures shape the behaviour of actors – the question is not so much whether to have second-order regulation but what type of second-order regulation is worth having. For example, a democracy has to choose *some* electoral system, and each system shapes the behaviour of politicians differently. In fact, the choice of the electoral system (majoritarian or proportionate, ranked or unranked, at large or constituency-based), the nature of executive-legislature relations (parliamentary, presidential, semi-presidential, semi-parliamentary), the number of legislative chambers, and the degree of centralisation or federation are all institutional choices that can significantly impact the nature of the party system in a polity. For example,

Michael Murakami, 'Divisive Primaries: Party Organizations, Ideological Groups, and the Battle of Party Purity', *Political Science and Politics* 41: 918 (2008).

65 *Ramakatsa v Magashule* [2012] ZACC 31 (South African Constitutional Court); *Bhutta v Pakistan* PLD 2018 Supreme Court 370 (Pakistani Supreme Court).

66 Khaitan, 'Constitutional Directives'.

67 Cass R. Sunstein, 'Nudging: A Very Short Guide', *Journal of Consumer Policy* 37: 583 (2014).

68 In other words, it is better to ensure compliance by making the realisation of some regulatory principles a precondition to accessing state support for parties, rather than through penalties.

69 Issacharoff and Pildes, 'Politics as Markets', 647.

majoritarian, cumulative, approval, and ranked voting systems are likely to incentivise centripetal parties, whereas proportionate representation is more conducive to factions. Parliamentary systems are likely to encourage collective party leadership, whereas presidential systems could encourage individual-centric parties. Bicameralism and federalism are probably better suited to protecting opposition rights than unicameralism and centralisation. The directionality of these precise connections is beside the point – if one concedes that a significant connection exists, in whatever direction, then many regulatory objectives in relation to parties can be achieved by the right combination of institutional design of state bodies. This indirect, second-order, regulation is generally more conducive to party autonomy than first-order legal regulation.

I am not suggesting that rule-based, judicially enforced, command-and-control first-order regulation will never be appropriate. Sometimes it will be. The party-state separation principle will normally require stringent, often legal, norms to protect the separation of the state from the ruling party/coalition. Most aspects of private law, such as the law of torts or contracts, should apply to parties, unless their public character demands an exception to be made. Anti-discrimination norms that support the anti-faction principle are usually already calibrated to justify judicial intervention against hybrid public-private actors[70] and will therefore be appropriate for judicial enforcement against parties in most jurisdictions. Consider *Smith v Allwright*, where the United States Supreme Court first determined that all-white primaries for the selection of Democratic Party candidates were so well-integrated in the electoral system of Texas that they amounted to state action, before applying the anti-discrimination principle to the Party and prohibiting all-white primaries.[71] This move may have been doctrinally necessary because of the quirks of the American legal system, but morally speaking, there is no reason why anti-discrimination norms should not apply to parties qua parties, that is, as hybrid public-private bodies, without needing to characterise them as state institutions. In general, however, where feasible and effective, second-order regulation is more likely to preserve the dual character of political parties. Extreme measures such as party bans are best avoided. Courts understandably struggle to condemn even the most clearly anti-democratic parties when the outcome is as far-reaching as a total ban.[72] What's worse, even when successfully deployed, party bans may be ineffective, or even

[70] See Khaitan, *A Theory of Discrimination Law*, 195–214.

[71] *Smith v Allwright* 321 US 649 (1944). See also Issacharoff and Pildes 'Politics as Markets', 654–660.

[72] On the difficulties in banning even plainly undemocratic parties, see *Nationaldemokratische Partei Deutschlands* 2 BvB 1/13 (German Constitutional Court): 'the prohibition of a political party by the Federal Constitutional Court is the sharpest weapon, albeit a double-edged one, a democratic state under the rule of law has against an organized enemy. The highest degree of legal certainty, transparency, predictability and reliability is therefore required in proceedings to prohibit a political party'.

counter-productive.[73] Having said that, second-order regulations would sometimes fail to achieve their desired purpose. While an independent guarantor institution like a boundaries commission may well ensure fair constituency determination in most cases,[74] even the best design can fail. If a captured boundaries commission produces a gerrymandered electoral map, there may well be strong reasons for first-order judicial intervention.[75]

The purposive autonomy principle is a meta-principle that dictates how constitutions should approach political party regulation. It demands a move away from a binary dichotomy that liberal constitutionalism is used to: rights for private persons, duties on public bodies. Instead, it draws attention to the need for a more nuanced approach, one that considers each right and duty in terms of its appropriateness for the hybrid character of political parties. The discussion above is not meant to be too directive: in constitutional practice, context matters a lot. Even in a given context, there may be many different ways of satisfying the purposive autonomy principle. The main point is that instead of trying to fit political parties into a ready-made template designed either for private individuals or for state bodies, an a la carte regulatory framework that works for them is required. The three following principles may be understood as facets of the purposive autonomy principle but merit separate discussion because of the important bearing they have on the constitutional regulation of parties.

4.3.2 *The Party System Optimality Principle*

Healthy parties tend to attract members, affiliates, and voters through their *ideologies*, rather than through clientelism or patronage. I understand 'ideology' in the sense that Converse explains it: a relatively wide-ranging *belief system*, which is relevant to political behaviour.[76] A belief system, in turn, is 'a configuration of ideas and attitudes in which the elements are bound together by some form of constraint or functional interdependence'.[77] The *centrality* of an element in a belief system is a measure of the likelihood that a voter will change her party preference if her party's stance regarding that element changes, rather than change her view on the element

[73] On party bans, see Tom Daly and Brian Jones, 'Parties versus Democracy: Addressing Today's Political-Party Threats to Democratic Rule', *International Journal of Constitutional Law* 18: 509 (2020).

[74] On the efficacy of the guarantor function of electoral and boundary commissions, see Malcolm Langford et al, 'The Rise of Electoral Management Bodies: Diffusion and Effects', *Asian Journal of Comparative Law* 16(S1): S60 (2021). Nicholas Stephanopoulas, 'Depoliticizing Redistricting', in *Comparative Election Law* ed. James Gardner. Elgar, 2022, 459–477.

[75] On a manageable judicial standard for detecting partisan gerrymandering, see Nicholas Stephanopoulas and Eric McGhee, 'Partisan Gerrymandering and the Efficiency Gap', *University of Chicago Law Review* 82: 831 (2015).

[76] Philip E. Converse, 'The Nature of Belief Systems in Mass Publics (1964)', *Critical Review* 18: 1, 4–5 (2006).

[77] Ibid. 3.

itself.[78] She may tolerate a party's change of position on less central elements in a belief system but give up on her partisan loyalty if the party reneges on a more central element. For Gerring, the quality of being 'bound together' (which he calls 'coherence') has two corollaries: *contrast* ('implying coherence vis-à-vis competing ideologies') and *stability* ('implying coherence through time').[79] Thus, competing political ideologies straddle the same ideological axis and are relatively stable over time. While much penumbral content of political ideologies is malleable, their most central elements are likely to be most relevant to contrasting them with other ideologies and determining their stability over time. Not all ideologies matter politically. Chhibber and Verma argue that politically salient ideologies not only need to be competing and stable but also possess two further features to structure a party system:

> First, there must be political, social, or economic *elites* with interests, vested or otherwise, who differentiate themselves on the basis of such ideas, offer resources to support the creation of a particular ideological position, and assist in the transmission of these ideas to the voters. And, second, the ideas thus transmitted, and the issues that embody them, must have the support of *enough people*.[80]

Without sufficient elite support, parties are unlikely to get off the ground. Without enough support in the electorate, they are unlikely to become meaningful political players. Sartori's classical account analysed party systems through this lens of salient ideological axes. His distinction between two-party systems, moderate pluralism systems, and polarised pluralism systems was based on two factors: the number of political parties in a system and the ideological distance between them.[81] In this model, a two-party system had two large, ideologically centrist parties (i.e., very little contrast between their ideologies); a moderate pluralism system had multiple parties organised around two broadly centrist ideological coalitions; and a polarised pluralism system had multiple parties pursuing ideologies cutting across the traditional left-right axis seen in the other two systems. The ideological distance between the parties/coalitions in the two-party system and the moderate pluralism system was relatively modest because each pursued the median voter organised on a single – macroeconomic policy – axis. On this account, the first two centripetal systems usually yielded stable and effective governments, whereas polarised pluralism often resulted in political as well as democratic instability.

This classical account needs an important revision in our times. As Scheppele has argued, politics is no longer organised on a single left-right ideological axis in

78 Ibid 4.

79 John Gerring, 'Ideology: A Definitional Analysis', *Political Research Quarterly* 50: 957, 980 (1997).

80 Pradeep K. Chhibber and Rahul Verma, *Ideology and Identity: The Changing Party Systems of India*. Oxford University Press, 2018, 15 (emphases in the original).

81 Sartori, *Parties and Party Systems* .

contemporary Western democracies. In the very least, a nativism-cosmopolitanism divide has strongly emerged as an additional, cross-cutting, axis for political alignment.[82] Chhibber and Verma argue that independent India has always had two salient political axes: the politics of statism ('the extent to which the state should dominate society, regulate social norms, and redistribute private property') and the politics of accommodation ('whether and how the state should accommodate the needs of various marginalised groups and protect minority rights from assertive majoritarian tendencies').[83] These insights scramble the tidiness of Sartori's single-axis classification. When two major ideological axes are salient to voters, there are at least four stable party types (and concomitant 'voter types') that can broadly capture the worldviews and political preferences of most voters in such systems: on Scheppele's classification, for example, one should expect left-nativist parties,[84] right-nativist parties,[85] left-cosmopolitan parties,[86] and right-cosmopolitan parties.[87] With each new salient axis, new permutations give rise to the possibility of an even larger number of voter types in search of distinctive political representation.

These ideological axes must be salient: political parties offer package deals, and they cannot be expected to customise their policy offerings to all the individual preferences of every voter. We should therefore understand key voter types only in relation to the politically *salient* ideological axes of division in a given polity, which in turn are defined by the most central belief elements in their belief system (such as nativism or redistribution). A salient political division comes to define the political preferences of voters in such a deep way that it becomes difficult for the same party to simultaneously represent the preferences of distinct voter types effectively. Such parties may try to speak in multiple voices to mutually incompatible constituencies (in the short term). However, if the salient divisions are abiding, these parties are either likely to split (if the system tolerates multiple parties) or have one group eventually come to dominate or decimate the other within the party (if it doesn't).

If the latter happens, and no party exists to cater to a particular voter type, the political participation costs of such voters will be extremely high, to the point that they may be totally excluded from representative politics. What is worse, even their efforts to start a party that caters to their voter type may be frustrated if the party system is structurally predisposed to a two-party system and does not facilitate the emergence of new parties. Their only remaining options will be either to capture one of the existing parties (and thereby deprive a different voter type of political

[82] Scheppele, 'The Party's Over'.

[83] Chhibber and Verma, *Ideology and Identity*, 2. Their name for the second axis is the 'politics of *recognition*'. I have called it the 'politics of *accommodation*' to avoid confusion with the recognition-redistribution debate, since accommodation can take distributive as well as expressive forms.

[84] Such as the Spanish Podemos Party.

[85] Such as the American Republican Party under Donal Trump's leadership.

[86] Such as the Indian Congress Party under Sonia Gandhi's leadership.

[87] Such as the British Conservative Party under David Cameron's leadership.

representation) or try to change the party system, or even the political system entirely, from the outside. Such excluded voters become especially vulnerable to a quick-fix populist rhetoric.[88] Such powerful, but unspent, political force is extremely dangerous to democracies. Furthermore, the near impossibility of political alliances in a two-party democracy – except when party discipline is extremely weak – is also not necessarily a good thing for democracy. This is the reason why a two-party system is more likely to encourage compromise-resistant tribalism in politics, accentuating the winner-takes-all feature of majoritarian politics.

What follows is that in any system that has more than one salient political axis, a two-party system simply cannot approximate the broad political worldviews of major voter types. A regime will establish 'the rule of the people' only if it facilitates the representation of the preferences of every major voter type in its party system, with two caveats: first, as I will argue later in this chapter, it is legitimate – albeit sometimes unwise – to restrict the likelihood of political representation – or, at least, the likelihood of political success – of factional voters who do not accept that a democracy is the rule of *all* the people, even if a factional-inclusivist axis has become salient in that polity. Just as I cannot rely on my autonomy to sell my children or my (future) self into slavery, rule of all the people cannot be relied upon to transform a democracy into the rule of *some* of the people. Neither autonomy nor democracy apply to themselves in this self-harming manner.[89]

The second caveat is that there is a feasibility limit to the total number of serious parties that a democracy can accommodate. It is true that the larger the number of distinctive parties in a system, the smaller the political participation costs are likely to be for a voter. In fact, if there is a party that mirrors every voter's customised set of political preferences, political participation costs will be non-existent for every voter. Needless to say, such single member 'parties' won't be parties in any meaningful sense. Furthermore, even as they reduce political participation costs, a large number of parties significantly increases voters' information costs. A voter who has to go through a list of fifty candidates belonging to fifty different serious parties is able to make an informed choice only after putting in considerable effort to educate herself on the distinctive ideological commitments and political platforms of all these fifty parties. She might as well focus her research on the fifty individual candidates in such cases (which would not be any less daunting, in any case). Too many choices may not matter when the stakes are low – such as when one is ordering a meal from a restaurant's menu – for one can make a reasonable choice having considered only the first five options. But when the stakes are as high as entrusting the government of one's polity, the voters' information costs

[88] Rogers Brubaker, 'Populism and Nationalism', *Nations and Nationalism* 26: 44 (2020); Rogers Brubaker, 'Why Populism?', *Theory and Society* 46: 357 (2017).

[89] Contrast them with freedom of expression, which typically includes the right to criticise freedom of expression itself.

must be reasonable enough to enable a judicious voter to consider the pros and cons of all candidates.

The sum of these concerns is the 'party system optimality principle': in contemporary democratic polities that divide along multiple salient axes, party systems should be optimised such that the total number of serious political parties is large enough to broadly represent every major 'voter type', but not so large that the information costs on judicious voters are too high. The choice of electoral system for the elected institutions and offices is probably the single most important regulatory tool to respect the party system optimality principle (although the party system can also become federalised in federal systems, since province-specific parties can emerge irrespective of the electoral system). Note that a polity can coherently adopt different electoral systems for different state institutions (especially in bicameral and federal systems), thus vastly expanding the regulatory permutations and combinations at its disposal.

4.3.3 *The Party-State Separation Principle*

One danger in approximating the democratic ideal through elections is the abiding possibility that we only manage to secure the rule of *some of* the people at any given point in time. The political exclusion of the losing parties – and potentially their voters – is more acute in winner-takes-all systems. We seek to solve this problem by temporally distinguishing between a state's *regime* and its *government*: a regime can still call itself democratic if, *over time*, it allows different parties to win political power. So long as there are no permanent winners, the regime can still claim to be ruled by *all* the people. This is the ideal that legitimises many power-sharing arrangements in deeply divided societies.[90] It also generates our third political principle: that a state should seek to ensure a separation of the ruling party/coalition and the state, so as to allow a genuine hope for today's losers to be tomorrow's winners. We will call this the 'party-state separation principle'. The basic argument is that if a party (usually the ruling party/coalition) becomes entrenched in the apparatus of the state, the political participation costs of the supporters of all other parties become insurmountable.

The party-state separation principle demands a recognition of a host of opposition rights: including a significant opposition voice – perhaps even a veto – in constitutional amendments and constitutional appointments. It requires the bureaucracy, police, prosecution, judiciary, and guarantor institutions to function in a nonpartisan manner. The principle also demands equity in state benefits given to the ruling party/coalition and to opposition parties – making it structurally difficult for a given party or parties to win state offices breaches the party-state separation principle

[90] See generally Sujit Choudhry, ed., *Constitutional Design for Divided Societies: Integration or Accommodation?* Oxford University Press, 2008.

as much as making it more likely for a given party or parties to win or retain state power. Recognising this principle is especially important given the salience of the *institutional* 'separation of powers' principle in constitutional theory – given how partisan loyalties can scramble institutional separation, it is essential that the party-state separation principle is considered alongside the institutional separation of powers principle and given the same weight in constitutional thought. Note, however, that the party-state separation principle does *not* require that the opposition be given the right to veto ordinary (as opposed to constitutional) policy objectives of a legitimate and democratically elected government. A balance has to be struck between allowing the opposition to perform its constitutional duties without thwarting the government's ability to govern.[91]

One way to appreciate the party-state separation principle is to think of it as a constraint imposed on the democratic rights of today's people by those of a *future* people. Constitutional theory has frequently worried about 'the dead hand of the past' in the context of entrenched fundamental rights but rarely considered constraints generated by the future people's right to democracy. Even if we assume that there are *a* people at a given point in time in a state, and that this people today unanimously wish to entrench the ruling party/coalition in the apparatus of the state, they cannot possibly obtain the consent of any future peoples to do so and must therefore lack this power. One might seek to respond to this claim by suggesting that it might at least be permissible to fuse a state and its ruling party/coalition for one generation, and the arrangement may be revisited by every future generation? The claim presupposes the all-too common, but mistaken, generational outlook to think of a 'people' in the temporal sense. A people – in its temporal sense – is not like The Doctor (from the famous British science-fiction show *Doctor Who*), who disintegrates and regenerates into a new version of him/herself at precise moments in time. Each version is the same eternal Doctor, but different, with clear and distinct temporal geneses and dissolutions. A people would be like The Doctor if everyone in a generation was born on the same day and died on the same day. In reality, a people – temporally – are better compared to a river. An ancient Greek philosopher, Heraclitus, is said to have posed the famous paradox: Can one step in the same river twice?[92] The paradox lies in the fact that anyone stepping into any given point in the course of a river twice – the two attempts separated by some interval of time – will be stepping into different waters of *the same* river. Just like a constantly flowing river that receives new waters from its source and loses old waters to the sea, a people are constantly gaining new individuals by birth or immigration and losing old ones to death and emigration. Even the separation of a day, therefore, will suffice to separate

[91] For a model for how this might be achieved, see Khaitan, 'Balancing Accountability and Effectiveness'.

[92] Daniel W. Graham, 'Heraclitus', *Stanford Encyclopedia of Philosophy* (3 September 2019), https://plato.stanford.edu/entries/heraclitus/.

the current people from a future one. As an ideational entity, they remain the same people over time; as a sum of their constituent individuals, they are constantly changing over time. Thus, even a single generational fusion of the ruling party/coalition and the state will be impermissible by the democratic ideal.

The party-state separation principle therefore requires that a state should preserve the genuine likelihood of different parties securing governmental power at different points in time. The transfer of power following elections should be peaceful, and the political opposition must be able to plausibly imagine itself as a government in waiting. It should therefore be hostile to a one-party system (where only one party is allowed to exist, de jure and de facto), or a hegemonic party system (where smaller parties are allowed to exist, but the system de facto and de jure favours a hegemonic party that remains in power) at all times.[93] It should even be hostile to the kind of two-party system in which the two parties operate like a cartel and make it structurally difficult for a third party to emerge.[94] Any such fusion of parties and the state is not only bad for democracy, it is also likely to make the regime unstable because any significant voter type without mainstream political representation is likely to find solace in anti-system parties. On the other hand, it is compatible with a predominant party system, where a single party or coalition de facto dominates all others, although de jure the system permits free and fair political competition and gives no structural advantage to the predominant party. That said, the purposive autonomy principle would still view a predominant party system as non-ideal and seek to enable opposition parties to rise and flourish in such a system. Even if the opposition does not win elections, a robust opposition is essential to check the political power of the ruling party/coalition (balanced against the need for effective government) and therefore to reduce the four democratic costs effectively. Recall that these costs remain high in a system with only one healthy political party. Hence the party-state separation principle.

4.3.4 *The Anti-faction Principle*

We can now consider the final principle. We must accept that an elected democratic government is unlikely to represent all the people of a state at any one given time, where representation is understood in terms of voters' electoral *preferences* as expressed on the ballot. But it does not follow that we should also accept that such an under-representative government only needs to serve the *interests* of those it represents. An under-representative government can, and should, still aspire to serve the interests of all its people. This is not drawn from an agenda for ensuring minority

93 On party systems, see Nwokora and Pelizzo, 'Sartori Reconsidered', 833.

94 Issacharoff and Pildes show how the two main parties have created an effective political duopoly in the United States: Issacharoff and Pildes, 'Politics as Markets', 644. Katz and Mair argue that the phenomenon of cartelisation extends to Europe as well: R. Katz and P. Mair, 'The Cartel Party Thesis: A Restatement', *Perspectives on Politics* 7: 753 (2009).

rights under a majoritarian government. Basic rights concern themselves with only the most fundamental human interests. Governments should never breach them unjustifiably. But governments do a lot more than not breach rights – when they work well, they facilitate human flourishing. Parties, in their idealised sense, work towards the flourishing of all the people of their state; factions care only for a sub-section thereof.[95] Factions a priori exclude the interests of their disfavoured section of the people from even being considered when framing policies – if these interests are considered at all, it is with a view to hurt them rather than to advance them. Importantly, given our capacity to threaten the very survival of humanity, at least in our times, factions would include parties that do not count the interests of the future people as legitimate concerns for their political calculations.

Factions fail to reduce the policy packaging costs for state institutions. We have seen that one of the key functions of political parties is to package the interests of all voters based on the party's value commitments. These policy packages are then tested in elections, and voters express their preferences for or against such packages, which information is then available to state institutions when framing policy. In the process, parties also translate any voter's factional interests into a subset of the common good through their policy packaging function, thereby moderating them to make them compatible with the interests of other citizens. Factions fail to do so. They also increase the political participation costs of the excluded voters – it is one thing to not have every party reflect one's voter type, quite another to have a party in a system not even consider one's interests as legitimate and relevant alongside the interests of all others.

This distinction between a party and a faction has been long recognised in political theory.[96] As Sartori put it, 'If a party is not a party capable of governing for the sake of the whole, that is, in view of a general interest, then it does not differ from a faction. Although a party only represents a part, this part must take a *non-partial* approach to the whole.'[97] Factions are concerned with the interests and well-being of only a sub-section of the people. Parties, even when they make claims on behalf of particular groups, 'must transcend the language of particularity and re-articulate the claims they represent in such a way that their demand for a share in political power is justified to the entire people and not only to that particular group of individuals that chooses to associate with them'.[98] The point of the distinction is normative rather than taxonomical: '[It] is very likely that the empirical analysis of existing practices will show how parties and factions are often entangled, with

[95] Barber characterises factions as 'sectarian parties': Barber, *The Principles of Constitutionalism*, 168. For a brief historical overview of the development of the conceptual distinction between parties and factions, see Bonotti, *Partisanship and Political Liberalism in Diverse Societies*, 103–105.

[96] White and Ypi, *The Meaning of Partisanship*, 32.

[97] Sartori, *Parties and Party Systems*, 50.

[98] White and Ypi, *The Meaning of Partisanship*, 34.

different political agents exhibiting features of both, to a greater or lesser extent.'[99] It is important to note that the distinction attaches itself to the entity as a whole and not to its individual actions. A party may have distinct policies catering to the interests of different sub-sections of the people – it will be a faction only if, *taken as a whole*, its political ideology and its policy platform is not justifiable to all the people. Any attempt to distinguish real-world parties from factions too sharply is likely to fail. Having said that, Rosenblum is probably right when she suggests that, even as an empirical matter, 'where it is an original identity, or at least not reducible to prior political identities, the "we" of partisanship is more inclusive than other political identities'.[100]

'Rule *of* the people' demands not only that political power is exercised by the people's representatives but also that it is exercised in the name of *all the people*. In the words of White and Ypi, 'the very ideal of collective self-rule implies that power is considered legitimate to the extent that it is justified to the *whole* people'.[101] It is this normative ideal that leads us to our final principle: that a state should seek to ensure that political parties do not operate as factions. We will call this the 'anti-faction principle' and amend White and Ypi's formulation somewhat to suggest that it requires political parties to ensure that their policies are objectively justifi*able* (rather than subjectively justifi*ed*) to all the people. The amendment is required because it may be that a party fails to even communicate, let alone actually justify, its policies to all the people. So long as its policies are justifiable to all of them, the anti-faction principle should be satisfied. The anti-faction principle, therefore, does *not* require parties to articulate their policies in Rawlsian 'public reason' terms.[102] Furthermore, a justifiab*ility*-standard is more tolerant of parties strategically appealing to particular sub-sections of the people as a matter of electoral tactics – so long as their packaged *policy platforms* are justifiable to all the people. Other independent moral and political constraints no doubt exist – such strategic appeals should not demonise any other section of the people, for example.

Unlike the purposive autonomy principle, which frowns upon single-issue parties, the anti-faction principle – on its own – does not require parties to have a plenary policy package. An anti-corruption party is not a faction. The party's size doesn't matter either, even if the party seeks only to influence policy rather than to govern. A small Green Party is likely to be a party, since its environmental objectives are justifiable to all. Even a party whose entire policy platform is devoted to advantaging a single societal group may not necessarily be a faction. A Workers' Party, a *Dalit* Party in India (for former 'untouchable' castes), or an African American Party in the United States can be parties, if they can justify the interests of their preferred groups

99 Ibid.

100 Rosenblum, *On the Side of Angels*, 356.

101 White and Ypi,*The Meaning of Partisanship*, 34 (emphasis in the original).

102 John Rawls, 'The Idea of Public Reason Revisited', *The University of Chicago Law Review* 64: 765 (1997).

by reference to the general interest (for example, that historically excluded groups have a greater claim on the state's resources). Furthermore, parties are allowed to make ideological and policy mistakes – the anti-faction principle does not demand that their policies actually work. But it does demand sincerity and plausibility – some obviously unworkable or implausible policies may evidence a lack of sincerity. A party that continues to deny the human impact on the global environment and its potential implications for future people, despite all the evidence to the contrary, is probably a faction because it is refusing to consider the interests of the future people, and its policies are unlikely to be justifiable to them. The one exception to the sincerity and plausibility test is this: even if a 'party' sincerely believes that the only interests that count are the interests of a sub-section of the people rather than those of all the people, its sincere rejection of democracy as rule-of-all-the-people is not enough to dodge its characterisation as a faction.

The hardest case is perhaps that of a party that claims that the sub-set of the people it represents is a distinct people – the Scottish National Party is a good example. Clearly, a full account of factionalism requires an understanding of who count as 'a people', as distinct from 'a nation' and 'a citizenry'. What may be relevant to the determination is whether the party at least represents all the people in the constituencies in which it puts up candidates for elections. If it does, it is less likely to be a faction, if it doesn't, more so. Perhaps the difficulty of this example demonstrates to us that it may well be parties, rather than constitutions, that constitute 'a people'. The shared experience of a people as an audience for a party's ideological and policy platform, in whose name and for whose benefit the party seeks to act, may well be constitutive. The failure of Europe to emerge as a robust polity may be owed to the absence of effective pan-European parties. This people-constituting feature of parties may well be the chief reason why factions are so problematic – they seek to redefine who the people that constitute a polity are by excluding a component thereof. Such redefinition may well be justified sometimes, such as when there is a legitimate right for internal or external self-determination. But outside this context, a majoritarian faction that excludes a minority from its concern is effectively seeking to exclude it from the polity by reconstituting its people on narrower, sectarian, terms.

The absence of a bright line dividing parties from factions may especially bother legal scholars: their fears are unfounded. I have already argued that apart from the application of anti-discrimination laws to parties, the anti-faction principle is best implemented by thorough second-order regulation: by creating a constitutional architecture – especially through the choice of an appropriate electoral system – which makes centrifugal factional behaviour politically less rewarding. Ranked-choice voting, cumulative voting, approval voting, and other such models, for example, are known especially to reward centripetal parties.[103] Such a regulatory

[103] Some Muslim members in the Indian constituent assembly (unsuccessfully) demanded ranked-choice or cumulative voting systems to be adopted and enshrined in the Constitution

architecture need *never* require a court to decide whether a party before it is a genuine party or a faction. This is precisely why the anti-faction principle demands that states 'encourage' anti-factionalism, unlike the party-state separation, which they ought to 'ensure'. It is best implemented through political nudges rather than legal command-and-control. While the anti-faction principle may not be necessary for satisfying a wholly procedural conception of a democracy, only a slightly thicker conception of democracy is needed to appreciate that, for example, the capture of the ruling party/coalition by a small set of wealthy donors transforms a democracy into a plutocracy.[104] The principle is compatible with even an interest-bargaining model of democracy – so long as the interests of *all* social groups matter in the bargain; it does not necessarily require an endorsement of the more demanding republican or deliberative conceptions of democracy.

4.4 CONCLUSION

In this chapter, I have provided an idealised account of the functions of a political party in a healthy democracy that can help diagnose the ailments of unhealthy parties and party-systems. That account emphasises their Janus-faced role as intermediaries between the state and its people, which they perform by lowering key information and transaction costs in a democracy. Parties are therefore simultaneously public and private. Party systems that successfully reduce political participation costs, voters' information costs, policy packaging costs, and ally prediction costs grease the wheels of representative democracy and are indispensable to its smooth operation. In order to aid parties in performing their intermediary function well, constitutions should seek to optimise four key principles in relation to political parties. First, they ought to protect the purposive autonomy of parties and align their rights and duties closely to their hybrid public-private character. Second, constitutions should optimise the number of parties such that there are enough parties to represent every salient voter-type, but not so many that voters' information costs become unaffordable. Third, constitutions should ensure the separation of the parties from the state so that no party is able to entrench itself in the institutions and offices of the state. Breach of this principle increases the political participation costs of the supporters of opposition parties. Finally, the anti-faction principle requires that constitutions should encourage parties to cater to the interests of all the people, rather than merely of a sub-section thereof. Factional parties increase the political participation costs of excluded minorities. They also make policy packaging difficult.

precisely because they were afraid on majoritarian Hindu factions flourishing under the first-past-the-post system: Neeti Nair, *Hurt Sentiments: Secularism and Belonging in South Asia*. Harvard University Press, 2023, 64.

[104] Khaitan, 'Political Insurance for the (Relative) Poor'.

Needless to say, these principles are compatible with many different ways of designing a constitution, but they are not compatible with all of them. How they apply precisely will obviously depend on the context. Note also that these principles may sometimes pull in opposite directions. For example, the anti-faction principle can be in tension with the party system optimality principle if a salient voter type demands factional representation. It is also in tension with the party state separation principle inasmuch as it demands that factions are structurally disadvantaged in the design of the state's political institutions. The goal is therefore to attempt their collective optimisation rather than any one principle's maximisation. In a separate article,[105] I have shown one set of institutional arrangements that might achieve such optimisation.

Political parties are the life-blood of representative democracy. Proposals seeking to respond to democratic deconsolidation have seen them as the problem, unnecessary middlemen who should be cut out of the system entirely in favour of direct democracy. These proposals fail to acknowledge the important function that parties perform in lowering key information and transaction costs that all-but-the-smallest democracies must contend with. If democracy is to survive, political parties need to be supported and improved, not eliminated. Despite all our advances in democratic technology, Schattschneider's famous claim that 'modern democracy is unthinkable save in terms of parties' remains as true as it ever was.[106] Hence the four political principles that I argue should inform constitutional designs of democracies. A party-less democracy, unless really small, is unlikely to remain democratic for very long.

[105] Khaitan, 'Political Parties, Electoral Systems, and the case for Semi-Parliamentarism'.
[106] E. E. Schattschneider, *Party Government*. Routledge, 1942.

5

The Constitutionalization of Parties and Politics

Tom Ginsburg and Mila Versteeg

5.1 INTRODUCTION

"War," said Ross Perot, "has rules. Mud wrestling has rules. Politics has no rules."[1] This view captures an increasingly common view of the political arena as one in which all bets are off, and any attempt to constrain the players is doomed to fail.

A moment's thought, however, exposes how facile that view is, at least for democracies. The metaphor of politics as a contest that takes place in a public arena is an evocation of a repeated game, in which the rules are themselves constitutive of play. Democratic politics may be dirty, but it relies on a set of structures that provide for competition, and its continued maintenance depends on some consensus on these underlying rules.

While the idea that politics has rules is probably uncontroversial, few have noticed that, over the past decades, these rules are increasingly specified in the text of the constitution itself. This was not always the case. Constitutions used to be mostly silent on key issues like the regulation of political parties, voting rights, or the details of holding and administering elections. But over the past decades, many constitutions have come to regulate core aspects of the democratic process, including political parties, details of elections and the electoral system, and voting rights. To illustrate, according to our data, 83 percent of constitutions in force today regulate political parties, 71 percent give a court or electoral body the power to oversee elections, and 44 percent specify rules for electing the lower house. Indeed, we find a sharp rise in the constitutionalization of democracy in three related areas: (1) the regulation of parties, (2) rules relating to voting and direct democracy, and (3) rules relating to administering elections and their oversight.

This is a partial reprint of Tom Ginsburg and Mila Versteeg, "The Constitutionalization of Democracy," *Journal of Democracy* (forthcoming). This version includes an expanded empirical analysis.

1 James Brooke, "Perot Attacks Political Process as Destructive," New York Times (September 10, 1996), www.nytimes.com/1996/09/10/us/perot-attacks-political-process-as-destructive.html.

This is a profound change, with potentially significant consequences. Constitutions are usually entrenched, meaning that they cannot be changed by ordinary democratic majorities, but instead require larger thresholds of legislative support for approval. Most constitutions also envision the practice of judicial review, meaning that courts can invalidate laws and regulations that contradict the constitution.[2] Constitutionalizing the rules relating to the democratic process, therefore, means that the rules of the democratic game will be harder to change and are subject to judicial oversight. This, in turn, implies a judicialization of democratic politics – core decisions about democracy are now made by constitutional and supreme courts.

Because of the nature of constitutions, the constitutionalization of democracy can aid democratic practices. After all, entrenching democratic rules and making them subject to judicial oversight means that ordinary majorities cannot tinker with them to create partisan advantage. Because of these qualities, constitutionalizing democracy can serve a hands-tying function; it allows constitution-makers to double down on their commitment to maintaining democracy.[3] In addition, writing down specific rules can also provide clarity on the rules of the game.[4] Such clarity is especially important when political conventions are weak, as is often the case during democratic transitions.

We find some evidence to support these ideas. We show how constitutional provisions protecting democracy served a clear hand-tying function in Kenya and that these same provisions appear to have helped prevent democratic backsliding. Looking at cross-national data, we find that constitutionalizing democracy is correlated with higher levels of democracy, which is consistent with the idea that constitutional rules on democracy can help protect democracy.

But we also add a note of caution. Constitutionalizing democracy gives an important role to high courts, in that they get to act as umpire over the rules of the democratic game. This might be a democracy-enhancing feature when courts are independent. But when courts are captured by the ruling coalition, they can interpret these same provisions in ways that are inconsistent with democracy.[5] This risk is especially present for provisions that give substantial discretion to courts, such as bans on undemocratic parties. We illustrate this possibility with the case of Thailand, where the constitutional provisions banning certain kinds of

2 Tom Ginsburg and Mila Versteeg, "Why Do Countries Adopt Constitutional Review?," *Journal of Law, Economics and Organizations* 30: 587–922 (2014).

3 Jon Elster, *Ulysses and the Sirens: Studies in Rationality and Irrationality*. Cambridge University Press, 1979, 94.

4 Russell Hardin, "Why a Constitution?," in *The Social and Political Foundations of Constitutions* ed. Denis J. Galligan and Mila Versteeg. Cambridge University Press 2013, 51, 59–60; Russell Hardin, *Liberalism, Constitutionalism and Democracy*. Oxford University Press, 2003, 103.

5 Dan Brinks and Abby Blass, *The DNA of Constitutional Justice in Latin America*. Cambridge University Press, 2018.

parties has been deployed by the Constitutional Court to ban democratic parties. Overall, we conclude that, while promising, constitutionalizing the rules of democracy is not a panacea to prevent democratic erosion. Under some conditions, particularly when the military plays a strong role in politics, constitutional provisions may have the opposite effect from their stated purpose of protecting democracy.

5.2 THE CONSTITUTIONALIZATION OF DEMOCRACY

One general trend in constitutional design over recent decades has been articulation: a growing propensity to regulate constitutionally with greater levels of specification. Constitutions written today tend to cover an ever-growing list of topics and deal with these topics in substantial detail. This trend has also been described as a move toward "constitutional codification," or growing "constitutional specificity."[6] The trend toward constitutional articulation affects many different areas of constitutional law, including constitutional rights, judicial power, foreign policy, the separation of powers, and "fourth branch" institutions. Here, we explore the same with respect to some of the core ingredients of democracy: political parties, voting, and elections.

5.2.1 *Data*

To map and explore the constitutional articulation of core aspects of democracy, we draw on data from the Comparative Constitutions Project to select some two dozen variables relating to democracy. We only selected those that arguably reflect rules compatible with democracy. To illustrate, we do not include provisions that ban specific parties or declare a one-party state; even though these provisions surely deal with parties and elections. At the same time, we do include provisions relating to militant democracy that ban certain *types* of parties and empower certain institutions to ban them. While one might argue that such rules are undemocratic, their goal, at least in theory, is to protect democracy.[7]

6 Rosalind Dixon, "Constitutional Drafting and Distrust," *International Journal of Constitutional Law* 13: 819–846 (2015); Mila Versteeg and Emily Zackin, "Constitutions Unentrenched: Toward an Alternative Theory of Constitutional Design," *American Political Science Review*, 110(4): 657–674 (2015); Zachary Elkins et al., *The Endurance of National Constitutions*. Cambridge University Press, 2009; Tom Ginsburg, "Constitutional Specificity, Unwritten Understandings and Constitutional Agreement," in *Constitutional Topography: Values and Constitutions* ed. Andras Sajo and Renata Utz. Eleven International, 2010, 66–93.

7 Karl Loewenstein, "Militant Democracy and Fundamental Rights I," *American Political Science Review* 31: 417–432(1937); Karl Loewenstein, "Militant Democracy and Fundamental Rights II," *American Political Science Review* 31: 638–658 (1937); Zachary Elkins, "Militant Democracy and the Pre-emptive Constitution: From Party Bans to Hardened Term Limits," *Democratization* 29: 174–198 (2022).

A first set of variables relates to the role of political parties: whether (1) the constitution refers to political parties; (2) creates a right to form political parties; (3) bans certain types of political parties (but not specific parties); (4) whether the legislature is given the power to ban certain types of unconstitutional parties (but not specific parties); (5) whether the constitutional court, supreme court, or the judiciary is given the power to ban certain types of unconstitutional parties (but not specific parties); (6) whether an electoral court or electoral commission is given the power to ban certain types of unconstitutional parties (but not specific parties); (7) whether the constitution guarantees equality of political parties; and (8) whether the constitution specifies that political parties can initiate general legislation.

A second set of variables relate to voting and direct democracy: (9) whether the constitution makes claims of universal suffrage; (10) whether there are any restrictions placed on the right to vote; (11) whether the constitution makes voting mandatory; (12) whether the constitution prescribes electoral ballots ought to be secret; and (13) whether the constitution gives individuals the ability to propose legislative initiatives.

A third, related set of variables describes to the electoral systems and the mechanics of elections. They include: (14) whether the constitution establishes a voting threshold of a certain proportion of the votes for a party to be able to take a seat in parliament; (15) whether ordinary (constitutional or supreme) courts have the power to supervise election; (16) whether an electoral commission, electoral court, or both, exist to oversee the election; (17) whether the constitution makes arrangements for scheduling the elections; (18) whether a specialized body (and not the executive or legislature) establishes the shape and size of electoral districts; (19) whether the constitution has provisions on the public financing of campaigns; (20) whether the constitution has provisions setting limits on the money used for campaigns; (21) whether the constitution prescribes the election timing for executive and legislature (either same or different days); (22) whether the constitution specifies the electoral system for the lower house; and (23) whether the constitution specifies the electoral system for the upper house.

5.2.2 *Trends*

A cursory look at the data reveals a growing constitutionalization of core features of democracy. Figure 5.1 shows the average number of all twenty-three democracy provisions over time. It shows a gradual increase in the number of electoral provisions in national constitutions. In 1810, the average number of provisions was 0.3; today, it is 6.9. But of course, there is substantial variation across countries. Even today, some constitutions do not enumerate any provisions relating to democracy, such as the absolute monarchies of Saudi Arabia, Brunei, and the United Arab Emirates.

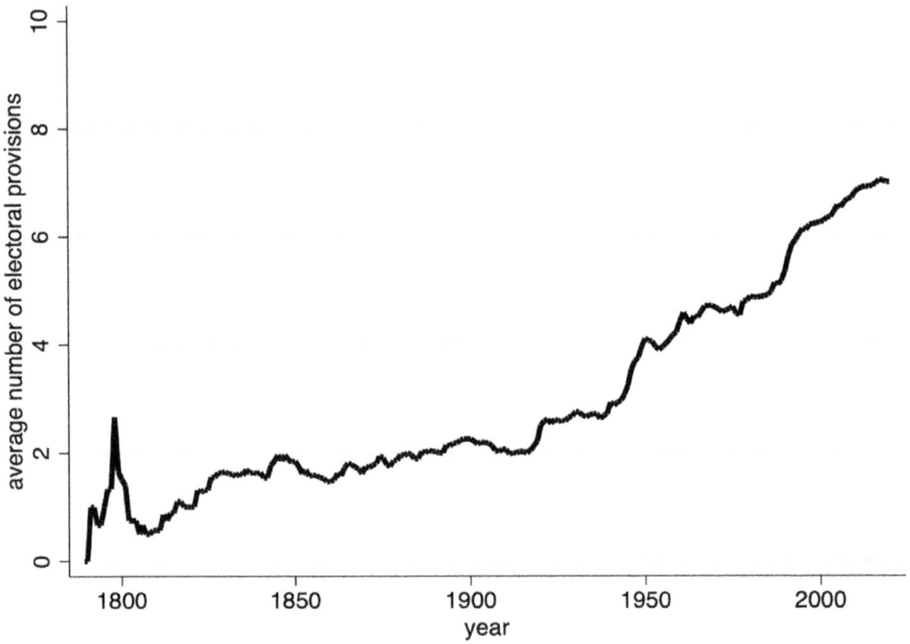

FIGURE 5.1 Number of democracy provisions on world map.

The US Constitution today includes only two democracy provisions – restrictions on abridging the right to vote under the Fifteenth, Nineteenth, and Twenty-Sixth amendments, which we code as being a claim to universal adult suffrage. But the US Constitution is notoriously silent on parties. In fact, the founders of the American republic sought to create a system of government that would protect liberty by *retarding* the formation of parties. As James Madison put it in Federalist 10, factions were a danger to popular government. These entities, composed of "some common impulse or passion, or of interest, adverse to the rights of other citizens," were an evil to be avoided through careful institutional design.[8] Despite Madison's best intentions, however, parties emerged early in the Republic as useful mechanisms to coordinate behavior in the legislature. As American democracy evolved and expanded in the nineteenth century, the party system changed as well, but constitutional language did not keep up. The Constitution was amended to provide for nondiscrimination in the provision of rights to vote for racial minorities, and later women and youth, but parties remain absent from the text. The time, place, and manner of congressional elections remain in the hands of state legislatures, which, contrary to Madison's expectations, have become hotbeds of partisan

[8] Federalist 10 (Madison).

self-dealing. In other settings, such questions are increasingly taken out of the realm of partisan politics and placed into the constitution.

On the other end of the spectrum, Kenya, starting in 2010, is the country with the largest number of constitutional democracy provisions. Its constitution contains no fewer than fifteen such provisions. It is followed by Liberia and Thailand (from 2007–2012), which both have fourteen democracy provisions.

When depicting the same data on a world map, we can see some regional trends, with a notable concentration of a high number of such provisions in both Latin America and Africa, which are areas with a good deal of constitutional turnover.

We see the same trends if we look at each of these categories separately. Consider, first, political parties. At the turn of the twenthieth century, exactly two constitutions referred to political parties: those of Colombia and Greece.[9] Today, 83 percent of the 193 national constitutions in force contain such a reference. As of 2020, 29 percent of constitutions prohibit certain parties or types of party programs, and some 13 percent provide that a court determine whether a political party is unconstitutional. These phenomena were unknown in 1900. Figure 5.2, Panel A shows the increase of provisions on political parties over time, a trend that accelerated after World War II.

We observe the same basic trends for voting and direct democracy. Figure 5.2, Panel B depicts the average number of provisions relating to voting. It is worth noting that these provisions are older than the political party provisions. We see them start appearing in the 1800s and steadily increase in number over time.

Finally, we also see the same trend for features of the electoral systems. Figure 5.2, Panel C depicts the average number of these provisions and reveals how they have increased over time. One increasingly popular constitutional design choice is to establish some form of electoral commission. This is a distinct body (or several) established to manage tasks like boundary delimitation and election management. In 1900, only Colombia and Liechtenstein provided for an electoral commission or/and court to oversee elections, but today 71 percent of constitutions constitutionally establish such a commission or give courts the power to oversee elections. Another noteworthy trend is to clarify the electoral system for parliamentary elections. In 1900, the four constitutions that clearly specified a voting rule for the lower house had a simple version of plurality or majority rule. Because of significant innovation in the understanding and design of voting systems during the twentieth century, contemporary constitutions not only have to choose between majoritarian and proportional representation but will sometimes specify a remainder formula, identify special constituencies for particular groups, or create a complex mixed system involving both proportional representation and districts. The five constitutional articles describing Sri Lanka's mixed method electoral system for the lower

[9] Constitution of Colombia (1886) Art. 47; Constitution of Greece (1864) Art. 11.

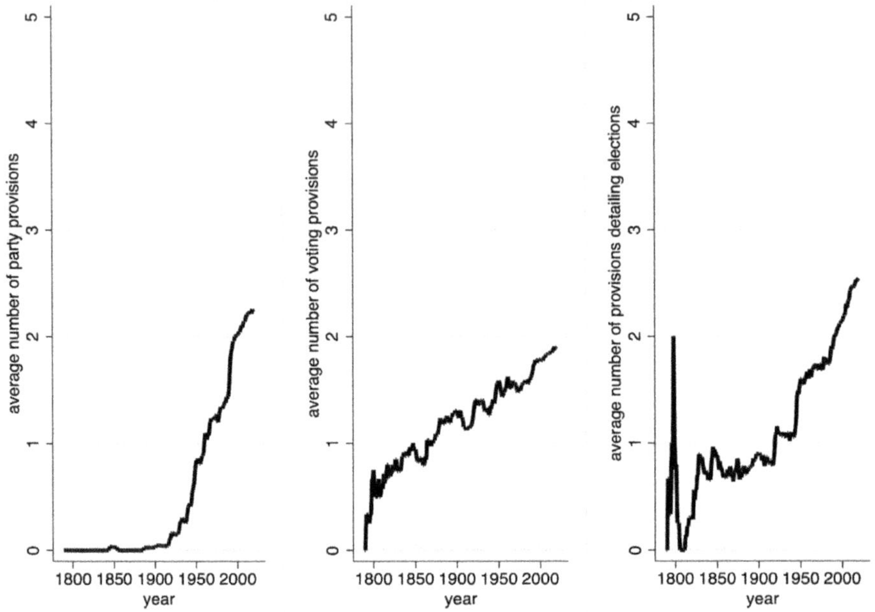

FIGURE 5.2 Average number of provisions relating to parties, voting, and elections.

house are nearly as long as some entire national constitutions.[10] They illustrate the tendency to constitutionalize the specifics of parliamentary elections.

5.2.3 *Relationship with Democracy*

Are these new constitutional features associated with regime type? The data reveals that these features can be found in democracies and autocracies alike, although they are somewhat more common in democracies.

We can observe this by analyzing the trends for democracies and autocracies separately. Figure 5.3 depicts the growing constitutionalization of democracy for autocratic and democratic regimes (we consider a country to be democratic if its polity2 democracy score is over 4 [on a scale from -10 to 10]). The dashed line denotes democracies; while the dotted denotes autocracies and solid captures the full sample. The first panel shows the trends for all democracy provisions, the second panel for parties, the third for voting, and the fourth for the electoral process. Overall, the graphs reveal that the trend toward constitutionalization is slightly more pronounced in democratic countries. By 2016, the average democracy constitutionally enumerated

[10] Libya's current document has 2,916 words, while Articles 95–99 of the Sri Lankan Constitution total 2,717.

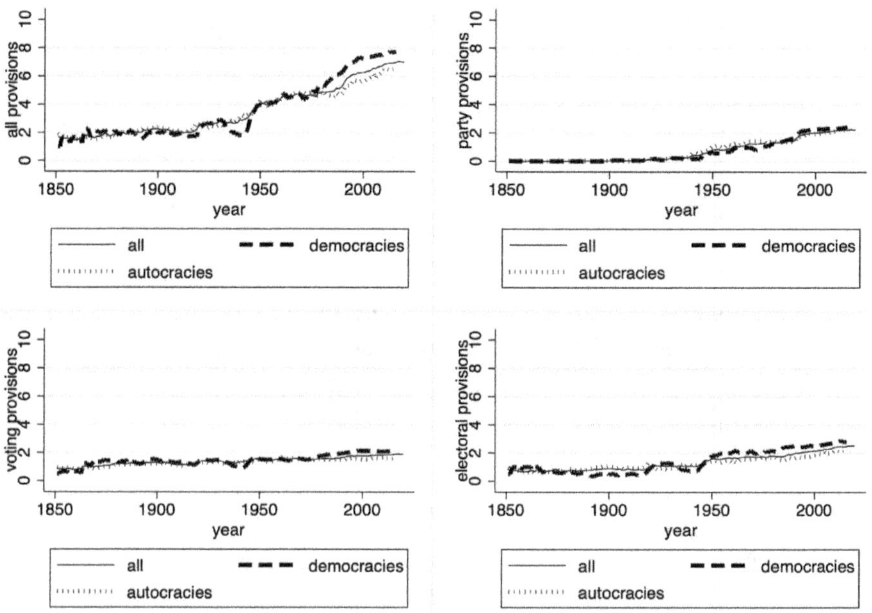

FIGURE 5.3 Average number of provisions relating to parties, voting, and elections by regime type.

7.7 of the variables we collected, while the average autocracy enumerated 6.5. But Figure 5.3 also reveals that this difference is mostly driven by constitutional provisions relating to the electoral process. By contrast, the second panel reveals that the constitutionalization of parties is just as common in democracies as autocracies.

Is the constitutionalization of democracy associated with higher levels of democracy de facto? It is notoriously difficult to sort out causation with cross-national data, and what follows is merely an initial exploration of whether constitutional provisions on democracy correlate with democracy de facto.

To explore the relationship between de facto democracy and constitutional rules relating to democracy, we estimate a simple OLS panel regression with the well-known polity2 democracy scale as the dependent variable. The model includes country-fixed effects, year-fixed effects, and a linear time trend. With these, we control for non-time varying country characteristics, common trends, and global shocks. We also experiment with adding a standard set of control variables: GDP per capita, population size, and civil war. Robust standard errors clustered are clustered by country to account for serial correlation.

Table 5.1 reports results from this exercise. It reveals that correlation between constitutionally entrenched rules relating democracy and de facto democracy is positive and statistically significant. For all the models capturing all provisions

TABLE 5.1 *Relationship with democracy*

	(1)	(2)	(3)	(4)	(5)	(6)	(7)	(8)
all provisions	0.455***	0.426***						
	(0.100)	(0.122)						
parties			0.585**	0.515**				
			(0.252)	(0.259)				
voting					0.925***	0.984**		
					(0.333)	(0.439)		
elections							0.707***	0.706***
							(0.180)	(0.225)
controls	no	yes	no	yes	no	yes	no	yes
country FE	yes	yes	yes	yes	yes	yes	yes	yes
year FE	yes	yes	yes	yes	yes	yes	yes	yes
time trend	yes	yes	yes	yes	yes	yes	yes	yes
Observations	12,849	8,712	12,858	8,721	12,893	8,756	12,889	8,752
R-squared	0.707	0.731	0.698	0.723	0.701	0.728	0.705	0.731

Note: the dependent variable is democracy. ***$p < 0.01$, **$p < 0.05$, *$p < 0.1$.

(columns 1 and 2), adding one additional constitutional feature (out of twenty-three) on democracy is associated with an increase of 0.455 on the 21-point democracy scale. While we should not interpret these as causal relationships, they are suggestive that these constitutional features are associated with somewhat higher levels of democracy.

5.3 WHY CONSTITUTIONALIZE DEMOCRACY? AN EXPLORATION

Hands-tying. What motivates drafters to regulate core aspects of democracy in the constitution? A likely reason is that constitutions are thought to serve as "pre-commitment devices."[11] The key idea here is that, when certain rules or values are constitutionalized, they are placed outside of the reach of ordinary politics. Because constitutions are harder to change than ordinary laws, ordinary democratic majorities cannot change constitutional rules. Additionally, courts are usually empowered to enforce these rules and to invalidate laws that contradict them. This also means that when disputes over interpretation or application arise, courts can further clarify and enforce these rules. The combination of entrenched and justiciable rules makes these rules harder to undermine and allows drafters to tie the hands of future democratic majorities.

This hands-tying logic reflects a certain amount of distrust of those who will govern under the constitution. Such distrust is often present during democratic transitions, when democracy is not taken for granted and constitution-makers use the constitution to attempt to lock in their commitments to a liberal democratic order.[12]

Under such conditions, creating a new machinery to run elections and to oversee democratic competition will make good deal of sense. The constitutionalization of parties likewise can serve a hand-tying function. The idea that constitutions should regulate and protect political parties can be traced back at least to Hans Kelsen, who noted that it is crucial "to anchor political parties *in the constitution* and give legal form de facto to what they have long since become: organs forming the will of the state."[13] On the one hand, modern constitutions protect parties. They do so through a right to form political parties, which ensures that constitutional mechanisms are available to prevent existing players from monopolizing the machinery of politics. Party rights usually also offer protections for smaller parties, preventing the state from intervening in a party's internal affairs or making party registration

[11] Elster, *Ulysses and the Sirens*.

[12] Andrew Moravcsik, "The Origins of Human Rights Regimes: Democratic Delegation in Postwar Europe," *International Organization* 54: 217, 218 (2000).

[13] Sujit Choudhry, "Resisting Democratic Backsliding: An Essay on Weimar, Self-enforcing Constitutions, and the Frankfurt School," *Global Constitutionalism* 7: 54–74, at 69 (2018).

requirements too arduous.[14] In some cases, it might also entail certain guarantees for opposition parties to be represented in the democratic process.[15] Empirical evidence suggests that rights to form parties are among those rights that are most likely to be effectively enforced, in part because parties themselves use these rights to protect their interests.[16]

But constitutions do not only protect parties; they also regulate them. The most common approach is to ban parties that propagate certain viewpoints. The practice of requiring parties to be democratic became relatively common after World War II. The rise of Nazism through mechanisms of parliamentary democracy led to great angst, and in 1937, the German political scientist Karl Loewenstein coined the term "militant democracy." Concerned with the inadequate democratic response to the rising threat of fascism, he called for a set of legislative and legal techniques that would allow democracy to defend itself against threats that emerge from within. "Constitutional scruples" he noted, "can no longer restrain from restrictions on democratic fundamentals, for the sake of ultimately preserving these very fundamentals."[17] Loewenstein went on to catalog techniques used by inter-war drafters that could constrain autocratic elements within society. But the prototype instrument of a militant democracy limits parties to those that are democratic. The design strategy of combining party rights with party bans, then, seems to reflect a simultaneous desire to recognize parties as important institutions of governance but also to set some boundaries on the ideological playing field.

Coordination. Another reason why constitutionalizing the rules of democracy can aid democratic practices is that constitutions can aid coordination around the rules of the game. If everyone has common understandings of the rules of politics, there is little additional advantage from writing them down. But there may be times when existing understandings break down, either because of exogenous change or because of the escalation of partisan competition. This can create incentives to clarify the rules of the game, so that parties can coordinate better in the future.

Coordination is especially important in the context of democratization. In such a context, new systems of elections and voting are often being set up from scratch. When starting from scratch, clarifying the basic rules of the game is particularly important as there are no preexisting political conventions to rely upon.

In a similar vein, coordination also becomes important when democratic political process become more open in character. The nineteenth century saw the rise of political parties around the world, be they the Colorados and Blancos in Uruguay, the Liberals and Farmers parties in Sweden, or the Liberals and Conservatives in Canada. What these party systems had in common at this time is that they are largely

[14] Adam Chilton and Mila Versteeg, *How Constitutional Rights Matter*. Oxford University Press, 2020.

[15] David Fontana, "Government in Opposition," *Yale Law Journal* 119: 384–647 (2009).

[16] Chilton and Versteeg, *How Constitutional Rights Matter*.

[17] Loewenstein, "Militant Democracy and Fundamental Rights I," 432.

elite affairs, in which parties regulated their interactions through reciprocity. But industrialization brought demands for an expansion of the franchise. As mass-based parties emerged out of labor movements in the early twentieth century, there was a sharp rise in polarization, putting pressure on norms of reciprocity among parties. In such a context, it made sense to start clarifying the rules of the political game and the role of parties within it. As democratic politics became more open and polarized, having clear rules helped parties to coordinate and channel their competition.

The explanations of hands-tying and coordination are not mutually exclusive, and likely work together in specific cases. For example, in the context of democratization, constitutionally specifying rules of the democratic process can be motivated by a joint desire to pre-commit to multiparty democracy as well as to clarify basic rules. Indeed, it is likely no coincidence that we see the constitutionalization of democracy take off during the wave of constitution-making in the 1990s.

5.4 THE CASE OF KENYA

We can see the importance of distrust of political elites in the constitution-making process undertaken in Kenya in the early 2000s, culminating in the Constitution of 2010. As noted above, this constitution is noteworthy because it has the largest number of provisions dealing with democracy of any constitution in force today. It is therefore worth probing the motivations behind this document and to explore how these provisions have been used in practice.

The Kenyan constitution-making process had followed an uneasy decade of democratization, during which longtime strongman Daniel Arap Moi retired in 2002. The prior text, adopted at independence in 1963, included an Electoral Commission, but had no mention of parties, and left the rules about voting to ordinary legislation. This document governed a rigged political process, and the Electoral Commission had no financial autonomy. Mass action in 1997 by civil society led to a constitutional amendment increasing the number of electoral commissioners and giving political parties more say in their selection. In addition, a Constitution of Kenya Review Act sought to "facilitate the comprehensive review of the Constitution by the people of Kenya."[18] This required the creation of the Constitution Review Commission (CKRC) to consult broadly and produce a draft. The draft would then be debated at a National Constitution Conference (NCC), made up of politicians and civil society, before going to parliament and the public for final approval.

Headed by famous civil society activist and scholar Yash Pal Ghai, the CKRC produced a draft after wide public participation. A summary of the public views presented to the CKRC included various criticisms of political parties: there were too many of them, they were too autocratic, and without internal democratic

[18] The Constitution of Kenya Review Act, 1997 (CAP 3A), long title.

procedures; they were vehicles for self-interest; they engaged in violence and hooliganism; and they did not seek to advance the national interest.[19] The solution, according to the report of the CKRC, was that "Political parties, as institutions of democratic and republican governance ... should be regarded as constitutional organs that should be provided for in and regulated by the Constitution."[20] Accordingly, the draft finally approved by the NCC in 2004 (known as the Bomas draft after the location of the NCC meetings) contained a major section on political parties, with rules, regulations, and provision for a code of conduct, as well as a fund for campaign expenditures, which included limits on party activities. Ghai and his colleagues sought to limit parties' ability to engage in corruption and to steer their activities toward democratic representation. In addition, the draft also fixed a time for parliamentary elections and introduced a clear right to vote.

However, as the process had been designed, the parliament had a chance to modify the draft before it went to public referendum for approval. Attorney General Amos Wako, a consummate political insider, was able to take control and watered-down key provisions in a process negotiated by the governing political parties without the opposition. The political-parties section shrank from ten articles to just two. The executive branch was made stronger. Civil society was outraged at this perceived capture of the draft by politicians, and the Wako version was rejected by public referendum in 2005 by a resounding vote of 58 to 42 percent. Subsequent elections were marred by significant violence, reflecting the largely tribal organization of Kenya's existing political parties. The country stood on the brink of unraveling, and the international community came in to broker a reset.

A second constitution-making process followed, in which initial drafting was done by a nonpartisan Committee of Experts, which included three foreigners. This body was charged with drawing the best of the earlier proposals into a new harmonized draft, which would presumably reflect a consensus. Its members were well aware of the need to reflect both public demand and elite consensus in this process.[21] The dynamics were similar to the prior episode, in which the Committee proposed a draft with an extensive section on political parties, but this was then submitted to a Parliamentary Select Committee, which reduced the number of articles on parties from nine to two. The draft then went back to the Committee of Experts for presentation to the public. The draft was ultimately approved by a referendum in August 2010, with more than 2/3 of voters supporting adoption, in a context of great distrust of politicians.

[19] Constitution of Kenya Review Commission, "The Final Report of the Constitution of Kenya Review Commission," Nairobi, Kenya (2005), at 141–143.

[20] Ibid. at 143.

[21] Christina Murray, "Making and Remaking Kenya's Constitution," in *Constitution-Makers on Constitution-Making* ed. Sumi Bisarya and Tom Ginsburg. Cambridge University Press, 2022, 37–76.

The resulting document included several global innovations, including a whole chapter on leadership and integrity, and established good governance, integrity, transparency, and accountability as national values. More specifically, the document creates a body to manage elections and oversee politics – an Independent Electoral and Boundaries Commission – and requires public participation in the process of delimitation of districts.

Even though the number of provisions regulating parties were reduced by politicians, the final document regulates parties substantially. Notably, the legislature is instructed to enact legislation regulating political parties, and Article 91 contains myriad constitutional rules about parties. These include requirements that parties have a national character and that they not be founded on ethnic, linguistic, regional, or other lines; that they have internal democracy in terms of their governing bodies and leadership; that they abide by principles of good governance; respect human rights, including those of minorities and marginalized groups to participate in the process; observe a code of conduct for parties; and several others.[22]

Overall, these new provisions can be best understood as efforts to tie the hands of politicians on behalf of the public, to constrain and channel political activity in beneficial ways. For parties, the provisions allowed for better coordination among themselves on the rules of the game: knowing that the rules were present, parties had some incentive to "play fair" under the new framework, rather than escalating competition in ways that violated the terms of the constitutional text.

Did the 2010 Constitution's strategy of "spelling things out" strategy work? Although Kenya's political class is among the world's most venal – the first act of parliament after approving the draft of new Constitution was to vote a pay raise for members – the text seems to have had an impact on the political system. A recent attempt by then-President Uhuru Kenyatta and his former rival Raila Odinga to cartelize the political system by unilaterally creating seventy new parliamentary constituencies and a new prime minister position was challenged by voters and minor parties. Among other provisions, the proposal – known as the Building Bridges Initiative – restricted judicial review of the boundary delimitation process and utilized a provision on popular initiative to propose the reforms. The courts rejected the attempt as procedurally flawed and incompatible with the Constitution, thereby foiling a partisan lock-up.[23] The High Court judgment in particular emphasized the role of the scheme in undermining the political process and the independence of the Commission, thus infringing on the rights of smaller parties and undermining the basic scheme of the Constitution. In August 2022, Odinga lost

[22] Constitution of Kenya, Art. 91.

[23] The African, "Kenya Supreme Court Declares BBI Unconstitutional," March 31, 2022, www.theeastafrican.co.ke/tea/news/east-africa/kenya-s-supreme-court-declares-bbi-unconstitutional-3766868; James Thuo Gathii, "The BBI Consolidated High Court of Kenya Judgment of the Constitutional and Human Rights Petition No. E282 of 2020" (Delivered May 13, 2021): Snap Overview

the presidential election to William Ruto, and outgoing incumbent Kenyatta peacefully turned over power to the latter – the first orderly alternation under the new charter.

To conclude, the Kenya story illustrates the democratic politics of constitutionalization: pressures for greater democratization led to the introduction of new ideas for regulation and strengthening constitutional protections for regulators. Both dimensions of parties and electoral mechanics were constitutionalized. The actual process took multiple iterations and involved civil society, technocrats, and sitting politicians, all under the supervision of courts at the phase of implementation. A major attempt to capture the process by two large parties, begun in 2020, was decisively rejected by the courts, using the constitutional text. In short, Kenya's democracy is far from perfect but no doubt in much better shape than when Moi stepped down two decades ago, and the constitutionalization of democracy helped to secure this.

5.5 A NOTE OF CAUTION

One important implication of constitutionalizing core features of democracy is that it empowers courts to police the boundaries of democratic politics. This is by design: when democracy is constitutionalized, constitution-makers envision that a neutral umpire can enforce constitutional boundaries in the face of partisan conflicts. Thus, high courts can now call out violations and clarify the rules of the democratic game when there is ambiguity on what these rules require.

When courts are independent, constitutionalizing the rules of democracy might make a whole lot of sense to protect democracy. But the central role for the court also comes with a vulnerability, which is that these same constitutional provisions can be used to accomplish partisan goals when courts are not independent. When the rules of democratic politics are constitutional in nature, then controlling a court becomes a powerful tool that allows would-be autocrats to stack the deck in their favor. Not only can courts reinterpret constitutional rules on democracy, their rulings enjoy priority over ordinary laws, which means that ordinary democratic majorities cannot simply alter them.

The pay-off of controlling the court might be highest for the provisions that represent broad and flexible standards. It is more difficult (though not impossible) to reinterpret clear rules, such as the day on which elections are to be held.[24] But other provisions give more discretion to courts. The ban on undemocratic parties is a prime example: it leaves to the courts to judge which policies and programs are undemocratic. When courts are captured, constitutional bans on undemocratic parties can become a tool to lock in current configurations. For example, in 2017,

[24] Mila Versteeg et al., "The Law and Politics of Presidential Term Limits," *Columbia Law Review*: 173 (2020).

the authoritarian government of Cambodia had the Supreme Court disband the country's main opposition group, the National Rescue Party, leaving strongman Hun Sen in control for an upcoming election. Individual members of the party were subjected to a five-year ban from running for office, as Hun Sen is reputed to be grooming his son to succeed him.

Thus, when courts become central to the functioning of democratic politics, it raises the stakes of controlling them. In the recent wave of democratic erosion, one of the first moves of would-be authoritarians is to control courts. When core features of democracy are constitutionalized, this only adds to the incentives to control courts.

Another factor that may lead to abuse of these provisions is a powerful role for the military in politics. Militaries often see themselves as the guardians of a set of fundamental values in the constitutional order, be they secularism (as in Turkey), religion and property (as in Chile under Pinochet), or the territorial integrity of the country (as in Pakistan or Nigeria). This self-conception can lead them to closely monitor civilian politics, even in a democratic era. They often align with judiciaries, with whom they share a hierarchical organization and technocratic orientation.[25]

There is a long history of military-aligned governments seeking to use the machinery of party bans to maintain power and shape politics. Perhaps the paradigm case is Turkey, which banned Islamist parties several times before the eventual success of Recep Tayip Erdogan. The case of Thailand illustrates how provisions constitutionalizing democracy can be a double-edged sword. As in Kenya, the Thai Constitutions of 1997 and 2007 contain a large number of provisions regulating democracy. But in the Thai case, the tools of constitutional regulation have been used to constrain democracy itself on behalf of military-bureaucratic institutions that are at the core of the political system.

Thailand is a country with a long history of alternating between corrupt civilian governments and military regimes, and in 1997, a new constitution was adopted to try to end this cycle. Known as the "People's Constitution" because it came out of a popularly elected constitutional assembly, the 1997 Constitution was the most democratic in Thai history. It contained numerous rights, political reforms to facilitate electoral majorities, and a network of "post-political" institutions to constrain and clean up democratic politics. Central here was a new Constitutional Court. Under Section 63 of the Constitution, the Court was given the power to disband any party found to be seeking to gain power by illegal means or to overthrow the "democratic regime of government with the King as Head of State." This is an old formula in Thailand, which seeks to balance the formal requirements of

[25] Irwin Stotzky, ed., *Transition to Democracy in Latin America: The Role of the Judiciary*. Westview Press, 1993.

democracy with a semi-divine monarchy.[26] We do not know who pushed for the inclusion of these provisions, but it likely reflected a combination of those with a genuine motive to protect democracy along with elements of the conservative bureaucratic-military elite.

Populist billionaire Thaksin Shinawatra dominated subsequent elections and held the premiership from 2001 to 2006, but conservative forces resisted him. Polarization increased sharply, and by the mid-2000s competing political factions were engaged in open and violent struggle in the streets of Bangkok. The Constitutional Court had dismissed corruption charges against Thaksin to allow him to take power in 2001, and sought to maintain a neutral role, but the rising political turmoil led the country's revered monarch to demand that courts address the problems. In 2006, a military coup sent Thaksin into exile. The Constitutional Court subsequently took up a case against Thaksin's Thai Rak Thai party, eventually deciding that it was banned under Section 63 of the Constitution. Polarization had drawn the courts into one side of a partisan divide.

The 2007 Constitution, produced by technocrats working with the military government, drew on the basic structures of 1997, with multiple regulatory institutions to govern elections, and contained an elaborately specified electoral system. It retained much of the language of the 1997 constitution with regard to parties, including the power of the Constitutional Court to ban parties under Section 68.[27] Section 65 of the 2007 document added new language, worth quoting in full:

> A person shall enjoy the liberty to unite and form a political party for the purpose of making political will of the people and carrying out political activities in fulfillment of such will through the democratic regime of government with the King as Head of the State as provided in this Constitution.
>
> The internal organization, management and regulations of a political party shall be consistent with fundamental principles of the democratic regime of government with the King as Head of the State.
>
> Members of the House of Representatives who are members of a political party, members of the Executive Committee of a political party, or members of a political party, as to the number prescribed by the organic law on political parties shall, if of the opinion that their political party's resolution or regulation on any matter is contrary to the status and performance of duties of a member of the House of Representatives under this Constitution, or contrary to or inconsistent with fundamental principles of the democratic regime of government with the King as Head of the State, have the rights to refer it to the Constitutional Court for decision thereon.

[26] Rawin Leelapatana, "The Thai-Style Democracy in Post-1932 Thailand and Its Challenges: A Quest for Nirvana of Constitutional Saṃs⊠ra in Thai Legal History before 1997," in *Thai Legal History: From Traditional to Modern Law* ed. Andrew Harding and Munin Pongsapan. Cambridge University Press, 2021, 217–232.

[27] Eugénie Mérieau, "Narratives of Buddhist Kingship in Thailand," in *Buddhism and Comparative Constitutional Law* ed. Tom Ginsburg and Benjamin Schonthal. Cambridge University Press, 2021, 181–197.

The motive for this section seems to reflect a deep distrust of political parties on the part of military technocrats, turning party members into monitors. When a member finds that the party leadership is acting outside the bounds of Thailand's democratic system, they can refer the case to the Constitutional Court. Section 68 goes on to provide the Constitutional Court with the power to disband unconstitutional parties for actions incompatible with the democratic regime with the King as Head of State. More broadly, the courts generally serve as guardians to limit the domain of politics, with power to strike resolutions of parties and channel their activities. One might describe this section as abusive from the outset – an attempt on the part of military leaders to control democratic politics.

The 2007 Constitution quickly became an instrument to limit democratic politics. Despite having left the country after his prior party was banned, Thaksin Shinawatra did not disappear as a political force. His allies reorganized Thai Rak Thai into a new People's Power Party, but this too was banned by the Constitutional Court in December 2008. Another successor party, Pheu Thai, won subsequent elections, and Thaksin's sister Yingluck took over as prime minister. Conflict continued, occasionally erupting in violence. While the courts had in the early years of Thaksin's ascendance sought to play a neutral role, they gradually took on the task of enforcing the demands of Thailand's traditional conservative elite against populist challengers. By 2014, a new coup sought to restrict the domain of elections and parties even further. Thaksin remained out of the country and seemed to have been defeated through the efforts of multiple party bans along with two military coups.

This meant that there was something of an opportunity for a fresh start in Thai politics. When the new Constitution of 2017 was adopted, several new parties formed to compete. A leading challenger was the Future Forward Party, which represented urban and young voters, and was led by a scion of a billionaire family, Thanathorn Juangroongruangkit. When this party proved to be fairly popular, however, it came to be seen as a threat to the party led by coup leader Prayuth Chan-Ocha. On relatively thin evidence, the Thai Constitutional Court found that Thanathorn had violated campaign laws and removed him from his seat in parliament in 2019. The next year, the Future Forward Party was disbanded by the Court. Its successor, the Move Forward Party that won an electoral victory in 2023, is currently facing a number of complaints asking for its dissolution.

The Thai story illustrates that constitutionalization of parties can be a two-edged sword and puts a great deal of faith in those who will make determinations of compliance with core norms. Even if adopted to protect democracy initially, constitutional provisions can be reinterpreted and repurposed. Party bans raise the stakes of controlling a constitutional adjudicator and increase the temptation to abuse the power. As always, when the institutions charged with protecting democracy become aligned with one faction in local politics, there is great potential for abuse.

5.6 CONCLUSION

Whether constitutionalizing democracy will serve a genuine hands-tying function or instead be subject to abuse will depend on context, and this can change over time within a single constitutional order.

In the case of Kenya, the ability of the courts to rely on constitutional principles and procedures was central to rebuffing an attempt by the two largest parties to cartelize the political system and to facilitating a transfer of presidential power in 2022. The constitutionalization of elections and parties has led to a vigorous jurisprudence, which simply would not have been possible absent the rules laid out in the 2010 Constitution . The broader positive correlation between constitutional regulation and measures of de facto democracy gives us reason to believe that this story is not confined to Kenya but that we might see similar dynamics at work in other cases such as Liberia and Nepal, which both have high levels of regulation.

However, constitutionalization is not a panacea. As our Thailand case study illustrates, the presence of provisions on elections, voting, and parties in a constitution can in practice be abused. In the wrong hands, constitutionalization might make things substantially worse for democracy. Hard limits on the political process are themselves a double-edged sword and may be subject to abuse by military-aligned governments in particular. This implies that, when considering whether or not to include constitutional provisions on the political process, democrats have to focus on who will be interpreting them down the road, and to choose the provisions least likely to be abused

6

Tackling Winner-Takes-All Politics in Africa

Inclusive Governance through Constitutional Empowerment of Opposition Parties

Adem Kassie Abebe

6.1 INTRODUCTION

Constitutions set the fundamental ground rules for democratic contestation and therefore influence the nature and outcomes of the dispensation. It is no wonder that the ground rules can be a point of serious contest among political groups, with dominant groups at times seeking ways to alter or entrench rules that favour their chances of victory. To check this self-serving temptation, the broad recognition, internalisation, acceptance and entrenchment of the ground rules and their relative stability and insulation from undue alterations and manipulations is critical for the legitimacy of democratic political systems.

Central to these ground rules are constitutional provisions guaranteeing multi-party democracy, universal suffrage and the right to stand for elections, rules governing elections (for the executive and legislature) and those regulating the establishment, operation, and rights and obligations of political parties. In connection with these, constitutions in Africa also often provide for election management bodies and courts to ensure the integrity and protection of electoral rights and multi-party democracy, including constraints on self-serving and capricious constitutional reforms. The constitutional recognition of these fundamental aspects of constitutional democracy is founded on the realisation that constitutional designers cannot simply assume that fair rules would be adopted and maintained by players with direct interest in the outcome.

Virtually all African constitutions directly or indirectly guarantee multi-party democracy and provide for the right to vote of citizens – even the 2005 Constitution of Eswatini (Swaziland), Africa's only absolute monarchy, recognises the right to vote of all adult citizens (article 85).[1] Moreover, while the African Charter on Human and Peoples' Rights (African Charter), does not specifically

[1] Nevertheless, although parties exist based on the right to association, electoral competition is based on a no-party system.

mention the right to vote, it guarantees the right to political participation (article 13), which has been interpreted to include the right to vote and stand for elections. The 2007 African Charter on Democracy, Elections and Governance (ACDEG) specifically recognises the right to participation through universal suffrage (article 4(2)).

To be sure, the right to vote has generated debates and litigation, particularly in relation to the right of prisoners to vote, which is increasingly recognised across the continent, on many occasions as a result of court decisions.[2] African constitutions also recognise the right of citizens to stand for elections, which often comes with more constraints in the form of citizenship, residency and other requirements. Notably, many constitutions in Africa still ban independent candidates, especially for presidential elections,[3] despite the fact that the African Court on Human and Peoples' Rights has found the ban on independent candidates incompatible with the African Charter.[4] Some constitutions in Africa also ban dual citizens or citizens of acquired nationality from running for certain high offices (e.g., 2016 Constitution of Cote d'Ivoire, article 55; 2010 Constitution of Angola, 110(2)), and in Muslim majority countries, candidates, particularly presidential candidates, are required to be Muslims (e.g., 2014 Constitution of Tunisia, article 74).

Perhaps more critical and contentious are provisions regarding the applicable electoral system and recognition and regulation of political parties. In general, African constitutions provide for key aspects of the electoral system for presidential elections. The detailed constitutional regulation of the electoral system for legislative elections is less prevalent, especially in Francophone Africa, where key aspects of the electoral system are left for legislative regulation. The recognition and regulation of political parties shows similar pattern to legislative election rules.

This contribution seeks to provide a broad overview of the constitutional regulation of the electoral system (Section 6.2) and political parties (Section 6.3) in African constitutions to identity any discernible patterns. Notably, it discusses how the relevant rules fared in times of democratic backsliding, using the example of Benin, one of the notable stories of democratic progress in Francophone Africa, which has recently witnessed downgrades in its democratic ranking (Section 6.4). The chapter also briefly discusses winner-takes-all politics (Section 6.5) as a fundamental scourge of both stability and democratisation in Africa and explores the importance of constitutional rules in ameliorating the challenge, with some examples. The Section 6.6 concludes.

[2] Adem Kassie Abebe, 'In Pursuit of Universal Suffrage: The Right of Prisoners in Africa to Vote', *The Comparative and International Law Journal of Southern Africa* 46: 410 (2013); African Criminal Justice Reform, 'The Right of Prisoners to Vote in Africa: An Update' (2020).

[3] Adem Kassie Abebe, 'Right to Stand for Elections as an Independent Candidate in the African Human Rights System: The Death of the Margin of Appreciation Doctrine?' *Africlaw* (2013).

[4] *Tanganyika Law Society and The Legal and Human Rights Centre and Reverend Christopher Mtikila v. The United Republic of Tanzania*, Applications 009 and 011/2011, Judgment of 14 June 2013.

6.2 OVERVIEW OF ELECTORAL SYSTEMS IN AFRICA

The large majority of African countries have established presidential and semi-presidential systems of government, with only a handful of countries adopting a parliamentary system. Most Anglophone African countries have established presidential systems, with the exception of some, such as Namibia and Tanzania, which establish semi-presidential systems (president-parliamentary), and Botswana and South Africa, which effectively have a parliamentary system where the position of president and prime minister are fused in a unified presidential office. In contrast, Francophone and Lusophone African countries have predominantly established semi-presidential systems. The only formally parliamentary systems in Africa are Ethiopia, Lesotho (under a king) and Mauritius. While Morocco has a powerful government led by a prime minister akin to parliamentary systems, the king exercises tremendous powers and is therefore not seen as parliamentary.[5]

The rules governing electoral rules to the executive and legislature, as well as the institutions charged with managing elections, show similarities across the systems of government. This section briefly discusses the applicable rules regarding presidential and legislative elections. While discussing electoral rules, it is important to note the existence of supranational constraints on substantive, procedural and institutional aspects. Notably, the ECOWAS Protocol on Democracy and Governance prohibits members states from altering electoral rules within six months of elections, except through broad agreement of political forces (article 2(1)). Substantively, a panoply of instruments, notably the African Charter and the ACDEG, provide additional external constraint on the content and change of electoral rules.

6.2.1 *Electing Presidents*

The applicable rules regarding presidents (both directly elected or otherwise) are largely regulated at the constitutional level across Africa (as well as around the world)[6] and generally not controversial. In countries with directly elected presidents, the rule is either plurality (first-past-the-post) or absolute majority (with a second round when necessary), with the latter dominating since the 1990s. Reforms have occurred both ways, with, for example, The Gambia (2001) and the Democratic Republic of Congo (2011) moving from absolute majority to plurality, while Togo (2019) shifted to the two-round system (which it had abolished in 2002) . Kenya and

[5] Inmaculada Szmolka, 'Bipolarisation of the Moroccan Political Party Arena? Refuting This Idea through an Analysis of the Party System', *Journal of North African Studies* 26: 73–102 (2021).

[6] Adem Kassie Abebe and Elliot Bulmer, 'Electing Presidents in Presidential and Semi-presidential Democracies', International IDEA Constitution Building Primer (2019), https://constitutionnet.org/vl/item/electing-presidents-presidential-and-semi-presidential-democracies.

Nigeria provide for a regional distribution of votes for winning presidential elections with a view to encourage inter-group/regional political formations. Accordingly, in Nigeria, a candidate must win both a plurality of the votes nationwide and at least 25 per cent of the votes in at least two-thirds of the thirty-six federal states (Constitution of Nigeria, 1999, section 134), and in Kenya a candidate must win an absolute majority nationwide and at least 25 per cent of the votes in at least half of the forty-seven counties (Constitution of Kenya, 2010, section 138). In both cases, if no candidate secures a win in the first round, a runoff is held where the regional distribution rule no longer applies.

In general, constitutions in Anglophone African countries include elaborate provisions governing presidential elections, largely avoiding serious controversies around the rules. An exception is Malawi. The Malawian constitution is not clear on whether the applicable rule is absolute majority or plurality. In practice, plurality was accepted as the rule, particularly following a decision of the highest court of the country.[7] Nevertheless, in 2020, the Supreme Court invalidated the May 2019 elections and crucially found that the applicable rule was an absolute majority, and not a plurality, effectively reversing its standing jurisprudence. In the absence of constitutional rules regarding the run-off election, the Court ordered parliament to clarify the applicable rules through reforms. Such reforms are yet to be enacted, and fortunately, the rerun election provided an opportunity for the second and third opposition candidates in the invalidated election to form an alliance, which secured a decisive absolute majority against the incumbent (who has been declared a winner of the invalidated election with a plurality of just over 38 per cent of the votes).

The constitutional rules for presidential elections are also generally broadly defined in constitutions of Francophone African countries, although the level of detail is comparably less than in Anglophone counterparts. Partly because of the relative constitutional minimalism, the rules in Francophone countries have been controversial in some cases. As indicted in Togo, the two-round system was restored in 2019 after persistent opposition demands and political instability. Perhaps most significantly, in Cote d'Ivoire, a rule that required presidential candidates to have both their parents born in the country proved extremely destabilizing, because most citizens in the north, who are also predominantly Muslims, often have cross-border links with people of Burkina Faso and other countries. The rule was ultimately abolished in constitutional reforms in 2016.[8]

7 Mwiza Jo Nkhata, 'Malawi's Nullified Presidential Elections and the Plurality vs Majoritarian (Run-off) Debate', ConstitutionNet (2020), https://constitutionnet.org/news/malawis-nullified-presidential-elections-and-plurality-vs-majoritarian-run-debate.

8 Pierre Olivier Lobe, 'Innovations of the Draft Constitution of Cote d'Ivoire: Towards Hyper-presidentialism?', ConstitutionNet (2016), https://constitutionnet.org/news/innovations-draft-constitution-cote-divoire-towards-hyper-presidentialism.

Another important aspect of presidential elections that continues to be a recurrent source of controversy relates to term limits.[9] Changes to applicable rules to extend incumbent terms represent the starkest manifestation of a decline in democratic space and autocratisation.[10] Because term limits represent clear rules that are hard to bypass otherwise, incumbents often target their amendment – either directly or indirectly through the adoption of ostensibly new constitutions and, in certain cases, through questionable judicial interpretations.[11]

Term limits are particularly often altered or removed in countries where power is personalised with weak parties (such as Congo Republic, Djibouti, Cameroon, Uganda) and less likely to occur in countries with equally dominant but strong parties or in competitive contexts. In countries with dominant but strong parties (such as Tanzania, Botswana and South Africa), term limits have been consistently respected, despite the parties having the numbers to change the rules, implying the importance of term limits in regulating intra-party power dynamics and alternation of power. Indeed, Tanzania became the first African country to witness an alternation of power as a result of term limits in 1995, while the country was still practically a one-party state. Similarly, in countries with relatively competitive contexts, term limits have largely remained stable, with efforts at altering them defeated, such as in Nigeria, Malawi and Zambia.

Other constitutional aspects of presidential electoral rules are not frequent subjects of reform, mainly because incumbents find ways to rig the applicability of the rules, without the need to change them. Even reforms related to the electoral system, with some countries shifting from runoff to plurality, may partly be explained by cost and other inconveniences, rather than simply as the last nail on the democratic coffin, as are changes to term limit provisions.

Additional aspects that have often generated controversy relate to registration fees for presidential candidates, which are not always regulated at the constitutional level but can prove a major hinderance to some candidates. Most recently, Nigeria's main opposition parties introduced a nomination fee for presidential aspirants of up to 100 million Nira (about USD 250,000) and lower amounts for other offices.[12] Interestingly, these fees are set by the parties, rather than by law.

Perhaps most notably, the introduction of a 'sponsorship' systems has become controversial in recent years in Senegal, Benin and Burkina Faso. A 2018 Senegalese law established a 'citizenship sponsorship' requiring presidential candidates to

[9] Joseph Siegle and Candace Cook, 'Circumvention of Term Limits Weakens Governance in Africa', Africa Center For Strategic Studies (2020, updated 2021), https://africacenter.org/spotlight/circumvention-of-term-limits-weakens-governance-in-africa/.

[10] Joseph Siegla and Candace Cook, 'Presidential Term Limits Key to Democratic progress and Security in Africa', *Orbis* 65: 467–482 (2021).

[11] Mauricio Guim et al., 'The Law and Politics of Presidential Term Limit Evasion', *Columbia Law Review* 120: 173–248 (2020).

[12] Johnbosco Agbakwuru, '2023: NNPP Condemns APC N100m Nomination Fees', *Vanguard* (2022), www.vanguardngr.com/2022/04/2023-nnpp-condemns-apc-n100m-nomination-fees/.

obtain the support of about 1 per cent of the voters in at least seven regions of the country.[13] While the law is intended to streamline electoral competition and ensure nationwide support for candidates (therefore reduce regionalised politics), it tends to benefit incumbent presidents and parties.

More seriously, in Burkina Faso, 2020 reforms to the electoral code require presidential candidates to be sponsored by at least fifty elected officials. When sponsors are municipal councillors, they must be located in at least seven of the thirteen regions of the country.[14]

Similarly, Benin introduced a party sponsorship system in 2018 requiring candidates to obtain endorsement of at least sixteen members of the National Assembly (of which there are eighty-three members) or mayors (of which there are seventy-seven).[15] While the number may seem relatively low, the requirement came after opposition parties boycotted the 2018 legislative elections because of alleged repressive tactics and changes to the electoral law establishing, among other rules, a requirement on political parties to receive a 'certificate of conformity' from the Ministry of Interior, to secure at least fifteen members from each municipality of Benin, as well as a ban on party alliances from presenting list of candidates for elections.

The rules in Benin were adopted ostensibly to stem the fragmentation and proliferation of candidates and parties (with the country of around 12 million people reportedly home to more than 200 parties before the changes) and encourage nationwide and ideological political formations, rather than regionalised identity-based parties. Nevertheless, in effect this meant that opposition candidates needed the endorsement of members of parliament and mayors aligned with the ruling coalition. These rules have proved extremely controversial partly because they are not regulated at the constitutional level and are therefore seen as unilateral and even opportunistic and capricious. Indeed, the Benin government has arrested and convicted key opposition leaders following instability after the latest elections where President Patrice Talon won re-election (despite promising during his presidential campaign not to run for re-election and even to amend the constitution to impose single terms on presidents).[16] Benin, once a paragon of democracy in Francophone Africa, is now classified as only partly democratic in all major democracy rankings.

[13] Paulin Maurice Toupane, Aissatou Kante and Adja Khadidiatou Faye, 'Suspicions Cloud Senegal's Upcoming Election', Institute for Security Studies (2019), https://issafrica.org/iss-today/suspicions-cloud-senegals-upcoming-election.

[14] Adewumi Mubin Bakare, 'Political Reforms and Implications for Democracy and Instability in West Africa: The Way Forward for ECOWAS Member States', ACCORD (2022), www.accord.org.za/conflict-trends/political-reforms-and-implications-for-democracy-and-instability-in-west-africa-the-way-forward-for-ecowas-and-member-states/.

[15] David Zounmenou, Jeannine Ella Abatan and Michael Matongbada, 'A Third Election without Main Opposition Parties in Benin', Institute for Security Studies (2021), https://issafrica.org/iss-today/a-third-election-without-main-opposition-parties-in-benin.

[16] Tim Hirschel-Burns, 'Benin's King of Cotton Makes Its Democracy a Sham', *Foreign Policy* (2021), https://foreignpolicy.com/2021/04/08/benin-election-democracy-sham-patrice-talon/.

Overall, provisions such as term limits and the two-round system were largely adopted in the 1990s in African constitutions as major concessions at moments of incumbent vulnerability and democratic euphoria during the transition towards democracy. Old and new dominant leaders and parties have since then sought to alter the rules and, on key occasions, succeeded, often marking a significant point in democratic backsliding.

6.2.2 *Electing Parliaments (for First Chamber)*

Unlike electoral rules for presidential elections, many African constitutions leave key aspects of parliamentary elections for legislative regulation. Notably, constitutions in Francophone African countries rarely even determine the applicable electoral system for the legislature, instead leaving it to determination through organic laws (which often required an absolute majority to enact). For instance, the 2016 Constitution of Cote d'Ivoire, one of the latest in Francophone Africa, provides that an organic law determines 'the number of members of each house, the conditions of eligibility and appointment, the system of ineligibilities and incompatibilities, the methods of voting and the conditions under which new elections should be organised' (article 90). Compare this with the 2010 Constitution of Kenya where the Constitution specifically determines the number of members of the National Assembly as well as manner of their election, including representation of women, as well as qualifications and disqualifications (articles 97–99).

Most countries in Africa have adopted a list proportional system (particularly common in civil law countries [Francophone and Lusophone], first-past-the-post system [mainly common in Anglophone countries] and mixed electoral system [parallel].[17] Constitutional rules regarding legislative elections have generally stayed stable, although it is not clear whether the rules are results of accident and historical colonial diffusion, or deliberation, reflection and consensus. While the legislative framework for the electoral system has changed on occasions, particularly with the transition to proportional systems in Francophone countries, it is unclear whether changes to legislative electoral rules have been tampered with to distort outcomes. This may partly be because incumbency advantages and outright election rigging often deliver tolerable results, while electoral reforms may be seen as unnecessary and even undesirable and visibly capricious.

Nevertheless, there are cases where electoral reforms have proved extremely contested. For instance, in 2018, Benin changed the electoral code imposing among other things a 10 per cent threshold for winning seats in the National Assembly.[18]

[17] For a list of countries and their system of government, see the International Institute for Democracy and Electoral Assistance Database on electoral systems, www.idea.int/data-tools/continent-view/Africa/44.

[18] Hirschel-Burns, 'Benin's King of Cotton Makes Its Democracy a Sham'.

While this was ostensibly intended to crack down on party fragmentation, it favoured the incumbent party and led to opposition boycott of the 2019 legislative elections. Indeed, following its observation of the elections, the African Union Election Observation Mission noted that the 10 per cent threshold 'appears to contradict the fundamental principles of fairness and equal suffrage'.[19] Regardless of the propriety of the applicable rules, the Benin experience shows that the lack of constitutionalisation of fundamental aspects of the electoral system could lead to unilateral alterations by incumbent parties without securing broad consensus. Indeed, in Benin, the incumbent party won all the legislative seats in 2019, which it then used to adopt constitutional amendments, without the need to submit them to a referendum – a referendum is only required if the proposed amendment does not secure a four-fifths majority in the National Assembly (Constitution of Benin, 1990, article 155).

6.3 POLITICAL PARTIES

Political parties are the principal engines of competitive democracy, straddling both the private and public spheres. The post-independence African constitutions largely left the issue of political parties unregulated. In any case, the post-independence period of multi-partyism was remarkably short and many of the countries, with the notable exception of Botswana, Mauritius and The Gambia, established de facto or de jure one-party systems.[20]

Multi-party politics returned in the 1990s as central to the waves of democratisation across Africa. Accordingly, the new constitutional frameworks recognised the right to political competition and opposition as critical to democratic dispensation and to peace and stability. Similarly, the ACDEG requires states to strengthen political pluralism and recognise 'the role, rights and responsibilities of legally constituted political parties, including opposition political parties, which should be given a status under national law' (article 3) . Fombad has argued that the constitutional recognition and regulation of political parties 'is not only imperative,

[19] 'Mission D'observation Electorale De L'union Africaine Pour Les Elections Legislatives Du 28 Avril 2019 En Republique Du Benin Conclusions Preliminaires', https://au.int/sites/default/files/pressreleases/36552-pr-conclusions_preliminaires_de_la_moeua_pour_des_elections_legislatives_du_28_avril_2019_au_benin.pdf.

[20] Fombad analyses constitutional recognition and regulation based on eight measures: formal recognition of multi-partyism, scope of rights and duties of political parties, principle of state-party separation, principle of free and fair political participation, internal party democracy principle, bans and regulatory restrictions principle, political party funding principle and compliance with democratic values and principles; Charles Fombad, 'Conceptualising a Framework for Inclusive, Fair and Robust Multiparty Democracy in Africa: The Constitutionalisation of the Rights of Political Parties', *Law and Politics in Africa, Asia & Latin America* 48: 3–27 (2015); Charles Fombad, 'Political Party Constitutionalization in Africa: Trends and Prospects for Deepening Constitutionalism', in *Comparative Constitutional Law in Africa* ed. Rosalind Dixon, Tom Ginsburg and Adem Abebe. Edward Edgar, 2022, 110–135.

but its broad scope to avert or at least limit the risks of one-party dictatorship is crucial'.[21] In this regard, Chilton and Versteeg have found that constitutional rules with natural constituencies, such as those applicable to political parties, are systematically associated with better practices and compliance.[22]

The level of detail with which African constitutions recognise and regulate political parties varies. In general, more recent constitutions across the continent and constitutions in Anglophone African countries tend to have more elaborate provisions, while Francophone countries tend to leave the regulation of parties to organic laws. Fombad has provided a useful analysis of twenty-four African constitutions partly drawing on a framework developed by Khaitan.[23] Notably, constitutional regulations of parties in Anglophone countries seem to aim at ensuring the democratic character of political parties in view of their public function, while in civil law countries, where it exists, the aim is mainly to protect parties from the state, in view of their private character.[24]

Many constitutions provide for equality of treatment of parties, principally through equitable access to publicly funded media, often during electoral periods, but in some cases all the time (Constitution of Gabon [article 95], Ghana [article 55 (11)] and South Africa [section 197]). For instance, the Ghanaian Supreme Court has ruled that opposition parties have the right to be granted access to public media to respond to an annual budget presentation by the government.[25] At the continental level, the African Commission on Human and Peoples' Rights has called on member states to ensure that political parties, especially opposition parties, 'are given equitable access to state controlled media and resources'.[26]

6.4 ELECTORAL AND PARTY RULES DURING BACKSLIDING: EXAMPLE OF BENIN

In general, changing the rules is too visible a strategy that incumbents with other options are likely to avoid. All things remaining equal, incumbents would arguably tend to prefer irregular means to undermine opposition and other critical groups. Nevertheless, constitutional and legal changes have been used to promote ostensibly legitimate political goals, while in practice unduly undermining opposition parties.

[21] Fombad, 'Political Party Constitutionalization in Africa', 116.

[22] Adam Chilton and Mila Versteeg, *How Constitutional Rights Matter*. Oxford University Press, 2020).

[23] Fombad, 'Political Party Constitutionalization in Africa'; Tarunabh Khaitan, 'Political Parties in Constitutional Theory', *Current Legal Problems* 73: 89–125 (2020).

[24] Samuel Issacharoff and Richard H. Pildes, 'Politics as Markets: Partisan Lockups of the Democratic Process', *Stanford Law Review* 50: 643–717 (1998).

[25] *New Patriotic Party v. Ghana Broadcasting Corporation* [1993–1994] 2 GLR 354.

[26] Resolution on Elections in Africa, ACHPR/Res.174(xlvii)10 (2010), www.achpr.org/sessions/resolutions?id=352.

Such changes are perhaps more likely in countries where irregular means are less readily acceptable, in view of the relatively open and politically competitive context.

Where constitutional rules exist, they can be effective even in largely authoritarian settings. For instance, in cases of presidential term limits, authoritarian incumbents often have no choice but to change the constitutional rules. Although term limit provisions have been bypassed in many countries, there are also cases where constitutional rules have worked in stymieing efforts at removing term limits – for example, Nigeria, Malawi, Zambia. Indeed, some incumbents opted to resort to courts (e.g., Senegal 2012) or simply delayed elections to practically extend their terms (DRC 2016), because of the political impracticality of constitutional change. In Burundi, the incumbent resorted to the constitutional court after failing to secure the numbers to amend the constitution to allow a third term.[27]

The limited scope or absence of constitutional regulation of key aspects of political parties, as well as broadly legislative electoral rules, means that they are rarely directly targeted through constitutional change. Instead, incumbents would either resort to irregular means or changes to the electoral laws to pursue their objectives. As a consequence, the political party and electoral rules tend to be relatively stable. But not everywhere.

In Benin, since 2018, a number of legislative reforms, noted above, were enacted, which the opposition objected to – including notably the requirement that political parties needed certificates of conformity from the Ministry of Interior, a duty to secure at least fifteen members from each municipality of Benin and a ban on party alliances from presenting list of candidates for elections. The law also exponentially increased the fee to field candidates.[28] This was in addition to reports of repressive government tactics.[29] Because of a combination of these tactics and legal changes, opposition parties boycotted the 2019 legislative elections, which contributed to a very low turnout of 27 per cent, but a total victory to the incumbent president's ruling coalition. The ruling coalition then used its dominance to adopt constitutional amendments through an accelerated/summary procedure, the first ever successful amendment since the adoption of the 1990 Constitution through a National Conference. Parliament adopted the amendments unanimously, which precluded the need for a national referendum, which is not necessary if the amendment receives a four-fifths majority in the unicameral National Assembly. While most of the amendments weren't too controversial – such as the establishment of position of vice president, increased quotas for women, banning of death

27 Ken Opalo, 'Term Limits and Democratic Consolidation in Sub-Saharan Africa: Lessons from Burundi', ConstitutionNet (2015), https://constitutionnet.org/news/term-limits-and-democratic-consolidation-sub-saharan-africa-lessons-burundi.

28 Olabisi D. Akinkugbe, 'International Decision Commentary: Houngue Éric Noudehouenou v. Republic of Benin', *American Journal of International Law* 115: 281–287 (2021).

29 Sarah Maslin Nir, 'It Was a Robust Democracy. Then the New President Took Power', *New York Times* (2019). www.nytimes.com/2019/07/04/world/africa/benin-protests-talon-yayi.html.

penalty, grouping of elections (holding them at the same time) – some were. Notably, the amendments effectively banned independent candidates from presidential elections, constitutionalising the party sponsorship system introduced in the earlier legislative reforms.

The amendments to the law and the constitution were challenged in the Constitutional Court but were approved. However, the Court was seen as captured by the incumbent president after he appointed his former personal lawyer as the chair of the Court. Two cases were then filed before the African Court on Human and Peoples' Rights challenging the reforms on both procedural and substantive grounds.[30] The African Court found that the constitutional amendments were not adopted through 'national consensus' as provided for in the ACDEG (article 10(2)). Interestingly, the principle was first formally propounded by the Constitutional Court of Benin[31] before its subsequent adoption as a continental standard in the ACDEG. Having found the entire amendment invalid on procedural grounds, the African Court did not deem it necessary to discuss the substantive compatibility of the amendments with continental standards. Nevertheless, the Court has ruled in another case involving Tanzania that a ban on independent candidates, even if done through the constitution, is incompatible with the African Charter.[32] While decisions of the African Court are technically only binding on the specific respondent state, they have crucial 'horizontal' importance in other contexts, especially when the decisions relate to the validity of legal and constitutional provisions, rather than merely their interpretation or application.[33]

Displeased with the cases before the African Court, Benin chose to withdraw the declaration allowing individuals and non-governmental organisations to submit cases before the Court – therefore preventing future cases against Benin – and has not implemented the decisions.[34] Interestingly, despite the fact that the African Union is required to enforce decisions of the African Court, the AU chose to send

[30] *XYZ v. Republic of Benin*, Application No. 010/2020, Judgment of 27 November 2020, https://africanlii.org/sites/default/files/judgment/afu/african-court/2020-afchpr-3//010-2020_XYZ_v_Benin_Judgment.pdf; and *Houngue Éric Noudehouenou v. Republic of Benin*, Application No. 003/2020, Judgment 4 December 2020, www.african-court.org/en/images/Cases/Judgment/003-2020-Houngue_Eric_Noudehouenou_v_Benin-_Judgment.pdf.

[31] Judgment No. DCC 06-074, 8 July 2006.

[32] *Tanganyika Law Society and the Legal and Human Rights Centre v. The United Republic of Tanzania*, application no 0009/2011, and *Reverend Christopher R. Mtikila v. The United Republic of Tanzania*, application No 011/2011, Judgment of 14 June 2013, www.african-court.org/en/images/Cases/Judgment/Judgment%20Application%20009-011-2011%20Rev%20Christopher%20Mtikila%20v.%20Tanzania.pdf.

[33] Adem Kassie Abebe, 'Horizontal Compliance with Decisions of the African Court on Human and Peoples' Rights', in *Compliance with International Human Rights Law in Africa: Essays in Honor of Frans Viljoen* ed. Aderomola Adeola. Oxford University Press, 2022, 168–182.

[34] Nicole De Silva, 'A Court in Crisis: African States Increasing Resistance to Africa's Human Rights Court', Opinio Juris (2020). http://opiniojuris.org/2020/05/19/a-court-in-crisis-african-states-increasing-resistance-to-africas-human-rights-court/.

election observers to the 2021 elections held under rules that were found to be incompatible with the African Charter.

6.5 ADDRESSING WINNER-TAKES-ALL POLITICS THROUGH INCLUSIVE MAJORITARIANISM

Electoral and political party rules are foundational to democratic contestation. In a context where electoral contests are often perceived as high stakes winner-takes-all politics – as former Nigerian President Olusegun Obasanjo quipped ahead of the 2007 elections, 'a matter of life and death'– incumbents often resort to subtle and non-subtle oppressive tactics and in certain cases use or change the rules to increase their chances of victory and dominance.[35] Winner-takes-all politics involves not only the overbearing dominance of the incumbent leader and party over status, power, governance and distribution of economic rents but also the active 'marginalization of perceived political opponents and the feeling of exclusion from the governance process [and access to resources] by those who do not belong to the government/ruling party',[36] rendering them spectators, rather than critical partners in governance and development. Accordingly, winner-takes-all thinking could lead to a situation where 'opposition parties may end up becoming desperate to win power by all means and at whatever cost; whilst the incumbents, mindful of the cost of losing elections, may also prepare to maintain power by all means and at anybody's expense'.[37]

It would not be an exaggeration to suggest that the most central challenge to democratisation and peace, intra- and inter-group tensions, stability and development in Africa lies in winner-takes-all, zero-sum politics. Accordingly, to enable progress in constitutional democracy in Africa, ensure the stability of the rules of the game and preclude their abusive changes, constitution makers need to recognise the manifestations of and tackle head-on the scourge of winner-takes-all politics. This political culture coexists with the widespread public support in Africa for 'consensual democracy', one that 'places limits on the extent of political competition, but without compromising the principle of political accountability'.[38]

This support for 'consensual democracy' arguably requires the recognition and empowerment of opposition groups, including in constitutional and legal reform processes, as well as in the exercise of constitutional powers. The issue of opposition

[35] Dayo Bensen, Rotimi Ajayi and Ben Agande, 'Nigeria: April Polls Are a Matter of Life and Death, Obasanjo Insists', *Vanguard* (2007), https://allafrica.com/stories/200702260525.html.

[36] Ransford Gyampo, 'Winner-Takes-All Politics in Ghana: The Case for Effective Council of State', *Journal of Politics and Governance* 4: 17–24 (2015).

[37] Andrews Atta-Asamoah, 'Winner-Takes-All Politics and Africa's Future, Institute for Security Studies (2010), www.polity.org.za/article/winner-takesall-politics-and-africas-future-2010-10-25.

[38] Nic Cheeseman and Sishuwam Sishuwa, 'African Studies Keyword: Democracy', *African Studies Review* 64: 704–732 (2021).

empowerment has received some scholarly attention,[39] broadly as necessary to encourage political moderation,[40] and also in the context of constitutional amendments.[41] Opposition empowerment not only enhances checks on the incumbent, it also increases the stakes for opposition groups in contributing to peaceful electoral and broadly democratic processes and accepting electoral outcomes – 'losers' consent'.[42]

This section briefly discusses existing mechanisms in African constitutions empowering the opposition, mainly using the implications of the principle of 'national consensus' as a precondition for legitimate constitutional amendments and the experience from Seychelles, which gives the opposition almost equal role as the incumbent in constituting courts and other democracy, rule of law and accountability promotion and protection institutions. In combination, the principle of national consensus and equitable role of the opposition in making key appointments reduce chances of abusive constitutional changes and incumbent capture of critical institutions and therefore can serve as a robust antibody against democratic backsliding. More positively, opposition empowerment rules necessitate a culture of regular engagement and cooperation among political rivals, which could enable trust, tame polarisation and winner-takes-all thinking and ultimately contribute to nurturing the legitimacy, stability and resilience of democratic systems. Normatively, as well, rules empowering the opposition 'ensure a more robust version of representation in politics, and hence a more robust version of legitimacy for democratic institutions'.[43]

The principle of national consensus in the adoption of constitutional amendments was formally adopted in the ACDEG[44] with a view to preclude opportunistic and abusive constitutional changes, mainly in view of a pattern of reversal of key concessions in the post-1990 democratisation and constitutional reform processes, notably presidential term limits. Nevertheless, the Constitutional Court of Benin

39 David Fontana, 'Government in Opposition', *Yale Law Journal* 119: 384–647 (2008).

40 Sumit Bisarya and Elliot W. Bulmer, 'Rule of Law, Democracy and Human Rights: The Paramountcy of Moderation', in *Constitutionalism and the Rule of Law: Bridging idealism and realism* ed. Maurice Adams, Anne Meuwese and Ernst Hirsch Ballin. Cambridge University Press, 2017, 123–158.

41 Adem Kassie Abebe, 'The Vulnerability of Constitutional Pacts: Inclusive Majoritarianism as Protection against Democratic Backsliding', in *Annual Review of Constitution-Building 2019*. International IDEA, 2019, https://constitutionnet.org/sites/default/files/2021-01/annual-review-of-constitution-building-2019.pdf.

42 Christopher Anderson, *Losers' Consent: Elections and Democratic Legitimacy*. Oxford University Press, 2005.

43 Fontana, 'Government in Opposition'.

44 Adem Kassie Abebe, 'The (Il)legitimacy of Constitutional Amendments in Africa and Democratic Backsliding', *Asian journal of Comparative Law* (2024), https://papers.ssrn.com/sol3/papers.cfm?abstract_id=4008355; Micha Wiebusch and Christina Murray, 'Presidential Term Limits and the African Union', *Journal of African Law* 63: 131–160 (2019).

had earlier adopted it as a fundamental principle of constitutional change, which likely inspired the drafters of the ACDEG.

The ACDEG requires state parties to 'ensure that the process of amendment or revision of their constitution reposes on national consensus, obtained if need be, through referendum' (article 10(2)). The principle of national consensus superimposes on the constitutional amendment procedures established in national constitutions.[45] Accordingly, countries cannot simply argue that they have followed the specific amendment procedures outlined in the respective constitutions to justify changes.

The principle of national consensus effectively empowers opposition groups beyond supermajority and other rules as it necessitates deliberation, dialogue and negotiation – and potentially consensus – beyond the four walls of parliament. The principle is particularly critical regarding electoral and party rules that should be protected from unilateral alterations, regardless of the dominance of any political group – considering that incumbent parties or coalitions have in many African countries secured absolute dominance in formal political institutions.

Indeed, in Benin after the 2019 legislative elections, the ruling alliance secured full control of the parliament. Nevertheless, arguably because of the principle of national consensus established by the Constitutional Court, and also because of escalating political tension, the president convened an ostensible national dialogue. The dialogue ultimately generated certain fundamental principles to provide the basis for reforms. Nevertheless, some opposition groups boycotted the dialogue and even some who attended complained that the unveiled outcomes did not reflect the deliberations in the dialogue. As noted above, although the Constitutional Court approved the amendments, the African Court found that the dialogue was insufficient to comply with the principle of national consensus.

The African Court – and broadly the African Union and the bodies monitoring compliance with the ACDEG – has not expounded on what national consensus exactly entails, particularly whether a critical mass of opposition groups should be on board with constitutional amendments. The 2000 Lomé Declaration on the Framework for an OAU Response to Unconstitutional Changes of Government recognises as fundamental principles the promotion of political pluralism, the principle of democratic change of government and '*recognition of a role for the opposition*' (emphasis added).[46] The Declaration also specifically calls for 'guaranteeing access to the media for all political stake-holders'.

In view of these continental standards, the value of the principle of national consensus would be maximised in protecting constitutional provisions, particularly

45 Adem Kassie Abebe, 'The (Il)legitimacy of Constitutional Amendments in Africa and Democratic Backsliding'.

46 Lomé Declaration of July 2000 on the framework for an OAU response to unconstitutional changes of government (AHG/Decl.5 (XXXVI), Principle V.

those relating to the democratic electoral game, where no player is allowed to change on their own the rules by which they must play, regardless of their dominance. In a different article, this author has argued that moving beyond supermajority and/or referendum rules and requiring direct cross-party approval of the most abused constitutional rules may be necessary to lead to a form of democracy founded on inclusive majoritarianism.[47] The legitimacy and validity of amendments to the 'democratic core' should depend not simply on the size/quantity of the supermajority but its quality/inclusiveness (of more than one group's voice).

Beyond constitutional change, the Seychelles Constitution perhaps has the most progressive and comprehensive guarantees for the involvement of opposition groups in governance, effectively precluding any incumbent from capturing rule of law, accountability and democracy protecting institutions. The Constitution provides for a Constitutional Appointments Authority with the mandate to propose names for key appointments and removals, including the Attorney General, members of the Electoral Commission, highest judges and the Ombudsperson (articles 139–142). The Authority has five members: two each selected by the President and the Leader of Opposition and a chairperson selected by the four members. The members serve guaranteed seven-year terms (which does not overlap with presidential terms) and may only be removed under strictly defined processes. The Leader of Opposition is elected by National Assembly members who are not from the party of the incumbent president, hence could be from the legislative majority or minority (article 84 (5)). The salary, allowances, gratuity or pension payable to the Leader of the Opposition are determined through legislation but 'shall be not less than those payable to a Minister and shall be a charge on the Consolidated Fund'. While other African countries have recognised the role of the opposition in the appointment of a handful of members of election management bodies, Seychelles stands out in building a representative and impartial appointment process to courts and other rule of law, accountability and democracy promoting institutions.

In addition to the principle of national consensus and role of the opposition in the Seychelles, African constitutions are increasingly recognising the status and roles of the opposition. In Burundi, the 2018 Constitution requires that the President and Vice President must belong to different political parties/coalitions, as well as different ethnic groups, or are independents of different ethnicities (article 124). A 2016 amendment to the Constitution of Senegal introduced the position of Head of Opposition and requires the adoption of an organic law outlining the rights and duties of the opposition (article 58). The 2016 Constitution of Cote d'Ivoire guarantees the

47 Abebe, 'The Vulnerability of Constitutional Pacts'. On the role of the opposition in relation to fourth branch institutions, see Tarunabh Khaitan 'Guarantor (or the So-called Fourth Branch) Institutions' in *Cambridge Handbook of Constitutional Theory* ed. Jeff King and Richard Bellamy (Cambridge University Press, 2024), https://ssrn.com/abstract=3997808 or http://dx.doi.org/10.2139/ssrn.3997808.

parliamentary opposition the right for adequate and effective representation in all the bodies of Parliament (article 100). The now repealed 2014 Constitution of Tunisia assigned the chair of the Finance Committee and rapporteur of the External Relations Committee to the opposition (article 60). The Tunisian opposition is also entitled to establish and head a parliamentary committee of enquiry annually. The Constitution of Rwanda establishes a National Consultative of Forum of Political Organizations as a permanent forum to bring together political organisations for the purposes of political dialogue and building consensus and national cohesion (article 59). While the focus of this chapter is on constitutional rules, which provide the most effective protection, many countries in Africa also empower the opposition, particularly in leading and representation in parliamentary committees, in various ways through the standing orders of parliament.

Overall, there is increasing recognition in Africa that winner-takes-all politics poses a fundamental challenge, and innovative approaches both at the national and continental level have emerged to institutionalise antidotes to the winner-takes-all thinking, principally through the empowerment of the opposition. In a way, constitution makers are starting to imagine and craft constitutions from the perspective of electoral losers, rather than merely the winners. In view of these developments, a more systematic deliberation on the issue is critical at national, sub-regional and continental levels to identify the various modalities of opposition empowerment at the constitutional, statute and legislative standing order levels to assess their performance in enabling stable, legitimate and resilient democratic and constitutional systems.

6.6 CONCLUSION

In summary, constitutions in Africa, as elsewhere, regulate to a different degree key aspects of the rules of the democratic game – electoral systems, political parties, courts and democracy and accountability promotion institutions. Constitutions in Anglophone African countries tend to have elaborate rules on the rules regulating the terms of democratic political contestation. In contrast, Francophone African countries tend to be constitutionally minimalist, leaving large aspects of these key issues, even with presidential elections, to organic law. Despite the differences, however, the constitutional rules have largely remained relatively stable. In most cases, democratic backsliding often happens through irregular processes, in some cases through legal reform and rarely through constitutional change, with the notable exception of presidential term limits.

Where there has been constitutional change, the pattern is decidedly towards better guarantees and protection of electoral rules. This is not to underestimate the importance of constitutionalisation of the fundamental rules to reduce the chances of formal backsliding. Indeed, the trend is that newer constitutions tend to regulate more of these rules of the democratic game than their predecessors.

Beyond the rules of contestation, this contribution argues that central to the battle against democratic backsliding may be the imagination of constitution design from the perspective of electoral losers, rather than merely electoral winners, more specifically, through ways of equitable participation of the opposition in governance, rather than merely opposing. The requirement of national consensus for the adoption and change of fundamental aspects of democratic competition ensures relative stability of the rules and prevents a dominant incumbent from self-servingly altering the rules of the game. The empowerment of the opposition in constituting the membership of the institutions central to rule of law, democracy and accountability – as in Seychelles – can reduce the chances of political capture, therefore enhancing the overall legitimacy of the political system, enhancing the stakes for all to accept electoral outcomes, enabling consistent engagement and dialogue and trust among rival political actors and, overall, building a stable foundation for constitutional democracy. This is not to say that the deliberate empowerment of the opposition is an unmitigated good. Such empowerment could potentially lead to political paralysis and deadlock. Accordingly, it is important to design systems that encourage deliberation, not blockade, which necessitates deadlock breaking mechanisms (European Commission for Democracy through Law [Venice Commission] 2018).[48] A balance must be struck to ensure that the desire to check the tyranny of the political majority through including the opposition in governance does not degenerate into the tyranny of the political minority.

Accordingly, constitutional designers in Africa (and beyond) should reimagine democracy beyond majoritarian conceptions and seek ways to empower the opposition through inclusive governance. Scholars should also explore ways through which countries in Africa and across the world have empowered the opposition, how particular approaches have operated in practice, and propose ways to refine the approaches based on comparative practice.

[48] Venice Commission, 'Compilation of Venice Commission Opinions and Reports Relating to Qualified Majorities and Anti-Deadlock Mechanisms'; CDL-PI(2018)003rev; 2018, www.venice.coe.int/webforms/documents/?pdf=CDL-PI(2018)003-e.

7

Parties versus Democracy

Addressing Today's Political Party Threats to Democratic Rule

Tom Gerald Daly and Brian Christopher Jones

7.1 INTRODUCTION: THE POLITICAL PARTY THREAT TO LIBERAL DEMOCRACY WORLDWIDE

The growing threat to liberal democracy worldwide is, in many ways, a political party threat. Recent years have seen the rise of a range of populist, illiberal, nativist, xenophobic, far-right, and neofascist parties.[1] In many places, parties with a questionable commitment to liberal democracy have entered government, while others remain outside government but are making gains.[2] We also see established democratic parties in government that have threatened or incrementally dismantled democratic structures through subversion by an outsider or the ascendance of an extremist wing. These threats are studied under rubrics including "constitutional retrogression,"[3] "constitutional capture,"[4] and "democratic

[1] See, e.g., Ron Inglehart and Pippa Norris, "Trump and the Populist Authoritarian Parties: The Silent Revolution in Reverse," *Perspectives on Politics* 15(2): 443–454 (2017); Andreas Johansson Heinö, "Timbro Authoritarian Populism Index 2017," *Timbro* (January 4, 2018), https://timbro.se/allmant/timbro-authoritarian-populism-index2017/; and Matthijs Rooduijn et al., "The PopuList: An Overview of Populist, Far Right, Far Left and Eurosceptic Parties in Europe," PopuList (2019), www.popu-list.org.

[2] A watershed moment, for both European and global democracy, was Germany's September 2017 elections, which brought a far-right-leaning party to parliament for the first time since the 1960s, with Alternativ für Deutschland (AfD) claiming 12.6 percent of the total vote and becoming the main opposition in the Bundestag following the formation of another CDU/CSU-SPD "grand coalition" between the mainstream Christian-democratic and social-democratic parties: Fredrik Erixon, "Merkel's Left-Right Coalition Has Given the AfD Exactly What It Wanted," *Spectator* (March 4, 2018), www.spectator.co.uk/article/merkel-s-left-right-coalition-has-given-the-afd-exactly-what-it-wanted.

[3] Aziz Z. Huq and Tom Ginsburg, *How to Save a Constitutional Democracy*. University of Chicago Press, 2019.

[4] See, e.g., Jan-Werner Müller, "Protecting the Rule of Law (and Democracy!) in the EU: The Idea of a Copenhagen Commission," in *Reinforcing Rule of Law Oversight in the European Union* ed. Carlos Closa and Dimitry Kochenov. Cambridge University Press, 2016, 206–224.

decay."[5] While this phenomenon is often framed as an executive-led problem, it also needs to be understood as a political party problem.

Parties and party leaders occupying an ill-defined space on the political spectrum between the center and extreme – the "far-right lite" – now present a much greater threat to democratic governance than overtly antidemocratic fringe outfits, such as Germany's neo-Nazi National Democratic Party (NPD). Such parties also frustrate, in new ways, the application of existing public law and policy mechanisms to address democracy-threatening parties, including refusal of registration, thresholds for entering parliament, application of the criminal law, outright banning, the erection of "cordons sanitaires" to freeze them out of governance, or a practice of considered engagement. Crucial features of contemporary political party threats include their ambiguous nature, their growing size, and the subversion of democratic parties by errant leaders or extremist factions.

This chapter makes the following central claims: that contemporary political party threats require us to more systematically map the key threats posed, to pay greater attention to crafting novel public law and policy solutions to address these threats, and to reflect anew on our fundamental assumptions about the relationship between political parties and the functioning of liberal constitutional democracy itself. At a time when political party systems are transforming worldwide, and certain parties' core function is shifting from a broadly rational vehicle for channeling citizen policy preferences to a more emotive representation of identity, this chapter aims to ignite discussion and debate on these developments.

The chapter contains four sections. Section 7.2 addresses the enduringly awkward relationship between democratic governance and political parties, as both essential mediators between the public and State and forces that can frustrate the design and functioning of the democratic system. Section 7.3 discusses conventional approaches to political parties perceived as threats to democratic governance. Section 7.4 highlights the inadequacies of existing approaches to address the threats posed by contemporary political parties. Section 7.5 canvasses a number of potential innovations in responding to such threats, with the aim of spurring deliberation on this crucial issue.

7.2 POLITICAL PARTIES: CENTRAL TO DEMOCRACY BUT ORPHANS OF CONSTITUTIONAL THOUGHT

Despite being central to contemporary understandings and conceptualizations of functioning liberal democracy, political parties occupy an enduringly awkward position in democratic governance and constitutional law, representing both a potential threat to democracy and a virtually unavoidable medium between the

[5] See, e.g., Tom Gerald Daly, "Democratic Decay: Conceptualising an Emerging Research Field," *Hague Journal on the Rule of Law* 11: 9–36 (2019).

state and the people in facilitating democratic governance in complex modern polities. This tension has deep historical roots. In crafting the US Constitution, James Madison warned of the "factional threat" represented by a group "who are united and actuated by some common impulse of passion, or of interest, adverse to the rights of other citizens, or to the permanent and aggregate interests of the community."[6] While the US Constitution itself says nothing of parties, its entry into force shortly predated, even spurred, the coalescence of the US political system into two clear groupings, centered on the issue of the extent of federal power, and prefiguring the enduring two-party system central to contemporary US democracy.[7]

Some 4,000 miles distant, political clubs in revolutionary France arose in the heady years of newly won political freedom following 1789, which saw a flowering of open political activity and exchange of ideas. However, Jacobin clubs, in particular, having played a key role in the height of The Terror from 1793–1794, during which the revolutionary government pursued its aim of countering its internal and external enemies through extreme violence, were closed down after the end of The Terror in 1794.[8] The terms "terrorism" and "terrorist" are said to have been invented retrospectively to describe the Jacobins and the methods they employed.[9] In France, then, the first (proto-)parties rapidly came to be viewed as antithetical to good governance. Yet, despite their increasing systemic importance, successive constitutions remained silent on the role of parties as the French Republic repeatedly foundered and renewed itself.

Despite the concurrent rise of constitutional government and political parties across the long nineteenth century (i.e., 1789–1914), constitutions worldwide largely overlooked parties as an essential element of the modern democratic state. As Aradhya Sethiya offers: "If political theory saw parties as anti-democratic, the eighteenth- century constitutions considered them constitutional externalities" or even "orphans of constitutional law."[10] In the post-1945 era, the most common early references to political parties in constitutional texts concern their registration and the constitutional power to ban parties opposed to democratic rule: originally found

6 See William Partlett and Zim Nwokora, "The Foundation of Democratic Dualism: Why Constitutional Politics and Ordinary Politics Are Different." *Constellations* 26(2): 177, 177–178 (2019); and James Madison, "Federalist No. 10" (1787), Bill of Rights Institute, https://billofrightsinstitute.org/founding-documents/primary-source-documents/the-federalist-papers/federalist-papers-no-10/.

7 Partlett and Nwokora, "The Foundation of Democratic Dualism," 182. See Russell Muirhead and Nancy L. Rosenblum, "The Uneasy Place of Parties in the Constitutional Order," in *The Oxford Handbook of the U.S. Constitution* ed. Mark Tushnet et al. Oxford University Press, 2015, 217–240.

8 Marisa Linton, "Jacobinism," in *1 Encyclopedia of Political Theory: A–E* ed. Mark Bevir. Sage, 2010, 725–726.

9 Ibid. at 726.

10 Aradhya Sethia, "Where's the Party? Towards a Constitutional Biography of Political Parties," *Indian Law Review* 3(1): 1 (2019).

in the 1949 Basic Law of West Germany and spreading in subsequent decades to states worldwide, including Spain, South Korea, Israel, and various states in Central and Eastern Europe after post-1989 transitions to democratic rule (e.g., Czech Republic and Poland).[11] In recent decades in continental Europe, thicker constitutional recognition has transformed political parties "from socio-political organizations into integral units of the democratic state," viewed as an attempt to shore up their legitimacy as their claim to democratic representation has weakened, not least due to declining membership.[12]

However, in constitutional law scholarship, parties have all too often been ignored or treated as an unwelcome guest, running amok around the three pristine pillars of ordered government sketched in the constitutional text. Not so in political science, where scholars, more interested in whomever exercises power and less hidebound by the niceties of constitutional texts and ideals, have expended much more energy on understanding precisely how political parties operate within the democratic system.[13] A rich literature analyzes everything from interparty relations to intraparty dynamics, to sweeping shifts in political party systems.[14] However, advances in legal actors' understanding of political parties as constitutional actors have been made in the past two decades.

Kommers has framed the Federal Constitutional Court of Germany's case law on political parties as a "jurisprudence of democracy,"[15] shaping the electoral system with the aim of ensuring a genuinely representative political system and bringing their roles within the constitutional realm. As well as insistently affirming the core democratic role of political opposition in its early decades and beyond, the court in key decisions granted political parties the power to defend their institutional rights before the court in a similar manner to other state organs, struck down restrictive candidacy laws, and upheld a law setting a 5 percent threshold of votes cast for parties to enter parliament, to ensure "orderly" governance in an electoral system characterized by diffuse voting patterns. The latter outcome reflected memories of the instability inflicted on Weimar's parliamentary system by a "chaotic carousel of shifting coalitions and collapsing governments, of immobile parliaments repeatedly dissolved."[16]

[11] Justin O. Frosini and Sara Pennicino, "Ban on Political Parties," in *The Max Planck Encyclopedia of Comparative Constitutional Law* ed. Rainer Grote et al. Oxford University Press, 2017, https://oxcon.ouplaw.com/display/10.1093/law-mpeccol/law-mpeccol-e598.

[12] Ingrid Van Biezen, "Constitutionalizing Party Democracy: The Constitutive Codification of Political Parties in Post-War Europe," *British Journal of Political Science* 42: 187 (2012).

[13] Kay Lawson, ed., *Political Parties and Democracy*. Bloomsbury, 2010.

[14] Zim Nwokora and Riccardo Pelizzo, "Measuring Party System Change: A Systems Perspective," *Political Studies* 66: 100 (2017).

[15] D. P. Kommers, "The Federal Constitutional Court: Guardian of German Democracy," *The Annals of the American Academy of Political and Social Science* 603: 111 (2006).

[16] Justin Collings, *Democracy's Guardians: A History of the German Federal Constitutional Court, 1951–2001*. Oxford University Press, 2015.

US scholars have crafted a "law of democracy" literature focused on an institutionalist analysis of the true workings of the democratic system, which underscores the serious tensions between real-world practice and the scheme set out in the venerable constitutional text. In a 2005 article, Pildes and Levinson argued that the original Madisonian design of the US Constitution, predicated on healthy interbranch competition as a means of preventing excessive concentration of political power and the concomitant risk of a tyrannical government, had been almost immediately superseded by the simultaneous emergence of the political party system.[17] For Levinson and Pildes, the continuing focus on this outmoded model of interbranch competition elides the ways in which disciplined political parties can functionally fuse executive-legislative branch operation, which has been exacerbated by the sharpening of ideological interparty divisions through factors including the rise of gerrymandering by both parties and the strengthening of internal party discipline, which renders branch interests "contingent upon shifting patterns of party control."[18]

This analysis is couched in a broader strain of recent US scholarship highlighting the way in which other long-term phenomena, including the growth of the administrative state and of (private) economic power, frustrate the ideals, understandings, and deep assumptions underlying the constitutional scheme and constitutional thought.[19] Yet, despite attempts to understand and reconceive political parties in constitutional terms due to their unavoidable centrality to the exercise of public state power, in the US system (and other states such as Australia and South Africa)[20] they are generally viewed in constitutional terms as private entities, under-regulated, or at best cuckoos in the constitutional nest.[21]

While the analysis above remains largely framed as analyzing the shortcomings of "ordinary" politics in systems populated by parties broadly committed to democratic governance,[22] public law scholars' focus on the centrality of parties to functional democratic governance has started to intensify as parties hostile to liberal democracy have gained ground and various governing parties worldwide

[17] Daryl J. Levinson and Richard H. Pildes, "Protecting Popular Self-Government from the People?," *Harvard Law Review* 119: 2312 (2005–2006).

[18] Ibid. at 2361.

[19] See D. A. Canteub, "Tyranny and Administrative Law," *Arizona Law Review* 59: 49 (2017); and Ginesh Sitaraman, "The Puzzling Absence of Economic Power in Constitutional Theory," *Cornell Law Review* 101: 1445 (2016).

[20] Graeme Orr, "Private Association and Public Brand: The Dualistic Conception of Political Parties in the Common Law World," *Critical Review of International Social and Political Philosophy* 17: 332 (2014); and Catherine O'Regan, "Political Parties: The Missing Link in our Constitution?," *South African Judicial Education Journal* 1: 61 (2018).

[21] Muirhead and Rosenblum, "The Uneasy Place of Parties in the Constitutional Order."

[22] Richard Pildes, "Romanticizing Democracy, Political Fragmentation, and the Decline of American Government," *Yale Law Journal* 124: 804 (2014).

have actively diminished accountability and rights-protecting organs (independent courts, media, and civil society organizations), while maintaining a veneer of legality and democratic rule through sophisticated manipulation of law and continued elections.[23] This presents a challenge of a different order and magnitude compared to the imperfect systemic functioning analyzed by Pildes and others, raising more intensely the risk of tyrannical government through excessive concentration of power and subversion of the constitutional framework.

In many states worldwide, the political party system is now unable to perform the essential mediating and representative role essential to adequately functioning representative democracy. This is due not only to long-established trends such as declining membership but also to the intensification of extreme polarization and "invidious partisanship,"[24] the prioritization of partisan advantage over fidelity to constitutional and democratic governance,[25] the fuller "capture" of parties by elite or sectoral interests, and party "capture" of the state itself through domination of all previously independent democratic institutions, often facilitated by the fragmentation or weakness of the opposition.

Further complicating the picture, perhaps the defining feature of the political party landscape in many states suffering democratic decay today is flux: marginal parties are growing, new parties are forming, long-dominant centrist parties are losing support, more extremist wings of large parties are in the ascendant, and – the greatest challenge of all – recent years have witnessed the rise of parties that are ambiguous in terms of their commitment to liberal democratic rule, rather than avowedly antidemocratic. The party system, quite settled for decades in many states, has become a churn of change. Given this churn, it is useful to briefly map existing approaches to problematic parties.

7.3 CONVENTIONAL APPROACHES TO ANTIDEMOCRATIC PARTIES

This section summarizes the three principal ways – legal, constitutional, and policy approaches – states have attempted to address parties perceived as threats to, or inimical to, the democratic system, and highlights their inadequacy in remedying the novel democratic threats posed by contemporary parties.

[23] Laurent Pech and Kim Scheppele, "Illiberalism Within: Rule of Law Backsliding in the EU," *Cambridge Yearbook of European Legal Studies* 19: 3 (2017); and Huq and Ginsburg, *How to Save a Constitutional Democracy*.

[24] Justin Levitt, "Intent Is Enough: Invidious Partisanship in Redistricting," *William & Mary Law Review* 59: 1993 (2018).

[25] See, e.g., Yasmin Dawood, "Democracy and the Problem of the Partisan State," in *Loyalty: NOMOS LIV* ed. Sanford Levinson et al. Oxford University Press, 2013, 257–292.

7.3.1 *Legal Approaches*

7.3.1.1 Registration Conditions

Registration requirements (and refusal to register) have been used to curtail threats by making it more difficult for fringe and extremist parties to gain ballot access. While in some states – especially in long-established common law democracies – these may only consist of "bureaucratic niceties," such as form- filling and fees,[26] in other jurisdictions requirements are "complex and lengthy."[27] Even if parties meet all the formal bureaucratic requirements, state authorities are often empowered to refuse registration based on the wider aims of the party or because of incongruity with party laws or constitutional standards – although such refusals can usually be appealed.[28] While research suggests that the types and forms of documentation required for political parties are becoming lengthier and more complex, this has not kept democracy-threatening parties off the ballot. Savvy parties are aware of these restrictions and are unlikely to divulge information that may lead to registration refusal.

7.3.1.2 Thresholds for Entering Parliament

Thresholds, defined as "the legally prescribed minimum number of votes needed for a party to take part in distribution of parliamentary seats,"[29] are designed to protect parliaments against extremist or fringe parties that may gain a small but not insignificant number of votes. Usually set between 3–7 percent, they can be higher or lower,[30] and can also relate to regional versus national vote percentage, or even for party coalitions.[31] Beyond the legal threshold, there is also a natural threshold that parties must surpass in order to gain seats, namely, the percentage needed to obtain one seat at the district level, which tend to be very significantly higher.[32] For example, in the United Kingdom's (UK) majoritarian system the natural threshold to secure a seat is 35 percent (preventing the UK Independence Party from gaining more than a single seat in the 2015 elections despite obtaining 12.6 percent of the

[26] Orr, "Private Association and Public Brand," 343.

[27] Pippa Norris, *Radical Right: Voters and Parties in the Electoral Market*. Cambridge University Press, 2006, 88.

[28] Criteria, Conditions and Procedures for Establishing a Political Party in the Member States of the European Union, European Parliament Document PE 462.512 (2012) at 20–23.

[29] Ibid.

[30] In the Netherlands, it is 0.67 percent. In Turkey, it is 10 percent. See Venice Commission, at 6–8.

[31] For example, in Germany parties need either three district seats or five percent of the national vote to enter the Bundestag.

[32] Venice Commission, at 9.

national vote).[33] As with registration requirements, elections in recent years have demonstrated that many state thresholds are not keeping threatening political parties out of power.

7.3.1.3 Applications of New and Existing Law

Jurisdictions are often hesitant to restrict specific parties because of the implications this could have for rights and liberties, such as freedom of association and expression, and foundational values such as democratic pluralism. Yet, states commonly punish extremist parties or party leaders through terrorism, hate speech or incitement laws,[34] criminal law,[35] tax fraud laws,[36] and campaign funding regulations,[37] which can lead to parties breaking down or voluntarily dissolving. However, this may not be the best strategy to defuse the long-term problem and may even prove advantageous – rather than debilitating – for the targeted party, by bolstering its status and electoral success, such as Jean-Marie Le Pen's success after his conviction for assault during a 1988 election campaign.[38] For states ordinarily less willing to tackle parties through the law, one-off restrictions include attempts in the 1950s to suppress or ban the main communist party in both the United States and Australia, which failed due to weak enforcement of a suppressive law (US)[39] or its being struck down by the apex court (Australia).[40] Alternative strategies, such as cutting off media access or government funding – which Germany's Bundestag opted for in 2017 after the Constitutional Court refused to dissolve the neo-Nazi National Democratic Party (NDP)[41] – have limited effect in the social media age and could even incentivize foreign or illegal funding strategies or the party dissolving and reregistering under a new name.

[33] Electoral Commission: 2015 UK General Election Results, www.electoralcommission.org.uk/find-information-by-subject/elections-and-referendums/past-elections-and-referendums/uk-general-elections/2015-uk-general-election-results.

[34] Vlaams Blok in Belgium in 2004 and Centrum Partij in the Netherlands in the 1990s. See William M. Downs, *Political Extremism in Democracies: Combating Intolerance*. Springer, 2012, 85.

[35] Reuters, "French Rightist Found Guilty of Assault in 1997 Campaign." *New York Times* (April 3, 1998), https://nyti.ms/2GFowkG.

[36] Mogens Glistrup, founder of the Danish Progress Party. See Downs, *Political Extremism in Democracies*, 139.

[37] E.g., the One Nation Party in Australia. See Norris, *Radical Right*, 69.

[38] See Norris, *Radical Right*, 91.

[39] Internal Security Act of 1950, Pub. L. No. 81-831, 64 Stat. 987.

[40] *Australian Communist Party v. The Commonwealth* [1951] HCA 5 (Australia).

[41] Tom Gerald Daly, "Germany's Move to Deprive Anti-Democratic Parties of Federal Funding: An Effective Response to the Populist Wave?" ConstitutionNet (July 26, 2017), www.constitutionnet.org/news/germanys-move-deprive-anti-democratic-parties-federal-funding-effective-response-populist-wave.

7.3.2 *Constitutional Approaches*

7.3.2.1 Election System Tinkering

Can particular election systems facilitate or diminish political party threats? While proportional systems have proliferated on the basis that they are more democratic by according voters a broader electoral choice and by constructing a more representative parliament after elections,[42] Rosenbluth and Shapiro argue that this can not only lead to haphazard, weak, or deceptively representative coalition governments but also permits fringe and extremist political parties into the system.[43] They argue that having two strong parties in a majoritarian single-member district (SMD) system produces the best democratic outcomes.[44] Counter-arguments here include: in many jurisdictions any wholesale electoral system change would be difficult and unlikely to be achieved within a short time-frame, fragmentation may be rooted in longstanding political traditions, major traditional political parties in majoritarian systems can still be captured by authoritarian-leaning populist candidates hostile to liberal democracy,; and the latter problem has been aggravated by changes to "democratize" party leadership election methods, which, compared to more traditional selection of leaders through party or parliamentary leadership, removes barriers for questionable candidates.[45] Thus, constitutional tinkering of the electoral system is at best a medium-term option and, even if successful, is no panacea.

7.3.2.2 Banning or Dissolving Political Parties

The power to dissolve political parties based on their purportedly antidemocratic platform or operation is a feature of many democratic constitutions globally, representing one of the most controversial weapons in the arsenal of a post–World War II "militant democracy" capable of protecting itself from threat or collapse by employing illiberal means. The most influential model has been the 1949 Basic Law of West Germany: Article 212(2) empowers the Federal Constitutional Court to ban political parties that "seek to undermine or abolish the free democratic basic order or to endanger the existence of the Federal Republic of Germany." While frequency of use varies considerably (from highly frequent in Turkey to not a single instance in Poland) and some sizeable parties have been dissolved (e.g., former ruling Communist parties in Latvia and Lithuania), they largely target fringe parties or specific state issues (e.g., secessionist parties).[46] One study indicates that twenty of

[42] Nils-Christian Bormann and Matt Golder, "Democratic Electoral Systems around the World, 1946–2011," *Electoral Studies* 32(2): 360, 363–365 (2013).

[43] Frances McCall Rosenbluth and Ian Shapiro, *Responsible Parties: Saving Democracy from Itself*. Yale University Press, 2018.

[44] Ibid. at 5.

[45] Ibid. at 81–89.

[46] Frosini and Pennicino, "Ban on Political Parties," at paragraph 16.

thirty-seven European states analyzed had banned at least one party since 1945, totaling fifty-two bans in all, including both post-authoritarian states and states without experience of authoritarian rule.[47] The core expressive and associative political freedoms such bans affect are not only recognized in national constitutions but also in international human rights instruments, including the International Covenant on Civil and Political Rights (ICCPR) and regional conventions such as the European Convention on Human Rights (ECHR).[48] In 2000, the Council of Europe's Venice Commission set out seven guidelines for political party dissolution,[49] drawing heavily from the case law of the European Court of Human Rights (ECtHR). However, these have not necessarily ensured clarity[50] and some of the ECtHR's judgments have come under heavy criticism.[51]

Bligh and Müller have argued for a reconsideration and new understanding of party bans on the basis that novel challenges and different types of authoritarianism have arisen.[52] As Bligh observes, "the dominant approach continues to be preoccupied with the Weimar scenario" of democratic breakdown in 1920s Germany, spurred by overtly antidemocratic actors.[53] Both public law and political science literature emphasizes the deficiencies of bans:[54] normatively, as being undemocratic and open to abuse, resting in intractable tension with adherence to democratic pluralism; and practically, as being "pointless", "counterproductive,"[55] and diverting attention from more effective methods, such as policy approaches.[56]

47 Angela K. Bourne and Fernando Casal Bértoa, "Mapping 'Militant Democracy': Variation in Party Ban Practices in European Democracies (1945–2015)," *European Constitutional Law Review* 13: 221, 230, 246 (2017).

48 Eva Brems, "Freedom of Political Association and the Question of Party Closures," in *Political Rights Under Stress in 21st century Europe* ed. Wojciech Sadurski. Oxford University Press, 2006, 120–128.

49 European Commission for Democracy Through Law (Venice Commission), "Guidelines on Prohibition and Dissolution of Political Parties and Analogous Measures," *CDL-INF* (2000), 1.

50 For example, Guideline 3 limits party bans to those advocating or using violence while Guideline 5 refers to the much broader criteria of "danger to the free and democratic political order or to the rights of individuals."

51 For instance, its upholding of the Welfare Party's dissolution by the Turkish Constitutional Court has been called "the largest single interference with freedom of association in European jurisprudence." (Paul Harvey, "Militant Democracy and the European Court of Human Rights," *European Law Review* 29: 407, 417 [2004]).

52 Gur Bligh, "Defending Democracy: A New Understanding of the Party-Banning Phenomenon," *Vanderbilt Journal of Transnational Law* 46: 1321 (2013); and Jan-Werner Müller, "Protecting Popular Self-Government from the People? New Normative Perspectives on Militant Democracy," *Annual Review of Political Science* 19: 249 (2016).

53 Bligh, "Defending Democracy," 1325.

54 See Downs, *Political Extremism in Democracies*, 199.

55 Tim Bale, "Will It All End in Tears? What Really Happens when Democracies Use Law to Ban Political Parties," in *Regulating Political Parties: European Democracies in Comparative Perspectives* ed. Ingrid van Biezen and Hans-Martien ten Napel. Leiden University Press, 2014, 195–196.

56 Angela Bourne, "Democratic Dilemmas: Why Democracies Ban Political Parties 3," Conference Paper, University of Montréal, European Consortium for Political Research General Conference (August 26–29, 2015).

7.3.3 *Policy Approaches*

7.3.3.1 Cordons sanitaires

"Cordons sanitaires" entail parliamentary parties adopting a policy of refusal to engage with extremist or threatening political parties that have entered parliament. There is little consensus that this is effective: some question the efficacy of "quarantining" in that targeted parties may not always become pariah parties and could exert influence through other means. Although repressive measures can have the effect of pushing out a "small minority" of members from extremist parties, such actions may also attract potential newcomers because of the party's "persecuted" status and can also lead to the establishment of clandestine networks and a hardening of extremist positions.[57] As Downs stresses, "denial, rejection, and repression have largely failed to mitigate extremism in the cases where they have been adopted as dominant strategies."[58]

7.4 DEMOCRATIC THREATS POSED BY CONTEMPORARY PARTIES

7.4.1 *The Rise of the "Far-right Lite" Party*

In recent years, the clearest global trend in political party systems is the rise of parties with a more ambiguous relationship to liberal democracy and more significant electoral support (e.g., France's Front National, Poland's Law and Justice Party (PiS), Brazil's Social Liberal Party (PSL), or India's Bharatiya Janata Party (BJP).[59] The nature of these larger parties is a key obstacle to addressing the threat they present. They often present a form of "far-right lite,"[60] with partially detoxified platforms that steer away from any overt challenge to democratic governance and tend to frame their racist, xenophobic, and illiberal views in a more sophisticated manner than previous problematic parties (although the Brazilian context has featured more overt authoritarianism at times).

Moreover, a party like the Alternativ für Deutschland (AfD) – like most parties – is not a monolithic bloc of one mind on all issues. Its success appears partly based on its ability to offer the electorate two political "flavors": a relatively moderate face, which frames anti-immigrant and other views as eminently sensible, and a much more strident and virulent face, which speaks against "an

57 Michael Minkenberg, "Repression and Reaction: Militant Democracy and the Radical Right in Germany and France," *Patterns Prejudice* 40: 25, 43 (2006).

58 Downs, *Political Extremism in Democracies*, 200.

59 Daly, "Democratic Decay."

60 Bale, "Will It All End in Tears?," 215.

invasion of foreigners" and is capable of shocking statements.[61] The AfD has made an art of walking back extreme statements with contrary statements from its more moderate wing. Thus, it is hard to fit the party into the established framework for addressing antidemocratic parties under the German Constitutional Court's case law or accepted understandings of such bans reflected in the Venice Commission's guidelines. Moreover, especially when the AfD has been the official opposition, a "cordon sanitaire" policy has been neither practically feasible nor democratically defensible.

Indeed, in the context of the Constitutional Court's refusal to ban the NPD in 2017 – strongly criticized by political actors, as discussed above – Stefan Thiel approved of the Constitutional Court's judgment as reflecting the view that German society "must adapt to fight extremist ideologies chiefly in the political, rather than the legal arena. First and foremost, this requires engaging with at times uncomfortable viewpoints, an active engagement of civil society in political debate and tolerance of dissent."[62]

7.4.2 *The Size of "Far-right Lite" Parties*

Second, and further undermining the potential application of existing mechanisms, is the size of contemporary democracy-threatening parties. While such "hybrid" parties long occupied the fringes of democratic political party systems, especially in Europe, it has been argued that they have now displaced liberal parties as the "third ideological authority" beyond Conservative and Christian Democrat parties, and Social Democrat Parties.[63] This means that Thiel's point above gains added force: the larger a potential antidemocratic party, the more foolhardy (and less justifiable) it may be to attempt to suppress it by legal means, or to attempt a policy of exclusion or containment. It is tempting to argue that such parties should be targeted before they have the chance to grow, through refusal to register, application of the criminal law, or outright bans. However, this would assume that a party's platform and views are explicitly antidemocratic, whereas contemporary parties present much more ambiguous fronts. It may only be when a party is in power that its true threat to democratic rule becomes apparent. Here, the "Weimar" scenario of overt aversion to democratic rule does not apply, which precludes the application of any banning mechanism.

61 Justin Huggler, "AfD Co-Leader Walks Out on Party on Day after German Election Success," *Telegraph* (September 25, 2017), www.telegraph.co.uk/news/2017/09/25/afd-co-leader-walks-party-day-electionannounces-fight-against/.

62 Stefan Theil, "A Vote of Confidence for the German Democratic Order: The German Federal Constitutional Court Ruling on the Application to Ban the National Democratic Party," UK Constitutional Law Association (January 31, 2017), https://ukconstitutionallaw.org/2017/01/31/stefan-theil-a-vote-of-confidence-for-the-germandemocratic-order/.

63 Timbro Authoritarian Populism Index 2017, 18.

7.4.3 *The Entry of Antidemocratic Parties into Government*

Apart from research on the banning of former ruling parties,[64] the majority of the literature on antidemocratic political parties focuses on contexts where the main political territory is occupied by "mainstream" parties within the acceptable ranges of the democratic political spectrum. However, in multiple states, parties hostile to liberal democracy have entered government, sometimes with significant majorities or in coalition. Some, like Hungary's Fidesz Party, Poland's Law and Justice Party or India's BJP have secured multiple terms in government while others have been ousted after one term (e.g., Bolsonaro's PSL in Brazil). The problems canvassed above regarding the futility of applying existing remedial measures to parties like the Front National and AfD are exacerbated in the case of a variety of parties that have, once in government, tended to incrementally hollow out democratic structures, crafting a hybrid governance system with few constraints on executive power but retaining elections. The examples of the Law and Justice (PiS) party in Poland and Fidesz party in Hungary demonstrate how difficult it is to deal with this issue before parties come to power. Indeed, both parties started as what seemed to be liberal-democratic parties; Fidesz (whose name comes from Fiatal Demokraták Szövetsége; Alliance of Young Democrats) emerged from a liberal student activist movement; PiS emerged from the Solidarity movement that spurred the Polish democratic transition ending Communist rule.

7.4.4 *The "Subversion" of a Democratic Party by an Outsider/Extreme Wing*

A different form of threat is posed by the takeover (or "populist capture")[65] of a long-established "good" party by a "bad" leadership, whether by an individual outsider or an extremist wing. This tends to be the only choice available to authoritarian-leaning political forces where the nature of the established party system precludes the formation of a new party.[66] Examples include Rodrigo Duterte in the Philippines and Donald Trump in the United States.

In neither scenario could existing mechanisms tackle the problematic rise of these individuals. In a two-party system such as the US, using criminal law, "cordon sanitaire" techniques, or other existing mechanisms against the subverted party simply could not work without distorting the entire political party system, and would inescapably be viewed as partisan in nature. It is important to emphasize the distinction between party leadership and the party itself. For instance, the 2011 Venice Commission guidelines on banning political parties emphasizes that

[64] Pieter Niesen, "Banning the Former Ruling Party," *Constellations* 19: 540 (2012).

[65] Lena Günther and Anna Lührmann, "Populism and Autocratization 1," V-Dem Policy Brief No. 19. University of Gothenburg, Varieties of Democracy Institute (December 2018).

[66] Ibid. at 1.

the activities of party members as individuals (including leaders) cannot provide the basis for dissolution, especially if such action runs counter to the political party's constitution or activities, unless it can be demonstrated that the activity was taken by the party's statutory body.[67]

In cases of "subversion" of a democratic party by an outsider, rather than the cost of measures that target the entire party, it may be more effective to wield the scalpel of targeted measures to remove a corruptive leader, such as impeachment.[68]

7.4.5 *The Dominance of a Party by Unaccountable or Shadow Insiders*

A "subverter" is not always an outsider, nor in a formal position of apex power in the State. In this connection, internal party dynamics appear increasingly important as a factor. This raises two difficult issues. First, to what extent can the activity of a dominant figure such as Poland's Jarosław Kaczyński be separated from the party itself? After all Kaczyński is leader of the PiS party but only joined cabinet in 2020 until PiS was ousted in 2023. Second, what democratic concerns are raised by the level of dominance exercised by an unaccountable individual or group of unaccountable individuals? Where government policy and activity is excessively influenced by one figure, this appears to cut against the most foundational safeguards of a democratic system, such as the separation of state powers – acutely heightening the concerns highlighted by Levinson and Pildes in the US context regarding the impact of party dynamics on excessive concentration of power. Effectively, the separate branches of government become simply different arms of the party, rather than separate "sovereign" entities that check and balance one another's power in concordance with the Constitution as well as acceptable constitutional practice in a democratic society. Such concentration of power in one individual also renders the link between the electorate and party more tenuous. It is an issue that requires much more attention in the literature.

7.5 CONTEMPLATING NEW PUBLIC LAW AND POLICY APPROACHES

Effectively addressing the novel challenges to democratic governance posed by contemporary political parties requires new mechanisms, based on key lessons from the debate concerning existing and historical approaches to antidemocratic parties, including: falling into the trap of mechanisms that can be characterized as elite or partisan frustration of the will of the people, assuming that antidemocratic parties will be easy to identify, and distinguishing between party leaderships and the parties

67 OSCE, ODIHR, & Venice Commission, Guidelines on Political Party Regulation 24: 48 (paragraph 94) (2011), www.osce.org/odihr/77812?download=true.

68 Bale, "Will It All End in Tears?," 218.

themselves. This section contemplates an indicative list of possible public law and policy options for addressing the difficult threats raised by contemporary political parties.

7.5.1 *Can We Just Trust Courts to Make the Right Call?*

A clear point of consensus across jurisprudence, scholarship, and practice is that the most serious forms of controlling political parties, such as bans, should be the responsibility of the constitutional court (or equivalent).[69] It therefore may be tempting to suggest that courts could be accorded much broader regulatory powers; for instance, to perform periodic party assessments for commitment to the constitution and rule-of-law principles or to assess parties' internal democratic procedures to prevent excessive dominance by one figure or faction. Grounds for regulation could be reframed in wider terms, allowing more discretion to constitutional courts to take a tailored approach to each party, with more flexible standards of scrutiny.

However, such an argument dissolves in the face of four issues. First, existing jurisprudence on party bans and regulation at both the national and international levels has attracted significant criticism, not least the inconsistencies in the ECtHR's case law, discussed above.[70] Second, courts may, for good reason, be unwilling to employ such an expanded regulatory power on the basis that it would mire them in partisan politics – especially regarding regulation of parties with more than marginal support. Third, packed courts in backsliding or fragile democracies might wield broad regulatory powers aggressively. As Cavanaugh and Hughes observe: "The use of [militant democracy] measures may well erode and devalue the very principles that they seek to protect."[71] Finally, even where independent courts remain in place, their characterization by authoritarian-leaning populist forces as elite liberal institutions could mean that intervention may strengthen support for such parties by allowing them to present themselves as victims of entrenched elites.

7.5.2 *Nonjudicial Options*

The party regulation model in states such as the United Kingdom may point to a less court-centered, approach. For instance, the UK's party proscription process under the Terrorism Act 2000 is wholly executive-based via the Home Secretary, but this is tempered by the Act's framework for deproscription. A proscribed party may apply to

69 See Frosini and Pennicino, "Ban on Political Parties"; Venice Commission, "Guidelines on Prohibition and Dissolution of Political Parties and Analogous Measures"; and Müller, "Protecting Popular Self-Government from the People?"

70 *United Communist Party of Turkey v. Turkey*, 1998 (26) European Human Rights Report 121.

71 Kathleen Cavanaugh and Edel Hughes, "Rethinking What Is Necessary in a Democratic Society: Militant Democracy and the Turkish State," *Human Rights Quarterly* 38: 623, 625 (2016).

the Home Secretary for deproscription and, if declined, may appeal to a Proscribed Organisations Appeal Commission (POAC) consisting of one senior judge and two other members of the Commission (usually accomplished lawyers),[72] with a right of further appeal to higher UK courts.[73] Thus, rather than court-centered from the beginning, the process of deproscription becomes increasingly court-focused only after decisions have been made again by the Secretary of State and then by an independent Commission. This may insulate the courts from accusations of political decision-making, as they are not the initial adjudicators on party dissolution.

Ideally, party regulation should involve multiple branches of government, incorporate quasi-judicial entities (e.g., independent commissions), and not place dissolution into the hands of one group or institution.

7.5.3 *Emerging International Mechanisms*

In the European Union (EU), approaches to contemporary illiberal parties, perhaps inescapably, have an international dimension. Alongside a long-standing but unsuccessful campaign to have the Hungarian and Polish governments sanctioned under Article 7 of the Treaty on European Union (TEU) for breach of fundamental values of the EU (e.g., democracy, rule of law) contained in Article 2 TEU,[74] and the pushback by both the Court of Justice of the European Union (CJEU) and national courts,[75] yet another gambit has emerged, focused on the parties themselves qua parties, rather than executive actors.

Pech and Alemanno in 2018 called on the European Parliament to request the EU party regulation body[76] to verify whether the European's People Party (EPP) (which groups together a range of national parties, including Fidesz, the ruling party in Hungary) is in compliance with the EU's fundamental values as set out in Article 2 TEU.[77] This legal mechanism (in a little-known EU Regulation)[78] had never been invoked and was perceived as potentially providing an avenue for Fidesz's deregistration as a European political party, thereby, at least by implication, diminishing its

[72] For example, a July 2007 case (*Lord Alton of Liverpool v. Secretary of the State for the Home Department* [2008] EWCA Civ 443) included was one senior Judge, Sir Harry Ognall, and two QCs, http://bit.ly/2pxsjtJ.

[73] Terrorism Act 2000, c. 11, §§ 4–6 (Eng.).

[74] A limited step forward was a positive vote on September 12, 2018 in the European Parliament to trigger article 7 against Hungary.

[75] Case C-216/18 PPU, Minister for Justice and Equality ECLI:EU:C:2018:586 (July 25, 2018); and Case C-619/18 *European Commission v. Republic of Poland* ECLI:EU:C:2019:531 (June 24, 2019).

[76] Authority for European Political Parties and European Political Foundations (APPF).

[77] Alberto Alemanno and Laurent Pech, "De-Registration of Europarties? Our Reasoned Request to Verify EPP's Continuing Compliance with EU Values," *The Good Lobby* (September 11, 2018), https://bit.ly/2SyUM1s.

[78] Regulation 1141/2014, 2014 O.J. (L 317) 1 (as amended by Regulation 2018/673, 2018 O.J. (L114) 1 (Euratom).

power and damaging its domestic standing. Interestingly, the request for review of a party by the EU regulator can be made not only by other EU organs (the Council and Commission) but also by "a group of citizens," although the latter is possible solely in the event of a "manifest and serious breach" of EU values. This option needs to be examined in light of the discussion above concerning the value and utility of repressive measures. Although it is not a party ban, with the relevant Regulation placing emphasis on political pluralism, it has not been pursued and appears as a measure of last resort from the EU law perspective.[79]

7.5.4 *Incentivizing Opposition Rights*

It is abundantly clear from the literature that, in countering governmental degradation of the democratic system, opposition parties matter. Levinson and Pildes have suggested that a key measure to address the democratic deficiencies of the US political party system would be to adopt the European notion of opposition rights, that is, "measures to empower the minority party to oversee government action, such as the power to initiate investigations, to obtain information through the subpoena power or other means, or to control audit or similar oversight committees."[80] More recently, this is a central plank of Huq and Ginsburg's argument for rendering the US political system more resilient against backsliding[81] and Khaitan's argument for pushing back against the illiberal agenda of the ruling BJP party under Prime Minister Modi in India (as well as multiparty appointments for, and greater independence of, fourth branch institutions).[82]

However, for some states, a focus on opposition rights is of little benefit where there is a seriously diminished or fragmented opposition. In the long term, these could be written into law, but for the short term – and again, as a measure of last resort due to democratic legitimacy concerns – the most effective approach may be to offer enhanced international funding for opposition coalitions that form a unified front against a ruling party that has demonstrably sought to entrench itself in power through the capture of independent accountability institutions and changes to electoral laws, although in many states this may be frustrated by laws against foreign funding.

[79] See Wouter Wolfs, *European Political Parties and Party Finance Reform Funding Democracy?* Springer International, 2022, 211, citing John Morijn, "Responding to 'Populist' Politics at EU Level: Regulation 1141/2014 and Beyond," *International Journal of Constitutional Law* 17(2): 617, 638 (2019).

[80] Levinson and Pildes, "Protecting Popular Self-Government from the People?," 2348.

[81] Aziz Huq and Tom Ginsburg, "Making Democratic Constitutions That Endure," in *How to Save a Constitutional Democracy*. University of Chicago Press, 2018, 164–204.

[82] Tarunabh Khaitan, "Killing a Constitution with a Thousand Cuts: The Incremental Fusion of Party and State in India," *Law and Ethics of Human Rights*, https://papers.ssrn.com/sol3/papers.cfm?abstract_id=3367266.

7.5.5 *Stronger Controls on Electoral Manipulation*

One of the greatest threats to the very core of democratic functioning is the use of law to degrade the fairness and transparency of the electoral process, such as state laws establishing extreme gerrymandering and voter suppression in the United States.[83] These measures, again, break the link of true representation that renders the party a legitimate channel of the electoral majority.

How can this be addressed? In the immediate term, the clearest backstop is international condemnation. However, this requires an in-depth understanding of often sophisticated manipulation of electoral laws, which can be a hard sell to foreign political leaders and organizations. In the longer term, new constitutional design options might be considered, drawing on Dixon and Landau's notion of "tiered constitutional amendment" – namely, creating different constitutional amendment requirements for different parts of the constitution,[84] which in the electoral arena, could require special and more onerous procedures or supermajorities to amend electoral law and transform electoral agencies.

7.6 CONCLUSION

This chapter sought to highlight key threats posed by political parties to the endurance of representative liberal democratic governance worldwide, to generate debate by putting a range of potential remedial options on the table, and to spur reflection on the need for a fundamental reorientation of deep constitutional assumptions concerning the role and democratic purpose of parties today. While it is impossible to be comprehensive or definitive regarding solutions, we have aimed to emphasize the urgent need for greater attention to the often ambiguous ways in which parties now threaten democratic governance. Despite prevalent analysis of the global authoritarian populist turn as based on a revolt of the electorate wrenching democracy from entrenched and out-of-touch elites – and there is considerable truth to that perspective – it is also a story of new elites delivering us charlatans, fake democrats, and fake democracy. Perhaps the most immediate lesson from this discussion is that to frame the challenges facing democratic rule worldwide as an executive, or even leadership, problem, is to miss the deep structural role that parties play in processes of democratic deterioration and decay. Worldwide, political parties are also learning from one another, as seen at the time of writing in how rapidly Slovakia's new government – a coalition of Direction – Social Democracy (Smer-SSD), Voice – Social Democracy (Hlas-SD), and the nationalist Slovak National Party (SNS) – is implementing the "authoritarian playbook" developed in large part by far-right lite

83 Levitt, "Intent Is Enough."

84 Rosalind Dixon and David Landau, "Tiered Constitutional Amendment," *George Washington Law Review* 86: 438 (2018).

party governments in Hungary and Poland.[85] These negative dynamics may remain even when specific democracy-threatening incumbents are ousted in elections across the world, as we have seen in states such as the USA, Brazil and, more recently, Poland. There is no doubt that contemporary democracy requires wider rethinking and renewal, and solutions must go far beyond trying to turn the clock back to the status quo ante. But we must start somewhere: democracy-threatening parties are going nowhere.

[85] See, e.g., Peter Čuroš, "Hundred Days of Fico IV Administration," Verfassungsblog, March 5, 2024.

8

What Is the Value of a Constitutionalized Right to Vote?

Yasmin Dawood

8.1 INTRODUCTION

In an era marked by democratic backsliding on the global stage, questions have been raised about the ability of constitutional safeguards to forestall authoritarian retrenchment.[1] Does the constitutional design of elections matter for the sustainability and functioning of democratic governance? This chapter seeks to address one aspect of this larger question by focusing on the right to vote. Given the norm of universal suffrage, the importance of the right to vote is virtually undisputed. What is the value, however, of a *constitutionally enshrined* right to vote? Does it matter whether or not the right to vote is constitutionalized?

It has long been accepted that the protection of constitutional rights is dependent, at least in part, on government enforcement and societal mobilization.[2] As James Madison famously noted in *The Federalist Papers*, liberty-protecting constitutional provisions amount to "parchment barriers" that are often unequal to the "encroaching spirit of power" embodied by the legislature.[3] Constitutional rights provisions do not necessarily translate into actual protections for citizens simply by virtue of being

I would like to thank Rohan Edrisinha, Tom Ginsburg, Aziz Huq, Sam Issacharoff, Tarunabh Khaitan, Christina Murray, Shamshad Pasarlay, Rick Pildes, Elizabeth Reese, Yvonne Tew, Mila Versteeg, and Shih-An Wang for very helpful comments and conversations.

[1] Wojciech Sadurski, *Poland's Constitutional Breakdown*. Oxford University Press, 2019; Tom Ginsburg and Aziz Z. Huq, *How to Save A Constitutional Democracy*. University of Chicago Press, 2018; Steven Levitsky and Daniel Ziblatt, *How Democracies Die*. Broadway Books, 2018; Mark A. Graber, Sanford Levinson, and Mark Tushnet, eds., *Constitutional Democracy in Crisis?* Oxford University Press, 2018.

[2] Stephen Holmes and Cass R. Sunstein, *The Cost of Rights: Why Liberty Depends on Taxes*. W. W. Norton & Company, 1999; Stuart A. Scheingold, *The Politics of Rights: Lawyers, Public Policy and Political Change*. Yale University Press, 1975; Gerald N. Rosenberg, *The Hollow Hope: Can Courts Bring About Social Change?* University of Chicago Press, 1991; Charles R. Epp, *The Rights Revolution: Lawyers, Activists, and Supreme Courts in Comparative Perspective*. University of Chicago Press, 1998.

[3] The Federalist No. 48, in Clinton Rossiter, ed., *The Federalist Papers*. Mentor, 1999.

included in the constitutional document.[4] Rights-protection is contingent upon the work of public institutions, such as the courts, and more generally upon effective government.[5]

A recent empirical study, while confirming the core insight that constitutional rights do not on their own protect citizens from a government's repressive actions, raises questions, however, about whether judicial independence and democratic accountability mechanisms are the prime causal factors leading to rights-protection.[6] Adam Chilton and Mila Versteeg argue that those rights that are organizational in character (in the sense that there are organizations that are invested in protecting the right) are harder for governments to violate than rights that are individual in character (in the sense that these rights are largely relied upon and defended by individuals).[7] That being said, they note that governments are usually successful when they are "determined to erode the protections provided by certain rights."[8]

In this chapter, I claim that the contingent nature of rights protection is particularly pronounced with respect to the right to vote – and this is the case for two reasons, both of which are tied to the distinctive features of the right to vote *qua* right. First, I suggest, the right to vote is multidimensional: it is composed of constitutional, statutory, regulatory, and jurisprudential elements that interact with one another to collectively produce "the right to vote." Second, the right to vote is a structural right in the sense that it is dependent upon an entire infrastructure of institutions to exist and perform its function. I suggest that these features of the right to vote – its multidimensional and institutional nature – make it uniquely susceptible to being undermined by political forces.

Although the constitutional enshrinement of the right to vote does not on its own protect voting rights, I claim that, as a normative matter, constitutions undoubtedly should recognize the right to vote. In addition to its potential impact on voting rights protection, I suggest that a constitutionally enshrined right to vote is crucially important for its expressive functions. A constitutionalized right to vote expresses a commitment to various democratic values and, in addition, establishes normative baselines regarding universal suffrage, political equality, and democratic representation. In democracies, these expressive functions can indirectly serve to protect voting rights.

4 David S. Law and Mila Versteeg, "Sham Constitutions," *California Law Review* 101: 863–952, 872, 880 (2013).

5 Vicki C. Jackson and Yasmin Dawood, "Constitutionalism and a Right to Effective Government: Rights, Institutions, and Values," in *Constitutionalism and a Right to Effective Government?* ed. Vicki C. Jackson and Yasmin Dawood. Cambridge University Press, 2022.

6 Adam S. Chilton and Mila Versteeg, *How Constitutional Rights Matter*. Oxford University Press, 2020, 7, 49.

7 Ibid., at 7.

8 Ibid.

However, the expressive functions of the right to vote can also, paradoxically, undermine democracy by furnishing autocrats in competitive authoritarian regimes with "democratic cover" while they are undermining the key determinants – competitive elections, rival political parties, freedoms of speech and association – that render voting meaningful. At a more general level, the expressive function of constitutional rights and structures raises questions about the ways in which authoritarian regimes use the mechanisms of democracy, such as voting rights and elections, to create the impression of democratic legitimacy while simultaneously eroding it in practice. However, the existence of democratic structures such as elections and voting, even when heavily manipulated, may nonetheless exert some constraints on elected autocrats, at least in comparison to the absence of such constraints in fully authoritarian regimes. For this reason, the claim that the right to vote ought to be constitutionalized remains normatively appealing, although the overall force of the claim is qualified in light of this paradox.

This chapter is organized in four sections. Section 8.2 introduces the multidimensional nature of the right to vote, while Section 8.3 focuses on the institutional dimension. Section 8.4 explores the claim that a constitutionalized right to vote can directly protect voting rights. Section 8.5 argues that a constitutionally enshrined right to vote is normatively valuable for its expressive function notwithstanding the potential that it will be used as a tool of autocratic entrenchment. The conclusion summarizes the main themes.

8.2 THE MULTIDIMENSIONAL RIGHT TO VOTE

The right to vote is multidimensional: it is composed of constitutional, statutory, regulatory, and jurisprudential elements and the interactions among them. In many democracies, the right to vote is constitutionally entrenched. Even when it is constitutionally recognized, the right to vote is also comprised by myriad statutory and regulatory provisions that determine the eligibility and opportunity to vote. Rules that impose citizenship or minimum age requirements on voters, or that require certain forms of voter identification, or that deny the franchise to those convicted of a crime exert an important influence on the contours of the right to vote. These statutory elements of the right to vote can also be described as a "legislative" or "political" component.[9] Statutes are enacted by political bodies to achieve certain political ends; hence a statute is both a legal and a political phenomenon. At times, the formal constitutional strand of the right to vote can be undermined by the statutory elements of the right to vote. This is particularly the case when the rules governing the eligibility and opportunity to vote are crafted to

[9] Grégoire C. N. Webber, *The Negotiable Constitution: On the Limitation of Rights*. Cambridge University Press, 2009; Franita Tolson, "Enforcing the Political Constitution," *Stanford Law Review Online* 74: 88–99 (2022).

augment or even entrench partisan advantage.[10] Judicial decisions that interpret these constitutional, statutory, and regulatory provisions likewise play a crucial role in delineating voting rights. As such, these various strands – constitutional, statutory, regulatory, and jurisprudential – taken together produce "the right to vote."

A snapshot view of the right to vote in Canada illustrates the multidimensional nature of the right to vote. In Canada, Section 3 of the Charter of Rights and Freedoms provides that "every citizen of Canada has the right to vote in an election of the members of the House of Commons or of a legislative assembly and to be qualified for membership therein."[11] In addition to the constitutional text, the right to vote is further specified in the Canada Elections Act,[12] which sets forth a vast array of rules governing federal elections. Most directly, these statutory rules determine the eligibility of voters and the mechanics of voting and vote counting. Provinces and municipalities have their own electoral statutes, which influence the right to vote at the local level. The right to vote is also comprises regulatory rules promulgated by Elections Canada, the electoral management body in charge of federal elections. Finally, the contours and content of the right to vote have also been determined by judicial decisions. The Supreme Court of Canada and lower courts have addressed various topics that bear directly on the right to vote, including voter qualification rules, voter identification requirements, the disenfranchisement of prisoners, residency rules, and the entitlement to vote.[13]

A cursory examination of global trends likewise suggests that many nations have enacted a complex array of rules and regulations that comprise the right to vote. For instance, citizenship is a qualification for registering to vote and for voting in national elections in over 95 percent of countries.[14] The vast majority (87 percent) of countries around the world set their minimum voting age at eighteen years of age.[15] An overwhelming majority of voters around the world are required to present some form of identification in order to vote.[16] As of 2004, approximately 72 percent of democracies impose restrictions on voting for those who have been convicted of a crime.[17] These statistics provide some indication of the complexity of rules that govern the right to vote in numerous countries.

[10] Samuel Issacharoff and Richard H. Pildes, "Politics as Markets: Partisan Lockups of the Democratic Process," *Stanford Law Review* 50: 643–717 (1998).

[11] Canadian Charter of Rights and Freedoms, s 3, Part I of the Constitution Act, being Schedule B to the Canada Act 1982 (UK), 1982 c 11.

[12] SC 2000 c 9.

[13] For a discussion of these decisions, see Yasmin Dawood, "Democratic Rights," in *The Oxford Handbook of the Canadian Constitution* ed. Peter Oliver, Patrick Macklem and Nathalie Des Rosiers. Oxford University Press, 2017, 717–735.

[14] ACE Electoral Knowledge Network, "Comparative Data," http://aceproject.org/epic-en.

[15] Ibid.

[16] Rodney Smith, *Multiple Voting and Voter Identification: A Research Report Prepared for the New South Wales Electoral Commission*. New South Wales Electoral Commission, 2014, 48.

[17] Louis Massicotte, André Blais, and Antoine Yoshinaka, *Establishing the Rules of the Game: Election Laws in Democracies*. University of Toronto Press, 2004, 32.

The complexity of the rules comprising the right to vote is also evident in the United States. While the US Constitution includes many provisions concerning voting and political participation, it does not contain an affirmative right to vote. The "most explicit protections of the franchise ... are phrased almost entirely in the negative – that is, they simply prohibit particular forms of disenfranchisement."[18] In addition to these constitutional provisions, there are countless statutory and regulatory rules governing the right to vote – a complexity that is amplified by the fact that individual states determine the qualifications for voting. Electoral regulations are likewise developed and applied at the state level. Every aspect of the right to vote is heavily specified by rules and regulations, including, for instance, the layout of a ballot, the methods for counting votes, the eligibility of voters, and the location of polling places. Court decisions, at both the federal and state levels, further specify the content and contours of the right to vote.[19]

The example of voter suppression in the United States illustrates not only how the right to vote is composed of various components but also how the statutory and jurisprudential strands of the right to vote can undermine the constitutional guarantee. The right to vote has had a long and turbulent history marked by racial discrimination and exclusion.[20] After the passage of the Fifteenth Amendment,[21] states turned to facially nondiscriminatory disenfranchising tactics – including poll taxes, literacy tests, character tests, property and residency requirements, secret ballots, all-white primaries, and voter registration rules – to prevent African Americans from voting.[22] Grandfather clauses waived such requirements for low-income and illiterate white voters. The Voting Rights Act of 1965, which prohibits racial discrimination in voting, was enacted to enforce the voting rights guaranteed by the Fifteenth Amendment of the US Constitution.[23]

[18] Pamela S. Karlan, "The Reconstruction of Voting Rights," in *Race, Reform, and Regulation of the Electoral Process: Recurring Puzzles in American Democracy* ed. Guy-Uriel E. Charles, Heather K. Gerken and Michael S. Kang. Cambridge University Press, 2011, 37.

[19] Richard Pildes argues, for instance, that the Supreme Court has engaged in the "constitutionalization" of various issues concerning elections and the institutions of democratic governance. See Richard H. Pildes, "Forward: The Constitutionalization of Democratic Politics," *Harvard Law Review* 118: 1–116, 6 (2004).

[20] Alexander Keyssar, *The Right to Vote: The Contested History of Democracy in the United States*. Basic Books, 2000.

[21] The Fifteenth Amendment provides that the "right of citizens of the United States to vote shall not be denied or abridged by the United States or by any state on account of race, color, or previous condition of servitude."

[22] Morgan J. Kouuser, *The Shaping of Southern Politics: Suffrage Restriction and the Establishment of the One-Party South, 1880–1910*. Yale University Press, 1974, 52–56.

[23] The Fifteenth Amendment provides: "The rights of citizens of the United States to vote shall not be denied or abridged by the United States or by any State on account of race, color, or previous condition of servitude," US Constitution.

Although the US Supreme Court was generally protective of voting rights after the advent of the civil rights era,[24] in recent years, the conservative majority of the Court has undermined voting rights. In the wake of the Court's decision in *Shelby County v. Holder*,[25] which effectively dismantled the preclearance process under the Voting Rights Act, states have passed a number of statutes that imposed new restrictions on the eligibility and opportunity to vote. These restrictions, which include stringent voter identification laws and complex registration requirements, amount to a new form of vote denial.[26] Given the confluence of racial identity and partisan affiliation in the United States, laws governing the eligibility and opportunity to vote are often designed to depress minority voting in order to achieve a certain partisan outcome.[27] In a recent case, *Brnovich v Democratic National Committee*,[28] the conservative majority of the Supreme Court considerably weakened another provision (section 2) of the Voting Rights Act, which prohibits voting regulations that have a disproportionate impact on minority voters. The Court announced a new approach to section 2 vote denial claims, which makes it arguably more difficult for plaintiff voters to prevail against voting restrictions.[29]

8.3 INSTITUTIONS AND THE RIGHT TO VOTE

A related point is that the right to vote has an institutional dimension. The right to vote is a "structural right" because its existence depends upon on an entire infrastructure of political institutions.[30] Structural rights are individual rights that take into account the broader institutional framework within which rights are defined, held, and exercised. Structural rights theory holds that the participation of individuals is key (hence the emphasis on rights) but that individuals participate within an institutional framework that is constituted by relations of power (hence the emphasis on structure). Rights do not exist in a vacuum but are instead exercised within a particular political, institutional, and societal context. While structural rights theory

[24] John Hart Ely, *Democracy and Distrust: A Theory of Judicial Review*. Harvard University Press, 1980.

[25] 570 U.S. 529 (2013).

[26] Daniel P. Tokaji, "The New Vote Denial: Where Election Reform Meets the Voting Rights Act," *South Carolina Law Review* 57: 689–733, 709 (2006).

[27] Keith G. Bentele and Erin E. O'Brien, "Jim Crow 2.0? Why States Consider and Adopt Restrictive Voter Access Policies," *Perspectives on Politics* 11: 1088–1116, 1103 (2013); Samuel Issacharoff, "Ballot Bedlam," *Duke Law Journal* 64: 1363–1410, 1370 (2015); Richard L. Hasen, "Race or Party? How Courts Should Think About Republican Efforts To Make It Harder to Vote in North Carolina and Elsewhere," *Harvard Law Review Forum* 127: 58–75, 63–64 (2014).

[28] 141 S. Ct. 2321 (2021).

[29] Yasmin Dawood, "The Right to Vote: Baselines and Defaults," *Stanford Law Review Online* 74: 37–54 (2022).

[30] Yasmin Dawood, "Electoral Fairness and the Law of Democracy: A Structural Rights Approach to Judicial Review," *University of Toronto Law Journal* 62: 499–561 (2012).

can be applied to many kinds of rights, it has particular salience for democratic rights.

For instance, the right to vote, while held by individuals, presupposes the existence of a wide array of institutions and actors, including elections, candidates, political parties, constituencies, candidates, legislatures, and so forth. By contrast, other individual rights, such as the right to liberty, necessarily inhere in individuals and are not dependent for their exercise upon the existence of a prior institutional framework. To be sure, and as described in Section 8.2, every right requires institutions in order to be enforced. However, the right to vote cannot even be conceived of as a right in the absence of an entire system of institutions. In addition, the right to vote is dependent upon effective democratic governance to provide not only voting but also the associated institutions and processes, in particular free and fair elections, that render such a right meaningful.[31] In this way, the right to vote confounds the usual distinctions between negative rights and positive rights; indeed, it comprises and combines elements of both.[32] Along with a properly functioning set of institutions, the right to vote is also dependent to a large degree on effective electoral administration.[33] As a caveat, the notion of a structural right is conceptual; it captures something relevant about the institutionalized nature of the right to vote but it does not imply that the holder of the right to vote is necessarily entitled to all the relevant institutions.

The political and institutional mechanisms by which votes are translated into power also have an impact on whether the right to vote is meaningful. The aggregation of votes,[34] the formation of electoral districts, and the influence of partisanship on electoral rules,[35] for example, can have an effect on how and whether votes count. Broader electoral rules – such as those affecting campaign finance – can undermine the relative power of citizens' votes. In the United States, for example, campaign finance rules have accentuated the disproportionate political influence of the wealthy. Political campaigns are largely funded by the so-called donor class, a wealthy and powerful minority.[36] Empirical research has shown that

[31] Yasmin Dawood, "Effective Government and the Two Faces of Constitutionalism," in *Constitutionalism and a Right to Effective Government?* ed. Vicki C. Jackson and Yasmin Dawood. Cambridge University Press, 2022.

[32] Karlan, "The Reconstruction of Voting Rights," 37–39.

[33] Mark Tushnet, *The New Fourth Branch: Institutions for Protecting Constitutional Democracy*. Cambridge University Press, 2021, 123–157.

[34] Heather K. Gerken, "Understanding the Right to an Undiluted Vote," *Harvard Law Review* 114: 1663–1743 (2001).

[35] Michael S. Kang, "Gerrymandering and the Norm against Government Partisanship," *Michigan Law Review* 116: 351–419 (2017).

[36] Spencer Overton, "The Donor Class: Campaign Finance, Democracy, and Participation," *University of Pennsylvania Law Review* 153: 73–118 (2004); Lawrence Lessig, *Republic, Lost: How Money Corrupts Congress – and a Plan to Stop It*. Twelve, 2011.

elected representatives are more responsive to the preferences of the affluent rather than those of most citizens,[37] which has distorted policymaking in Congress.[38]

A meaningful right to vote is also arguably dependent on more diffuse sociological factors, such as the availability of informed voting. While social media has provided citizens with new venues for expression and information-gathering, it has also flooded public discourse with disinformation and fake news. Social media produces echo chambers, exacerbates polarization, and creates bias.[39] Individual actors and foreign governments have used social media to influence elections by targeting citizens with fake news.[40]

8.4 CONSTITUTIONALIZING THE RIGHT TO VOTE

To summarize thus far: the right to vote is comprised of multiple strands – constitutional, statutory, regulatory, jurisprudential – and is inextricably embedded in an institutional framework. Two implications emerge from these observations. First, the "right to vote" is heavily specified by rules and regulations that determine not only its outer boundaries but also its internal content. It is also unintelligible as a right in the absence of an array of institutions and processes. These two features of the right to vote distinguish it, I suggest, from other kinds of rights, such as the freedom of speech. To be sure, the difference is one of degree, not kind: while other constitutional rights, such as the freedom of speech, are determined to some extent by laws and judgments and are exercised within an institutional context, they are, in comparison to the right to vote, relatively less dependent on legislative and judicial specification and relatively less dependent on institutional mechanisms for their realization.[41] The second implication stems from the first, namely, that the multidimensional and institutional features of the right to vote impose certain constraints on how effectively a bare constitutional right to vote can protect voting rights.

That being said, does the constitutional backstop of a right to vote make a difference? There is no question that constitutional structures matter, but it has proven to be difficult to reach a consensus about which structures matter and why. For instance, there are long-standing debates about whether presidential or

[37] Larry Bartels, *Unequal Democracy: The Political Economy of the New Gilded Age*. Russell Sage Foundation, 2008; Martin Gilens, *Affluence and Influence: Economic Inequality and Political Power in America*. Russell Sage Foundation, 2012.

[38] Lessig, *Republic, Lost*; Nicholas Stephanopoulos, "Aligning Campaign Finance Law," *Virginia Law Review* 101: 1425–1500 (2015).

[39] Cass R. Sunstein, *#Republic: Divided Democracy in the Age of Social Media*. Princeton University Press, 2017.

[40] Yasmin Dawood, "Combatting Foreign Election Interference: Canada's Electoral Ecosystem Approach to Disinformation and Cyber Threats," *Election Law Journal* 20: 10–31 (2021).

[41] One caveat is that these distinctions are likely to be more evident in stable democracies as compared to competitive authoritarian or fully authoritarian regimes.

parliamentary systems are more stable,[42] whether the variation is a function of institutional factors other than regime type and the separation of powers,[43] or whether economic or cultural factors matter more than institutional ones.[44] Leaving aside questions of regime stability, institutional features, such as presidential or prime ministerial selection devices, may matter a great deal for other sorts of issues, such as the kind of democratic politics that results.[45] Or it may be the case that in other circumstances it is not possible to draw valid inferences from institutional rules alone.[46] A constitution may not even mention key institutional features, such as political parties, which have proven to be indispensable to politics.[47] And finally, constitutions may provide the legal framework for democracy,[48] at varying degrees of success,[49] but they may be fully compatible with competitive authoritarian regimes and fully authoritarian regimes.[50]

Another way to approach this issue is to ask whether the *absence* of an affirmative right to vote, for instance in the US Constitution, makes a difference to the protection of voting rights. It is possible that a generalized and affirmative right to vote in the US Constitution would have made it easier for legislators to enact pro-voting rights legislation, or alternatively, would have furnished courts with greater tools to strike down legislation that undermined voting rights. It may be the case, however, that the protection of voting rights is more dependent on non-constitutional factors, such as statutory rules, political forces, and legal norms, which buttress the right to vote. For instance, the existence of compulsory voting in

42 Juan J. Linz, "The Perils of Presidentialism," *Journal of Democracy* 1: 51–69, 63 (1990); Donald L. Horowitz, "Comparing Democratic Systems," *Journal of Democracy* 1: 73–79 (1990).

43 Jose A. Cheibub, *Presidentialism, Parliamentarism, and Democracy*. Cambridge University Press, 2007; Robert Elgie, "From Linz to Tsebelis: Three Waves of Presidential / Parliamentary Studies?," *Democratization* 21: 106–122, 107 (2005); Jose A. Cheibub and Fernando Limongi, "Democratic Institutions and Regime Survival: Parliamentary and Presidential Democracies Reconsidered," *Annual Review of Political Science* 5: 151–179 (2002).

44 Seymour M. Lipset, "The Centrality of Political Culture," *Journal of Democracy* 1: 80–83 (1990).

45 Stephen Gardbaum and Richard H. Pildes, "Populism and Institutional Design: Methods of Selecting Candidates for Chief Executive," *New York University Law Review* 93: 647–708 (2018).

46 Thomas H. Hammond and Christopher K. Butler, "Some Complex Answers to the Simple Question 'Do Institutions Matter?': Policy Choice and Policy Change in Presidential and Parliamentary Systems," *Journal of Theoretical Politics* 15: 145–200 (2003).

47 Daryl J. Levinson and Richard H. Pildes, "Separation of Parties, Not Powers," *Harvard Law Review* 119: 2311–2386 (2006).

48 Cass R. Sunstein, *Designing Democracy: What Constitutions Do*. Oxford University Press, 2001.

49 Sanford Levinson, *Our Undemocratic Constitution: Where the Constitution Goes Wrong (And How We the People Can Correct It)*. Oxford University Press, 2006.

50 Tom Ginsburg and Alberto Simpser, "Introduction: Constitutions in Authoritarian Regimes," in *Constitutions in Authoritarian Regimes* ed. Tom Ginsburg and Alberto Simpser. Cambridge University Press, 2014; Mark Tushnet, "Authoritarian Constitutionalism," *Cornell Law Review* 100: 391–461 (2015).

Australia[51] suggests that non-constitutional rules can play an important role in safeguarding the right to vote. Indeed, in democracies without written constitutions, the franchise is protected by statute, as in the United Kingdom. International legal norms may also serve as a safeguard for the right to vote. For example, Article 25 of the International Convention on Civil and Political Rights provides every citizen with the right and the opportunity to "vote and be elected at genuine periodic elections which shall be by universal and equal suffrage and shall be held by secret ballot, guaranteeing the free expression of the will of the electors."[52] Broader cultural and social norms around the right to vote may provide important safeguards for voting even if formal franchise rights are weakly protected. In sum, contextual factors and the non-constitutional elements of the right to vote must be considered when evaluating the impact of the formal constitutional guarantee of the franchise in any given jurisdiction.

Given this complexity, it may be more useful to conceive of a constitutionalized right to vote as part of the "minimum core," which is defined by Rosalind Dixon and David Landau as those institutions and rights that are required to preserve competitive democracy.[53] This minimum core can be used to assess and compare the performance of different constitutions. On this view, it may be less important to disaggregate the individual effect of each component of competitive elections and more important to focus instead on the extent to which constitutional structures, taken as a whole, protect democracy.[54] While I am in favor of minimalist approaches to democracy,[55] I think that even the most minimalist version of competitive democracy is actually fairly "thick" with respect to the complex interplay of rules, processes, and institutions that are inevitably at stake. In this chapter, I have defended, as a conceptual matter, a thicker multidimensional conception of the right to vote, which emphasizes the myriad details that underlie the seemingly

51 For a discussion of how compulsory voting transforms the right to vote from a formal right to an instantiated one that is exercised, see Lisa Hill, "Compulsory Voting and the Promotion of Human Rights in Australia," *Australian Journal of Human Rights* 23: 188–202 (2017).

52 For a discussion of the international legal standards and norms respecting voting and democratic participation, see Tom Ginsburg, *Democracies and International Law*. Cambridge University Press, 2021, 21–22.

53 Rosalind Dixon and David Landau, "Competitive Democracy and the Constitutional Minimum Core," in *Assessing Constitutional Performance* ed. Tom Ginsburg and Aziz Z. Huq. Cambridge University Press, 2016, 276.

54 Ibid., at 277.

55 Schumpeter defined democracy as "that institutional arrangement for arriving at political decisions in which individuals acquire the power to decide by means of a competitive struggle got the people's vote." Joseph A. Schumpeter, *Capitalism, Socialism and Democracy*. Harper & Row, 1950, 269. An alternative minimalist conception describes democracy as a system of government that allows for the peaceful transfer of power. Adam Przeworski, "Minimalist Conception of Democracy: A Defense," in *Democracy's Value* ed. Ian Shapiro and Casiano Hacker-Cordón. Cambridge University Press, 1999, 45.

simple act of casting a ballot. This thicker conception, I suggest, would still fall under minimalist conceptions of democracy.

8.5 THE EXPRESSIVE FUNCTIONS OF A CONSTITUTIONALIZED RIGHT TO VOTE

The multidimensional and institutional features of the right to vote have the potential to impose significant constraints on voting rights. While the constitutional enshrinement of the right to vote can have a protective impact on voting rights, it provides no guarantee that it will do so. That being said, a constitution should protect the right to vote. I claim that a constitutionally enshrined right to vote is normatively valuable inasmuch for its expressive functions as it is for its direct impact on voting rights.

Legal rules have an expressive dimension.[56] The constitutional right to vote expresses and symbolizes the values of political equality, respect, and belonging. As Judith Shklar observed, the right to vote is a "certificate of full membership in society" that "confers, and in some ways, defines, full citizenship."[57] Those who are denied the vote "feel dishonored, not just powerless."[58] Individuals who are excluded from the franchise are, according to Charles Beitz, "socially dead" as they are "not publicly recognized as persons at all."[59] Not only does the right to vote confer belonging and dignity, it is also closely connected to the principle of equality.[60] The right to vote is a "minimal condition of political equality";[61] it is also, crucially, a public expression of that civic equality.[62] In the United States, the right to vote has long been connected to the principle of racial equality but in recent years it has also been understood through the lens of universalist principles of equal voting, which apply regardless of race.[63] To be sure, the expressive value of a

[56] Cass R. Sunstein, "On the Expressive Function of Law," *University of Pennsylvannia Law Review* 144: 2021 (1996); Elizabeth S. Anderson and Richard H. Pildes, "Expressive Theories of Law: A General Restatement," *University of Pennsylvania Law Review* 148: 1503–1575 (2000).

[57] Judith Shklar, *American Citizenship: The Quest for Inclusion*. Harvard University Press, 1991, 2, 27.

[58] Ibid., at 3.

[59] Charles R. Beitz, *Political Equality: An Essay in Democratic Theory*. Princeton University Press, 1989, 109.

[60] Joseph Fishkin, "Equal Citizenship and the Individual Right to Vote," *Indiana Law Journal* 86: 1289–1360, 1333 (2011).

[61] Iris Marion Young, *Inclusion and Democracy*. Oxford University Press, 2000, 6.

[62] Amy Gutmann, "Responding to Racial Injustice," in *Color Conscious: The Political Morality of Race* ed. Anthony K. Appiah and Amy Gutmann. Princeton University Press, 1996, 156.

[63] Guy-Uriel E. Charles and Luis E. Fuentes-Rohwer, "Slouching towards Universality: A Brief History of Race, Voting, and Political Participation," *Howard Law Journal* 62: 809–853 (2019); Samuel Issacharoff, "Voter Welfare: An Emerging Rule of Reason in Voting Rights Cases," *Indiana Law Journal* 92: 299–325 (2016).

constitutionally enshrined right to vote may change depending on the wording of the guarantee and the culture and history of the relevant jurisdiction.

In addition to expressing certain values, the right to vote also expresses and thereby establishes normative baselines concerning universal suffrage, political equality, and democratic representation. It is a fundamental normative commitment of a democracy that all citizens should have the right to vote.[64] The right to vote is viewed as a preservative right because it enables the protection of all other rights through the mechanisms of political participation, democratic representation, and accountable government.[65] These normative baselines of universal suffrage and political equality can set an outer limit for subconstitutional regulation. That is, the expressive value of the right to vote lies in serving as an outer boundary – at least in theory – for statutory and judicial restrictions on the right to vote. While these restrictions may undermine the right to vote, the existence of the normative baseline of universal suffrage would make it costly as a reputational matter to eradicate the constitutional protection altogether. A more general observation is that the aspirational dimension of constitutions and constitutional rights[66] can have a real-world impact on politics. The effect of aspirational constitutions may be subtle in that they help to thwart decay.[67] Or they may, as in the case of the right to vote, serve as a rallying point to mobilize citizens and bring about progressive political change.

To be sure, there are empirical difficulties associated with the claim that a constitutionally enshrined right to vote establishes a normative baseline of universal suffrage that can serve as an outer boundary for subconstitutional regulation. One challenge with assessing this claim is that it would be difficult to disentangle the effect of the constitutional dimension of the right to vote from the effects of its other aspects in a manner that would produce a definitive conclusion. Another complication is that legislatures and courts can undermine voting rights while still protecting universal suffrage. Even though all citizens may nominally have the right to vote, a state can enact voting rules that place considerable restrictions on the eligibility and opportunity to vote. It may be difficult to ascertain the extent to which the normative signal of constitutionally endorsed universal suffrage is constraining legislatures and courts.

A more significant challenge is that a constitutionally enshrined right to vote can also, paradoxically, undermine democracy. The electoral route to competitive

64 Dennis F. Thompson, *Just Elections: Creating a Fair Electoral Process in the United States*. Chicago University Press, 2002, 4.

65 The right to vote is a "fundamental political right, because preservative of all rights." *Yick Wo v. Hopkins*, 118 U.S. 356, 370 (1886).

66 Chilton and Versteeg, *How Constitutional Rights Matter*, 20.

67 Zachary Elkins, Tom Ginsburg and James Melton, "Time and Constitutional Efficacy," in *Assessing Constitutional Performance* ed. Tom Ginsburg and Aziz Z. Huq. Cambridge University Press, 2016, 260.

authoritarianism is a well-documented avenue to democratic backsliding.[68] Once the autocrat is elected to office, the right to vote and associated constitutional rights and structures provide "democratic cover" to autocrats, furnishing them with democratic legitimacy as they strip out democratic safeguards. Competitive authoritarian regimes retain the trappings of an electoral system, including the right to vote, while going to considerable lengths to manipulate the election to entrench themselves in power.[69] Thus, they "practice authoritarianism behind the institutional facades of representative democracy."[70] Although they hold regular multiparty elections with universal suffrage, they deploy a range of manipulative strategies to win elections, including prosecuting candidates, banning parties, intimidating voters, harassing journalists, and forging election results.[71] Political parties and candidates in opposition face significant hurdles.[72] Constitutional rules and entities, including the courts, are subverted to entrench the autocrat in power.[73] Private entities, such as the media, are likewise co-opted to support the regime.[74] Rather than providing for accountability and the possibility of new leadership, elections are designed to entrench the incumbent autocrats.

Autocrats hope that these periodic elections provide a "semblance of democratic legitimacy" for both domestic and foreign actors.[75] The expressive function of the right to vote and elections confers democratic legitimacy on autocrats even as they ensure their continued grip on power by undermining democracy. At the same time, the existence of even nominally competitive elections may incentivize autocrats to be somewhat more attentive to the needs of the people, at least in comparison to the leaders of fully authoritarian regimes. A formal recognition of a universal right of suffrage in the constitution could increase the costs for autocrats who might otherwise be tempted to eradicate elections. For this reason, a constitutionalized right to vote is normatively appealing notwithstanding its paradoxical nature.

68 These regimes are defined as "civilian regimes in which formal democratic institutions exist and are widely viewed as the primary means of gaining power, but in which incumbents' abuse of the state places them at a significant advantage vis-à-vis their opponents." Steven Levitsky and Lucan Way, *Competitive Authoritarianism: Hybrid Regimes After the Cold War*. Cambridge University Press, 2010, 5.

69 Andreas Schedler, *The Politics of Uncertainty: Sustaining and Subverting Electoral Authoritarianism*. Oxford University Press, 2013, 2.

70 Ibid., at 1.

71 Ibid.

72 Levitsky and Ziblatt, *How Democracies Die*, 1–10, 97–109.

73 David Landau, "Abusive Constitutionalism," *University of California Davis Law Review* 47: 189–260, 191 (2013); Kim Scheppele, "Autocratic Legalism," *University of Chicago Law Review* 85: 545–583, 557 (2018); Ginsburg and Huq, *How to Save a Constitutional Democracy*, 23.

74 Ginsburg and Huq, *How to Save A Constitutional Democracy*, 108–109.

75 Andreas Schedler, "Elections without Democracy: The Menu of Manipulation," *Journal of Democracy* 13: 36–50, 36–37 (2002).

8.6 CONCLUSION

In this chapter, I have claimed that while a constitutionally enshrined right to vote can help to strengthen voting rights in practice, it does not on its own provide a guarantee that the right to vote will be meaningful. The right to vote is both multidimensional and institutional, which suggests that the sub-constitutional components of the right make a far greater difference to the reality of voting than the bare fact that the right is constitutionalized. That being said, I have argued that, as a normative matter, constitutions should recognize the right to vote. A constitutionalized right to vote plays a crucial expressive function by promoting democratic values and establishing normative baselines concerning representation, universal suffrage, and political equality. These values and baselines can indirectly protect voting rights in a democracy.

However, the expressive function of constitutional rights and structures can, paradoxically, undermine democracy by providing autocrats in competitive authoritarian regimes with democratic cover while they are undermining constitutional safeguards. That being said, the reality of elections and voting, even when heavily manipulated, may exert some beneficial constraints on elected autocrats. For this reason, the claim that the right to vote ought to be constitutionalized is normatively justifiable.

PART III

Specific Institutions

9

Democratic Design and the Twin Contemporary Challenges of Fragmented and Unduly Concentrated Political Power

Stephen Gardbaum

There are (at least) four key values or principles of democratic governance. These are: (1) effective and responsive government, (2) stable government, (3) accountable government, and (4) representative and deliberative legislative bodies. Given the trade-offs among them, democratic polities cannot achieve all of these values equally but they are expected to attain at least a "minimum core" of each and to aim at balancing or perhaps jointly optimizing them.

This goal faces both a general problem and a more specific contemporary one. The general, and long-standing, problem is the central role and importance of political parties in modern democracies. Because political parties and their leaders compete to occupy two of the major governance institutions (the executive and legislature) and exercise public power, they can concentrate such power where the same party controls both and also disperse it where it does not, regardless of the formal or constitutional relationship between these institutions.[1] In this way, concentration of power threatens the values of continuously accountable government (i.e., not only at elections) and a genuinely deliberative legislature and, in so doing, increases the chances of various types of "misrule."[2] On the other hand, dispersal of power risks undermining the values of effective and (sometimes also) stable government. For this reason, we cannot think of state institutions alone in analyzing or designing systems of democratic governance.

This general background problem or complexity is exacerbated by specific features of the contemporary political party systems in many democracies today. Party systems should not only be thought about in terms of numbers – a single, dominant,

Many thanks to Steffen Ganghof and to participants at the workshop, especially commentator George Tsebelis, for helpful questions and comments on a previous draft.

1 Stephen Gardbaum, "Political Parties, Voting Systems, and the Separation of Powers," *American Journal of Comparative Law* 65: 229 (2017).

2 Jonathan Gould characterizes one dilemma faced by progressives in thinking about constitutional design as "the tension between enabling effective lawmaking and preventing misrule." Jonathan S. Gould, "Puzzles of Progressive Constitutionalism (book review)," *Harvard Law Review* 135: 2053, 2094 (2022).

two-party or multiparty system – or the type of political regime in which they operate – presidential versus parliamentary parties[3] – but also in terms of certain pathologies to which they are vulnerable. So, whether and to what extent a political party system is polarized, fragmented, or subject to hyper-partisanship also affects the difficulty of balancing and reconciling the four values. Polarization and hyper-partisanship can render both effective and accountable government, as well as deliberative legislative processes, harder to achieve because there is less, or no, overlapping middle ground. A fragmented party system makes effective and stable government less likely, as it is more difficult to obtain and sustain a governing majority.[4] All three features undermine the political center and the types of consensus building and accommodation that tend to be important for the optimization of all four values. They also help to create the type of alienation from democratic politics "as usual" that has fueled various types of populism over the past decade.[5]

Both the general and the special problems can and do arise in all democratic regime types, of which there are at least six (and not only three), depending on the combination of (a) form of government and (b) political party and electoral systems. These are two party/majoritarian presidential, parliamentary, and semi-presidential systems and multiparty/PR versions of each.[6] In all cases, the operation of both "ordinary" party politics and the special consequences of polarized, fragmented, and/or hyper partisan party politics complicates the task of balancing the four key values of democratic governance and skew polities toward either the fragmentation or the undue concentration of political power.

A recent strand within political science and constitutional scholarship has identified "semi-parliamentarism" as a new and alternative democratic regime type and also argued for its superiority to existing ones.[7] The precise nature of this claimed superiority (as well as some of the institutional details) varies somewhat among its main proponents and could also benefit from being further developed but, at least

[3] See David Samuels and Matthew Shugart, *Presidents, Parties, and Prime Ministers: How the Separation of Powers Affects Party Organization and Behavior*. Cambridge University Press, 2010.

[4] See Richard Pildes, "Political Fragmentation in Democracies of the West," https://papers.ssrn.com/sol3/papers.cfm?abstract_id=3935012.

[5] On the variety of populisms, see Mark Tushnet and Bojan Bugaric, *Power to the People: Constitutionalism in the Age of Populism*. Oxford University Press, 2021.

[6] I do not include the recently identified "crown-presidential" form of government, as it is characteristic of non-democratic, or only partially democratic, political systems. See William Partlett, "Crown-Presidentialism," *International Journal of Constitutional Law* 20: 204 (2022).

[7] See Steffen Ganghof, *Beyond Presidentialism and Parliamentarism: Democratic Design and the Separation of Powers*. Oxford University Press, 2022; Steffen Ganghof, "A New Political System Model: Semi-Parliamentary Government," *European Journal of Political Research* 57: 261 (2018); Steffen Ganghof, Sebastian Eppner, and Alexander Porschke, "Australian Bicameralism as Semi-Parliamentarism: Patterns of Majority Formation in 29 Democracies," *Australian Journal of Political Science* 53: 211 (2018); Tarunabh Khaitan, "Balancing Accountability and Effectiveness: A Case for Moderated Parliamentarism," *Canadian. Journal of Comparative & Contemporary Law* 7: 81 (2021).

implicitly or in part, the claim is that it better balances the four values.[8] Semi-parliamentarism is presented as a distinct variation on two-party and multiparty parliamentary regimes. It is defined by the absence of the direct election of the chief executive and the existence of two directly elected and co-equal legislative chambers in which only the first can dismiss the cabinet in a no-confidence vote, while the second has veto power over legislation that cannot be overridden by an ordinary or absolute majority of the first. Importantly, its final key feature is the incorporation of different voting systems for each of the two chambers, to try and ensure that the governing party does not control both. Whereas for pure parliamentarism in either its two-party or multiparty versions, reconciling the first two values with the second two is notoriously difficult, it is potentially achievable with semi-parliamentarism.

I agree that semi-parliamentarism is a promising regime type. In this chapter, my primary aim is to explore whether the insights of its proponents can be adapted to suggest versions of *non*-parliamentary democratic regimes that better reconcile and optimize the four values and address the specific challenges of political party polarization, fragmentation, and hyper-partisanship. In other words, my focus is not on the question of which regime type is superior overall but rather on how to maximize the potential benefits of the semi-parliamentary model through ambitious, but not wholesale or root and branch, design reforms in the face of current democratic challenges. Pragmatically, given the well-known "stickiness" or path dependence of forms of government,[9] ruling out these potential benefits to the roughly two-thirds of non-parliamentary democratic polities seems like a waste. Specifically, I will argue that semi-parliamentarism's core feature of "symmetrical" and "incongruent"[10] bicameralism is detachable from parliamentarism and that, with suitably customized modifications and reforms, is available in presidential and semi-presidential versions that may similarly reduce the contemporary pathologies of party systems and better balance the underlying values of democratic governance than existing regimes of these types. In so doing, all three adapted forms may also address some of the causes, and resist some of the consequences, of democratic backsliding in general and authoritarian populism in particular. The secondary aim of the chapter is to consider whether the design features of these versions that involve political parties and voting systems, rather than institutional powers and relations, should be constitutionalized and, if so, which.

8 For further details, see Section 9.4.

9 See, for example, Arend Lijphart, "Democratization and Constitutional Choices in Czechoslovakia, Hungary and Poland: 1989–1991," *Journal of Theoretical Politics* 4: 207, 208 (1992) (noting that changes to "fundamental constitutional structure" are rare in established democracies); Ozan Varol, "Constitutional Stickiness," *UC Davis Law Review* 49:899 (2016).

10 According to Lijphart's terminology, "symmetrical" refers to equal legislative powers and "incongruent" to the two chambers being likely to have different partisan make-ups. See Arend Liphart, *Patterns of Democracy*. Yale University Press, 1999, 198.

9.1 THE GENERAL AND SPECIAL PROBLEMS THAT POLITICAL PARTIES POSE TO OPTIMIZING THE FOUR KEY VALUES OF DEMOCRATIC GOVERNANCE

It is widely accepted that democratic governance seeks to promote at least four key values or principles. The first is effective and responsive government. Political parties and their leaders campaign during elections not simply to occupy public office but to offer voters a meaningful choice of policies on issues that matter to them that they will seek to put into effect if elected. This capacity to bridge, translate, and aggregate voters' policy preferences into governing and legislative agendas is perhaps the central function and justification of political parties in a democracy.[11] Being elected to power and obtaining the relevant majority support legitimizes one policy agenda over another and, ceteris paribus, this is what a democratic government is expected to act on: elections have consequences. The ability of a government to effectuate the policies for which it was elected, as well as deal with ongoing and unexpected issues as they arise, is the hallmark of a functional democratic polity; the inability to do so is a sign of dysfunction.[12] The perceptions that democratic governments have been dysfunctional and/or more responsive to the interests of various elites than ordinary voters have, of course, been one of the main factors driving populisms of left and right over the past decade.

Government stability during the course of an election cycle is a second key value. Ongoing fragility or frequent turnover undermines the kind of mid-term planning that effectiveness requires and distracts voters and politicians by elevating office over policy. It also renders polities vulnerable in the face of new and unexpected crises that may arise. Obviously, too much stability is also problematic – if not always or necessarily inconsistent with democratic governance[13] – as periodic (rather than frequent) turnover is another hallmark of a functional democratic polity. This, in turn, is partly driven by the third value of continuous governmental accountability, as without periodic turnover, party-state fusion[14] and entrenchment across all institutions risks impunity and the inability to meaningfully question those in power. Putting into practice this third value is one of the key functions of democratic legislatures, although it is shared with other actors, public and private, including free and independent media outlets. The other key function of democratic legislatures is to promote the fourth value, by directly representing a broader range of voters and

[11] See Nancy Rosenblum, *On the Side of the Angeles: An Appreciation of Parties and Partisanship*. Princeton University Press, 2008; Tarunabh Khaitan, "Political Parties in Constitutional Theory," *Current Legal Problems* 73: 89 (2020).

[12] Obviously, these (or even balancing the four values) are not the only things desirable in, or required of, a democratic government; others include respecting the rule of law, rights, etc.

[13] As shown in dominant party democracies, such as South Africa, at least in the short and medium term.

[14] Khaitan, "Political Parties in Constitutional Theory."

political positions than the executive and bringing these to bear in inclusive and collective deliberation over legislative priorities and content.

These four values exist in some tension with each other and inevitably involve some trade-offs in practice, as no single democratic polity could maximize all of them. A realistic normative goal is rather to balance or jointly optimize them in a way that ensures at least a "minimum core" of each is achieved, even if certain polities afford greater weight to some than others. Indeed, each of the three widely adopted modern forms of democratic government can be thought of as designed to achieve such a balance, albeit with different emphases resulting from the particular allocation of powers and functions between the executive and legislative branches. As referenced in the introduction, the general problem is that these modern forms of government were designed (or evolved) in ways that focused only on institutional relations and either ignored or were openly hostile to political parties.[15] But the rise and role of modern political parties changes a great deal about how these forms operate in practice and complicates their actual ability to balance the values. And this general problem has been exacerbated in recent years by the particular nature of many party systems in democracies as polarized, hyper-partisan, and/or fragmented.

Starting with the general problem, institutions are occupied by leaders and representatives of political parties rather than by individuals per se, and this means that parties can effectively merge what is intended to be separate, as well as separate what is intended to be fused. This way in which parties can function like a sort of political holding company or conglomerate was well captured by Maurice Duverger in his classic work on the subject:

> Officially Great Britain has a parliamentary system . . . in practice the existence of a majority governing party transforms this constitutional pattern from top to bottom. The party holds in its hands the essential prerogatives of the legislature and the executive . . . Parliament and Government are like two machines driven by the same motor – the party. The regime is not so very different in this respect from the single party system. Executive and legislature, Government and Parliament are constitutional facades: in reality the party alone exercises power.[16]

So, despite the classic British separation of power between King and Parliament, or its modern version between the King's ministers in parliament and its ordinary members, as early as Bagehot it was recognized that the "efficient secret of the English Constitution" is "the close union, the nearly complete fusion of the executive and legislature powers" in the cabinet,[17] stemming from the existential need of the government to retain the confidence of parliament. With the subsequent introduction or evolution of modern political parties, party discipline, and

[15] Gardbaum, "Political Parties, Voting Systems."

[16] Maurice Duverger, *Political Parties: Their Organization and Activity in the Modern State*. John Wiley & Sons, 1954, 124.

[17] Walter Bagehot, *The English Constitution*. William Collins Sons & Co (Fontana ed.), 1963, 65.

control over their legislators, the effectiveness and stability of Westminster-style parliamentary governments was increasingly achieved at the expense of genuine accountability to, and deliberativeness of, the legislative body. But even where executive and legislative branches are designed to be more separated and independent than in modern parliamentary systems, where and when the same political party controls both, a broadly similar concentration of power occurs with analogous effects on the third and fourth values.[18] By contrast, where and when different parties control these two branches, or there is no majority party in the legislature, then accountability of the executive to the legislature and the latter's independence to deliberate over proposed bills are often achieved at the expense of effective governance, due to the resulting gridlock and/or fragmentation of power.

This general background problem for reconciling the values of democratic governance is exacerbated by certain specific features of contemporary party systems. As referenced above, party systems should not only be categorized by the number of parties – single, dominant, two-party, multiparty, etc. – or by the regime they operate in – presidential versus parliamentary parties – but also by whether political parties are polarized, hyper-partisan, and/or fragmented. These are, obviously, distinct but overlapping pathologies. Although parties typically occupy different spaces on the relevant policy and ideological spectrum(s), polarization refers to a situation where the major parties or blocs are close to the opposite poles and far apart in their basic platforms and orientations, leaving the center of the spectrum relatively vacant. Hyper-partisanship generally references the way that parties and their supporters interact with, and treat, each other: do they engage in "hardball," eschew cooperation and accommodation, act as if unconstrained by practical norms of bi-/multipartisanship, treat opponents as enemies or traitors, maximize the use of power for partisan ends. Although such hyper-partisanship is more likely to occur where polarization exists, it can happen without (for example, where one party breaks away from another, where the major parties cluster around a similar space on the spectrum and need to distinguish themselves, or where parties are personality rather than policy based) and need not happen with. A fragmented party system is one in which either (a) popular support is divided among several or many parties, without any one party or coalition of parties achieving majority or clear plurality support, or (b) such division takes place within, rather than between, the major parties.

These features of many contemporary democratic party systems are making the task of achieving and reconciling the four values significantly more difficult. Polarization and hyper-partisanship can render the task of forming and maintaining a government where no single party has a majority more complex and time-consuming, undermines the accountability and deliberative functions of the legislature where one party controls both branches, and makes gridlock worse during

[18] See Daryl Levinson and Richard Pildes, "Separation of Parties, Not Powers," *Harvard Law Review* 119: 2311 (2007).

divided government. Fragmentation undermines effective and stable government, making it more difficult to obtain and sustain a governing majority and legitimate authority. Fragmentation and splintering of political power in general, and of party systems in particular, may currently be the most challenging problem bedeviling democracies around the world and has several causes.[19] These include alienation of ordinary voters from the mainstream center-left and center-right parties that have mostly governed since the end of World War II for a mix of economic and cultural reasons, a realignment of party politics away from the traditional left-right axis based on socio-economic position and educational level, and the communication revolution that has enabled new parties, individual politicians, and even single citizens to bypass traditional parties and media outlets to reach mass audiences via social media, etc.[20]

9.2 HOW THE GENERAL AND SPECIAL PROBLEMS ARISE IN ALL WIDELY ADOPTED DEMOCRATIC REGIME TYPES

Although the three basic and most common forms of democratic government were, in principle, intended to achieve and balance all four values, albeit in different ways, once the operative effects of electoral and party systems are taken into account, reconciliation is more difficult. Let us briefly see how and why for each of the six major democratic regime types, looking first at the "general problem" and then superimposing the contemporary special one.

In practice, the promotion and reconciliation of all four values has been hardest to achieve in parliamentary systems. In theory, as with the other forms, this is not so. The partial fusing of executive and legislative powers bolsters the effectiveness and stability of government, while still retaining full political accountability to a representative and deliberative legislature. But factoring in the impact of the electoral and party systems substantially changes the equation and balance. In two party, Westminster-style parliamentary systems resulting primarily from the majoritarian (and usually first past the post) voting system, effective and stable government is achieved at the expense of both genuine (as distinct from formal) political accountability to the legislature and inclusive, collective deliberation of the contents of legislative proposals. As indicated in the Duverger quotation above, this is due to the power and control of the typical governing (i.e., majority) party. Because of the necessary party discipline resulting from the "sink or swim together" political logic of the single election for both the executive and legislature, this regime type standardly concentrates power in the governing party, of which the prime minister is the leader, so that it typically controls the legislature through its majority. This, in turn, means that its survival is more or less assured (unless it acts in ways that cause a rebellion

[19] Pildes, "Political Fragmentation in Democracies of the West."
[20] Ibid.

among its backbench members), political accountability is mostly reduced to somewhat theatrical exchanges with the official opposition party, and "government bills" that dominate the timetable are ordinarily steamrollered through the legislative process. This "ordinary" concentration of power in a majority party and its leadership (which has on occasion been referred to as an "elective dictatorship")[21] has been extended and abused by authoritarian populist regimes in parliamentary systems, such as those led by Orban and Erdogan (pre-2017), to further consolidate and entrench their power by undermining all independent institutions and sources of power.

With recent fragmentations of party systems, and the resulting greater likelihood and experience of coalition or minority governments,[22] legislatures have become somewhat more independent of government control, leading to greater political accountability, representativeness (through the greater influence of smaller parties), and deliberation. But, as reflected in the chaotic period in the United Kingdom before Brexit occurred, this was very much at the expense of effective and stable government.

In other words, the United Kingdom at this time looked more like the second type of parliamentary regime, the multiparty one resulting from having a proportional representation election system. Here, and especially where there are not two blocs formed by allied parties, the traditional difficulty of reconciling the four values is the converse of the two-party version. Without a single majority party, effective and stable government can be difficult to achieve, in some cases notoriously so, but, on the other hand, the lesser concentration of power and its greater dispersal among parties may lead to a more independent and representative legislature with more scope for holding the executive accountable (including parties withdrawing support from a coalition government) and assembling ad hoc (rather than preordained) legislative majorities on particular bills. With polarization and/or fragmentation, the risks to effective and stable (coalition or minority) government are that much greater and the probabilities of ad hoc majorities for accountability or legislative purposes are smaller.

The presidential form of government, invented out of necessity in the United States, was designed to create effective and stable government through the direct election[23] of a legislatively irremovable single-person executive for a fixed term of office, while a separated, independent, and more representative legislature would

[21] The phrase was popularized by the former Lord Chancellor of the United Kingdom, Lord Hailsham, in a Richard Dimbleby Lecture at the BBC in 1976.

[22] The United Kingdom had its first coalition government since World War II between 2010 and 2015, followed shortly thereafter by its longest period of minority government (led first by Theresa May and then by Boris Johnson) in modern times: two and a half years in between the June 2017 and December 2019 general elections. In Canada, five of the last seven governments have been minority governments.

[23] In contrasting presidentialism's direct election of the chief executive with parliamentarism's indirect election, I am putting to one side the complications created by the role of the Electoral

engage in executive oversight and have the institutional freedom to exercise its major, legislative, function in a deliberative manner. Under majoritarian, two-party presidential systems, the reality has long been "separation of parties, not powers": either a unified government where the same party controls both branches, with a high concentration of power and significant control of legislative outcomes, or a divided government with different parties in control of the two branches and the resulting risk of legislative gridlock.[24] As with two-party parliamentary systems, which they resemble,[25] unified presidential governments are often effective and stable but at the price of legislative accountability and deliberativeness. Divided governments are frequently ineffective, if stable, due to legislative paralysis, although oversight of (the often-increased reliance on) presidential unilateral authority is typically robust.

With polarized, hyper-partisan parties, the concerns about overly concentrated power in a unified government tend to be even greater, as bipartisan accommodation and restraints disappear, and the gridlock resulting from divided government is that much deeper and insurmountable. In this regime type, fragmentation tends to occur within, rather than between, parties so that even unified governments may be ineffective and unresponsive, as presidents find themselves unable to fulfill their legislative agendas due to internal opposition, as prominently recently in the first terms of Presidents Trump and Biden.

Apart from the United States and the Philippines, all other countries adopting pure presidentialism employ PR for legislative elections, as here the claims of representation that this voting system maximizes appear to trump the less relevant governance benefits of majoritarian systems. And yet such benefits turn out to be highly relevant as multiparty/PR presidential systems often suffer from the absence of a presidential party, or any party, majority in the legislature resulting sometimes in ad hoc support for presidentially sponsored bills in the absence of the more continuous coalitions needed to sustain the executive in parliamentary systems but sometimes in paralysis and ineffective government.[26] This is one of the well-known recipes for the "Linzian nightmare"[27] of presidential coups in Latin America and elsewhere. Although such ad hoc majority-building may suggest the potential for more independent, deliberative legislative processes and presidential oversight, achievement of these values is frequently undermined by weakly institutionalized, more personality-focused presidentialist parties, as compared with at least

College in the United States. For my purpose here, "direct election" means election (normally) by a body or entity other than the legislature, usually but not necessarily by popular vote.

24 Levinson and Pildes, "Separation of Parties, Not Powers."

25 Resemble, but are not identical, given the lesser fusion of executive and legislative power in practice, stemming from their separate elections and terms of office. See Gardbaum, "Political Parties, Voting Systems."

26 Bolsonaro's government Brazil is a recent example.

27 Bruce Ackerman, "The New Separation of Powers," *Harvard Law Review* 113: 663 (2000).

mainstream parliamentary ones. With fragmentation in particular, these particular pathologies of multiparty presidentialism tend to increase.

As the newest widely adopted form of democratic government,[28] semi-presidentialism also in theory promotes all four values.[29] A directly elected president who is not politically removable by the legislature ensures stability for the full length of the fixed term, even where the prime ministerial government that is fully accountable to parliament falls and changes beforehand. There are, as it were, two paths to effective government as either of the chief executives, or better both working together, can provide it. At the same time, having two chief executives produces less concentrated power than the "executive personalism"[30] of the fully presidential model and, at least vis-a-vis the president, a more separated legislature to engage in both oversight and deliberation of executive legislative proposals.

As with the other forms, however, factoring in electoral and party systems often renders achievement and reconciliation of these value a more complex and difficult task. The two party/majoritarian version of semi-presidentialism risks the most highly concentrated political power of all, where the president's party controls the legislature, for here a president is effectively (although not formally) also the head of a parliamentary party and government. In earlier work, I have referred to this possibility as "super-presidentialism."[31] In this scenario, effective and stable government comes at an even higher cost in terms of accountability between elections and legislative deliberateness than in majoritarian parliamentary systems.

Where the prime minister is from the other major party, this resembles the situation in such parliamentary systems, with the exception that here, the effective leader of the opposition is the more powerful figure of the president. The timing of presidential and legislative elections, whether or not they are simultaneous, tends to be key to the probability of these two outcomes,[32] as it is with unified or divided government under pure presidentialism. With polarization, such "cohabitation"

[28] Cindy Skach, "The 'Newest' Separation of Powers: Semipresidentialism," *International Journal of Constitutional Law* 5: 93 (2007).

[29] As with presidentialism and parliamentarism, there are institutional variations on the form. With semi-presidentialism, at least two sub-types have been identified – premier-presidentialism and president-parliamentarism – depending on whether the prime minister and cabinet are exclusively responsible to parliament or also to the president, who may dismiss them. The division of powers between the president and prime minister also varies considerably. See, for example, Robert Elgie, *Semi-Presidentialism: Subtypes and Democratic Performance*. Oxford University Press, 2011.

[30] Ganghof, *Beyond Presidentialism and Parliamentarism*.

[31] Gardbaum, "Political Parties, Voting Systems."

[32] Although near-simultaneous elections are no guarantee that the president's party will have a majority in the legislature, as France showed us in 2022 for the first time since the shift from non-simultaneous elections in 2002, when Macron's party lost its previous majority six weeks after his re-election.

risks further undermining the effectiveness of this regime type,[33] and fragmentation can leave even a newly elected president with reduced legitimacy,[34] as well as heading an internally divided majority party, although the constraint of sustaining the parliamentary government means that these divisions are likely to play out less than in pure presidentialism. A Senator Manchin veto may doom a presidential legislative policy or nominee but not the party's hold on governmental office itself.

Finally, multiparty semi-presidentialism raises a risk to effective government that the two-party version rarely does; namely, fragmentation of power to the extent that neither presidential nor prime ministerial authority can be sustained. This risk, which characterized the Weimar Republic for the final half of its existence,[35] in a sense combines that of both other multiparty regime types. On the other hand, where this risk does not materialize and where the party system is more parliamentary than presidential in nature, legislatures may be in a better position to fulfill their accountability and deliberative functions. Again, polarization and hyper-partisanship may undermine the bases for necessary inter-party alliances and agreements, and the contemporary fragmentation of political power makes the risk of this regime type even greater.

9.3 SEMI-PARLIAMENTARISM

As noted above, parliamentary systems of both two-party and multiparty versions have traditionally found it hard to reconcile the four values, with each version prioritizing two different ones in ways that risk failing to achieve the "minimum core" of the other two. This is perhaps even more pronounced in the two-party, Westminster-style version because the normal majority party required for effective and stable government combined with the sink or swim political logic of the single election typically enables it to control and dominate the legislature and the legislative agenda. The resulting loss of genuine political accountability has been a major reason that many parliamentary systems have enhanced the legal accountability of government by establishing forms of judicial review for the first time.[36]

In the last few years, an alternative to the standard two types of parliamentary regime has been proposed that it is claimed better reconciles and optimizes the four values.[37] This alternative has been labeled "semi-parliamentarism." It is generally

33 Imagine if Jean-Luc Mélenchon's party, La France Insoumise, had won a majority in the French legislative elections in June and he had become prime minister (or Le Pen's National Rally).

34 As happened to Macron soon after his first presidential election victory in 2017; see Pildes, "Political Fragmentation in Democracies of the West."

35 Skach, "The 'Newest' Separation of Powers."

36 Stephen Gardbaum, "Separation of Powers and the Growth of Judicial Review in Established Democracies (or Why Has the Model of Legislative Supremacy Mostly Been Withdrawn from Sale?)," *American Journal of Comparative Law* 62: 613 (2014).

37 Primarily Ganghof and Khaitan, see n. 7.

based on, although a modification of, the closest real-world examples, at both the national and state levels in Australia, and its main proponents have advanced a couple of different versions or sub-types. As stated above, the four defining components of this regime type are: (1) the absence of the direct election of the chief executive, (2) two directly elected legislative chambers, (3) only the first chamber can dismiss the cabinet in a no-confidence vote, and (4) both chambers have equal legislative power and exercise of the second chamber's veto cannot be overridden by an ordinary or absolute majority of the first.[38] In addition to these purely institutional arrangements, the key to the claimed advantage of this regime type in better reconciling the values is the requirement of different voting systems for the two chambers in an attempt to ensure that the same party does not control or have a majority in both: specifically, a majoritarian voting system for the first chamber, to promote effective and stable government, but a PR voting system for the second chamber, to promote accountability and legislative deliberativeness.

I find semi-parliamentarism to be an innovative and promising democratic regime type that has the potential to offer a superior version of parliamentarism to the two existing ones. Part of its merits are the internal resources it brings to bear for addressing the contemporary challenges of polarization, hyper-partisanship, and/or fragmentation that render the balancing of values more difficult. The composition and legislative powers of the second chamber create incentives for multipartisan, ad hoc, issue-specific negotiation and accommodation among represented parties that might temper polarization. In a sense, it also deals with the contemporary problem of fragmentation of power by both channeling and celebrating it. So, the attempt is to contain the inter-party version in the first chamber through a majoritarian voting system that over-rewards the two leading parties but to increase the number of parties (and so representation) in the second chamber through PR.

Among its principal expositors, Steffen Ganghof argues that semi-parliamentarism is clearly superior to presidentialism because it provides the same benefits of separated powers between the executive and (here, the second chamber of the) legislature but without the unnecessary costs of "executive personalism."[39] Although he is less clear or categorical about this, it also appears to be superior for him to both pure parliamentarism (because of the absence of separated powers) and semi-presidentialism (because most of the costs of executive personalism survive, in terms of a directly elected, irremovable chief executive, despite the existence of a second,

[38] Khaitan proposes a party weighted conference committee system to break legislative ties, in which a single opposition party would not be able to veto legislation and the governing party must gain the votes of some other parties. Khaitan, "Balancing Accountability and Effectiveness." On the full range of tie-breaker mechanisms employed in bicameral systems, including various conference committee arrangements, see George Tsebelis and Jeannette Money, *Bicameralism*. Cambridge University Press, 1997, 54–69, 176–208.

[39] Ganghof, *Beyond Presidentialism and Parliamentarism*.

parliamentary one).[40] Tarunabh Khaitan also suggests that (his "moderated parliamentarism sub-type" of) semi-parliamentarism is superior to the alternatives because it "combines the most attractive elements of each" while still yielding a stable regime.[41] But he also makes the more modest claim that moderated parliamentarism is *one way* to optimize what he has identified as four constitutional principles relating to political parties,[42] as well as to balance governmental effectiveness and accountability.

For reasons of space, my aim here is not to discuss whether or not Ganghof's arguments for the superiority of semi-parliamentarism over all three widely adopted forms of government are compelling. For what it is worth, I believe that his conception of the separation of powers is somewhat narrow and constrained; it seems to imply, for example, that pure parliamentary systems lack this value altogether.[43] I also think the contrast between presidential and (modern) parliamentary systems in terms of the "executive personalism" of the former – that is, executive power being located in a single person versus a collectivity – is overdrawn in the modern era in which prime ministers are no longer simply "first among equals" and the office has become "presidentialized" in many countries.[44] But I do think his work is insightful and illuminating, so much so that it is worth exploring whether the principles and institutional ingenuity of semi-parliamentarism are perhaps exportable to other regime types . Similarly, in terms of Khaitan's (more modest) claim that his version of semi-parliamentarism is one way to reconcile effectiveness and accountability, I want to ask whether there might be *other ways* and, in particular, whether the insights of the semi-parliamentary model that he has helped to develop are capable of being adapted for other regime types. Moreover, would some of the inherent features of semi-parliamentarism that might reduce current party pathologies be exportable to these others? Are there any independent design features that might be helpful in this regard?

9.4 DOES SEMI-PARLIAMENTARISM SUGGEST THERE MAY BE WAYS TO BETTER BALANCE THE FOUR VALUES IN NON-PARLIAMENTARY REGIMES?

As we have seen, from the perspective of optimizing the four values, semi-presidentialism and (even more) presidentialism tend to achieve stable government

40 Ibid.

41 Khaitan, "Balancing Accountability and Effectiveness," 94.

42 Ibid.

43 For him, separation of powers appears to be equated with the executive not being subject to a vote of no-confidence and ouster by the legislature. See Ganghof, *Beyond Presidentialism and Parliamentarism*.

44 See, for example, Thomas Poguntke and Paul Webb, eds., *The Presidentialization of Politics: A Comparative Study of Modern Democracies*. Oxford University Press, 2005; Anthony Mughan, *Media and the Presisdentialzation of Parliamentary Elections*. Palgrave Macmillan, 2000.

for the duration of the presidential term – at least, absent the "Linzian nightmare" scenario – but, depending on political party strength and alignment, risk significant underperforming on the others.

Starting with presidentialism, a bicameral legislature with the same equal powers and separate voting systems as under semi-parliamentarism would likely, with a few additional modifications, have similar potentially beneficial effects. Effective and responsive governance would be bolstered by more or less ensuring that the president's party has a majority in the first chamber for the full duration of the president's term. This could be achieved by combining (a) a majoritarian voting system with (b) simultaneous executive and first chamber legislative elections and (c) making the first chamber term the same as that of the president (for example, four years). Importantly, this latter feature obviously rules out midterm legislative elections that often create divided presidential government and gridlock. To the extent that ineffective and unresponsive government is driving the current alienation from the more mainstream or centrist parties, this would help to address the problem. Given the presidential party's likely majority in the first chamber, a presidential legislative veto – as a check on a potentially hostile, runaway, or "all-powerful" legislature – is likely unnecessary,

As with semi-parliamentarism, PR elections for the second chamber will likely enhance multipartisan, and so potentially more effective, executive oversight and accountability, as well as overall legislative representation of voters' preferences and the deliberativeness of legislative processes. With likely no presidential or *any* single party majority, the prospects of both rubber stamping and continuous institutional gridlock are much reduced and the incentives for multipartisan, ad hoc, issue specific negotiations and accommodations for presidentially sponsored (and other) bills greatly increased. PR thus appears to be key to the values-optimizing goals of an "incongruent" second chamber. Other institutional permutations, such as different (and possibly staggered) terms and being elected at a different time from the simultaneous presidential and first chamber elections, seem less central than under semi-parliamentarism itself,[45] although certainly could be considered as potential supplements.

As for addressing and reducing the special problems, a number of inherent and possible additional features of such a regime hold promise. To push candidates away from the extremes and so reduce polarization (as well as increase responsiveness and representation), presidential elections should, as they do almost everywhere, require a direct national majority of voters. As the PR voting system for the second chamber is likely to result in the existence of more than two main political parties and

45 Unlike in semi-parliamentarism, where the first chamber (alone) has the power to withhold confidence and oust the government, there is no additional reason of "breaking the legitimacy tie" between the two chambers for longer second chamber terms, i.e., ensuring the first chamber is always the most recently elected. Similarly, there is also no need to give the first chamber an advantage in the legislative tie-breaking rule.

presidential candidates, an instant or two-round run-off system would therefore need to be employed for presidential elections. Although not of course guaranteed, this increases the chances of an anti-polar majority at the second round, as we have now seen three times in France. The method of selecting party candidates for presidential (as well as legislative) office should similarly not reward more extreme or outlier positions, as, for example, the US system of party primaries can do by effectively bypassing both more knowledgeable party insiders and less motivated/partisan, ordinary party voters.[46]

At the legislative level, this type of presidential regime again inherently counters polarization and hyper-partisanship by reducing the risk of general gridlock and creating incentives for issue-specific coalitions engendering multipartisanship and accommodation. Additionally, in terms of the majoritarian voting system for the first chamber, ranked choice voting (or a run-off system) is to be preferred to first past the post, for, as a true majoritarian rather than plurality system, it increases the prospects of less extreme positions and candidates. Again, party primaries that tend to be dominated by more motivated, partisan, and extreme party members/voters are part of the current problem and should either not be the method of selection at all or replaced by a "top four"[47] or equivalent method, to counter this effect. Independent redistricting commissions are also important, as having competitive *general* elections, rather than only primaries due to partisan gerrymandering, is key to reducing polarization.

In terms of fragmentation, again in a sense PR in the second chamber is designed to channel and reap its systemic benefits as compared with some of the costs of a two-party system that we have seen. If the risk or reality is of an overly fragmented second chamber exists, the common technique of capping it by employing voting thresholds for seats can be instituted. To the extent that the current fragmentation of parties and party authority is the result of the greater independence of legislative representatives stemming from the communications revolution and the potential for individual following and fundraising it has created,[48] this independence could be reduced in at least two ways. First, a closed list PR system for the second chamber would make individuals more dependent on the party, for their ranking on the list, and in this way replace older, intra-party seniority control systems. Second, whether through law (where possible) or internal regulation, funding and campaign finance rules for all elective offices could also render politicians more dependent on party and less on their own, individual fundraising.

46 See Stephen Gardbaum and Richard Pildes, "Populism and Institutional Design, Methods of Selecting Party Candidates for Chief Executive," *New York University Law Review* 93: 647 (2018).

47 More than two candidates are needed if, as suggested, the majoritarian voting system for the general election to the first chamber employs ranked choice voting or a run-off.

48 See Pildes, "Political Fragmentation in Democracies of the West."

With semi-presidentialism, the goal of achieving greater optimization of the four values revolves around attempting to avoid both the undue concentration that occurs when a president is effectively also the head of a parliamentary government, as party leader and the undue fragmentation where no party or stable bloc has a legislative majority. Essentially the same set of institutions, powers, voting systems, and reforms as with presidentialism just discussed would increase the probability of such an intermediate outcome. With simultaneous first chamber and executive elections, same terms of office, and a majoritarian (preferably ranked choice or two round) voting system, the result is likely to be presidential control,[49] but the key difference from the "super-presidential" scenario is the likely absence of a presidential, or any single, party majority in the directly elected and co-equal second chamber, where PR is employed. Combined with most of the other features and reforms discussed above for presidentialism, the potential result is to support effective and responsive government but without either undue concentration of power or built-in gridlock, enhance accountability to, and the representativeness of, the legislature, to create incentives for issue specific deliberation and accommodation across parties, and thereby also lower the risk of extreme fragmentation.

9.5 THE ROLE OF CONSTITUTIONAL LAW

Democratic regime types are constituted by the combination of form of government (institutional powers and relations) and the operative voting and party system. This is why, for example, two-party and multiparty parliamentary systems are distinct types (or sub-types), generally furthering opposite values of democratic polities. It is a traditional blind spot of constitutional scholars to focus on the first part of the combination only, without the second. But a constitution should ordain and establish a regime type and not merely a form of government and so should presumptively include the key party and voting variables of the chosen type. Not only does this render it more difficult for elected officials to deliberately change or undermine a given democratic regime, but it also protects that regime from more unintended, serendipitous, or gradual alterations in its constituent parts.

As we have seen, the versions of presidentialism and semi-presidentialism that may better balance the four values and address some of the pathologies of contemporary party systems contain a distinctive set of institutional powers and relations that should presumptively be constitutionalized, as per the modern norm. To recap, these include direct national election of the president by a majority of the popular vote; two co-equal and directly elected legislative chambers, with the first having the

[49] Again, "likely," but not guaranteed, as the recent first French experience since the 2002 reforms with a divided National Assembly elected six weeks after the president illustrates. Here, the forces of party fragmentation, which have reduced the previously dominant center-left and center-right parties to minor actors and undermined the appeal of Macron's new party, have been extremely powerful.

same term as the president and a simultaneous or nearby election day, whereas members of the second chamber have different (and possible staggered) terms and/or are elected at a different time.

The key party/voting feature that is co-constitutive of these distinct democratic regime types is the employment of different voting systems for the two chambers, a majoritarian system – and preferably ranked choice voting – for the first, and PR – presumptively the closed-list variety – for the second. It is key, in significant part, because the respective party systems, two governing party contenders in the first house and multiparty in the second, largely follow from this choice. Accordingly, this should also be constitutionalized. Otherwise, depending in part on the legislative tie-breaker rule employed,[50] it might be possible for the first chamber to repeal an ordinary statute PR requirement for the second. Given the design requirement of single-member constituencies for the first chamber, the polarizing possibility of artificially eliminating competitive general elections through partisan gerrymandering should be minimized by also enshrining independent districting commissions in the constitution. This would likely have a knock-on effect of reducing partisan incentives for holding party primaries that select more extreme candidates, so that constitutional regulation of parties in this regard may be unnecessary.

9.6 CONCLUSION

This chapter represents an initial exploration of the possibilities of incorporating variations of political party and electoral systems into constitutional design for the purpose of addressing the twin contemporary democratic challenges of fragmented and unduly concentrated political power. It generalizes from the insights of proponents of semi-parliamentarism to suggest that its core promising feature of "symmetrical and incongruent" bicameralism can usefully be adapted to create equivalent versions of presidentialism and semi-presidentialism. By seeking ways to render all types of democratic government more effective and responsive, the chapter aims to counter the fragmentation and dysfunction that is helping to drive the appeal of more polar political forces, including authoritarian populisms of left and right. At the same time, it also seeks to curb the overly concentrated power that single party (or alliance) control of executive and legislative branches risks. For not only does this undermine the democratic values of accountability and legislative deliberation, but such concentrated power has been exploited and abused in recent years by various authoritarian populist regimes, both those with and without clear electoral majorities. In these ways, the aim is also to address some of the causes and consequences of such regimes. Obviously much remains to be done in terms of filling in the details.

[50] See, for example, nn. 37 and 44.

10

Courts as Constitutional Rule-Makers for Elections and Parties

Some Comparative Evidence

Aziz Z. Huq

10.1 INTRODUCTION

After declaring independence in 1960, the people of Côte d'Ivoire have faced the legacy of a long and difficult struggle to achieve democratic self-rule. Impeding their path was thirty-plus years of single-party rule by President Félix Houphouët-Boigny, successful and failed coup attempts, and a bloody civil war that ripped the country apart along a north-south line. Against this fractious backdrop, the presidential election of 2010 pitted incumbent Laurent Gbagbo against his former minister Alassane Ouattara and other candidates. When a runoff between Gbagbo and Ouattara was called in the challenger's favor (54.1 percent to 45.9 percent), Gbagbo appealed to the national Conseil constitutionnel, alleging fraud. The Conseil, a judicial body patterned on the French model, threw out 600,000 votes and declared Gbagbo the winner. This decision struck many impartial observers as fraudulent and counter democratic.[1]

A year later, the Awami League government of Bangladesh repealed the Thirteenth Amendment of that nation's Constitution. This provision had created a system of non-party "caretaker" regimes prior to national elections, headed by a former chief justice, charged with the impartial management of polls. Under these caretaker regimes, Bangladesh experienced three elections (in 1996, 2001, and 2008) "widely lauded as free and fair."[2] The later polls in 2014 and 2018, without a caretaker regime, were marked not just by declining competitiveness and captured legislative bodies but also sharp increases in "legal and extralegal measures to silence critics,

[1] O'Brien Kaaba, "The Challenges of Adjudicating Presidential Election Disputes in Africa: Exploring the Viability of Establishing an African Supranational Elections Tribunal," Doctor of Laws (LLD) thesis University of South Africa, 2015.

[2] M. Ehteshamul Bari, "The Incorporation of the System of Non-party Caretaker Government in the Constitution of Bangladesh in 1996 as a Means of Strengthening Democracy, Its Deletion in 2011 and the Lapse of Bangladesh into Tyranny following the Non-participatory General Election of 2014: A Critical Appraisal," *Transnational Law & Contemporary Problems* 28(1): 52 (2018).

weaken the opposition, and create a culture of fear."[3] In effect, the involvement of a judicial actor – albeit in a nontraditional, and arguably non-judicial role – allowed democracy to thrive.

In both Côte d'Ivoire and Bangladesh, an actor identified with the higher judiciary – either an apex court or its former chief – exercised a constitutionally defined power over the administration of national elections and parties. In the first case, judicial involvement arguably derailed fair democratic choice. In the second, a judicial actor's involvement enabled a fairer measuring of popular judgment. At minimum, therefore, these cases caution against a rush to judgment for or against a robust judicial presence in the constitutional law of parties and elections. A global answer to this question quickly meets powerful counterexamples.

More modestly, this chapter explores theoretical and analytic foundations of these questions. It first aims to clarify some theoretical premises of this significant constitutional design choice. It then develops an analytic taxonomy of potential judicial tasks in managing elections with an eye toward democratic stability. This is complemented with an enumeration of potential risks. I make no claim that this theoretical and analytic ground-clearing yields sharp prescriptions about the role of courts in protecting democracies, although it does clarify the stakes of that functionality. This chapter offers, in the end, a crisper, less obstructed vantage upon the choices at play, rather than a decisive prescription.

Four other limits to the chapter's scope need emphasis. First, I focus on the role of *apex* courts (broadly defined) in setting out basic ground rules for democratic choice. I do not address the interaction between ordinary litigation and election management. Almost any kind of jurisdiction *can* yield litigation that somehow "affects" an election. When a visiting session of the Lefortovo court sentenced the late Alexei Navalny to nine years' imprisonment in March 2022 on fraud charges,[4] for example, it was clearly influencing the possibility of democratic competition in Russia – perhaps in deep ways that were not evident at the moment of judgment. But it was not defining or applying the ground rules for elections or parties as such.

Second, and relatedly, there are many other aspects of intergovernmental relations and legislative process that might be thought essential to a functioning democracy beyond elections and parties. Gardbaum, for example, rightly singles out the legislative failure to hold an executive accountable as a political-process

[3] Ali Riaz, "The Pathway to Democratic Backsliding in Bangladesh," *Democratization* 28(1): 190 (2021).

[4] Council of Europe, "Russia: Declaration by the High Representative on behalf of the EU on the ruling to extend Alexei Navalny's politically motivated imprisonment by an additional 9 years," Press Release 305/22 (March 22, 2022), www.consilium.europa.eu/en/press/press-releases/2022/03/22/russia-declaration-by-the-high-representative-on-behalf-of-the-eu-on-the-ruling-to-extend-alexei-navalny-s-politically-motivated-imprisonment-by-an-additional-9-years/pdf.

failure.[5] Keeping with the more limited focus of this volume. I will home in more narrowly on the immediate accoutrements of democratic choice.

Third, I am concerned with courts' function in democratic contexts, broadly defined to include some instances of competitive authoritarianism but not purely authoritarian ones. (The latter do run elections of a sort. And when de facto independent courts in non-democratic contexts are allowed, these do seem to mitigate the risk of illegal manipulation.)[6]

Finally, I focus on constitutional, not statutory, rules and institutions. The last distinction is a touch artificial. Constitutions can be entrenched to greater or lesser extents than statutes. Entrenchment can vary within a single document, for instance, via targeted eternity clauses. Whole constitutions can be self-consciously styled as "temporary,"[7] just as institutions – think of Bangladesh's caretaker governments – can be "intermittent."[8] To assume a stable variation in the entrenchment of statutes and constitutions, therefore, is unjustified. My use of the term "constitutional," therefore, should be understood to connote a relatively high degree of entrenchment compared to other state institutions in a given polity.

10.2 THEORETICAL COORDINATES

What role should apex courts play in the constitutional law of elections and parties? Is theirs a function other bodies can serve equally well? And if there's choice between courts and alternative constitutional institutions, what considerations should guide designers? In the first instance, these questions sound in constitutional theory, oriented to offer guidance on the different functions necessitated by a commitment to democracy. Often, constitutional theory implicitly adopts the position of an imaginary constitutional designer. It implicitly assumes that theoretical and empirical work can, in tandem, at least narrow the range of plausible design choices. What is "optimal" may depend heavily on political and economic context, so specific prescription can be infeasible. A minimal "Hippocratic" insight into the range of feasible options that "do no harm" may be the best normative constitutional theory can do.[9]

It is a mistake to think that a democratic constitution must be composed solely of democratic parts. To the contrary, institutions insulated from partisan politics play

[5] Stephen Gardbaum, "Comparative Political Process Theory," *International Journal of Constitutional Law* 18(4): 1435–1457 (2020).

[6] See Cole J. Harvey, "Can Courts in Nondemocracies Deter Election Fraud? De Jure Judicial Independence, Political Competition, and Election Integrity," *American Political Science Review* 116(4): 1325–1339 (2022).

[7] Ozan Varol, "Temporary Constitutions," *California Law Review* 102(2): 409–464 (2014).

[8] Adrian Vermeule, "Intermittent Institutions," *Politics, Philosophy, and Economics* 10(4): 420–444 (2011).

[9] Aziz Z. Huq, "Hippocratic Constitutional Design," in *Assessing Constitutional Performance* ed. Tom Ginsburg and Aziz Z. Huq. Cambridge University Press, 2016, 39–70.

necessary roles in fostering the persistence over time of democratic choice.[10] A polity in which police and election officials responded to every whim of elected actors would not be democratic very long. Recent work by Gardbaum and Khaitan builds on this basic premise. Both start from the Madisonian intuition that constitutions invest individuals with legal and political authority, which can be used to advance or undermine the structural presuppositions of future popular choice under a stable constitutional frame. Even if some policy choices inevitably commit future actors,[11] a democratic constitution at least requires that electors retain the ability to change their minds at least about *who* is in power – although perhaps this is not alone enough[12] – so as to yield a tolerable measure of uncertainty and hence rotation of political office. To the extent it is conceptualized as intertemporally durable, democracy demands constraints at odds with elected actors' incentives.

Gardbaum's theory of "comparative political process theory" identifies the defense of "institutional structures and political processes within which democratic politics operates" from "erosion, corruption, and capture" as a distinctive design problem.[13] Echoing Hans Kelsen's celebration of the judiciary as the "guardian" of constitutional norms,[14] Gardbaum isolates "judicial review" as the institutional vessel for that defense.[15] Khaitan echoes Gardbaum's concern about the instability of non-self-executing constitutional norms. In contrast to Gardbaum's focus upon courts, though, he posits a need for "guarantor institutions" (or "fourth branch" bodies) with legislative and executive functions. He criticizes the "lawyerly blinkers" that lead scholars to "ignore" actors other than judges. The latter have both expressive and also material capacity (which courts are said to lack). They act either before or after a constitutional norm is violated.[16] Khaitan's point has empirical resonance: by 2019, some 64 percent of states had some kind of independently managed electoral system.[17]

Written constitutions have in the last fifty years taken up both Gardbaum's judicial path and Khaitan's fourth-branch proposal. Figures 10.1 and 10.2 plot the percentage of constitutions in force at any given time that contain respectively, a court explicitly tasked to resolve election disputes, or some form of election

10 Aziz Z. Huq and Tom Ginsburg, "Democracy without Democrats," *Constitutional Studies* 6 (1): 165–188 (2020).

11 Paul Pierson, "When Effect Becomes Cause: Policy Feedback and Political Change," *World Politics* 45(4): 595–628 (1993).

12 Compare Norberto Bobbio, *The Future of Democracy: A Defence of the Rules of the Game*. University of Minnesota Press, 1987.

13 See Gardbaum, "Comparative Political Process Theory," 1453.

14 Hans Kelson and Carl Schmidt, *The Guardian of the Constitution*. Cambridge University Press, 2015.

15 See Gardbaum, "Comparative Political Process Theory," 1411.

16 Tarunabh Khaitan, "Guarantor Institutions," *Asian Journal of Comparative Law*, 16: S43 (2021).

17 Malcolm Langford, Rebecca Schiel, and Bruce M. Wilson. "The Rise of Electoral Management Bodies: Diffusion and Effects," *Asian Journal of Comparative Law* 16: S62 (2021).

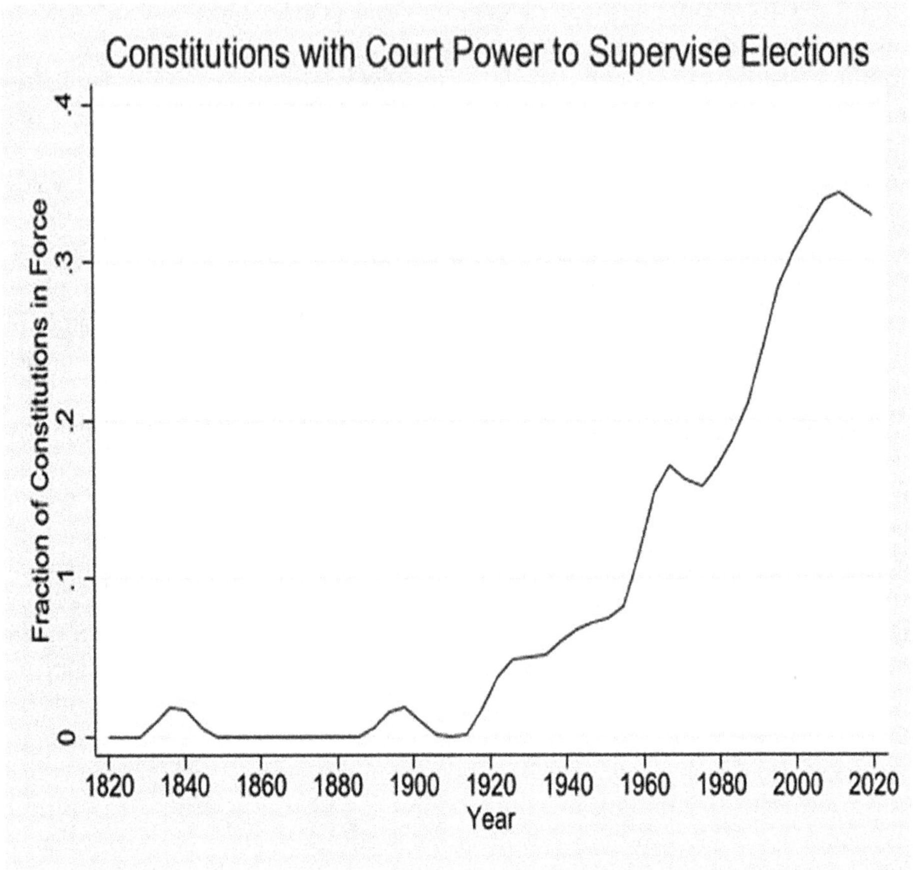

FIGURE 10.1 Percentage of extant constitutions with courts engaged in electoral supervision.

management body.* They show how the adoption of courts preceded that of election commissions globally by about twenty years and, further, how neither model is obviously numerically dominant. The choice between courts and fourth-branch institutions (if imagined as a matter of substitutes and not as possible complements) hence remains a live one.

Both accounts leave questions open. Gardbaum, for example, does not address the possibility, illustrated in the Côte d'Ivoire case, that courts can be instruments of entrenchment. It thus does not explain how to stymie judicial capture. Khaitan also invites inquiry into how to create institutions insulated from ordinary politics, how to maintain such insulation, and to how to respond in the event of capture. He further

* Thanks to Morgen Miller for help with the charts in this chapter.

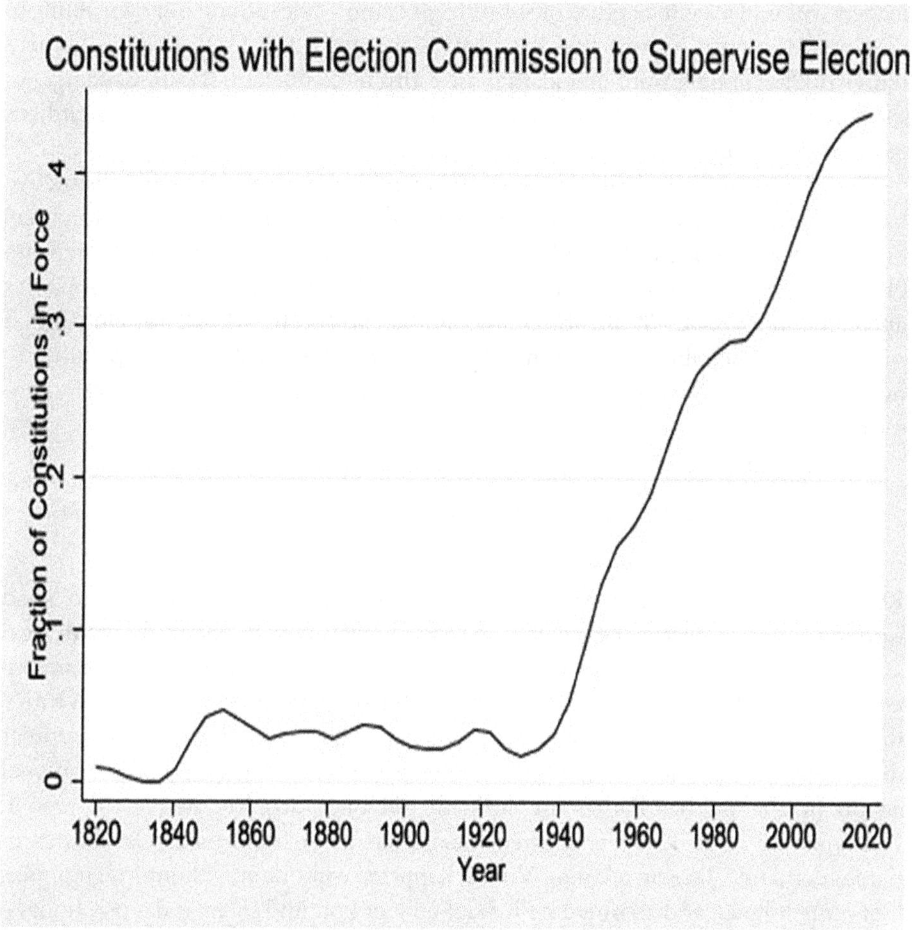

FIGURE 10.2 Percentage of extant constitutions with commissions engaged in electoral supervision.

leaves open the question of whether (or which) guarantor institutions are "normatively desirable" at all.[18] If the Côte d'Ivoire case invites the thought that courts, acting alone, cannot alone be assumed to be faithful guardians in a Kelsenian mold, a different study of election commissions in four Central American countries paints a rather dismaying picture of slow decay and partisan capture.[19] More generally, a designer may be uncertain about the nature of future threats to democracy (which might bare differently on courts as opposed to commissions), the risk that political

[18] Khaitan, "Guarantor Institutions," S59.

[19] Antonio Ugues, "Electoral Management Bodies in Central America," in *Advancing Electoral Integrity* ed. Pippa Norris et. al. Cambridge University Press, 2014, 118–134.

leaders will find ways to capture or subvert "guarantor" bodies, and her own ability to memorialize norms in ways that have consistent effect over time. Even as tremendous work has gone toward elucidating the forms of democratic failure writ large, in short, there is relatively little systematic work on how or why institutional guardians of democracy founder.

Current theoretical work further leaves open how to taxonomize the distinctive tasks involved in electoral guarantorship and the related puzzle of how to parcel out those tasks among different bodies. In part, this gap abides because there is no clear sense of what, quite specifically, "democratic maintenance" work on parties and elections involves. With a more fine-grained taxonomy of such tasks in hand, it may well be possible to discern whether and when institutional parallelism overlap, or even monopoly control by one body is desirable, or at least not a serious error.

10.3 A TAXONOMY OF JUDICIAL RESPONSIBILITIES RELATED TO ELECTIONS AND PARTIES

Keeping a system of competitive political parties and electoral choice in good working order is no simple matter. It requires attention to many different legal and constitutional mechanisms. There are many sharp corners during any representative process at which a hazardous and destabilizing political judgment can throw the democratic project off track. Election-related activity often begins when popular discontent with an incumbent regime bubbles over into oppositional associational action by the public. Parties are formed; old ones dissolve, merge, or reboot. Platforms are drafted, voters courted. Coalitions must be formed. Candidates or parties demand a line on a ballot. Voting happens, without or without irregularities. Counting follows, and an outcome is reached – or not. And so on and – one hopes – on, again and again: The promise of democracy resides in its endless capacity for iterative revision, of messing up, and starting again. From the ex ante perspective of the constitutional designer, a choice must be made about which of these diverse moments falls under constitutional regulation.

This section organized the heterogeneous range of such possible platforms for election regulation in a constitution into four broad categories. Setting these out, I avoid the assumption that each one must be subject to judicial supervision. Rather, there is a wide range of possible forms of choices about what to regulate and also how. Hence, a specific problem might be under a court's supervision, regulated by a constitutional (or statutory) fourth-branch body, left without any regulation at all, or even insulated from state regulation via negative constitutional rights against the state. I bracket this choice of regulatory instruments and instead offer a taxonomy of moments in the democratic process in which judicial intervention can be imagined. A four-prong taxonomy, in my view, captures the range of potential issues in a tractable way. To the extent feasible, I illustrate this taxonomy with examples from outside the American context: The latter is relatively familiar and well-studied, and in many ways "exceptional."[20]

a. Entry rules for voters, candidates and parties. Constitutional regimes for voters, candidates, and parties tend to point in different directions. Respecting voters, constitutions tend to be inclusive. Article 42 of the Ghanaian Constitution, for example, declares that "every citizen of Ghana of eighteen years of age or above and of sound mind has the right to vote and is entitled to be registered as a voter for the purposes of public elections and referenda."[21] Until a 2012 Supreme Court decision, however, adult prisoners in Ghana were not permitted to vote. As in South Africa and Kenya, a constitutional judgment redrew the electorate's boundaries to draw in the incarcerated.[22] By way of counterpoint, the Indian high court has invalidated a statutory prohibition that negated felon disenfranchisement *only* for legislators.[23] The right to vote might also be implicated by practical hurdles, such as registration deadline, residency rules, and identification demands.

Voters are numerous and candidates, to some extent, replaceable. In contrast, parties tend to be fewer and far less fungible. As Schattschneider famously said, "political parties created democracy, and modern democracy is unthinkable without them."[24] So constitutional regulation of parties has higher stakes for democratic stability. The risks of both their regulation and their freedom are acute. One implication is the allocation of constitutional rights to associate to parties, which appear to have generally positive effects.[25] Another is the possible prohibition of parties that would otherwise command meaningful public support. I focus on the latter here.

Starting with the German Basic Law, constitutions have included "militant democratic" party bans as prophylactics against anti-democratic political formations (as discussed at more length in the Introduction to this volume). Article 21(2) of Germany's Basic Law, their locus classicus, flatly bans political parties that "seek to impair or abolish the free democratic basic order or endanger the existence of the Federal Republic of Germany."[26] A recent survey of legislative and constitutional party-ban provisions in Europe found around thirty-six examples, excluding prohibitions on parties on ideological grounds (65 percent), for violent activity (56 percent),

[20] Nicholas O. Stephanopoulos, "Our Electoral Exceptionalism," *University of Chicago Law Review* 80(2): 769–858 (2013).

[21] Constitution of Ghana, art. 42. (1992 [rev.1996]).

[22] Adem Kassie Abebe, "In Pursuit of Universal Suffrage: The Right of Prisoners in Africa to Vote," *Comparative and International Law Journal of Southern Africa* 46(3): 410–446 (2013).

[23] Surya Deva, "Democracy and Elections in India," in *Judicial Review of Elections in Asia* ed. Po Jen Yap. Routledge, 2016, 49.

[24] Elmer Eric Schattschneider, *Party Government: American Government in Action*. Routledge, 1942, 1.

[25] Adam S. Chilton and Mila Versteeg, "Do Constitutional Rights Make a Difference?," *American Journal of Political Science* 60(3): 575–589 (2016).

[26] Grundgesetz [GG] [Basic Law] art. 21(2), translation at www.gesetze-im-internet.de/englisch_gg/index.html.

as a means to protect the political order (44 percent), or for undemocratic internal party functioning (5 percent).[27] These provisions are largely enforced by courts, which rely for evidence on parties' platforms, leaders' statements, and members' activities.[28] Administrative agencies play a larger role within individualized lustration regimes, addressed below.[29] It is worth considering whether this forum choice influences the way in which democratic threats are evaluated. An administrative process, for example, might focus less on ostensible policy ambitions (courts' core concern) and more on empirical evidence of, say, party linkages to foreign, anti-democratic forces (e.g., the Russian government) or paramilitary formations.

A variant on "militant democracy" bans is the use of rules setting a threshold, or floor, of votes before a party obtains any legislative representation. Thresholds of 3 to 5 percent are common in party-list proportional representation systems.[30] In 1952, the German Bundesverfassungsgericht invalidated a Schleswig-Holstein law that imposed a 7 percent threshold, citing grounds of political equality and the need for a compelling justification for thresholds greater than 5 percent. It subsequently invalidated vote threshold rules that disfavored smaller parties from the former East Germany in the wake of reunification. The Bundestag responded by amending the election law to ameliorate the constitutionally flawed threshold rule.[31] The net result of these cases is that changes to Germany's election framework that seem likely to fence out smaller parties receive close judicial scrutiny, at the same time as the basic law raises the specter of judicial exclusion. This implies a judgment that courts, and not legislatures alone, should manage party disqualification. Germany is not alone in this practice. In 1998, the apex court of Italy invalidated a threshold that disfavored the representation of linguistic minorities in the Trentino-Alto Adigo region.[32]

One reason to favor judicial settlement of individual and party bans is that such prohibitions implicate considerations of due process that are familiar to judges and well-suited to resolution by courts. The law is singling out a person or association for a handicap not imposed on similarly situated actors. Courts may be able to draw on deeper jurisprudential resources to elaborate fitting procedural safeguards and

[27] Angela K. Bourne and Fernando Casal Bértoa, "Mapping 'Militant Democracy': Variation in Party Ban Practices in European Democracies (1945–2015)," *European Constitutional Law Review* 13(2): 221–247 (2017).

[28] Yigal Mersel, "The Dissolution of Political Parties: The Problem of Internal Democracy," *International Journal of Constitutional Law* 4(1): 86 (2006).

[29] Tom Ginsburg, David Landau, and Aziz Z. Huq, "Democracy's Other Boundary Problem: The Law of Disqualification," *California Law Review* 111, forthcoming, available at https://papers.ssrn.com/sol3/papers.cfm?abstract_id=3938600.

[30] Arend Lijphart, *Electoral Systems and Party Systems. A Study of Twenty-seven Democracies, 1945–1900*. Oxford University Press, 1994, 20–35.

[31] Donald P. Kommers and Russell A. Miller, *The Constitutional Jurisprudence of the Federal Republic of Germany*. Duke University Press, 2012, 186–191.

[32] Kieran Williams, "Judicial Review of Electoral Thresholds in Germany, Russia, and the Czech Republic," *Election Law Journal* 4(3): 193 (2005).

evidentiary thresholds. The existence of a familiar template for judicial involvement lowers the expected adoption and error costs associated with courts' intervention. The same, however, may well not be true for challenges to vote thresholds – which instead implicate questions of judicial competence in respect to more synoptic judgments about election systems in the round.

b. Electoral system review. The cases concerning the validity of vote thresholds in proportional representation systems are a reminder that constitutional courts can exercise jurisdiction over abstract (otherwise known as "facial") challenges to different elements of electoral systems. These cases present the question of conformity between a constitutional norm and the verbal contents of election law, bracketing any inquiry into how that law is applied on the ground. Generally, such challenges are adjudicated before an election. They seem less common than more specific charges of fraud or malfeasance in a particular election, a class of jurisprudence that I take up below. But the two categories obviously overlap.

A common question for review involves the carving up of a polity into geographic districts for representational purposes. In 1961, Ireland's High Court struck down a districting plan characterized by "grave inequalities."[33] Between 1986 and 2010, France's Conseil Constitutionnel invalidated several electoral districting statutes with large deviations from an equal population baseline. It twice instructed the French legislature to redraw all the nation's districts.[34] Other electoral system features can also be subject to judicial review. In 2008, for example, Indonesia's Constitutional Court upheld a mandatory gender quota for party lists but invalidated a vote threshold for party-list candidates.[35] In 2013, Italy's Constitutional Court struck down a 2005 election law because it used closed party lists and assigned a majority party a "bonus" in seats. These features, reasoned the Court, violated Article I of Italy's Constitution (popular sovereignty), Article 3 (equality before the law), Article 67 (representation as national, not local); and Article 48 (freedom of the vote). In an unusual further step, the Italian court issued a remedy in the form of a new, purely proportional, electoral system using a preference voting system. This system served the interest of neither party coalition. Their leaders Matteo Renzi and Silvio Berlusconi quickly negotiated an alternative scheme.[36]

Systemic challenges can also be lodged in international judicial bodies. Since 1986, the European Court of Human Rights has also permitted challenges to European law concerning elections to the European parliament.[37] And in 2016,

33 O'Donovan v. Attorney General, High Court of Ireland (January 1, 1962), https://ie.vlex.com/vid/donovan-v-attorney-general-806302841.

34 Stephanopoulos, "Our Electoral Exceptionalism," 781–782.

35 Stefanus Henrianto, "The Curious Case of Quasi-weak-form Review," in *Judicial Review of Elections in Asia* ed. Po Jen Yap. Routledge, 2016, 101–102.

36 Gianfranco Baldini and Alan Renwick, "Italy toward (Yet Another) Electoral Reform," *Italian Politics* 30(1): 164–166 (2015).

37 Francis G. Jacobs, "Constitutional Control of European Elections: The Scope of Judicial Review," *Fordham International Law Journal* 28: 1034–1036 (2005).

the African Court of Human and People's Rights ordered Côte d'Ivoire to amend its electoral commission law to bring it into compliance with an impartiality principle in the African Charter on Democracy, Elections and Governance. The international court, though, stepped in only after a substantial challenge had been filed and rejected by the nation's high court.[38]

A final relevant class of cases involves the legal environment in which elections are run. Constitutions might extend a positive constitutional protection to speech, spending, and conduct constituting a campaign. Alternatively, they can impose negative restraints on how and when campaigns are conducted. Litigation of such rights that yields judgments of general scope will shape the electoral environment. They may indirectly change outcomes, but the frequency and identity of outcome-dispositive voting rules is hard to evaluate.

c. Election integrity claims. Specific complaints about election integrity seem more common than abstract challenges. A "surprisingly large" number of elections are closely fought.[39] Emotions are likely to run higher during such heated contests, with accusations of impropriety (or perhaps even its appearance) being more common. Across Anglophone democracies, moreover, partisan identification – both negative and also positive – appears to play an increasingly large role in national politics.[40]

The judicial reversal of a national election result on grounds of specific illegality or malfeasance seems rare. (The invalidation of *subnational* elections, by contrast, is more common, as Camby illustrates).[41] The example of Côte d'Ivoire's 2010 poll seems exceptional, not illustrative. Hence, when presidential polls in Taiwan in March 2004 led to an incumbent victory by 0.22 percent, the loser sought and obtained a court-ordered recount that reduced, but did not flip, the margin of victory.[42] In 2013, the Kenyan Supreme Court declined to set aside Uhuru Kenyatta's first-round victory in a presidential race against Raila Odinga.[43] Four years later, in 2017, after yet another closely fought election between Kenyatta and Odinga, the same Court accepted the latter's complaints of election irregularities, nullified the poll, and ordered fresh voting within sixty days. Because Odinga refused to participate in this second round – citing concerns about the election commission's integrity – judicial intervention did not ultimately change the

38 Ben Kioko, "The African Charter on Democracy, Elections and Governance as a Justiciable Instrument," *Journal of African Law* 63(S1): 53 (2019).

39 Laurence Whitehead, "The Challenge of Closely Fought Elections," *Journal of Democracy* 18 (2): 14 (2007).

40 Mike Medeiros and Alain Noël, "The Forgotten Side of Partisanship: Negative Party Identification in Four Anglo-American Democracies," *Comparative Political Studies* 47(7): 1022–1046 (2014).

41 Jean-Pierre Camby, *Le Conseil constitutionnel, juge électoral*. Dalloz, 2013.

42 Tun-jen Cheng and Da-chi Liao, "Testing the Immune System of a Newly Born Democracy: The 2004 Presidential Election in Taiwan," *Taiwan Journal of Democracy* 2(1): 81–101 (2006).

43 Kaaba, "The Challenges of Adjudicating Presidential Election Disputes in Africa," 93–94.

election's outcome.[44] In a variant on this dynamic, international courts in Africa, rather than their domestic counterparts, have been reviewing election disputes in Burkina Faso, Nigeria, Kenya, and Tanzania.[45]

The logical limit-case of these possibilities is Bangladesh's caretaker government regime. Recall that this looked to a former chief justice to administer government during the run-up to an election.[46] In effect, it assumed that the risk of illegal self-dealing by the incumbent government would be unacceptably large. Rather than adjudicate challenges after the fact, it imposed a blanket prophylactic remedy of control by judicial personnel. The judicial character of the caretaker regime, indeed, seems to have been important to its success.

Such widespread practice aside, there is also good reason to doubt that judges generally do a good job catching or preventing irregularities. A threshold reason is their lack of relevant expertise in recondite and technical matters of election administration. A second problem is impuissance. The path of the 2017 Kenyan election suggests that even when a court perceives irregularities, it may lack the political capital to force a change in election outcomes. The latter also illustrates the possibility of tension, even conflict, between a judiciary and a fourth branch institution with different views of a vote's legality – a point to which I return below.

On the other hand, the power to consider specific allegations of fraud or malfeasance in respect to a particular election is distinct from the power to consider whether, in the abstract, a legal framework contained in statutes and regulations comports with constitutional norms. The two genres of litigation usually turn on different evidentiary grounds and demand different kinds of judicial competencies. The distinction between specific and abstract review, though, should not obscure a more profound connection between these two genres of litigation: A well-designed and well-functioning legal structure for parties and elections minimizes the opportunity for strategic action by powerful state actors intended to derail an anticipated electoral defeat. Post hoc judicial review of specific objections might usefully identify vulnerabilities in the electoral framework, providing the legislature with the information necessary to "patch" the system. Alternatively, such review might have a corrosive "moral hazard" effect: Elected officials know that they can appeal, after the fact, to the bench in cases where something goes awry. Ex ante, therefore, they have less urgent reasons to anticipate and fix vulnerabilities in an electoral system. The exercise of judicial review, which is often assumed to be the sine qua non of legality, hence creates a dynamic unravelling of the rule of law around

44 Richard Stacey and Victoria Miyandazi, "Constituting and Regulating Democracy: Kenya's Electoral Commission and the Courts in the 2010s," *Asian Journal of Comparative Law* 16: 1–18 (2021).

45 James Thuo Gathii and Olabisi D. Akinkugbe, "Judicialization of Election Disputes in Africa's International Courts," *Law and Contemporary Problems* 84(1): 181–218 (2022).

46 See Bari, "The Incorporation of the System of Non-party Caretaker Government in the Constitution of Bangladesh."

elections. A possible way to mitigate the force of such incentive effects is the judicial use of a "penalty default" remedy. This is a judicial solution disfavored by all – perhaps akin to the Italian constitutional court's ruling in 2013 – that forces hegemonic partisan actors to revise the election law rather than compete under an intolerable disposition.

Ginsburg and Elkins offer a more minimalist justification of the judicial role in settling close elections.[47] Likening a closely contested election to the game-theory model of "chicken," they posit that a judicial resolution can operate as a "self-enforcing focal point" that mitigates the risk of overt conflict even if it is not a particularly accurate factfinder. This role, they note, need not be played by a court; the latter is just a "convenient third-party [that] draws on the imagery of a neutral dispute resolver."[48] This logic, though, assumes a relatively narrow temporal focus on the moment after a close election. It does not account for the risk of strategic false claims by a likely loser that an election is closer than it really is: Again, the problem can be characterized in terms of moral hazard, with the risk of upstream strategic action rising as the expected accuracy of the third-party adjudicator decreases.

d. "Exit" rules for candidates and parties. Just as law can impose front-end hurdles to entering the political process so too can law create chutes for expelling individuals or groups that pose a threat to the democratic process. Democratic exclusion varies not only by whether it operates at a granular, individual level or a coarser group level but also whether it hinges on past "bad" conduct or a prediction of future harm. I have addressed party bans above because they can be thought of as ex ante barriers to participation. I hence focus on individual disqualification here because they commonly hinge on a finding of "bad" past action.

At one end of this spectrum is the familiar impeachment remedy. Almost all (90 percent) of constitutions with a presidency speak to impeachment. Crimes and constitutional violations are the most common bases for removal. A lower legislative chamber usually begins an impeachment by a supermajority vote, and ex post judicial review is often, albeit not always, available. Between 1990 and 2018, impeachment was proposed at least 210 times in 61 countries, against 128 different heads of state. But only ten removals were ultimately carried out, some of which involved judicial review of a legislative removal decision.[49] Impeachment is not the only pathway for exclusion. Israeli courts have adopted an aggressive program of removing officials and blocking appointments based on a judge-made concept of "good character," deeming officials ineligible from remaining in or holding office if

[47] Tom Ginsburg and Zachary Elkins, "Ancillary Powers of Constitutional Courts," *Texas Law Review* 87(7): 1456–1457 (2008).

[48] Ibid. at 1457.

[49] Tom Ginsburg, Aziz Z. Huq, and David Landau, "The Comparative Constitutional Law of Presidential Impeachment," *University of Chicago Law Review* 88(1): 81–164 (2021).

currently under indictment.[50] On the other side of the ledger, lustration rules might be subject to constitutional challenge rather than simply being enforced. In 2003, for instance, Indonesia's Constitutional Court invalidated a prohibition on the election of Communist Party members.[51]

Given their stakes, disqualification disputes unsurprisingly can spill into larger questions of institutional power. India provides an example. After the Allahabad High Court invalidated the election of Indira Gandhi on corruption-related grounds, the Indian parliament enacted a constitutional provision making election disputes involving the prime minister and speaker non-justiciable. In 1975, the Indian Supreme Court invalidated that amendment, citing its "basic structure" doctrine.[52] Hence, a discrete dispute about one politician become the basis for a more sweeping ruling about judicial power.

e. Summary. Apex courts are in practice involved in a wide range of election and party-related disputes. In some instances, they perform tasks assigned by a constitution (e.g., enforcing rights, resolving factual claims of irregularity, and disqualifying parties or candidates). At other times, they clarify the meaning of the organic law (e.g., in abstract challenges to the constitutionality of election-related provisions). A minimal conclusion from this survey is negative: Given the heterogeneity and numerosity of potential disputes, there is unlikely to be a single "right answer" to the question of when courts should be involved, or not, in the constitutional regulation of parties and polling. The world is too complex for a single, simple solution of that kind.

10.4 INSTITUTIONAL CHOICE IN THE CONSTITUTIONAL SUPERVISION OF ELECTIONS AND PARTIES

If there is no "one size fits all" institutional choice covering all of these examples, the question arises whether there are reasons to assign some tasks to courts and some to fourth-branch bodies. The choice is nonbinary: Courts might be either substitutes or complements for fourth-branch bodies, such as election commissions. Indeed, as Figure 10.3 shows, a nontrivial number of constitutions contain both election-specific judicial powers and also an election commission. This overlap creates the possibility of both cooperation and conflict.

The case studies discussed above push in different directions as to this choice. The Côte d'Ivoire example points toward skepticism about courts and hence an emphasis on nonjudicial bodies. In South Africa, the Constitutional Court and the Public Protector have worked in tandem in respect to high-level corruption relevant

[50] Yoav Dotan, "Impeachment by Judicial Review: Israel's Odd System of Checks and Balances," *Theoretical Inquiries in Law* 19(2): 705–744 (2018).

[51] See Henrianto, "The Curious Case of Quasi-weak-form Review," 98.

[52] See Deva, "Democracy and Elections in India."

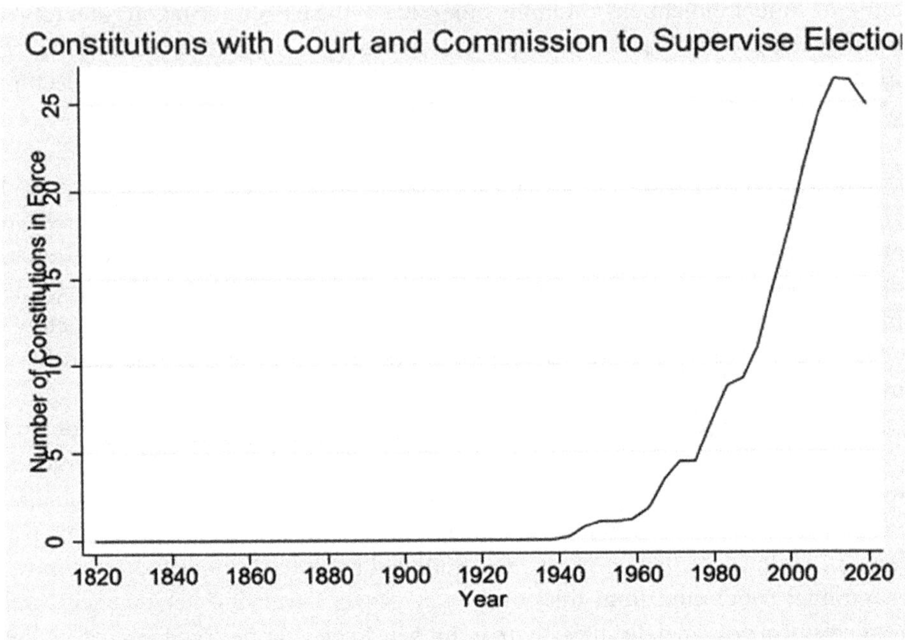

FIGURE 10.3 Proportion of extant constitutions with both judicial and fourth-branch electoral bodies.

to the potential disqualification of the prime minister.[53] Or an election commission might be subject to judicial oversight, as was the case in Kenya in 2017. That oversight can be intense or mild. In Taiwan, for example, courts "respect[] the regulatory authority" of the Election Commission by deferring to its judgment.[54] The Bangladesh example further hints that judicial actors can be embedded within an election management infrastructure to sustain constitutional norms. There is, in short, a quite wide array of potential relationships between courts and other bodies: cooperative, adversarial, entangled, or dominating.

There is good reason for resisting a strong presumption in favor of courts or fourth-branch bodies. To see this, consider three obstacles confronted by any constitutional body charged with maintaining democratic hygiene in and around elections: All three afflict both courts and non-judicial bodies in roughly equal measure. First, an institution with sufficient insulation from contemporaneous partisan pressures must get off the ground. Not only must that institution be designed with robust insulation from the very beginning, but that design feature must prove enduringly effective.

53 Aziz Z. Huq, "A Tactical Separation of Powers Doctrine," *Constitutional Court Review* 9(1): 19–44 (2019).

54 Wen-Chen Chang and Yi-Li Lee, "Judicial Strategies in Resolving Presidential Election Disputes," in *Judicial Review of Elections in Asia* ed. Po Jen Yap. Routledge, 2016, 147–172.

The initial constitutional design of either a judicial or a fourth-branch body can be flawed. In a study of election management bodies, Michael Pal identifies gaps in their organic documents that facilitate capture.[55] Similarly, the American federal judiciary was designed with two assumptions in mind: that the nation's Senate would be a nonpartisan body and that the supply of potential judges would be limited enough that selection could not be used to partisan ends. Both assumptions faltered within a decade of ratification. As a result, the American system for appointing federal judges is directly partisan, and partisan projects infuse the operation of the national judiciary.[56] One sort of democratic success, that is, engendered a different kind of democracy-related failure in another element of the Constitution.

Good design requires constitutional founders who eschew a partisan cast of mind and who are capable of anticipating evolving and as-yet unanticipated strains on the democratic process. Obviously, these won't always be to hand. Perhaps the most obvious circumstances in which good design will come to the fore arise after a widely maligned (e.g., a fascist or apartheid) regime has collapsed, and there is intense public and geopolitical pressure for a fresh start.

Second, even a well-designed court or fourth-branch body institution can be subject to overweening informal (or illegal) pressures that compromises their good operation. For the past three decades, the Indian judiciary has exercised almost complete control over the formal processes for appointments to the higher bench. This insulates it from direct partisan pressure. The Supreme Court, indeed, invalidated a 2014 statute creating a National Judicial Appointments Commission. Yet the judiciary has recently turned a "blind eye" to controversial steps by the Bharatiya Janata Party (BNP) of Prime Minister Narenda Modi, such as a controversial campaign finance law, extrajudicial detentions in Jammu and Kashmir, and the construction of a Hindu temple on the site of the Babri Masjid. Judicial quiescence appears to be the result of "subtle" administrative measures, such as slow-walking promotions and background checks and resisting calls for better funding.[57] More troubling allegations of corruption on the part of a new chief justice and blackmail by the BNP suggest that even most robust legal defenses of institutional independence might be vulnerable to circumvention by sufficiently unscrupulous political operatives.[58] Similarly, Zambian Chief Justice Mathew Ngulube was forced to resign in 2002 after it was found out that he had received bribes from incumbent President Fredrick Chiluba while deliberating on an election-related petition.[59]

[55] Michael Pal, "Electoral Management Bodies as a Fourth Branch of Government," *Review of Constitutional Studies* 21(1): 85–113 (2016).

[56] Aziz Z Huq, "Why Judicial Independence Fails," *Northwestern University Law Review* 115 (4):1055–1122 (2020).

[57] Madhav Khosla and Milan Vaishnav, "The Three Faces of the Indian State," *Journal of Democracy* 32(1), 117 (2021).

[58] Atul Dev, "India's Supreme Court Is Teetering on the Edge," *The Atlantic* (April 29, 2019), www.theatlantic.com/international/archive/2019/04/india-supreme-court-corruption/587152/.

[59] Kaaba, "The Challenges of Adjudicating Presidential Election Disputes in Africa," 115.

Where an incumbent resorts to extralegal measures to undermine democratic choice, the institutional choice between guardianship bodies will have limited salvific effect. What is more important is the strength of the larger supervisory regime of criminal law pertaining to political corruption.

It is not clear whether courts or fourth-branch bodies can best resist this pressure. Tushnet[60] has suggested that the modal adjudicative tasks of an apex court often force it to take positions that have inescapable partisan connotations. Tasking judges with election-related dispute resolution may amplify the risk they will be tarred as "party-political".[61] And Tushnet's concern clearly extends, as he recognizes, to fourth branch institutions. And it may be that apex courts are more vulnerable because their ordinary docket has high political stakes. Or it might be that an apex court has a sufficiently large load of non-partisan-coded cases that it has a *greater* capacity to absorb or deflect "party-political" criticism. It is hard to know which way this consideration cuts in advance.

Third, it is well known that a verbal specification of a norm may be an imperfect proxy for an underlying constitutional value. Over time, a specific formulation may do an increasingly bad job of tracking that value. A more general verbal formulation, in contrast, may require new judgments over time as to how best to apply it across new and different circumstances over time. The negative right to speak free of governmental coercion, for example, is plausibly thought to be necessary to a well-functioning democracy. But that negative right may become increasingly irrelevant if it is possible for government to crowd or drown out critical, adversarial speech.[62] As a result, a court or guarantor institution tasked with maintaining a healthy democratic public sphere must revise radically how "democratic debate" is realized to avoid obsolescence at the hands of new digital media technologies. Again, a potentially paradoxical dynamic can be traced: A court that has successfully defended a negative-rights account of the democratic sphere may be so beholden to that history, intellectually or as a matter of institutional pride, that it is unable to recognize a decisive evolution in the sociopolitical environment. Blinded by success, it is driven to failure.[63]

There is, in short, a complex blend of countervailing pressures at play across a range of constitutional design decisions. It is, in particular, difficult to see an overwhelming case for either courts or fourth-branch bodies. Both courts and non-judicial bodies are vulnerable to threshold design flaws and illegal influence.

60 Mark V. Tushnet, *The New Fourth Branch: Institutions for Protecting Constitutional Democracy*. Cambridge University Press, 2021, 32–33.

61 Ibid.; compare Olabisi D. Akinkugbe and James Thuo Gathii, "Judicial Nullification of Presidential Elections in Africa: *Peter Mutharika v Lazarus Chakera and Saulos Chilima* in Context" (2020), https://papers.ssrn.com/sol3/papers.cfm?abstract_id=3642709.

62 Zeynep Tufekci, *Twitter and Tear Gas*. Yale University Press, 2017.

63 Stephen Holmes, "Saved by Danger/Destroyed by Success. The Argument of Tocqueville's Souvenirs," *European Journal of Sociology* 50(2):171–199 (2009).

Perhaps the longer historical pedigree of judicial independence offers a more secure psychological and social foundation for resisting drift and corruption; or perhaps the *bien-pensant* myth of judges who stand above the fray makes their partisan allegiance more difficult to discern and critique. In respect to the third concern raised above, it is easy (but probably wrong) to assume that courts are worse than legislative or executive bodies at updating principles' legal entailments under new circumstances. The Canadian Charter of Rights and Freedom has famously been viewed as a "living tree," capable of fruitful adaption to new environments.[64] Max Weber's idea that bureaucracy can be hindered by an "iron cage" of rigid doxa and habit has grown into cliché – but holds more than a grain of truth. The dominance of either "living tree" or "originalist" metaphors in the high-level legal culture of a polity may have a greater impact than the abstract choice between judge and bureaucrat.

To the extent that even a rough cut at the question of institutional choice is appropriate, Tushnet's suggestion that overlapping guarantor institutions may well be ex ante desirable seems a good starting point.[65] Rather than trying to read the tea leaves to discern the political future, a designer might write in multiple, seemingly redundant bodies so that at least one does not fail when confronted by an unexpected challenge.[66] Yet even this guidance requires caveats: Where particularized election disputes are concerned, a plurality of forums for contesting an outcome may induce forum-shopping, inconsistent judgments, and even outright conflict because of the lack of a focal-point resolution.[67] Where an election-related dispute requires a quick answer therefore – usually because operative power hangs in the balance – it is likely better to avoid overlap and second-guessing. Perhaps this will lead to a higher rate of erroneous decision-making, but that may be better than a higher-rate of election-related conflicts.

10.5 CONCLUSION

Apex judiciaries have played a significant part in administering elections in many jurisdictions. Success stories as well as cautionary tales abound. To an extent, the courts are likely capable of being replaced by fourth-branch bodies. But the design of the latter raises many of the same questions about "independence" as a judiciary's design. Reinventing the wheel might do little to improve the quality of democracy. For this reason, there may be some small reason to prefer courts in a jurisdiction where de facto judicial independence has been achieved, and more reason to look to fourth-branch institutions where that public good remains an elusive and unrealized goal.

64 Wilfred J. Waluchow, "The Living Tree, Very Much Alive and Still Bearing Fruit: A Reply to the Honourable Bradley W Miller," *Queen's Law Journal* 46: 281 (2020).

65 Tushnet, *The New Fourth Branch*, 22.

66 Aziz Z. Huq, "Forum Choice for Terrorism Suspects," *Duke Law Journal* 61: 1415–1519 (2011).

67 Compare Ginsburg and Elkins, "Ancillary Powers of Constitutional Courts."

11

The Durability and Dynamism of American Indian Constitutional Reform

Elizabeth H. Reese

11.1 INTRODUCTION

There are hundreds of self-governing tribes in the United States. Not all are democracies. Not all have constitutions. But because of cultural and colonial forces, the constitutional democracy is undoubtedly the most common form of tribal government. The constitutional provisions that structure the democracies of American Indian tribes are not only strikingly different from one another, they are by in large far more in flux than the constitutions of United States federal and state governments that colonized them. Within their constitutional structures, tribes are trying out different representative structures, different qualifications for their elected leaders, different restrictions on the right to vote, different practices for voting, and granting different parts of their governments the power to oversee elections.

As this chapter will discuss, many tribes are dynamically remolding their constitutional structures. In doing so they are demonstrating what I suggest is a notably high tolerance for reform or failures that catalyze reform. Nowhere is this dynamism more on display than in the different ways that tribes now politically order themselves – in the reshaping and restructuring of their representative democratic institutions. The takeaway from this chapter is that these tribal governments are carefully experimenting with democracy and that they view the need for institutional change as a moment of *growth* rather than a *failure* in their practice of self-government. Reforms have become an almost natural – if not celebrated – part of perfecting their government structure.

Part of this story of different attitudes to constitutional change is undoubtedly tied to complex origins of many tribal constitutions as well as a humility about the role of law and institutions within the identity of a nation. The two tribes profiled in this chapter demonstrate how tribes have survived and avoided democratic crises – not by having *constitutional structures* that are durable but by having *constitutional cultures* that accept the need for change and value resilience.

11.2 UNINSPIRING CONSTITUTIONAL ORIGINS STORIES

With a few exceptions,[1] the hundreds of self-governance documents that are tribal constitutions began as post-contact creations, written under complex political circumstances often involving varying degrees of pressure, or even oversight from the United States. Most prominently, under the Indian Reorganization Act (IRA) of 1934, Indian tribes were encouraged to adopt, by majority vote, written constitutions that were generally reminiscent of the US federal constitution.[2] The IRA not only made it clear that adopting tribal constitutions was the clear policy preference of the United States but also created an incentive for tribal governments to adopt a constitution: power.

The IRA specified that: "In addition to all powers vested in any Indian tribe or tribal council by existing law, the constitution adopted by said tribe shall also vest in such tribe or its tribal council the following rights and powers: To employ legal counsel; to prevent the sale, disposition, lease, or encumbrance of tribal lands, interests in lands, or other tribal assets without the consent of the tribe; and to negotiate with the Federal, State, and local governments."[3] While the right to retain counsel and negotiate with other governments were arguably rights that tribes already had or were exercising, the right to prevent the further sale of their lands without their consent loomed large against the backdrop of recent federal policies that resulted in the dramatic loss of tribal lands. Ultimately, 181 tribes accepted the IRA, while 77 rejected it.[4] Today, around 60 percent of the 574 federally recognized Indian tribes have a constitutional system with origins in the IRA.[5]

Some tribes who did not adopt IRA constitutions nevertheless adopted written constitutions as a result of efforts from within the tribe to transform their government systems. This, of course, did not happen in a vacuum. The pressures of American colonialism and norms of American democracy had a tremendous effect on tribal

1 Most famously, the Iroquois Confederacy had a constitution, recorded in wampum, that predated the arrival of Europeans to the Americas. See Robert B. Porter, "Building a New Longhouse: The Case for Government Reform within the Six Nations of the Haudenosaunee," *Buffalo Law Review* 46: 805, 814 (1998) (discussing the origins and history of the Iroquois or Haudenosaunee Constitution and contemporary prospects for reform.)

2 Indian Reorganization Act of 1934, Pub. L. No. 73-383, 8 Stat. 984 (1934), Sec. 16; The Harvard Project on American Indian Economic Development, "Introduction," in *The State of the Native Nations: Conditions Under U.S. Policies of Self-Determination*. Oxford University Press, 2008, 19. Following considerable scholarly debate, it is now generally accepted that there was no "model" constitution that the Bureau of Indian Affairs suggested tribes adopt, though several tribes did receive some kind of model document. Elmer R. Rusco, A *Fateful Time: The Background and Legislative History of the Indian Reorganization Act*. University of Nevada Press, 2000; David Wilkins, "Introduction," to *On the Drafting of Tribal Constitutions* ed. Felix S. Cohen. University of Oklahoma Press, 2006.

3 Indian Reorganization Act of 1934, Pub. L. No. 73-383, 8 Stat. 984 (1934), Sec. 16(e).

4 Theodore H. Haas, "Ten Years of Tribal Government Under the I.R.A.," Department of the Interior – United States Indian Service (1947), 3.

5 National Congress of American Indians, "Tribal Nations and the United States: An Introduction" (2020), 22.

decision-making. Some tribes chose American-style constitutional democracies more out of a desire to win favor or approval from the United States than out of genuine admiration for the system or a belief that it was best suited to their project of self-governance. For that reason, even tribes that seemed to have independently chosen constitutional democracies often harbored seeds of structural instability or doubts about the suitability of their constitutions for their own people.[6] Many tribal governments' initial constitutions were not an accurate, or even workable, expression of a tribe's political culture or priorities.[7] That is why the wave of tribal constitutional reforms in the last fifty years is both expected and vital.[8]

Because of these initial circumstances surrounding the adoption of their written constitutions, constitutional reform has become a highly conscientious reckoning for tribes. A reckoning about their past, present, and future identity as Nations.[9] Many, if not most all of these tribes fit the description of postcolonial constitutionalism developed to describe the experience of many other newly independent nations in Africa and Asia who adopted nominal constitutions that largely reflected the constitutional order of their former colonizer and then entered into "a dialectical process involving an ongoing struggle between absorption and rejection of the former colonizer's" institutions, political culture, and identity.[10]

What the constitutional design and reform process of American Indian tribal governments brings to the fore, however, is just how important and transformative *the dialectical process itself* is for political communities who are struggling not only with their relationships to their colonial past (and present), but with their connections to their precolonial past and the character of their hopes for a postcolonial

6 See Robert B. Porter, "Strengthening Tribal Sovereignty through Government Reform: What Are the Issues?," *Kansas Journal Law & Public Policy*: 72, 82 (Winter 1997) (describing such nations as autonomous constitutional governments).

7 Harvard Project, "State of the Native Nations," 19–20 (contrasting several Apache nations who made IRA constitutions work with several Lakota tribes who continue to struggle with political instability).

8 See also, Jason P. Hipp, "Rethinking, Rewriting: Tribal Constitutional Amendment and Reform," *Columbia Journal Race & Law* 4: 73, 81 (2013) (examining tribal constitution drafting as subnational constitutions drafted in the federal framework's shadow or responsive to it); Eric Lemont, "Developing Effective Processes of American Indian Constitutional and Governmental Reform: Lessons from the Cherokee Nation of Oklahoma, Hualapai Nation, Navajo Nation, and Northern Cheyenne Tribe," *American Indian Law Review* 26: 147, 148 (2002).

9 See generally Eric D. Lemont, ed., *American Indian Constitutional Reform and the Rebuilding of Native Nations*. University of Texas Press, 2006; see also Jean Dennison, *Colonial Entanglement: Constituting a Twenty-First-Century Osage Nation*. University of North Carolina Press, 2012; Keith Richotte Jr., *Claiming Turtle Mountain's Constitution: The History, Legacy, and Future of a Tribal Nation's Founding Documents*. University of North Carolina Press, 2017; Gerald Vizenor and Jill Doerfler, *The White Earth Nation: Ratification of a Native Democratic Constitution*. University of Nebraska Press, 2012.

10 Michael Rosenfeld, "Constitutional Identity," in *The Oxford Handbook of Comparative Constitutional Law* ed. Michael Rosenfeld and Andras Sajo. Oxford University Press, 2012, 765–766.

future. Telling a story of political and cultural *continuity* throughout all these changes is a vital part of what holds these nations together. There is no sense that tribes have *failed* as nations if they did not get it right the first time or need to revisit their constitutional structure. Tribal political identities and pride in their self-governance persist despite moments where it was clear that their current government structure was failing them. Instead, there is comfort with recognizing and accepting the need for change – a comfort that has made them remarkably resilient.

The source of this comfort is no mystery. It developed as a reaction to the number of forced changes that tribal governments have experienced already and will undoubtedly continue to experience going forward. Throughout all these changes, these tribes describe their nations as political survivors. These reforms are not simply questions of what form of political ordering can best safeguard rights or express the interests of the people but who the people are now compared to who they were and who they hope to become.[11] No matter what path they choose, the narrative of continuity and survival in the face of change is an animating part of the tribal constitutional reform process. Even when the underlying reforms are quite drastic and could be characterized as re-foundings, they are, importantly, not viewed as such.

11.3 STORIES OF REFORM

The remainder of this chapter showcases two examples of tribal constitutional reform concerning democratic rights and orderings and how the constitutional culture of continuity I described above got them through the democratic reform process, including constitutional crises provoked by factionalism. It presents how these tribes – the Cherokee Nation and the Citizen Potawatomi Nation – have remade the structure of their democratic institutions from the laws delineating citizenship, voting, and office holding to the configuration of their representative institutions themselves.[12] Specifically, it describes how both tribes pulled themselves out of periods of democratic crisis by reforming their constitutions.

[11] Joseph Kalt, "Constitutional Rule and the Effective Governance of Native Nations," in *American Indian Constitutional Reform and the Rebuilding of Native Nations* ed. University of Texas Press, 2006, 185–219; Eric Lemont, "Overcoming the Politics of Reform: The Story of the Cherokee Nation of Oklahoma Constitutional Convention," *American Indian Law Review* 28: 1, 3 (2004) (describing how tribes are "engaged in a fundamental rethinking over how to balance entrenched, western institutions with often competing traditional, cultural and political values"); David E. Wilkins, "Sovereignty, Democracy, Constitution: An Introduction," in *The White Earth Nation: Ratification of a Native Democratic Constitution* ed. Gerald Vizenor and Jill Doerfler. University of Nebraska Press, 2012, 8.

[12] One question that looms in the background of these reforms and their diversity or creativity is just how much tribal nations have been explicitly borrowing from other models, usually foreign ones, or coming up with solutions independently. While this is difficult to know for certain, Eric Lemont has suggested, and my experience largely confirms the intuition that "most

These two tribes have notable differences. While they are both presently located in Oklahoma, they are originally from very different parts of the United States and had quite different precolonial political cultures. They are very different sizes – Citizen Potawatomi has approximately 37,000 citizens,[13] while Cherokee Nation has 430,000 citizens.[14] Although both are constitutional democracies today, Cherokee Nation became one long before the IRA, while Citizen Potawatomi is an IRA tribe.

11.3.1 *Cherokee Nation*

The Cherokee originally occupied territory that extended across seven states in what is now the American South. After a series of treaties between the Cherokee and various southern colonies and, then, eventually, the United States, the tribe had lost a great deal of land but secured promises that their remaining lands and the sovereignty of their borders would be protected thereafter.[15] But the United States broke these treaty promises against the mounting pressure for land in the south and consistent attempts by the southern states to claim authority over Cherokee lands.[16]

Many of Cherokee Nation's leaders hoped that by adapting to American ways, they could bolster the legitimacy of Cherokee Nation's government and its land claims in the eyes of the United States – and maybe even prevent forced removal out west. The Cherokee developed a written form of the Cherokee language that was used to print a tribal newspaper, and in 1827, adopted a written constitution that established a republican form of government for the Cherokee.[17] But removal came despite these changes. Congress, at the urging of newly elected President Andrew Jackson, passed the Indian Removal Act of 1830, and the Cherokee signed the Treaty of New Echota, which relinquished all their original territory in exchange for lands in present-day Oklahoma.

The 1827 Cherokee Nation Constitution created a three-branch system of government with a legislature, executive, and judiciary.[18] The Cherokee legislature, known as the General Council, was composed of two separate bodies, a Committee and Council.[19] Two representatives to the Committee and three representatives to the Council, were each selected by the same eight districts of the Cherokee nation that

American Indian nations have traveled along their own roads of reform in a context of informational isolation." Lemont, "Overcoming the Politics of Reform," 4.

13 "Tribal Rolls," Citizen Potawatomi Nation (2002), www.potawatomi.org/government/tribal-rolls/.

14 "Home," Cherokee Nation of Oklahoma, www.cherokee.org/.

15 Ben O. Bridgers, "An Historical Analysis of the Legal Status of the North Carolina Cherokees," *North Carolina Law Review* 58: 1075, 1077–1078 (1980).

16 Ibid. 1079–1082.

17 Ibid. 1082.

18 Cherokee Nation Constitution of 1827, art. II, sec. 1.

19 Ibid. art. III, sec. 1.

sent delegates to the constitutional convention.[20] The General Council was given the power to select the executive branch leader, the Principal Chief,[21] and to make the laws governing Cherokee elections after the initial election of 1828, other than the requirement that elections be conducted via voice vote.[22] The right to vote was extended to all free male citizens over eighteen[23] and eligibility for General Council was further limited to those over twenty-five.[24] Eligibility for the office of Principal chief was limited to men over thirty-five, and – like the United States Constitution – who were natural born citizens.[25] Though the constitution did not have a Cherokee Nation residency requirement, it specified that citizens who move away from the Nation and "become citizens of any other government" would lose the rights and privileges of Cherokee citizenship unless they petitioned the General Council for readmission.[26]

After removal, the Cherokee Nation was reunited with the Western Cherokee who were already settled out west. The two governments passed a formal act of union[27] and held a new constitutional convention. The constitution ratified in 1839 was quite similar to the one that preceded it.[28] The legislature, now called the National Council, was tasked with dividing the new lands of Cherokee Nation into a new set of eight districts and given the power to add one or two more "if subsequently it should be deemed expedient."[29] They also kept the practice of voice voting.[30] The largest change was to the method of selecting a Principal Chief. The office was now chosen by an at-large vote instead of by the National Council.[31]

The 1839 Constitution governed the Cherokee for about sixty years before the Curtis Act dissolved tribal governments in Indian Territory in 1907 as part of the preparation for transitioning the territory into the State of Oklahoma.[32] The tribe

20 Ibid. preamble, art. III, sec. 2–3.

21 Ibid. art. IV, sec. 1.

22 Ibid. art. III, sec. 6.

23 Ibid. art. III, sec. 7. The Constitution also acknowledged the rights and privileges of the Nation would extend to all descendants of Cherokee women, and those descendants of Cherokee men from a marriage recognized by Cherokee Nation – excluding those offspring that were mixed with Black or non-free persons. Ibid. art. III, sec. 4. There have been considerable disputes about the role of race in Cherokee citizenship, including the rights of former Cherokee Nation Slaves, known as the Freedmen. This includes their rights to citizenship, to vote, and hold political office. This issue – though certainly part of the story of Cherokee reform, particularly since it led to constitutional amendments in 2007, is simply too complex to cover in sufficient detail in this article. For this reason, the rights of Black Cherokees are set aside as beyond the scope of this chapter.

24 Ibid. art. III, sec. 4.

25 Ibid. art. IV, sec. 2.

26 Ibid. art. I, sec. 2.

27 Act of Union between the Eastern and Western Cherokees, July 12, 1838.

28 Cherokee Nation Constitution of 1939, art. II, sec. 1; art. III, sec. 1, 3.

29 Ibid. art. III, sec. 2.

30 Ibid. art. III, sec. 7.

31 Ibid. art. IV, sec. 1.

32 Curtis Act, ch. 517, 30 Stat. 495 (1907).

elected a Chief for the first time since the Curtis Act in 1971, and his first order of business was for the Cherokee Nation to draft a new Constitution[33] for the reconstituted nation that would grow from a mostly defunct entity that funneled resources to members, into robust government once again.[34]

The Cherokee Constitution of 1975 enacted substantial changes to the political arrangements of Cherokee Nation. These changes reflected the vastly changed political circumstances of the Nation, and a very different relationship to the United States than the one the Nation had in the nineteenth century. It did away with the bicameral legislature, instead providing for a single Council composed of fifteen council members who were all elected at-large.[35] This constitution also included the first membership definition, limiting Cherokee citizenship to those persons with ties to the Dawes Commission rolls.[36] The 1975 constitution lowered the age requirement for Principal Chief to thirty and a Cherokee "by blood" requirement was added to the qualifications for both Council and Principal Chief.[37] Voice voting was also eliminated, and secret balloting was adopted instead.[38]

The Council retained the power to regulate elections,[39] however, the most notable change to democratic governance was the inclusion of an entirely new article dedicated to popular referendums, initiatives, and amendments. The people now retained the power to enact referendums, legislation, and constitutional amendments by majority vote and to independently place them on the ballot after obtaining the signatures of 5, 10, or 15 percent of registered Cherokee voters – calculated based on the "total number of votes cast at the last general election for the officer receiving the highest number of votes at such election" – respectively.[40] The constitution specified careful rules for the inclusion and presentation of measures in a popular election, ensuring that overlapping subject matters or measures included on one ballot could not confuse voters.[41] Crucially, the people also retained the exclusive power to call for a constitutional convention and the

33 Will Chavez, "1839 Cherokee Constitution born from Act of Union," *Cherokee Phoenix* (August 26, 2014), www.cherokeephoenix.org/news/1839-cherokee-constitution-born-from-act-of-union/article_5621e3f8-f65c-5990-8af2-c889b21b0abc.html.

34 Lemont, "Overcoming the Politics of Reform," 9–10.

35 According to Chief Swimmer, a bicameral legislature was too "unwieldy" and ill-suited for some of the quick needs to respond and disperse federal funding. Ibid. at 9 (citing Ross Swimmer, former Principal Chief, Cherokee Nation of Oklahoma, Address at John F. Kennedy School of Government Symposium on American Indian Constitutional and Governmental Reform (April 2, 2001) (transcript on file with Eric Lemont).

36 Cherokee Nation Constitution of 1975, art. III, sec. 1–2.

37 Ibid. art. VI, sec. 2; art. IX, sec. 2.

38 Ibid. art. IX, sec. 3.

39 Ibid. art. IX, sec. 3.

40 Ibid. art. XV, sec. 1–3.

41 Ibid. art. XV, sec. 6–8.

possibility of a constitutional convention was required to be submitted to the people at least once every twenty years.[42]

An unconventional change was a few instances of self-imposed subornation to the US federal government. The 1975 Constitution adopted US Constitutional supremacy, stating that "the Cherokee Nation is an inseparable part of the Federal Union. The Constitution of the United States is the Supreme law of the land; therefore, the Cherokee Nation shall never enact any law which is in conflict with any Federal law."[43] Moreover, the 1975 Constitution required that all constitutional amendments be approved by the president of the United States before they could take effect.[44]

After the passage of this new constitution, a series of amendments and Cherokee tribal court cases further tweaked or clarified the Nation's democratic structure. In 1987, the people amended the constitution via referendum to do away with at-large voting for the Tribal Council and return to the old system of representation by legislative districts. The Tribal Council was directed to "establish representative districts which shall be within the historical boundaries of the Cherokee Nation of Oklahoma" that were to be "apportioned to afford a reasonably equal division of tribal membership among the districts."[45] Some voters were taken aback by the Council's decision to require citizens to register in their new districts for the 1995 election and initially challenged the Council's power to institute such a requirement under its new constitutional authority.[46] The Nation's Judicial Appeals Tribunal upheld the Council's actions as a valid exercise of their newly specified powers.[47]

The Cherokee Courts also upheld legislation implementing district-specific residency requirements on Cherokee political candidates as contained within the Council's power to create districts rather than exceeding its power by creating another affirmative qualification for office not otherwise specified in the constitution.[48] Councilmen also brought a lawsuit challenging the Council's decision to pass a law delaying the reapportionment that was necessary after 1994 until 2002 and successfully struck down the district maps that would have been in place in 1999. Council was ordered to draw new maps reapportioned to reflect a

42 Ibid. art. XV, sec. 9.
43 Ibid. art. IX, sec 1.
44 Ibid. art. XV, sec. 10.
45 Ibid. art. V, sec. 3. (amended by Referendum on June 20, 1987, pursuant to Cherokee Nation Council Resolution No. 9-87).
46 *Pfichett v. Cherokee Nation & Election Commission*, No. JAT 95-6 (Cherokee Nation Judicial Appeals Tribunal, July 24, 1995).
47 Ibid.
48 *Terrell v. Cherokee Nation Election Commmission*, No. JAT-99-03, 1999 WL 33589130, at *3 (Cherokee January 27, 1999).

constitutional right to equal representation contained within the 1987 constitutional amendments.[49]

During this period of judicial volleys and reform, however, the Cherokee Nation suffered through a widely publicized constitutional crisis.[50] In the 1995 general election, none of the candidates for Principal Chief received a majority of the votes, and so a runoff was scheduled between the top two candidates, George Bearpaw (38 percent) and Joe Byrd (29 percent).[51] However, ten days before the runoff, two petitions were filed in Cherokee Courts claiming that Bearpaw was ineligible to serve as Principal Chief since he had an Oklahoma felony conviction from twenty years prior.[52] The Tribal Election Commission disqualified Bearpaw and effectively handed the office to Byrd after setting aside all votes Bearpaw received in the runoff.[53] Based on this initial election conflict, battle lines were drawn, distrust was deeply ingrained, and a long shadow was cast over Byrd's administration.

Once he took office, Byrd's political opponents accused him of financial misconduct. Rather than cooperating with the investigators, Byrd delayed turning over documents, forcing the Cherokee Courts to order a search of his office. Byrd responded by first firing all the Cherokee marshals involved in the search and then – once he had been charged with obstruction of justice – leaning on his supporters on Tribal Council to impeach all three members of the Judicial Appeals Tribunal.[54] The marshals and justices kept showing up to work until Byrd sent officers to confiscate the marshals weapons and close down the courthouse. The tribal prosecutor who protested the shutdown was arrested for resisting and then Byrd fired the tribe's other prosecutor – leaving the courthouse entirely empty as of August 1997.[55] Outraged, the minority of the Tribal Council who opposed Byrd's actions started boycotting Council meetings in April 1998, denying them a quorum to conduct business for over a year until the courts were reopened.[56]

What saved the nation from this political crisis was an unlikely provision of their constitution and a decision that predated the crisis. In the same 1995 general election that led to the Bearpaw–Byrd runoff, the question of a constitutional convention was on the ballot, as article XV, section 9 of the constitution requires

49 *Lay v. Cherokee Nation*, No. JAT-97-05, 1998 WL 34067267 (Cherokee December 9, 1998) (striking down Cherokee Legislative Act 7–97, Section 4(C), (D) codified as 26 CNCA Section 4(C), (D), as unconstitutional under Cherokee Nation Constitution of 1975, art. V, sec 3).

50 Lemont, "Developing Effective Processes," 157.

51 *In Re: Contest of Joe Byrd as Announced Elected Candidate for Principal Chief v. Joe Byrd (or Chad Smith v. Joe Byrd)*, No. JAT-95-09 (Cherokee Nation J. App. Tribunal, August 25, 1995), slip op at 5 n.1.

52 Lois Romano, "A Nation Divided," *Washington Post* (July 17, 1997), www.washingtonpost.com/archive/lifestyle/1997/07/17/a-nation-divided/209aae32-9fc5-459f-8897-00328a9e7b64/.

53 *In Re: Contest of Joe Byrd as Announced Elected Candidate for Principal Chief v. Joe Byrd (or Chad Smith v. Joe Byrd)*, No. JAT-95-09 (Cherokee Nation J. App. Tribunal, August 25, 1995).

54 Romano, "A Nation Divided."

55 Ibid.

56 Lemont, "Overcoming the Politics of Reform," 11.

must happen at least once every twenty years.[57] The Cherokee people had voted overwhelmingly for a constitutional convention, and after languishing for several years as a lower priority for the tribal council, the opportunity for reform coincided with the political crisis.

After consulting with outside experts on how to avoid letting the divisions take over the reform process, the Rules Committee decided to create a commission that would be composed of two representatives appointed from each branch and a seventh member chosen collectively by the first six.[58] Byrd loyalists would control the executive appointments, and the judiciary was staunchly anti-Byrd after his attempts to oust them. With the Tribal Council splitting their two members between Byrd and anti-Byrd factions that divided the body, the selection process ensured that the commission would be evenly divided. To further give credibility to the commission, the commissioners agreed to hold open meetings, took an oath of political neutrality, to act only upon unanimity, and to promise not to hold political offices in the new government. The Council attempted to limit the commission's authority to an advisory role for the Council, but the commission successfully preserved its independence by threatening to walk away entirely.[59] The commission's enabling legislation thus made it an entirely "independent commission" with the authority to put either a new constitution or set of amendments directly on the ballot.[60]

The commissioners set about their work, holding twenty meetings across Cherokee nation and in major US cities where a large number of Cherokee citizens lived.[61] The commission cataloged suggestions for reform by topic and frequency, accepted written testimony, and ultimately created an eight-hundred-page record of testimony from Cherokee citizens.[62]

The next task was selecting delegates for the convention. The commission decided on seventy-nine delegates composed of the seven commissioners, eight delegates each selected by the current branches of government, twenty-four delegates selected from a pool of those citizens who testified at the hearings, and twenty-four chosen by lottery from a pool of citizens who had either submitted a written request to serve as a delegate or had given oral or written testimony.[63] The constitutional convention was called to order on February 26, 1999. After nine days

57 Cherokee Nation Constitution of 1975, art. XV, sec. 9.

58 Lemont, "Overcoming the Politics of Reform," 12–13.

59 Ibid. 14.

60 Act Creating a Constitution Convention Commission § 4A, Legislative Act No. 10-98 (Cherokee Nation May 15, 1998).

61 D. Jay Hannah, "The 1999 Constitution Convention of the Cherokee Nation," 35 *Arizona State Law Journal* 35: 1, 7 (2003).

62 Ibid. 7–8.

63 Ibid. 8.

of deliberation – the records of which capture around three-thousand pages of discussion – a new constitution was adopted by the convention on March 6, 1999.[64]

The new constitution, notably, created term limits for both the executive and legislative officers,[65] as well as staggered terms for the appointed judiciary to avoid court-stacking.[66] It also addressed the removal problems that had so quickly escalated in the recent political crisis. The Tribal Council kept its power to remove all elected and appointed officials, but this power was now limited to specific for cause failings such as willful neglect or a felony, requiring a two-thirds majority vote for removal and only after a trial before the Tribal Council that afforded the accused officials due process.[67] The judiciary, moreover, was given an additional removal protection in the creation of a Court of the Judiciary – made-up of seven persons using the same appointment process as the constitutional commissioners – that had the power to recommend removal of judicial officers.[68] On top of all of these new removal protections, the people were given the power to separately recall any elected official.[69]

To address the reality that 40 percent of Cherokee Nation citizens now lived outside the boundaries of the reservation, the 1999 Constitution created two new Council seats,[70] which would be chosen at-large by the off-reservation members of Cherokee Nation.[71] A separate election commission was also created to independently administer elections.[72] Finally, the 1999 Constitution removed the incorporation of the United States Constitution and the requirement that the president approve any amendments to the Constitution.

This last change, however, put the Nation in a bit of a legal bind. Article XV, Section 10 of the 1975 Constitution plainly required that no amendment or new Constitution shall become effective without the approval of the president of the United States or his authorized representative. The draft 1999 constitution had been submitted to the BIA, but the Nation spent years in an elaborate and, at times, contentious back and forth over its approval. At one point the Nation sought more limited approval for simply an amendment removing the presidential approval requirement. Talks eventually broke down in 2002, leading the Nation to give up and set elections for removing BIA oversight on May 24, 2003, and then the new

64 Ibid. 11–12.
65 Cherokee Nation Constitution, art. VI, sec. 3; art. VII, sec 1.
66 Ibid. art. VIII, sec. 3.
67 Ibid. art. VIII, sec. 8; art. XI, sec 1–3.
68 Ibid. art. VIII, sec. 5.
69 Ibid. art. VIII, sec. 8; art. XI, sec 4.
70 Lemont, "Developing Effective Processes," 163–164.
71 Cherokee Nation Constitution, art. VI, sec. 3.
72 Ibid. art. IX, sec. 1–2.

constitution on July 26, 2003.[73] The 1999 Cherokee Constitution passed – narrowly – via popular vote on July 26, 2003.[74]

Though the constitutionality of the new constitution's adoption without presidential consent was challenged, the Nation's Supreme Court ultimately held that the people had the "inherent sovereign power" to "remove the self-imposed requirement" of presidential approval,[75] and thus, "the 1999 Constitution of the Cherokee Nation became effective on July 26, 2003."[76]

Per the requirements of the 1999 Constitution, the Council has been tasked with drawing and redrawing the fifteen legislative districts. On one occasion, their map was struck down by the Cherokee Courts since the districts deviated by 22.8 percent from equal representation.[77] On another occasion, the districts were upheld when they came close to 10 percent deviation, as the court acknowledged both deference to the Council where possible and that the 10 percent rule was persuasive guidance.[78]

Since 2003, the Nation has continued to have disputes over elections, but none have resulted in a similar crisis. In perhaps one of the best tests of the new Constitution's institutions, history closely repeated itself, but the nation avoided the political turmoil and crisis that followed the Byrd–Bearpaw crisis. In 2019, just days before the election, the Cherokee Nation Supreme Court upheld the Election Commission's decision, just a few weeks previously, to disqualify one of the leading candidates for Principal Chief for accepting illegal campaign contributions.[79] The candidate, councilmen David Walkingstick, had run a divisive campaign that criticized the Nation's ties to the Democratic Party[80] and though he claimed the election was "stolen,"[81] nothing else came of it. And more recently, in the 2021 election, a candidate for Tribal Council was disqualified by the Election Commission for accepting improper campaign contributions but did not contest the election even though he lost by only seven votes.[82] The Nation even survived a

[73] Hannah, "The 1999 Constitution Convention," 13–19.

[74] *In re Status & Implementation of 1999 Constitution of Cherokee Nation*, 65 American Tribal Law 63, 65 No. JAT 05-04, 2006 WL 5940407 (Cherokee Nation Sup. Ct, June 7, 2006).

[75] Ibid.

[76] Ibid. 67

[77] *Cowan-Watts v. Smith*, 10 American Tribal Law 297, 299 (Cherokee Nation Sup. Ct., November 18, 2010).

[78] *Anglen v. Council of the Cherokee Nation*, 12 American Tribal Law 140, 142 (2013).

[79] *In Re: the Protest of Chelsea Huber to Disqualify David Walkingstick as a candidate for Principal Chief*, No. SC-2019-07 (Cherokee Nation Sup. Ct., May 29, 2019).

[80] Graham Lee Brewer, "The Cherokee Nation's Next Chief Will Have a Big Footprint in Indian Country," *High Country News* (May 29, 2019), www.hcn.org/articles/tribal-affairs-the-cherokee-nations-next-chief-will-have-a-big-footprint-in-indian-country.

[81] "A 'Stolen' Election? Cherokee Nation Proceeds to Vote without Candidate David Walkingstick," Indianz.com (May 19, 2019), www.indianz.com/News/2019/05/29/a-stolen-election-cherokee-nation-procee.asp.

[82] Joe Tomlinson, "Cherokee Nation Election Concludes with Disqualified Candidate, Failed Legal Challenge," Nondoc (August 10, 2021), https://nondoc.com/2021/08/10/cherokee-nation-election-concludes/.

Bush–Gore style election in 2011, where the election was so close that the winner changed several times in various recounts[83] and so the Supreme Court threw out the election and ordered a new one after deciding that it would be "impossible to determine the results with mathematical certainty."[84]

Through all of these election showdowns that tested the current formulation of Cherokee Nation's institutions, they have held strong. And the legacy of Cherokee Nationhood remains one of change, continuity, and resilience all the way back to their original constitution. As their current Principal Chief, Chuck Hoskin, describes: "As the U.S. was growing around the Cherokee Nation … we changed how we governed ourselves …. We developed a written constitution. We elected a chief. We centralized in strength and our government so we could deal with what was happening around us."[85]

11.3.2 *Citizen Potawatomi Nation of Oklahoma*

The people who currently make up the Citizen Potawatomi Nation were once part of a confederation of tribes that included the Anishinaabe Nations of the Potawatomi, Ojibwe, and Odawa that originally controlled a large territory in the Great Lakes region of the United States.[86] However, by the late eighteenth century, white settlers and US treaties had eroded the Confederacy's land base such that the United States was able to forcibly remove the three Nations.[87] In 1838, the Potawatomi were removed by the US military on what is called the "Trail of Death" from northern Indiana to Kansas.[88] In 1861, the Potawatomi in Kansas were offered a treaty that would require them to surrender tribal membership in exchange for US citizenship and private land ownership in Oklahoma.[89] Those who took the deal and moved to Oklahoma are now the Indians who make up the Citizen Potawatomi.

The Citizen Potawatomi's original 1938 constitution was based on the Oklahoma Indian Welfare Act[90] model – an Oklahoma-specific IRA. It left all major decisions

[83] Will Chavez, "2011 Chief's Race Tumultuous, 2015 Election Decided !uickly," *Cherokee Phoenix* (May 16, 2019), www.cherokeephoenix.org/news/2011-chiefs-race-tumultuous-2015-election-decided-quickly/article_5a12bde0-3316-5efd-baaf-832552e6bb03.html.

[84] *In the Matter of the 2011 General Election*, No. SC-11-06 (Cherokee Nation Sup. Ct., July 2, 2011).

[85] "Cherokee Nation Chief Speaks on Tribal History at OSU," *Oklahoma State University News* (February 3, 2020), https://news.okstate.edu/articles/communications/2020/cherokee-nation-chief-speaks-on-tribal-history-at-osu.html.

[86] "Culture," Citizen Potawatomi Nation, www.potawatomi.org/culture/.

[87] Ibid.

[88] "Native History: Potawatomi Removed at Gunpoint, Trail of Death Begins," *Indian Country Today* (September 4, 2014).

[89] "The Treaty of 1861 Is CPN Origin Story," Citizen Potawatomi Nation, (November 16, 2016), www.potawatomi.org/the-treaty-of-1861-is-cpn-origin-story/.

[90] 25 USC. §§ 501–509.

up to a "Council," which was composed of all members over the age of twenty-one who attended a meeting on the last Thursday in June.[91] The meetings were chaotic and unproductive, and so in 1985 the tribe passed a constitutional amendment that redefined its supreme governing body as the entire voting electorate allowed for referendums by ballot. This reform allowed absentee voters to participate for the first time, a vital change given the diaspora of their population.[92]

In 1930, the vast majority of Indian people continued to live in rural reservation communities, with barely 10 percent of the total Native population living in urban areas.[93] However, as a result of federal relocation policies[94] and high rates of Native military service in World War II, by 1980 nearly half the population of Native people lived in urban areas.[95] The Citizen Potowatomi were no exception to this phenomenon. The Dust Bowl in the 1930s also contributed to their citizens moving away from Oklahoma, such that by the 2000s, two-thirds of the Citizen Potawatomi Nation's citizens moved far from the tribe's lands in Oklahoma and lived throughout the rest of the United States.[96] By this time, the tribe had politically stabilized and was experiencing rapid economic growth.[97] However, the Nation struggled with low voter turnout – especially from absentee voters – and a general sense of "apathy" about the nation's government.[98] The Nation "decided to take the government to the people" and held meetings throughout the United States to solicit input from the large populations of off-reservation Citizen Potawatomi.[99] The result was a decision to completely overhaul the government in order to reengage the nation's off-reservation population.

In 2007, the Nation amended its constitution to include a legislature comprising sixteen legislators.[100] Eight of these legislators are chosen from new legislative

[91] Citizen Potowatami Constitution art. iii; art. iv (1938).

[92] "Modern Tribal Governments, Constitutions, and Sovereignty: John 'Rocky' Barrett," NCAI, www.youtube.com/watch?v=XzbGOny8IS8 (hereinafter Rocky Video).

[93] C. Matthew Snipp, "The Size and Distribution of the American Indian Population: Fertility, Mortality, Migration, and Residence," in *National Research Council (US) Committee on Population, Changing Numbers, Changing Needs: American Indian Demography and Public Health* ed. Gary D. Sandefur, Ronald R. Rindfuss, and Barney Cohen. National Academy Press, 1996, www.ncbi.nlm.nih.gov/books/NBK233098/.

[94] See, generally, The Indian Relocation Act of 1956, Pub. L. No. 84-959, 70 Stat. 986 (1956) (federal program offering reservation Indians financial assistance and job training if they moved to cities in the hopes of assimilating Indians into the population of major urban areas).

[95] See Snipp, "Size and Distribution," 13.

[96] "Constitutional Reform," Citizen Potowatomi Nation – 2010 and 2014 Honoring Nations Award (July 1, 2010), The Harvard Project on American Indian Economic Development, https://embed.culturalspot.org/embed/exhibit/pwJyYYg1eea1Lg; Rocky Video.

[97] "Honoring Nations All Stars Profile: Constitutional Reform Citizen Potawatomi Nation," Harvard Program on American Indian Economic Development 5 (2014) (hereinafter All Stars) (the tribe went from contributing $55 million to the Oklahoma economy in 2001, to $350 million in 2006).

[98] Ibid. 6.

[99] Rocky Video.

[100] All Stars, 1.

districts drawn to equally represent citizens who live outside the state of Oklahoma, while five are chosen from districts within the state of Oklahoma and three belong to the at-large elected executive officials.[101] The tribe recognized that there was a risk that out-of-state constituents would be incentivized to undervalue in-state interests (such as land purchases) and so divided the legislature's weighted representation. Although out-of-state citizens make up two-thirds of the population, they receive only half of the seats on the legislature.[102] Similarly, an Oklahoma residency requirement ensures that executive positions are tied to in-state interests, although they are elected by Nation-wide popular vote.[103]

In 2017, Citizen Potawatomi conducted its first ten-year constitutionally mandated redistricting to reflect population growth.[104] Overall voter participation for the nation doubled as a result of these changes in the structure of the legislature. Moreover, the Nation saw significant increases in other forms of civic engagement and cultural participation. With these reforms, the Nation also achieved geographic participation parity, with out-of-state voters comprising 67 percent of the vote.[105]

The scope and impact of the Citizen Potawatomi system make it unique even compared to the handful of international examples of expatriate voting districts or other tribes such as the Cherokee Nation, which also provides for off-Reservation representation. Unlike in these cases, extraterritorial resident citizens are far from the exception. The Citizen Potawatomi extraterritorial districts make up half of their legislature. As such, Potawatomi legislative restructuring was not only a way to increase voter turnout and grant more of a voice to extraterritorial citizens, it was also a bold statement about how the Citizen Potawatomi view citizens across the country. These citizens are an important part of the Nation, as opposed to citizens who left the Nation by leaving its geographic borders.[106] Citizen Potawatomi pulled themselves out of a period of dysfunctional governance and voter apathy, like the Cherokee, through not only simple swift constitutional fixes but also constitutional changes that involved elaborate processes and rigorous processes that engaged their entire electorate.

11.4 CONCLUSION

The choices that the two tribes have made reveals the strange boon that the chaos of colonialism has been for them. There have been countless disruptions or

[101] Citizen Potawatomi Constitution art. 7; art. 12.
[102] Rocky Video.
[103] Ibid.
[104] Ibid.
[105] All Stars, 9.
[106] See Peter J. Spiro, "Perfecting Political Diaspora," *New York University Law Review* 81: 207, 207 (2006) ("political rights of nonresident citizens" indicates a "changed conception of citizenship and nationhood, as political membership decouples from territorial location").

interference with their ability to freely self-govern, and yet, the tribe's political identity and will to self-govern persisted. The undeniable limitations and even outright failings of some of their governing documents allows for tribal constitutional reform efforts to not only be easier to achieve but seems to have allowed for tribes to think more creatively about their reforms than they would have if they were more strictly wedded to their prior version of democratic ordering. This complex postcolonial dialectic of institution building through constitutional reordering seems to be, in short, liberating for tribes who can contemplate and implement creative solutions to even their most basic political orderings problems.

The constitutional structure of representation and elections, in other words, has become one of the most important sites for American Indian tribal nations to set the boundaries and substance of their identities as nations. As Citizen Potowatomi Chairman Barrett puts it: "If you're not in the constitution-fixing business, you're not in economic development, you're not in self-governance; you're not sovereign."[107] And as Cherokee Nation Principal Chief Hoskin describes, the resilience of tribal governments is a key part of their identity as nations: "We were torn apart politically; our economy was destroyed, [and y]ou would predict it would take decades or generations to come back if they ever did. But what happened next is I think is one of the most remarkable stories in the history . . . of this country and the world. We rebuilt within about a decade. We invested in a system of law and justice. We have to remember, and we have to remind people . . . what the Indian nations have gone through."[108]

A key takeaway from these experiences, is the value of seeing the usefulness of failure – even in a democracy or a constitution – and the durability of the commitment to self-governance as a continual process rather than a singular ideal that can be perfected and captured in a single document.

[107] All Stars, 9.
[108] "Cherokee Nation Chief Speaks on Tribal History at OSU."

12

Eternity Clauses and Electoral Democracy

Silvia Suteu

Whether in the 'old' key of militant democracy or in the newer one of democratic backsliding, the question of how constitutions can insulate against the erosion of democratic institutions remains ever fresh. Much has changed in this landscape, however. Experiences with populists in power and authoritarian takeovers the world over have cast doubt on long-standing certainties. The faith in courts and constitutional review as preeminent tools of legal protection of democracy and fundamental rights has been shaken by the reality of captured courts and eroded judicial independence. With it, too, the belief that detailed constitutional bills of rights would reign in arbitrary power.

The search for legal institutions to uphold and strengthen democracy's foundations has instead turned to other horizons. One of these, explored in this chapter, is the turn to eternity clauses and the prospect that constitutional unamendability could act as a stronger barrier against democratic erosion through otherwise legal means. The hope is a familiar one: that when faced with procedurally legitimate constitutional amendments that undermine or even 'dismember' the constitution, substantive hurdles should remain in place that sanction these amendments as illegitimate and unconstitutional.[1] We saw this hope raised and swiftly dashed in Hungary after the Orban government embarked on constitutional change to entrench its hold on power and before the disempowerment of the Hungarian Constitutional Court. During that period, some hoped the Court would embrace an unconstitutional constitutional amendment doctrine to allow it to prevent, delay, or at least signal the authoritarian takeover veiled in legality.[2] More recently, we

[1] Yaniv Roznai, *Unconstitutional Constitutional Amendments: The Limits of Amendment Powers*. Oxford University Press, 2017; Richard Albert, *Constitutional Amendments: Making, Breaking, and Changing Constitutions*. Oxford University Press, 2019; Silvia Suteu, *Eternity Clauses in Democratic Constitutionalism*. Oxford University Press, 2021.

[2] Gábor Halmai, 'Unconstitutional Constitutional Amendments: Constitutional Courts as Guardians of the Constitution?', *Constellations* 19(2): 182–203 (2012); Fruzsina Gárdos-Orosz, 'Unamendability as a Judicial Discovery? Inductive Learning Lessons from Hungary', in *An Unamendable Constitution? Unamendability in Constitutional Democracies* ed. Richard Albert and Bertil Emrah Oder. Springer, 2018, 231; Rosalind Dixon and David Landau, 'Transnational

witnessed Kenyan courts embrace the idea of substantive limits on constitutional amendment and even consider embracing a basic structure doctrine to block the president-initiated Building Bridges Initiative (BBI) package that would have transformed the Kenyan Constitution.[3] We have also seen calls for the unconstitutional constitutional amendment doctrine itself to be adapted to the realities of our populist/authoritarian times, such as by renouncing judicial self-restraint in reviewing amendments and adopting a more holistic interpretation of their cumulative effects.[4]

Doubts have remained, however, including expressed by this author, as to whether unamendability is indeed the answer to democratic backsliding, or whether it is itself salvageable from the clutches of populists and authoritarians in power.[5] That scepticism has been grounded in the ambivalent operation of unamendability in practice, whether as a bargaining tool during constitution-making processes or when enforced judicially. This reality includes the propensity of eternity clauses to entrench partisan hold on power as well as to essentialise political identity. As we will see, this ties into the complex relationship between eternity clauses and electoral democracy. The tension between unamendability and democracy has of course received ample attention. Comparatively underexplored has been the particular type of democracy eternity clauses seek to protect, how that relates to the specific constitutional context in which they are adopted, and how this more specific understanding of democracy influences the unconstitutional constitutional amendment doctrines developed by local courts. In particular, the relationship between unamendable democratic commitments and the electoral arena is ripe for close examination.

This chapter seeks to fill this gap. It explores the link between eternity clauses and electoral democracy by looking at two instances of applied unamendable democracy: party bans, whether direct or indirect, and the protection of parliamentary mandates. Both types of interventions are operated in the name of guarding democracy, whether against anti-democratic forces, as in the case of party bans, or against weakening core democratic institutions, as in the case of parliamentary mandates. These two approaches are illustrated via a range of case studies: the ban of anti-democratic parties in Germany; bans of ethnic, separatist, and religious parties in Turkey; indirect unamendability and its chilling effect on party competition in Israel; and the judicial protection of parliamentary mandates as unamendable in

Constitutionalism and a Limited Doctrine of Unconstitutional Constitutional Amendment', *International Journal of Constitutional Law* 13(3): 606 (2015).

3 Tom Ginsburg, Adem K. Abebe, and Rosalind Dixon, 'Constitutional Amendment and Term Limit Evasion in Africa', in *Comparative Constitutional Law in Africa* ed. Rosalind Dixon, Tom Ginsburg, and Adem K. Abebe. Edward Elgar, 2022, 54.

4 Yaniv Roznai and Tamar Hostovsky Brandes, 'Democratic Erosion, Populist Constitutionalism, and the Unconstitutional Constitutional Amendments Doctrine', *Law & Ethics of Human Rights* 14(1): 19–48 (2020).

5 Suteu, *Eternity Clauses in Democratic Constitutionalism.*

Czechia. These are indeed meant to be illustrations of the problems I discuss, rather than to be taken as prototypical examples. The wide range of democracy type covered provides insights into the very different understanding, enforcement, and effects of unamendability in consolidated, transitional, and hybrid democracies.

Underpinning this work is the belief that unamendability cannot be adequately understood, and its propensity as democratic defence evaluated, divorced from the constitutional politics within which it is embedded. As part of that politics, questions of electoral balance of power, health of the party system, and politicisation of court intervention must be faced head on. Doing so engenders scepticism about unamendability as an unquestionable ally in the fight to protect democracy. I hope to show that unamendability's propensity to be misused and to lead to distorted outcomes is greater precisely in those contexts where it is most likely to be adopted: incomplete or fragile democracies seeking to entrench a path towards consolidation (hence also my choice of case studies). I also argue, however, that the bluntness and open-ended nature of unamendability risks having a chilling effect on electoral democracy in stable democratic contexts as well. Thus, we should not merely assume that eternity clauses and the judicial doctrines surrounding them will be democracy-enhancing. When we instead investigate their operation in context and across time, including by evaluating their effect upon the electoral arena, we find them to sometimes misfire or even backfire as democratic defences.

12.1 UNAMENDABILITY AND ELECTORAL COMPETITION: PARTY BANS

One could say the very essence of eternity clauses is to protect democracy from its enemies. We can view such provisions as a prime legal embodiment of the ethos of militant democracy: a constitutional democracy should be able to defend itself against those who seek to undermine its very foundations, including against those who seek to do so via constitutional amendment. In language that has now become the norm, eternity clauses would thus be viewed as prime weapons against 'abusive constitutionalism'.[6] They would thus complement other measures, such as electoral thresholds, designed to prevent the fragmentation of parliamentary politics as led to the downfall of the Weimar Republic, as well as party bans, aimed at preventing anti-democratic forces from even operating on the electoral arena.[7] A recent attempt at classifying the constitutional elements of militant democracy listed unamendability alongside other tools such as term limits, loyalty oaths, the right to resist,

6 David Landau, 'Abusive Constitutionalism', *UC Davis Law Review* 47: 189–260 (2013).

7 Rivka Weil, 'On the Nexus of Eternity Clauses, Proportional Representation, and Banned Political Parties', *Election Law Journal* 16(2): 237–246 (2017).

emergency provisions, and civilian control of the military, to be deployed depending on the nature of the threat.[8]

The logic of party bans overlaps with that of unconstitutional constitutional amendment doctrines. Just as the latter seeks to prevent otherwise procedurally sound amendments when they substantively undermine democracy and the rule of law, so too party bans seek to prevent not just parties that advocate or engage in violence but also those that threaten 'a "legal" anti-democratic takeover of the state apparatus'.[9] The hope is that when such subterfuge is afoot, there remain legal resources for courts to intervene before the whole democratic edifice is taken down.

However, we can find more direct connections between party bans and eternity clauses. One of the distinctions between rationales for party bans traces a shift from Weimar-inspired bans to a 'legitimacy paradigm'.[10] The former are aimed at parties that seek to abolish democracy wholesale and have been enforced against Nazi, fascist, communist, and, more recently, Islamist parties. The latter seeks to justify the proscription of those parties that 'threaten certain elements within the liberal constitutional order, such as commitment to equality and non-discrimination, the absolute commitment to a nonviolent resolution of disputes or secularism'.[11] This has led to bans on ethnic and religious parties, which have assumed the place of ideological parties in the postwar period.[12] However, the logic of Weimar – the fear that mass parties gone awry would destroy democracy wholesale – does not apply neatly to religious and ethnic parties, particularly in a pluralist, multicultural society.[13] Challenges to political identity are vaguer, more diffuse, and therefore more elusive than frontal attacks on democratic institutions, and the danger of essentialising identity – itself a catch-all concept – may be inherent in such bans.[14] Eternity clauses, especially those insulating state characteristics such as the form of government, territorial integrity or unity, official language or religion/secularism, are precisely aimed at defining such a political identity and placing it beyond the reach of political contestation.[15]

[8] Zachary Elkins, 'Militant Democracy and the Pre-emptive Constitution: From Party Bans to Hardened Term Limits', *Democratization* 29(1): 174–198 (2022).

[9] Matthijs Bogaards, Matthias Basedau, and Christof Hartmann. 'Ethnic Party Bans in Africa: An Introduction', *Democratization* 17(4): 605 (2010).

[10] Gur Bligh, 'Defending Democracy: A New Understanding of the Party-Banning Phenomenon', *Vanderbilt Journal of Transnational Law*: 1321–1380 (2013); Angela K. Bourne and Fernando Casal Bértoa, 'Mapping "Militant Democracy": Variation in Party Ban Practices in European Democracies (1945–2015)', *European Constitutional Law Review* 13: 221, 243 (2017).

[11] Bligh, 'Defending Democracy', 1345.

[12] Nancy L. Rosenblum, 'Banning Parties: Religious and Ethnic Partisanship in Multicultural Democracies', *Law & Ethics of Human Rights* 1(1): 17–59, 22 (2007).

[13] Ibid., 23.

[14] Ibid., 59.

[15] Suteu, *Eternity Clauses in Democratic Constitutionalism*, ch. 1.

The move away from the Weimar paradigm, then, elevates the risk that party bans be abused for partisan purposes.[16] One example would be government self-entrenchment against political opponents, the latter recast as enemies of liberal democracy and as such eliminated from political competition. There is also a heightened danger that party proscription follows a process of 'securitisation', such as bans in the name of protecting 'national communities from challenges to core identities and values'.[17] Religious, ethnic, and regional parties, whose banning may compound discrimination already experienced by the communities they represent, are most likely to be cast as 'existential threats' to the state and as a consequence would also see legitimate avenues for political expression and contestation closed off.[18] Insofar as the status quo is the baseline against which unlawful party ideology and behaviour is to be measured, parties organised precisely to contest that status quo become pariahs by default.[19] As we will see, party bans in conjunction with constitutional unamendability compound these dangers and judicial oversight may not in fact act as the neutral safeguard some have hoped it to be.[20]

I will discuss three instantiations of these different rationales: party bans in the name of a democratic principle enshrined in an eternity clause, illustrated by Germany; bans of ethnic, separatist, or religious parties in the name of unamendable secularism or territorial integrity and unity, such as in Turkey; and indirect restrictions, where parties are not banned outright but prevented from standing for elections for alleged breaches of state ideology, as in Israel. Insights from other national contexts are brought in where relevant. These examples show how unamendability has been deployed to reinforce democracy not just at a high level of abstraction or in its minimal understanding but in response to locally specific evaluations of democratic threats, sometimes with the effect of significantly skewing the electoral arena. In some cases, such as Germany's, courts have been astute at modulating the forcefulness of their intervention over time, balancing the threat posed by a given party against the anti-democratic effects of its ban. In other instances, however, such as Turkey's, courts have adopted a much more rigid approach, reinforced by an extensive eternity clause. In others still, such as Israel's, party bans have reinforced an ever more exclusionary notion of citizenship.

I will show that the entrenchment of democracy through eternity clauses, whether explicit or implicit, is not always limited to minimal conceptions of democracy. Nor, indeed, is it always interpreted by courts and other constitutional actors as leaving room for the contestation of a single, sometimes exclusionary conception of democracy. In practice, such interpretations have led to party bans and interventions in parliamentary politics that at least in some instances have

16 Bligh, 'Defending Democracy', 1377.
17 Bourne and Casal Bértoa 'Mapping "Militant Democracy"', 246.
18 Bligh 'Defending Democracy', 1378; Rosenblum 'Banning Parties', 58.
19 Rosenblum 'Banning Parties', 60.
20 See Bligh 'Defending Democracy', 1378–1379.

silenced reasonable disagreement and reduced electoral competition. As such, and like other types of eternity clauses, there is a dark side to democratic unamendability of which it is imperative we remain vigilant.[21] Put differently, the constitutional entrenchment of democratic commitments to the point of rendering them unamendable may yet undermine rather than strengthen those same commitments.

12.1.1 *Anti-democratic Parties*

The most straightforward case for a democratic defence involving prohibiting parties would seem to be that involving those organisations advocating for democracy's very demise. Germany's Basic Law is often analysed as the epitome of a constitution that embraces militant democratic goals. It does so, among other means, by enshrining the democratic principle (Article 20(1)), which it then renders unamendable through the *Ewigkeitsklausel* in Article 79(3). Importantly, however, the Basic Law for the first time recognised political parties as constitutional actors and enshrined their protection as well as their duties in Article 21. Thus, they are recognised as opinion formers but also required to be internally democratic, publicly accountable financially, and – according to Article 21(2) – they are subject to the Federal Constitutional Court which can rule them unconstitutional should 'their aims or the behaviour of their adherents, seek to undermine or abolish the free democratic basic order or to endanger the existence of the' state. Article 21 therefore aims to walk the tightrope between extending constitutional protection to parties, in direct response to the perceived failures of Weimar and its poorly institutionalised party structure,[22] while at the same time requiring them to abide by the democratic rules of the game under threat of unconstitutionality.

There have been two successful party ban cases in Germany: the Socialist Reich Party (the party-heir to the Nazis) and the Communist Party, both in the immediate post-war years.[23] In banning both parties, the Constitutional Court laid out its test in such cases as involving assessing a party's internal structure and public actions and statements and opting for the ban only when the party seeks to topple supreme fundamental values of the free democratic order that are embodied in the Basic Law. The Court did not, in the two cases, rely on Article 79(3) for its determination. The link to the eternity clause was indirect, insofar as the democratic principle under threat was unamendable. Its unamendability signalled its centrality to the constitutional order, as well as its non-negotiable status.

[21] Suteu, *Eternity Clauses in Democratic Constitutionalism*, 3.

[22] Cindy Skach, *Borrowing Constitutional Designs: Constitutional Law in Weimar Germany and the French Fifth Republic*. Princeton University Press, 2005, 38, 52–57, 68; Cindy Skach, 'Political Parties and the Constitution', in *The Oxford Handbook of Comparative Constitutional Law* ed. Michel Rosenfeld and András Sajó. Oxford University Press, 2012, 878.

[23] 2 BVerfGE 1 (1952) ('*Socialist Reich Party*') and 5 BVerfGE 85 (1956) ('*Communist Party*').

More recently, the German Constitutional Court changed its approach to party bans. This was seen in the 2017 attempt to ban the Neo-Nazi Nationaldemokratische Partei Deutschlands (NPD), which the Court declined to do on account of the party's perceived electoral insignificance and the strength of German democracy against such threats.[24] The Court no longer found it sufficient for a party to be shown to pursue anti-constitutional aims; proof of its potential to be successful would now also be required: 'a presumption that the criterion of "seeking" has been met only if there are specific weighty indications suggesting that it is at least possible that a political party's actions directed against the goods protected under Article 21(2) GG may succeed (potentiality)'.[25] Given the extreme nature of a ban, the Court would henceforth impose one only if the political party has sufficient means to exert influence due to which it does not appear to be entirely unlikely that the party will succeed in achieving its anti-constitutional aims, and if it actually makes use of its means to exert influence.[26]

In other words, even while the criteria developed in the 1950s cases might have otherwise led to a ban, the Court balanced this against the perceived consolidation of German democracy, which was deemed robust enough not to need to go down the more militant route of a ban.

Importantly, the 2017 judgment for the first time clarified the relationship between Article 21(2) and the eternity clause in Article 79(3). Insofar as specifying the meaning of "free democratic basic order" in the former, the Court explained that 'its regulatory content cannot be defined by means of general recourse to Art. 79 (3) GG but is limited to those principles which are absolutely indispensable for the free democratic constitutional state'; instead, the Court anchored its meaning in 'the principle of human dignity (Art. 1(1) GG), which is specified in greater detail by the principles of democracy and the rule of law'.[27] The Court thus explained that it would read Article 21(2) in a more limited manner, concentrating 'on a few central fundamental principles which are absolutely indispensable for the free constitutional state', invoking the importance of the political will–formation role of parties.[28] The content of the eternity clause goes beyond this minimal conception of democracy, the Court said, such as by protecting republicanism and federalism.[29] Given that 'constitutional monarchies and centralised states can also be in accordance with the guiding principle of a free democracy', the Court would not ban parties on account of challenging these unamendable features of German democracy.[30]

[24] BVerfG 17 January 2017, 2 BvB 1/13 (2017) ('*National Democratic Party II*'). An earlier attempt to ban the NPD had failed in 2003 on procedural grounds. See BVerfG 18 March 2003, 2 BVB 1/01 ('*National Democratic Party I*').

[25] *National Democratic Party II*, para. 585.

[26] Ibid., para. 586.

[27] Ibid., para. 529.

[28] Ibid., para. 535.

[29] Ibid., para. 537.

[30] Ibid.

This aspect of the 2017 judgment has been termed 'surprising' and 'certainly not warranted by the case at hand'.[31] The narrower interpretation of Article 21(2) aimed at aligning of German law with European human rights law in this area. The European Court of Human Rights (ECtHR) has assessed party bans to include both acceptance of democratic contestation of the current dispensation of state principles and structures[32] and a higher 'imminent threat' standard for assessing the danger posed.[33] With this move, however, the German Constitutional Court has been viewed as selecting a 'core of the core of the Grundgesetz' that in practice might allow a party to advocate unconstitutional change that could only be achieved by violating the eternity clause – a 'stunning' result.[34]

The 2017 judgment also had a series of important consequences. In doctrinal terms, it means the German Federal Constitutional Court has now added a timing, contextual element to its assessments of party ban requests. Thus, the substantive test of whether the party opposes the democratic order is now complemented by a 'risk calculation' test that looks at the potential of that party to realise its goals.[35] It has been argued that the Court created a new category of party in Germany: one that engages in anti-constitutional activity but lacks the potential to realise its aims.[36] Article 21 has also been amended to enable the removal of funding from this new category of 'anti-constitutional but not unconstitutional' parties,[37] with the Federal Constitutional Court retaining sole competence to decide on such funding stripping. The practical effects of this change, as we know from the literature on indirect party bans achieved via restrictive regulation, may yet amount to a de facto ban.

These changes have been controversial, with some viewing Article 21's amendment as introducing a form of party differentiation that breaches the principle of party equality in German constitutional law.[38] The German eternity clause comes back into the picture insofar as it insulates from amendment the principle of democracy enshrined in Article 20(1), which could be seen as preventing such unequal treatment among parties. Following this line of interpretation might even lead to a finding that the amended text of Article 21 amounts to 'unconstitutional constitutional law'.[39] At the very least, the 2017 judgment introduced an element of

[31] Lasse Schuldt, 'Mixed Signals of Europeanization: Revisiting the NPD Decision in Light of the European Court of Human Rights' Jurisprudence', *German Law Journal* 19(4): 817–844, 826 (2018).

[32] *Socialist Party v. Turkey* (Application No. 21237/93), Grand Chamber Judgment, 25 May 1998, para. 47.

[33] See discussion of the Refah Partisi case in Section 12.1.2.

[34] Schuldt, 'Mixed Signals of Europeanization', 825.

[35] Gelijn Molier and Bastiaan Rijpkema, 'Germany's New Militant Democracy Regime: National Democratic Party II and the German Federal Constitutional Court's "Potentiality" Criterion for Party Bans', *European Constitutional Law Review* 14: 394–409, 408 (2018).

[36] Ibid.

[37] Schuldt, 'Mixed Signals of Europeanization', 837.

[38] See ibid., 844.

[39] Ibid.

uncertainty regarding the interpretation of the core of the Basic Law. Uncertainty also now exists about the application of the new standard for determining when a ban is to be imposed, insofar as the Court left open the questions of how many seats should a party have or how close to power should it be before it is deemed dangerous are now open-ended questions.[40]

12.1.2 *Ethnic, Separatist, and Religious Parties*

A more complex case is that of parties said to be organised along ethnic or separatist lines, whose purported threat to the democratic state would amount to their challenging of its territorial makeup, as well as that of religious parties, whose attack on secularism has been viewed as an attack on state foundations. Turkey is infamous for its rich experience with both types of party bans. According to one study, there have been twenty-seven party bans in Turkey between 1961 and 2019, banning either Kurdish separatist parties (said to breach unamendable territorial integrity) or parties seen to promote political Islam (said to breach unamendable secularism).[41] Another study looking at the 1983–2015 period, found Turkey overrepresented among European party bans with sixteen out of fifty-two (31 per cent).[42] A recurrent feature of Turkey's democratisation process,[43] party bans have not been limited to electorally insignificant actors. They have included parties with significant parliamentary presence and even part of ruling government coalitions.[44]

One might wonder about the relevance of including an 'incomplete democracy' such as Turkey's in this analysis. However, party ban studies have found such 'incomplete democracy bans' to be the largest category of party bans (at least in Europe), especially when it comes to sub-state nationalist parties.[45] Turkey's example is also illustrative for how bans on salient parties come about and their effects, whether we consider national (as in the case of the Welfare Party) or sub-national salience (as in the case of Kurdish parties). Especially when considering party success at the sub-national level, we find similar considerations present when banning parties in Germany, Spain, Belgium, or Greece.[46] Moreover, in terms of

[40] Molier and Rijpkema, 'Germany's New Militant Democracy Regime', 409.

[41] Gözde Böcü and Felix Petersen, 'Debating State Organization Principles in the Constitutional Conciliation Commission', in *The Failure of Popular Constitution Making in Turkey: Regressing Towards Autocracy* ed. Felix Petersen and Zeynep Yanaşmayan. Cambridge University Press, 2019, 150.

[42] Bourne and Casal Bértoa, 'Mapping "Militant Democracy"', 230.

[43] Sabri Sayarı, 'Party System and Democratic Consolidation in Turkey: Problems and Prospects', in *Turkey's Democratization Process* ed. Carmen Rodríguez, Antonio Ávalos, Hakan Yılmaz, and Ana I. Planet. Routledge, 2014, 101.

[44] Dicle Koğacıoğlu, 'Progress, Unity, and Democracy: Dissolving Political Parties in Turkey', *Law & Society Review* 38(3): 433–462, 443 (2004).

[45] However, 'fewer incomplete democracies have banned parties than those that have not banned parties'. Bourne and Casal Bértoa 'Mapping "Militant Democracy"', 233.

[46] Ibid., 232.

the link to unamendability, a democratising context such as Turkey's is fertile ground to test eternity clauses' ability to protect fragile democratic gains and foster abidance to constitutional democracy.

Turkey's constitution contains several unamendable provisions. Article 4 renders unamendable the republican character of the state as well as Articles 2 and 3, which in turn entrench, among others, the state's democratic and secular character as well as its territorial integrity. These principles are embedded in the constitutional text also outside these two provisions, however. Thus, secularism is further protected by the preamble that mandates 'that sacred religious feelings shall absolutely not be involved in state affairs and politics as required by the principle of secularism', by Article 13 as a ground for rights limitations, and by Article 14 on the abuse of rights, among others. Article 68 of the Turkish Constitution explicitly requires party statutes and programmes to respect the independence of the state, its indivisible territorial and national integrity, human rights, equality and the rule of law, national sovereignty, and the principles of the democratic and secular republic. The Turkish Constitutional Court thus had a rich textual panoply on which to construct not only its unamendable constitutional amendment doctrine[47] but also its party ban case law.

When it comes to bans on separatist parties, the case of Halkin Emek Partisi (HEP), the People's Labour Party,[48] is instructive. The court found the Kurdish party, having promoted Kurdish political and cultural rights, to have threatened the unity of the nation-state and thus to be in breach of several constitutional provisions, including unamendable ones. The preamble of the Turkish Constitution declares 'the eternal existence of the Turkish Motherland and Nation and the indivisible unity of the Sublime Turkish State', while unamendable Article 3 declares the state, with its territory and nation, 'an indivisible entity' and the national language Turkish. Other constitutional provisions also mention territorial integrity, such as Article 14 on the prohibition of abuse of fundamental rights.

Roznai and I have argued elsewhere that declaring territorial integrity unamendable tends to occur in the face of internal contestation of the constitutional dispensation and of external threats to the state's boundaries, illustrating our argument with the (sadly, since all too relevant) example of Ukraine.[49] But whereas courts will be powerless against the latter, they can and have exercised their interpretive powers to operationalise unamendable territorial integrity internally. In the words of one

[47] Kemal Gözler, *Judicial Review of Constitutional Amendments: A Comparative Study*. Ekin Press, 2008; Tarik Olcay, 'The Unamendability of Amendable Clauses: The Case of the Turkish Constitution', in *An Unamendable Constitution? Unamendability in Constitutional Democracies* ed. Richard Albert and Bertil Emrah Oder. Springer, 2018, 313–343.

[48] Case No. 1992/1 (Political Party Dissolution), Decision No.: 1993/1, 14 July 1993.

[49] Yaniv Roznai and Silvia Suteu, 'The Eternal Territory? The Crimean Crisis and Ukraine's Territorial Integrity as an Unamendable Constitutional Principle', *German Law Journal* 16(3): 542–580 (2015).

author, the Turkish court invoked constitutional text and the history of post-Ataturk Turkey to find that ethnic or language groups would be denied minority status on account of its incompatibility with national unity: 'The state was unitary, the nation was a whole, and arguments to the contrary could only be seen as unwarranted foreign influences intensified by the rhetoric of human rights and freedoms.'[50] In the party ban literature, Turkey's would be an example of the 'legitimacy paradigm' casting Kurdish parties as an 'existential threat' to the state for demanding cultural and territorial accommodation.

It should be noted that bans on Kurdish parties coexist with other measures that limit political representation in practice. A 10 per cent electoral threshold for gaining seats in Parliament was in place until 2022, having been introduced by generals after the 1980 coup in a bid to address political fragmentation. This unusually high threshold curtailed the political representation of not only the Kurdish community but wider Turkish society insofar as it precluded the parliamentary voice of numerous smaller (mainly leftist) parties. By one study, as many as a quarter of voters were disenfranchised as a result of the 10 per cent threshold.[51] Its effects also extended to increasing the share of parliamentary seats allocated to the AKP, which enjoyed repeat absolute and even supermajorities that in turn allowed it to push through constitutional reform. For example, the AKP held over two-thirds of seats on only 34 per cent of the votes cast following the 2002 election, when some 46 per cent of votes had been redistributed. The threshold has only been reduced to 7 per cent in 2022 following a split in the Nationalist Movement Party (MHP), the AKP's traditional coalition partner, which would have seen it remain outside parliament had the 10 per cent bar stayed in place.

Interestingly, two candidates in the 2002 election whose party did not enter parliament lodged an application with the European Court of Human Rights alleging that the threshold of 10 per cent imposed nationally for parliamentary elections interfered with the free expression of the opinion of the people in the choice of the legislature, relying on Article 3 of Protocol No. 1 to the European Convention on Human Rights. The ECtHR Grand Chamber disagreed and accepted the Turkish Government's justification of the threshold as aimed at 'avoiding excessive and debilitating parliamentary fragmentation and thus of strengthening governmental stability'.[52]

[50] Koğacıoğlu, 'Progress, Unity, and Democracy', 447; for a similar discussion of the Romanian Constitutional Court interpreting unamendable provisions on territory to block administrative territorial reorganisation, see Silvia Suteu, 'The Multinational State That Wasn't: The Constitutional Definition of Romania as a National State', *Vienna Journal on International Constitutional Law* 11(3): 413–435 (2017).

[51] Soner Cagaptay, 'Turkey's Threshold', The Washington Institute (9 May 2011), www.washingtoninstitute.org/policy-analysis/turkeys-threshold.

[52] *Yumak & Sadak v. Turkey* (Application no. 10226/03), Grand Chamber Judgment, 8 July 2008.

An even more famous instance of a party ban in Turkey was the prohibition of the Refah Partisi, the Welfare Party.[53] The threat the Constitutional Court identified to the democratic system was said to be the party's embrace of *Shari'a* law, contradicting the unamendable secularism enshrined in the Turkish Constitution. The court defined secularism as 'a way of life that has destroyed the medieval scholastic dogmatism and has become the basis of the vision of democracy that develops with the enlightenment of science, nation, independence, national sovereignty, and the ideal of humanity'.[54] The court proceeded to defend this understanding of secularism as reinforcing the protection of religion itself, insofar as by separating it from politics, religion 'is saved from politicization, saved from being a tool of administration and kept in its real respectable place which is the conscience of the people'.[55] The same logic was later invoked in the even more famous *Headscarf* decision.[56] There, the Turkish Constitutional Court invalidated an amendment meant to abolish the ban on headscarves in universities on grounds of equality and the right to education in the name of secularism, said to be an essential condition for democracy and 'a guarantor of freedom of religion and of equality before the law'.[57]

The court invoked the language of militant democracy and stayed silent on the political implications of banning what by then had become the most electorally significant party in the country, in power for two years. In fact, according to some observers, reducing electoral competition had been precisely the point, revealing the Constitutional Court's own political bias in favour of secularist elites.[58] Even on the face of the judgment, we find its discussion of the notion of democracy it was defending to have been limited and unsystematic[59] and its assessment of democratic threats black and white. The court's reasoning left no room for democracy's inner tensions and only saw it as 'a formal category, an abstract entity in need of protection'.[60]

On this occasion again the European Court of Human Rights endorsed the Turkish Constitutional Court's decision. In its own highly contested Refah Partisi case, the ECtHR accepted the militant democratic argument once more.[61] It found

53 Case No. 1997/1 (Political Party Dissolution), Decision No.: 1998/1, 16 January 1998.

54 Cited in Koğacıoğlu, 'Progress, Unity, and Democracy', 450.

55 Ibid.

56 Decision of 5 June 2008, E. 2008/16; K. 2008/116, Resmi Gazete, 22 October 2008, No. 27032, 109-52. See a fuller discussion of the case in Yaniv Roznai and Serkan Yolcu, 'An Unconstitutional Constitutional Amendment – The Turkish Perspective: A Comment on the Turkish Constitutional Court's Headscarf Decision', *International Journal of Constitutional Law* 10(1): 175–207 (2012).

57 Ibid., 179.

58 Böcü and Petersen, 'Debating State Organization Principles in the Constitutional Conciliation Commission', 150 and 159.

59 Ibid., 153.

60 Koğacıoğlu, 'Progress, Unity, and Democracy', 453 and 457.

61 *Refah Partisi (the Welfare Party) and Others v. Turkey* (Applications Nos. 41340/98, 41342/98, 41343/98 et al.), Grand Chamber Judgment, 13 February 2003.

Shari'a to be incompatible with the fundamental principles of democracy, legal pluralism meant to implement it to undermine individual rights, and the possibility of recourse to force to gain political power – read into the ambiguity of *jihad* – to justify forceful state action, including a party ban. The fact of Refah's being in power was actually read as even more reason to intervene, insofar as the ECtHR saw it as making the party more likely to implement its agenda.

Turkey's experience is illustrative of the ways in which eternity clauses can underpin party bans with at times far-reaching effects on electoral democracy. Democracy itself may be part of the Turkish Constitution's unamendable core, but it is a particular understanding of it: certainly secular and, via unamendable territorial integrity and official language, also nationalist and majoritarian. The constitution works in tandem with other tools to restrict access to the electoral arena, such as electoral thresholds. Interestingly, the Constitutional Court has adopted an expansive reading of the reach of these unamendable provisions, applying them to party ban cases and not only unconstitutional constitutional amendment cases. Moreover, we see that appeals to supranational standards of human rights protection reinforced the Turkish Court's reading of the constitution and militant defence of it. The ECtHR was concerned with showing due regard to Turkey's history of political fragmentation – when the 10 per cent electoral threshold was challenged – and to the rigid understanding of secularism that justified banning even a governing party that had not taken steps to implement an Islamist agenda. In so doing, both the national and the supranational court narrowed the scope of what Turkish democracy could mean, ironically contributing to the erosion of multi-party democracy in the country over the long term and facilitating the political dominance of the AKP.[62]

12.1.3 *Indirect Party Bans*

It is not always the case that parties are restricted from the electoral arena through an outright legal ban. Instead, they may be prevented from standing for elections or accessing public funding indirectly, such as through restrictions on ideological commitments. This is arguably the case in Israel, where parties that would seek to challenge the Jewish and democratic definition of the state are not permitted to stand for elections. From one perspective, this could be added to the examples of anti-democratic party bans discussed above. However, the particular Israeli situation warrants a separate examination: not only are we dealing with an incompletely codified constitutional system, where the constitutional basis for restricting political

[62] Fernando Casal Bértoa and Angela K. Bourne, 'Prescribing Democracy? Party Proscription and Party System Stability in Germany, Spain and Turkey', *European Journal of Political Research* 56(2): 440–465 (2017); Pelin Ayan Musil, 'Emergence of a Dominant Party System after Multipartyism: Theoretical Implications from the Case of the AKP in Turkey', *South European Society and Politics* 20(1): 71–92 (2015).

parties is thus less clear-cut, but the country's ethno-religious definition and political division make it a unique case.

One may be sceptical from the outset as to whether the question of unamendability even arises in Israel. Given the Israeli system's incomplete constitutionalisation via a series of Basic Laws, all arguably open to amendment by the Knesset, one might think unamendability foreign to Israeli legal thought or judicial practice. Moreover, the Israeli Supreme Court has recognised the Knesset as sitting not only as a legislative assembly but also as a constituent body.[63] This would seem to suggest its legislative powers limitless, including in the constitutional realm. However, already in the famous *Bank Mizrahi* judgment, the Supreme Court indicated that only another Basic Law could alter a previously enacted one and also that certain constitutional values would operate as limits on the Knesset's constituent power.[64] Later case law clarifying that those limits embodied the Jewish and democratic nature of the state.[65]

Thus, even in the absence of a formal eternity clause, it has been argued that Israel does exhibit a form of implied unamendability. Aharon Barak has claimed Israel to be an example of a narrower form of unamendability, one operating in the absence of a textual eternity clause but whose object was the Jewish and democratic nature of the state as laid out in the country's Declaration of Independence.[66] Consequently, while a future Israeli constitution might expand the scope of unamendability to include things like judicial review or independence, until the process of constitutionalisation is completed, Barak has argued, only the state's definition would amount to a substantive limit on Basic Laws.[67] More recently, Mazen Masri has argued that two forms of unamendability operate in the Israeli system: one concealed, through controlling the composition of the Knesset, and one unwritten and judicially created.[68] Like Barak, he views these as resulting in the entrenchment of the definition of the state. Additionally, however, Masri finds unamendability also to be a vehicle through which to embed a hierarchy among citizens and to reinforce favourable status for certain groups.

Understanding how this form of unamendability has impacted the electoral and parliamentary arenas in Israel requires a trip back in time. In the 1965 *Yeredor* case,

[63] CA 6821/93 *Bank Mizrahi HaMe'ouha v. Migdal Kfar Shitofui* (1995), IsrSC 49 (2) 221.

[64] *Bank Mizrahi*, 394. See also discussion in Suzie Navot and Yaniv Roznai, 'From Supra-Constitutional Principles to the Misuse of Constituent Power in Israel', *European Journal of Law Reform* 21(3): 403–423 (2019).

[65] HCJ 6427/02 *The Movement for the Quality of Governance in Israel v. The Knesset* (2006) and HCJ 4908/10 *Bar-On v. The Knesset* (2010).

[66] Aharon Barak, 'Unconstitutional Constitutional Amendments', *Israel Law Review* 44: 321 (2011).

[67] Ibid.

[68] Mazen Masri, *The Dynamics of Exclusionary Constitutionalism: Israel as a Jewish and Democratic State*. Hart, 2017; Mazen Masri, 'Unamendability in Israel: A Critical Perspective', in *An Unamendable Constitution? Unamendability in Constitutional Democracies* ed. Richard Albert and Bertil Emrah Oder. Springer, 2018, 169–193.

the Supreme Court upheld the electoral disqualification of the Socialist List, a principally left-wing Arab list.[69] The ground invoked was that the party did not respect the 'fact' of Israel's founding as an eternal Jewish state, fulfilling the right to self-determination of the Jewish people.[70] The party's programme was seen as sharing premises with that of the previously banned *Al-Ard* pan-Arab movement. The state saw the movement as a threat to Zionism and as such to its own existence and the Central Elections Committee agreed, despite no formal statutory basis to block the party's candidacy; the Supreme Court nevertheless endorsed the Committee's decision.[71] The Weimar experience and the concept of militant or defensive democracy, respectively, were invoked by the majority justices in their opinions. Neither the unlikely electoral success of the party nor its emphasis that it was contesting the Jewish but not the democratic nature of the state factored into the decision.[72]

While the Supreme Court later adopted a narrow interpretation of this judgment, the case already at the time raised the question of whether a judicially created 'supra-constitution' had emerged.[73] Others see it as creating an implicit eternity clause whose effect is pre-emptive, by screening in advance ideas that can enter the Knesset.[74] The implications are especially significant given the Knesset's double role as ordinary legislature and constituent assembly. It has thus been argued that in Israel, revolutionary amendments are neutralised before even entering the constituent arena, insofar as their very initiators are precluded from even attempting to enter its gates.[75]

The Knesset adopted Amendment 7A to The Knesset Basic Law in 1985. It enshrined in law the self-defensive understanding of Israeli democracy, which 'allows Israel to ban a list or candidate who supports armed struggle against the state of Israel, who negates the existence of the *state of Israel as the state of the Jewish people*, or incites to racism'. In 1988, the extreme right-wing anti-Arab party Kach was prevented from contesting elections on this new legal basis, as a racist party. Despite the passing of Amendment 7A, no party has been banned on the second ground since 1965.[76] The Israeli Supreme Court in later cases distinguished the *Yeredor* case as an extreme measure, whereas in other instances – such as the

69 Ami Pedahzur, *The Israeli Response to Jewish Extremism and Violence: Defending Democracy*. Manchester University Press, 2018, 33.

70 Masri, 'Unamendability in Israel', 176, citing EA 1/65 *Yeredor v. Chairman of the Central Elections Committee for the Sixth Knesset* (1965), IsrSC 19 (3) 365.

71 Masri 'Unamendability in Israel', 176.

72 Pedahzur, *The Israeli Response to Jewish Extremism and Violence*, 33.

73 Shlomo Guberman, 'Israel's Supra-constitution', *Israel Law Review* 2: 455–474, 460 (1967).

74 Masri 'Unamendability in Israel', 178.

75 Sharon Weintal, 'The Challenge of Reconciling Constitutional Eternity Clauses with Popular Sovereignty: Toward Three-track Democracy in Israel as a Universal Holistic Constitutional System and Theory', *Israel Law Review* 44: 449–497, 468 (2011).

76 Pedahzur, *The Israeli Response to Jewish Extremism and Violence*, 34; Nir Kedar, *Law and Identity in Israel: A Century of Debate*. Cambridge University Press, 2019, 125.

attempted ban of the Progressive List for Peace – it declined to find evidence of the impugned party seeking the dissolution of the state.[77] The Supreme Court attempted to ground the definition of the state in universalist, liberal values, with its former Chief Justice Barak equating Jewish values not with religious values but with Western democratic principles.[78] In 2002, the Knesset amended 7A and changed this second ground for party proscription to a ban on negating 'the existence of the state of Israel as a Jewish and democratic state', part of the growing shift towards entrenching a particular view of state identity in law.

Kedar, reconstructing the origins of the catchphrase 'Jewish and democratic' in Israeli legislation, refers to it as having been born 'almost inadvertently'.[79] The language was introduced during negotiations for the 1992 Basic Law: Human Dignity and Liberty and Basic Law: Freedom of Occupation to placate fears that religious practices previously accommodated would now risk being found discriminatory.[80] Thus, it was a matter of political compromise, as part of 'a fight over the division of political power between the state and the religious establishment'.[81] The expression was seen as ambiguous enough to appease different sides in the debate and the courts remained reluctant to give it effect.[82] The task of constitutionally defining state identity and building consensus could be once more relegated to another day.

However, developments since 2014 moved away from this universalist logic. With the passing of the Basic Law: Referendum that year, strict restrictions were placed on governmental action affecting the territory of Israel, which in turn limits possible routes to a peace agreement.[83] Then in 2018, the Basic Law: Israel as the Nation State of the Jewish People was adopted. In addition to listing state symbols, recognising Hebrew as the official language (with Arabic afforded a special status) and recognising Jewish settlement as a national value, the law controversially declared the Jewish nature of the state without making reference to its democratic character, or indeed to a principle of equality. Many saw the 2018 law as entrenching the state definition as well as the erosion of equality rights of both individuals and non-Jewish groups in Israel.[84] At the very least, it 'create[d] the impression that the Jewish

77 *Neiman v. The Chairman of Central Elections Committee for the Eleventh Knesset* [1984] IsrSC 39 (2) 225.

78 Hanna Lerner, 'Permissive and Unpremissive Constitution Making', *Law & Ethics of Human Rights* 16(2): 321–346, 330 (2022).

79 Kedar, *Law and Identity in Israel*, 123.

80 Ibid.

81 Ibid.

82 Ibid.

83 Lerner, 'Permissive and Unpremissive Constitution Making', 330–331.

84 Yousef T. Jabareen, 'Enshrining Exclusion: The Nation-State Law and the Arab-Palestinian Minority in Israel' in *Jewish State, Democracy, and the Law* ed. Simon Rabinovitch. Hebrew Union College Press, 2018, 249–264; Roznai and Brandes, 'Democratic Erosion, Populist Constitutionalism, and the Unconstitutional Constitutional Amendments Doctrine'.

character of the state takes precedence over democracy'.[85] This impression was hard to escape given that the law's supporters had expressed hope it 'would end the Supreme Court's increasing bias, since the 1990s, in favour of human rights and democracy and against the states' Jewish identity'.[86]

Fifteen petitions were lodged with the Supreme Court challenging the Basic Law as an unconstitutional constitutional amendment. In 2021, the Supreme Court rejected the petitions and found the legislation compatible with the other Basic Laws of Israel.[87] It emphasised the declaratory nature of the law and rejected its interpretation as discriminatory in light of other guarantees of individual rights in Israeli law. The only Arab judge on the Court was the sole dissenting voice. In his view, the law contradicted the state's democratic nature and undermined equality by ignoring Arab and Druze citizens.

The 2021 decision was an attempt by the Supreme Court to square the circle: neither to outright reject the petitions nor to find in their favour by, for the first time, striking down a basic law as unconstitutional. The Court attempted to neutralise the potentially discriminatory nature of the law via interpretation by emphasising its declaratory nature. There are certainly those who believe it would have been 'an extremely unfortunate move' for the Court to strike down the law as an unconstitutional constitutional amendment before it was ever applied.[88] However, when viewed as one piece of a larger puzzle, the 2021 decision does little to assuage fears that the 2018 law further eroded the purposeful ambiguity of the 'Jewish and democratic' definition of the state. We see instead the trajectory being an ever more exclusionary understanding of the state, one that fuses the democratic and Jewish characteristics thus making it impossible for the latter to be challenged without the former also being presumed attacked. Moreover, reforms were introduced in early 2023 to curb the Supreme Court's powers of judicial review, introduce government control over judicial appointments, and give the Knesset powers to override Supreme Court rulings. If adopted, the prospect of a politicised Court far less inclined to walk the interpretive tightrope discussed above becomes near certainty.

12.2 UNAMENDABILITY AND PARLIAMENTARY POLITICS: PARLIAMENTARY MANDATES

I wish also briefly to discuss another type of judicial intervention in electoral politics facilitated by unamendability: instances in which courts intervene to protect the electoral or parliamentary arena in the name of an eternity clause. The case I will discuss here is by now famous in the literature and concerns a Czech Constitutional

85 Kedar, *Law and Identity in Israel*, 133.

86 Ibid.

87 HCJ 5555/18 *Hassoun v. The Knesset* and 14 other petitions (2021).

88 Ruth Gavison, 'Reflections on the Nation-State Law Debate', in *Jewish State, Democracy, and the Law* ed. Simon Rabinovitch. Hebrew Union College Press, 2018, 346.

Court decision from 2009.[89] This was the decision setting out the material core doctrine of the court, grounded in Article 9(2) of the Czech Constitution, which reads: 'Any changes in the essential requirements for a democratic state governed by the rule of law are impermissible.'

But first, some background to the 2009 crisis resulting in the case. In March 2009, after four failed attempts, the parliamentary opposition succeeded in passing a no confidence vote against the Government. An early dissolution of the Assembly of Deputies and early elections was seen as desirable. The constitutional procedure to follow would have involved first proving that the legislative body was unable to function effectively, which in turn involved one of three scenarios: either three failed consecutive attempts at confidence votes in a new Government, or a failed vote on a government bill on which the Government had attached the issue of confidence, or, finally, when the Assembly had been adjourned for a longer period than permitted by the constitution (Article 35(1)). Even under these scenarios, the procedure is not automatic but merely empowers the President to act. The cumbersome procedure was seen as too time-consuming by all political sides, with cross-party consensus emerging that early elections were preferable.[90] As a consequence, an ad hoc constitutional amendment, Constitutional Act No. 195/2009/Coll. was adopted (with a 172:9 vote in the Assembly and 56:8 vote in the Senate) to procedurally pave the way for early parliamentary elections in October 2009.[91] This would have shortened the mandate of the existing Parliament, given that normally elections would have been held in May 2010.

This was not, in fact, the first time such an ad hoc path was chosen to deal with a political crisis. In 1997/1998, a similar political compromise emerged in the aftermath of the breakdown of the ruling coalition Government. A constitutional amendment was passed then similarly to enable the running of early elections and resulting in the shortening of that parliamentary term by two years. In that instance, however,

[89] Decision Pl. ÚS 27/09: Constitutional Act on Shortening the Term of Office of the Chamber of Deputies, 10 September 2009. For analyses of the decision, see Maxim Tomoszek, 'The Czech Republic', in *How Constitutions Change: A Comparative Study* ed. Dawn Oliver and Carlo Fusaro. Hart, 2011, 41–68; Kieran Williams, 'When a Constitutional Amendment Violates the "Substantive Core": The Czech Constitutional Court's September 2009 Early Elections Decision', *Review of Central and Eastern European Law* 36: 33–51 (2011); Ivo Šlosarčik, 'Czech Republic 2009–2012: On Unconstitutional Amendment of the Constitution, Limits of EU Law and Direct Presidential Elections', *European Public Law* 19 (3): 435–448 (2013); Yaniv Roznai, 'Legisprudence Limitations on Constitutional Amendments? Reflections on the Czech Constitutional Court's Declaration of Unconstitutional Constitutional Act', *Vienna Journal on International Constitutional Law* 8 (1): 29–57 (2014); and Ivo Pospíšil, 'Activist Constitutional Court as Utility Tool for Correcting Politics. Structure, Composition and Case-law', in *Czech Democracy in Crisis* ed. Astrid Lorenz and Hana Formánková. Palgrave Macmillan, 2020, 133–155.

[90] See Šlosarčik, 'Czech Republic 2009–2012', 436.

[91] Ibid., 437.

the amendment was not challenged before the Constitutional Court and the early elections proceeded as planned.[92]

In 2009, however, one of the MPs standing to lose his mandate challenged the amendment before the Court, arguing that it violated his right to participate in the administration of public affairs and that any exception to his carrying his mandate to the full four-year term needed to be prescribed by the Constitution at the time of his election. He also challenged the nature of the Act in question, arguing it was not a real constitutional amendment because it violated the material core of the Czech Constitution. Specifically, he claimed it breached principles of non-retroactivity, generality, and predictability of laws, which come under the umbrella of respect for the rule of law.

The Constitutional Court agreed and voided the Act. Its decision involved several important steps. First, the Court had to establish its power to review constitutional acts, whereas the Constitution and Constitutional Court Act only stipulated its power to review the constitutionality of 'laws'. However, relying on its constitutional role as guardian of the constitution (Article 83), the Czech Constitutional Court proceeded with its review. Second, it challenged the nature of the 2009 Act, calling it constitutional only in form and not in substance. Given that it referred to a specific rather than general situation, the Act was closer to an administrative act and in breach of principles of equality, non-arbitrariness, and right to an independent judge, in addition to the principle of separation of powers.[93] Third, the Court established a link to the Constitution's 'material core' as enshrined by Article 9(2) by accepting the claimant's rule of law arguments (while ignoring his rights-based claims). Additionally, the Court emphasised the irregular parliamentary procedure followed for adopting the amendment as itself evidence of the breach of the 'material core'. It sought to ground its decision in both precedent and appeals to history. It thus cited case law having recognised 'popular sovereignty, a right of resistance, and the basic principles of election law' as 'fundamental inviolable values of a democratic society' and as such part of the 'material core' of the constitutional order.[94] The Court also invoked the Weimar experience together with Czech experience with communist semblance of legality to justify its intervention.[95]

It should be noted that, hitherto, the enforceability and practical implications of the Czech eternity clause had been disputed. Some had seen it as purely declaratory or else directed to the Senate as the chamber responsible for revising legislation passed by the Assembly.[96] In its decision, however, the Court removed any doubt about the teeth of the eternity clause, declaring it 'non-changeable . . . not a mere

92 Ibid.

93 Šlosarčik, 'Czech Republic 2009–2012', 439.

94 Williams, 'When a Constitutional Amendment Violates the "Substantive Core"', 42.

95 Ibid.; Kieran Williams, 'Judicial Review of Electoral Thresholds in Germany, Russia and the Czech Republic', *Election Law Journal* 4(3): 191–206 (2005).

96 Tomoszek 'The Czech Republic'.

slogan or proclamation, but a constitutional provision with normative consequences'.[97] In stepping in to enforce it, the Court saw itself as guarding not just the rule of law but also the whole democratic order and the integrity of the Czech constitutional system.[98] It would go on to build its constitutional identity doctrine in later case law, all the while resisting calls to provide an exhaustive list of the elements constituting this constitutional 'material core'.[99]

The literature on unamendability has long debated such judicial self-empowerment when it comes to enforcing eternity clauses. What I wish to focus on here is rather the necessity and implications of the Czech Court's intervention in the concrete case at hand. The proportionality of the Court's intervention is dubious.[100] Clearly, its invocation of a Weimar-like threat signals the Court saw a real danger to parliamentary politics in the country. However, when looking at the political context surrounding the passing of the 2009 Act, it is difficult to conclude that Czech democracy had really been endangered to the point implied by the Court. The bicameral political consensus underpinning the adoption of the Act, as well as its support from both the prime minister and president, are evidence of wide agreement – among the same MPs that would stand to have their mandates shortened – that early elections were desirable. One could also argue that parliament itself choosing to cut short its term is far less likely to amount to an abuse of process than were it to have done the opposite and extend its mandate or were the curtailment to have occurred at the hands of the executive alone. Additionally, while the 1997/1998 precedent may not have completely excluded the possibility of unconstitutionality, it certainly undermined the existential threat rhetoric employed in 2009. Finally, ignoring the individual rights claims in the case also seems a weakness of the judgment.

The practical consequences of the 2009 decision were manifold. A new constitutional act was adopted in September 2009 that creates a route to early elections involving the self-dissolution of the Assembly by a three-fifths vote (Article 35(2)), thus rendering the amendment in general terms. However, to avoid another constitutional challenge, the new procedure was not relied upon in 2009 and the existing Parliament carried out its full term. It has been argued that the delay 'hanged the Czech political landscape and probably also the victor of the elections', seriously denting the vote share of Social Democrats – previously frontrunners in the polls –

97 Decision Pl. ÚS 27/09, Part IV.

98 Ibid., Part VI(a).

99 Pl. ÚS 19/08: Treaty of Lisbon I, 26 November 2008 and Pl. ÚS 29/09: Treaty of Lisbon II, 3 November 2009. See discussion in Bříza, Petr. 'The Czech Constitutional Court on the Lisbon Treaty', European Constitutional Law Review 5:1 (2009) 143–164; and further discussion of the rise of constitutional identity review in Suteu, *Eternity Clauses in Democratic Constitutionalism*, ch. 3.

100 Radim Dragomaca, 'Constitutional Amendments and the Limits of Judicial Activism: The Case of the Czech Republic', in *The Jurisprudence of Aharon Barak: Views from Europe* ed. Willem Witteveen and Maartje de Visser. Wolf Legal, 2011, 198.

and allowing the rise of new 'pro-business parties' such as Public Affairs in the 2010 elections.[101] The wide eternity clause was thus the hook on which the Czech Constitutional Court anchored its 'material core' doctrine. In 2009, the Court deployed the doctrine ostensibly in the name of protecting parliamentary politics against a Weimar-like threat. It did so, however, at a high political cost and against the wishes of all political actors.

12.3 CONCLUSION

This chapter has aimed to examine, through a selective range of case studies, the complex interplay between eternity clauses and electoral democracy. It has sought not to take at face value unamendability's claim to be democracy enhancing, even where the unamendable provisions in question embody a militant ethos and explicitly aim to protect multi-party democracy. Party bans and election invalidations have the potential seriously to affect political competition and parliamentary democracy, so court intervention resulting in such measures deserves very careful scrutiny.

Germany's example illustrates a seemingly clear-cut commitment to militant democracy that combines constitutional tools including an eternity clause and party bans. The early years of German post-war democracy saw it ban both Nazi and communist parties seen to seek to destroy the democratic constitutional order. As German democracy consolidated, the need for such drastic measures might be said to have decreased, in recognition of which the Constitutional Court stopped short of banning the Neo-Nazi NPD in 2017. However, the Court's attempt to delimit the constitutional grounds for proscribing parties from the normative content of the eternity clause may have introduced uncertainty both about the standard for banning anti-constitutional parties and about the constitutional core of the Basic Law. As the rise of the AfD has shown, moreover, the threat of extremist parties – also well-versed in avoiding falling foul of constitutional rules[102] – may yet test the German constitutional system's militant democratic commitments.

In Turkey's case, we have witnessed numerous party bans on grounds rooted in the constitutional eternity clause, with far-reaching implications for electoral politics. On the one hand, bans on Kurdish parties have operated in tandem with other rules, not least the long-standing 10 per cent parliamentary threshold, to preclude their ability to enter the electoral arena. On the other, the ban on (sometimes salient) religious parties would not appear to have weakened them, given that

[101] David Kosař and Ladislav Vyhnánek, '*The Constitutional Court of Czechia*', in *The Max Planck Handbooks in European Public Law: Volume III: Constitutional Adjudication: Institutions* ed. Armin von Bogdandy, Peter Huber, and Christoph Grabenwarter. Oxford University Press, 2020, 121.

[102] Franziska Brandmann, 'Radical-right Parties in Militant Democracies: How the Alternative for Germany's Strategic Frontstage Moderation Undermines Militant Measures', *European Constitutional Law Review* 18(3): 412–439 (2022).

Erdogan's AKP has been in power since 2003. However, a different interpretation is possible. As Rosenblum has argued, the separation of state and religion in Turkey, to which we can add the constitutional arrangements entrenching secularism, was 'uniquely one-directional: government was protected from religion but not vice versa'.[103] As a consequence, no contestation of the balance between state and religion was possible, which in turn could be viewed as having provoked the politicisation of religion.[104]

Israel's trajectory is less typical for studies of unamendability, insofar as its constitution is fragmentary and its unamendable core must be pieced together from different legislative and judicial sources. Nevertheless, the definition of the state as Jewish and democratic is clearly part of this core. For decades, its ambiguity served to stave off conflict over political identity, not just between the Jewish majority and non-Jewish minorities but also with religious Jewish groups. The Supreme Court's universalist, human rights–based approach during that period mitigated the exclusionary potential of this definition. In party ban cases, this meant developing a more restrained approach that upheld bans against racist parties but not those accused of denying the existence of the state as Jewish and democratic. The increasing polarisation in Israeli politics, however, and the entrenchment of this state definition in legislation culminating in the 2018 Nation-State Law have shifted the terms of the debate. It has made it much more difficult to defend this entrenched political identity as anything other than exclusionary, especially in the absence of a similarly entrenched equality guarantee.

Czechia's experience reveals another side to the story of unamendability's potential impact on electoral politics. In a context of serious political crisis but also rare political consensus, a political solution was found to pave the way for early parliamentary elections. The constitutional amendment it was enshrined in, however, was invalidated by the Czech Constitutional Court on the grounds that it violated the Constitution's 'material core'. A close reading of the decision reveals more concern with building the legitimacy of the Court's unconstitutional constitutional amendment doctrine than sensitivity to the political context within which the invalidation would produce effects. There are serious reasons to believe the Court's assessment of the Weimar-like threat to Czech parliamentary democracy was overblown. Moreover, while Czech political actors respected the judgment, its impact on the electoral balance of power was significant.

The examples above show that courts will not always strike the right balance between protecting and unduly narrowing democratic commitments. In some cases, they may even unintentionally undermine multi-partyism itself or significantly influence electoral outcomes. With its bluntness, unamendability may hinder rather than help bring nuance to these difficult decisions.

[103] Rosenblum, 'Banning Parties', 63.

[104] Ibid.

13

Monarchy and Democracy in Modern Malaysia

Yvonne Tew

13.1 INTRODUCTION

No country in the world has as many monarchs as Malaysia. Among the monarchies in the world today,[1] Malaysia is unique in its system of a rotating, elected monarchy. Within the Malaysian Federation, nine Malay Rulers are sovereign as the constitutional head of their respective states. Every five years, the King who serves as Supreme Head of the Federation – known by the title of the Yang di-pertuan Agong – is elected in a rotating system from among these nine Rulers. The Federal Constitution of Malaysia set up a Westminster-style parliamentary system, with a constitutional monarch as the head of state. The written document explicitly sets out the monarch's powers, which limits the powers of the King in most areas of governance. As a matter of design, the constitutional text created at independence in 1957 contemplated the monarch as a constitutional figurehead with a largely symbolic role.

Not so in practice. In recent times, the contemporary monarch in Malaysia has emerged as a critical actor in the formation and functioning of the federal government. The monarch assumed a key role during a period of unprecedented democratic transition and disintegration in modern Malaysia.

In 2018, Malaysia experienced a historic national election that resulted in the ousting of the Barisan Nasional ruling coalition that had governed the country for more than sixty years since independence.[2] Malaysia's political transition was hailed as a democratic breakthrough, ending decades of dominance by a single political

Johanna Mintz, Hana Kassem, and Austin Lowe provided excellent research assistance.

1 Tom Ginsburg, "East Asian Monarchy in Comparative Perspective," *The Long East Asia*. Springer, 2023, 199 (noting that "22% of the countries today are monarchies").

2 See "After Six Decades in Power, BN falls to 'Malaysian Tsunami,'" *Malaysiakini* (May 10, 2018), www.malaysiakini.com/news/423990; "Malaysia Election: Opposition Scores Historic Victory," BBC (May 10, 2018), www.bbc.com/news/world-asia-44036178; see also Yvonne Tew, *Constitutional Statecraft in Asian Courts*. Oxford University Press, 2020, 1–5.

coalition.[3] Twenty-two months after being elected, however, the newly elected Pakatan Harapan government disintegrated following a series of political defections. A divisive battle for government leadership ensued among former prime minister Mahathir Mohamad, his supposed successor Anwar Ibrahim, and senior politician Muhyiddin Yassin. The King intervened directly into this government crisis by deciding to appoint Muhyiddin Yassin as the new prime minister, cementing a government turnover to a coalition that returned to power many from the previously deposed ruling political party.

In the months that followed, the monarch played a central role in the country's governance. As the Perikatan Nasional government under Muhyiddin Yassin struggled to deal with the COVID-19 pandemic while maintaining its fragile grasp on power, the Agong refused the new premier's bid to declare emergency rule. Later, in July 2021, the Agong publicly rebuked Muhyiddin's administration for announcing that the emergency proclamations had been revoked without the monarch's consent.

This chapter explores the central part the monarch played in facilitating the political transition and in the constitutional governance of Malaysia's contemporary political order. Doing so raises broader questions about the role of the monarchy in a democracy and its institutional capacity to safeguard against incumbent capture or to accelerate democratic erosion. It begins in Section 13.2 by setting out the historical context for Malay kingship and its eventual transformation into a constitutional monarchy after Malaya's independence in 1957 from British colonial rule. It examines the constitutional design of Malaysia's federal parliamentary system and the design choices made regarding the ways in which the Federal Constitution structures the relationship between the monarchy and the other branches of government.

Section 13.3 tells the story of the monarch's rise during Malaysia's first change of government following a general election and the subsequent collapse of two successive governments. The political crises that occurred amidst these government transitions and during the COVID-19 pandemic have left the country's political parties and electoral institutions highly fragile. Meanwhile, following the royal interventions between 2018 and 2021, the monarchy has emerged with an enhanced position in Malaysia's contemporary constitutional order. Far from being an outdated or anachronistic institution, the story that emerges is that monarchy in Malaysia is not just surviving, it is thriving – a story that has broader resonance in other parts of Southeast Asia. Section 13.4 offers some concluding reflections on the role that the monarch can play in protecting or undermining constitutional democracy.

[3] See Shadi Hamid, "'What Democracies Can Learn From Malaysia' Malaysia," *The Atlantic* (May 16, 2018), www.theatlantic.com/international/archive/2018/05/malaysia-democracy-najib/560534/; Larry Diamond, "Malaysia's 'Malaysia's Democratic Breakthrough' Breakthrough," *American Interest* (May 15, 2018), www.the-american-interest.com/2018/05/18/malaysias-democratic-breakthrough/.

13.2 OF SULTANS AND KINGS: HISTORY AND CONSTITUTIONAL DESIGN

13.2.1 *Malay(sian) Kingship: Historical Background*

Malaysia does not have one monarchy; it has nine. The origins of the nine Malay Rulers have their roots in the sultanate that presided over the famed port city of Malacca. The city rose to glory in the fifteenth century as one of the region's preeminent trading centers, situated at the crossroads of the spice route between the East and West. Following the fall of the Malacca empire in 1511 to the Portuguese, sons of the Malacca sultan established empires in Perak and Johor, and other new sultanates modeled on Malacca's emerged across the Malay peninsula.[4] Malay ideas of kingship drew on influences from Islamic traditions infused with local customs and Hindu and Buddhist elements.[5]

The Portuguese colonial powers were followed by the Dutch, and then the British. Between 1874 and 1930, the British established a series of treaties with the sultans of the nine Malay states. This system of indirect rule required the state Rulers to act on the advice of a British Resident, except in matters relating to Malay religion and custom. After the Second World War, during which the Japanese occupied the Malayan states for a few years, the British sought to unify the nine Malay states, along with Penang and Malacca, into a unitary entity – the Malayan Union – in 1946. Vehement opposition to the Malayan Union consolidated into a rallying point for Malay political leaders to form the United Malays National Organisation (UMNO), the political party that would dominate Malaysian politics for the next seven decades. The political rebellion against the proposed Malayan Union was due to many reasons, but a main objection was that the sovereignty of the Malay monarchs over their individual states would be abolished by the creation of a unitary state.

The British relented. The Federation of Malaya was created in 1948, replacing the proposed Malayan Union structure with a federal system of government that preserved the powers of the Malay sultans as the Rulers of their respective states. This federal arrangement would form the basis for the design of the constitutional system put in place at the Federation's independence.

In 1956, a constitutional commission consisting of five Commonwealth legal experts, chaired by Britain's Lord Reid, began the constitution drafting process based on terms of reference that had been agreed on by representatives of the Malayan

4 See Andrew Harding and Harshan Kumarasingham, "The Malay Monarchies in Constitutional and Social Conception," *Asian Journal of Law and Society* 9(3): 399–417 (Special Issue), 2022.

5 Kobkua Suwannathat-Pian, *Palace, Political Party, and Power: A Story of the Socio-political Development of Malay Kingship*. National University of Singapore Press, 2011, 7.

government, the Malay Rulers, and the British government.[6] The draft constitutional text was modified in several aspects after scrutiny by a local working party and eventually ratified by the federal legislative council. The Constitution came into force on August 31, 1957, when the Federation of Malaya became fully independent. In 1963, when Sabah, Sarawak, and Singapore joined the Federation, it became the Federal Constitution of Malaysia.[7]

13.2.2 *Constitutional Design and Constitutional Politics*

The Malaysian Constitution provides for a constitutional monarchy, as well as a Westminster-style parliamentary system with a bicameral legislature, executive, and independent judiciary. It proclaims the Supreme Head of the Federation as the King, officially called the Yang di-Pertuan Agong[8] – quite literally, "One who is Made Supreme Lord." Federalism remains at the core of the design of the political system and the constitutional monarchy. The Constitution cemented the position of the Malay Rulers as the constitutional heads of their respective states. It guarantees the sovereignty of the Malay Rulers within their territories,[9] and the rights and privileges of each Ruler as the head of their states and as the head of the religion of Islam in those states.[10]

Malaysia has a unique system of rotating, elected constitutional monarchy.[11] The position of the Yang di-Pertuan Agong (Agong) rotates every five years among the sultans of the nine states traditionally headed by Malay Rulers. Electing the federal constitutional monarch is a matter for the Conference of Rulers, a body comprising the nine Malay Rulers and the governors of the other four states.[12] That task is carried out typically once every five years or when there is a vacancy, which may

6 See generally Joseph M. Fernando, *The Making of the Malayan Constitution*. The Malaysian Branch of the Royal Asiatic Society, 2002.

7 Malaysia is a federation consisting of nine states, with Malay Rulers, four states with governors, and three federal territories.

8 Federal Constitution of Malaysia 1957, Article 32(1).

9 Federal Constitution of Malaysia 1957, Article 181(1).

10 Federal Constitution of Malaysia 1957, Article 71(1); 3(2). The Yang di-Pertuan Agong is the head of the religion of Islam in his own state and in the federal territories and states without a Malay Ruler. Federal Constitution of Malaysia 1957, Articles 3(3)–(5).

11 Historical examples of elective monarchies include the Polish-Lithuanian Commonwealth, the Holy Roman Empire, the Mongol Empire, and the African Kingdom of Kongo. Today, Malaysia is one of the very few elective monarchies in the world (and the only one where the federal monarchy rotates among nine kings). Another (rare) example is Cambodia, where the king is elected for a life term by the Royal Council of the Throne.

12 Federal Constitution of Malaysia 1957, Article 38. The nine states headed by Malay Rulers are Kedah, Kelantan, Johor, Perak, Perlis, Pahang, Selangor, Negeri Sembilan, and Terengganu. The four states that are headed by Governors, instead of monarchs, are Penang, Malacca, Sabah, and Sarawak.

occur due to death or, more uncommonly, resignation.[13] In addition to the power to elect – and remove – the King, the consent of the Conference of Rulers is required to amend certain provisions of the Federal Constitution, such as those dealing with the status of the Rulers, the Conference of Rulers, the Malay national language, and the special position of the Malays and the natives of Sabah and Sarawak.[14]

The role of Malaysia's Agong was loosely modeled on that of a constitutional monarch in a Westminster-style political system. Unlike Britain's uncodified constitution, however, the powers of the Malaysian Agong are expressly set out in the Federal Constitution. The Malaysian Constitution vests executive authority in the Agong,[15] but specifies that the King "shall act in accordance with the advice of the Cabinet or of a Minister acting under the general authority of the Cabinet, except as otherwise provided by this Constitution."[16] According to the Constitution, the Agong also possesses legislative authority as a constituent part of Parliament, which consists of the Agong and the two Houses of Parliament.[17] The King is constitutionally empowered to summon, prorogue, and dissolve (or decline to dissolve) Parliament.[18]

The monarchy in Malaysia has always been bound up with constitutional politics. Post-independence, the Rulers clashed with the governments ruling their states in several episodes in the 1970s and 1980s; ultimately, tensions and conflicts between the Rulers and the federal government resulted in a constitutional confrontation.[19] During the first Mahathir Mohamad administration, which spanned the 1980s and 1990s, the federal government pushed to amend the Federal Constitution to constrain the powers of the Rulers. Constitutional amendments passed in 1984 and 1994 limited the King's power to refuse assent to laws passed by Parliament, removed the royal immunity of the Rulers from suit, and required the Rulers to act on executive advice.[20]

Nonetheless, the Constitution specifies several areas in which the King "may act in his discretion," including: "(a) the appointment of a Prime Minister; (b) the withholding of consent to a request for dissolution of Parliament."[21] Those who view the sovereign as occupying a largely symbolic position in a Westminster-style parliamentary system consider the monarch's function to be primarily formal and ceremonial, with the head of state having no real discretion even in these circumstances.

13 Federal Constitution of Malaysia 1957, Article 32(3). For a recent high-profile royal resignation, see Mike Ives, "Malaysia's King, an Unusual Monarch, Abruptly Leaves His Job," *New York Times* (January 7, 2019), www.nytimes.com/2019/01/07/world/asia/malaysia-king-muhammad-abdicates.html.
14 Federal Constitution of Malaysia 1957, Article 159(5).
15 Federal Constitution of Malaysia 1957, Article 39.
16 Federal Constitution of Malaysia 1957, Article 40(1).
17 Federal Constitution of Malaysia 1957, Article 44.
18 Federal Constitution of Malaysia 1957, Articles 43(4), 55(1)–(2).
19 See H. P. Lee, *Constitutional Conflicts in Contemporary Malaysia*, 2nd ed. Oxford University Press, 2017, 31–62; Suwannathat-Pian, *Palace, Political Party, and Power*, 345–370.
20 Federal Constitution of Malaysia 1957, Articles 66(4A), 181(2), 71(1).
21 Federal Constitution of Malaysia 1957, Article 40(2).

Yet, in recent times, Malaysia's monarch has emerged to play a critical role in the formation and functioning of government in the country. As we will see, the Agong's appointment of the prime minister and the monarch's consent (or lack thereof) to emergency rule during the COVID-19 pandemic would turn out to be crucial turning points during Malaysia's 2020 government transition and in subsequent political crises.

13.3 CONSTITUTIONAL MONARCHY IN CONTEMPORARY PRACTICE

13.3.1 *Formation of Government*

The future of democracy in Malaysia was being decided in February 2020, so it appeared, inside a room in the palace. At half past two o'clock on a Wednesday afternoon, on February 25, the first wave of parliamentary members began arriving at the palace gates in Kuala Lumpur to be interviewed by the King. Over the course of that day and the next, they would meet one by one with the Agong. The palace announced that "his majesty himself" would interview each of the 222 members of the lower house of Parliament to determine which candidate the parliamentarians supported as prime minister.[22]

Days before, the Pakatan Harapan government had collapsed, after less than two years in power following its democratic triumph in the 2018 national elections. Initially triggered by several key members defecting from the governing Pakatan Harapan alliance to join forces with rival political blocs, a confounding political drama played out over the last week of February. Mahathir Mohamad resigned as prime minister, the Agong named him as interim prime minister, and then Mahathir sought to resume the mantle of prime minister. A battle for the country's premiership ensued between Mahathir Mohamad, the supposed premier-in-waiting Anwar Ibrahim, and Muhyiddin Yassin, a senior politician from Mahathir's own political party. Days of confusion followed as parliamentarians switched support for the contenders vying for the prime ministership in a series of bewildering political twists and turns.[23]

The King intervened at the heart of the political turmoil, seeking to exercise his constitutional power to appoint a prime minister. Never in the history of the country

[22] See Radzi Razak, "In Unprecedented Move, Agong to Interview Each MP to Determine Who Commands Majority,"*Malay Mail* (February 25, 2020), www.malaymail.com/news/malaysia/2020/02/25/in-unprecedented-move-agong-to-interview-each-mp-to-determine-who-commands/1840697.

[23] See James Massola, "'Somewhere between Game of Thrones and The Crown': Malaysia's Political Soap Opera," *Sydney Morning Herald* (February 28, 2020), www.smh.com.au/world/asia/somewhere-between-game-of-thrones-and-the-crown-malaysia-s-political-soap-opera-20200227-p54568.html.

had the monarch's constitutional task seemed so fraught. What followed was a high-profile two-day interview process at the palace, during which the King met with all the members of Parliament to determine who commanded the support of the majority of the house. At the end of the two days, though, the King professed himself unable to reach a resolution, declaring that he was not confident that a single parliamentarian had the majority support to form a new government.[24] The Agong then asked for various party leaders to nominate their candidates for prime minister, and met with the party leaders as well as with the Conference of Rulers.

Soon after, the King announced that he had determined, based on the representations of the party leaders, that Muhyiddin Yassin had the support of the majority and that he would appoint Muhyiddin to the premiership. Even as the palace made its announcement, Mahathir Mohamad claimed that he had majority support, releasing a list of 114 parliamentarians who had allegedly signed statutory declarations in his support.[25] Nevertheless, the King refused to grant him an audience. As things turned out, Mahathir never got to be in the room where it happened.

On March 1, 2020, Muhyiddin Yassin was sworn in as the new prime minister. He took power at the helm of a hurriedly assembled Perikatan Nasional governing coalition containing many politicians from the United Malays National Organisation, which had been the key party bloc in the previously deposed Barisan Nasional government.

Malaysia's political crisis in 2020 resulted in an unusual government transition in a country that had hitherto experienced six decades of one-party rule and one (short-lived) democratic changeover when voters ousted the ruling Barisan Nasional coalition from governance for the first time.[26] Also unprecedented was the King's role in deciding who to appoint as prime minister. The events brought to the fore constitutional issues and constitutional conventions that had never been tested at the level of the federal government.

Begin with the constitutional text. The King's role in appointing a prime minister is laid out in Malaysia's Federal Constitution; Article 43(1)(a) states that "the Yang di-Pertuan Agong shall … appoint as Prime Minister to preside over the Cabinet a member of the House of Representatives who in his judgment is likely to command the confidence of the majority of the members of that House." Up to this point in Malaysia's political history, which had been dominated for decades by a ruling

[24] "No One Has the Majority to Be New PM, Party Leaders to Nominate PM Candidate: Malaysian King," *Today Online* (February 28, 2020), www.todayonline.com/world/no-one-has-majority-be-new-pm-party-leaders-nominate-pm-candidate-malaysian-king.

[25] 114 members of Parliament constituted a (bare) majority of the 222-member lower house of Parliament. Jason Thomas, "Dr M Released List of 114 MPs Backing Him," *Free Malaysia Today* (February 29, 2020), www.freemalaysiatoday.com/category/nation/2020/02/29/dr-m-releases-list-of-mps-backing-him/.

[26] See Yvonne Tew, "Malaysia's 2020 Government Crisis: Revealing the New Emperor's Clothes," *International Journal of Constitutional Law Blog* (April 15, 2020), https://perma.cc/7NZR-ZMP7.

coalition that controlled a vast majority of legislative seats, the monarch's appointment of the prime minister in Malaysia had been merely a pro forma task.

Not so in 2020. The government upheaval of February 2020, with political shenanigans resulting in razor thin, constantly shifting margins of support for each of the vying prime minister candidates, raised questions that had never come to the fore at the federal level. How was the King to exercise his "judgment" as to who was "likely to command the confidence of the majority" in appointing the new prime minister? And what evidence could the constitutional monarch rely on in making that determination?

The Malaysian monarch decided to directly intervene into the midst of the political crisis. The Agong took the extraordinary step of interviewing each individual member of Parliament and then met with the leaders of the competing political parties to hear their representations – a move that the palace itself characterized as going "beyond the call of obligation."[27]

Malaysia's case offers a striking example of a non-majoritarian institution playing an assertive role in influencing the government's formation. Textually, of course, the monarch is constitutionally empowered to appoint the person who "in his judgment" is likely to command majority support in Parliament.[28] But as Asanga Welikala observes, "the king's actions do raise a question that often arises in Westminster-style systems: a course of action that may be strictly legal may nevertheless be regarded as unconstitutional."[29]

Malaysia's unusual government transition in 2020 implicates fundamental questions of constitutional design. Under the constitutional framework of a Westminster-style parliamentary democracy, the monarch's role in appointing a prime minister is normally to affirm the outcome of the political process.[30]

Of course, times of political crisis are not the normal circumstances under which a monarch appoints a prime minister.[31] In extraordinary circumstances, the head of state may be pressed to draw on various sources of evidence to try to measure majority support.[32]

[27] Bernama, "Istana Negara's Statement on The Guardian's editorial," *New Straits Times* (March 8, 2020), www.nst.com.my/news/nation/2020/03/572767/istana-negaras-statement-guardians-editorial.

[28] Federal Constitution of Malaysia 1957, Article 43(1).

[29] Asanga Welikala, "The Dismissal of Prime Ministers in the Asian Commonwealth," *Political Quarterly* 91: 793 (2020).

[30] Vernon Bogdanor, *The Monarchy and the Constitution*. Clarendon Press, 1997, 84.

[31] Ibid., 89.

[32] While this question had not been addressed before at the federal level in Malaysia, in a dispute dealing with a state government, the High Court has held that the state Menteri Besar (a position equivalent to the governor of a state) can only be removed through a vote of confidence in the state legislative assembly. However, the Court of Appeal later overturned the lower appellate court's decision, determining that a formal vote of no confidence is not required by the state's constitution and thus a loss of confidence in the Menteri Besar can be determined from extraneous evidence, including representations made by the lower assembly

In a situation of highly fraught political uncertainty, though, when there is serious dispute as to which candidate in fact commands majority support, there are strong arguments of democratic accountability and constitutional structure for allowing the political process to play out, rather than being resolved through premature royal intervention. When the palace announced the King's decision, effectively sealing the premiership, Muhyiddin and Mahathir both claimed to command majority support, and Mahathir had produced a list of members of Parliament declaring their support for him.

Had the monarch not decisively named a prime minister, the contenders might have continued to battle it out in the wider political sphere through negotiations, compromise, or political horse-trading.[33] Or the contentious matter could have been resolved in Parliament through a vote of confidence (or no confidence) to determine majority support openly on the floor of the legislature.

Amidst the political crisis, the King was thrust with the circumstances to play kingmaker.

Still, a constitutional monarch intervening too precipitously into a political controversy may end up being perceived as overturning the country's democratic mandate.[34] Royal assertiveness in the formation of government of the sort that resulted in the Malaysian government transition in early 2020 risks undermining, rather than promoting, democracy. The events that unfolded thereafter appeared to underscore this point. When Muhyiddin was appointed prime minister, Mahathir and the opposition parties immediately called for a vote of confidence to be held in Parliament – a call that was repeated throughout Muhyiddin's premiership.

Yet, as the next section describes, that vote of confidence never happened.

members and the Menteri Besar. The Court of Appeal's decision was upheld by the Federal Court. Dato' Seri Ir Hj Mohammad Nizar bin Jamaluddin lwn Dato' Dr Zambry bin Abd Kadir [2009] 5 Malayan L.J. 108 (High Court, Kuala Lumpur); Dato' Dr Zambry bin Abd Kadir v Dato'Seri Ir Hj Mohammad Nizar bin Jamaluddin (Attorney General of Malaysia, intervener) [2009] 5 Malayan L.J. 464 (Court of Appeal, Malaysia); Dato' Seri Ir Hj Mohammad Nizar bin Jamaluddin v Dato' Seri Dr Zambry bin Abdul Kadir (Attorney General, intervener) [2010] 2 Malayan L.J. 285 (Federal Court, Malaysia).

Although this case might suggest that the head of state may make his decision based on evidence beyond the support expressed on the floor of the state legislative assembly, the upper appellate court decisions are viewed as controversial and problematic. See, e.g., Jaclyn Neo, "Change and Continuity: The Constitutional Head of State and Democratic Transitions in Malaysia," *Malayan Law Journal* 5: i, viii (2012).

33 See Dian Shah and Andrew Harding, "Constitutional Quantum Mechanics and a Change of Government in Malaysia," *International Journal of Constitutional Law Blog* (April 8, 2020), www.iconnectblog.com/2020/04/constitutional-quantum-mechanics-and-a-change-of-government-in-malaysia/ (arguing "that a less proactive approach might in fact have been more appropriate and more usual in the context of a Westminster system of government, allowing the political elites to resolve the issue amongst themselves").

34 See, e.g., Editorial, "The Guardian View on a Royal Coup: A King Overturns a Historic Election," *The Guardian* (March 3, 2020), www.theguardian.com/commentisfree/2020/mar/03/the-guardian-view-on-a-royal-coup-a-king-overturns-a-historic-election#maincontent.

13.3.2 *Suspension of Government*

On May 18, 2020, after a prolonged period of suspension, members of Malaysia's Parliament convened for an unusual one-day parliamentary sitting.[35] Barely an hour after the parliamentarians had assembled in the lower house chamber, the meeting was over and Parliament adjourned yet again.

That one-day sitting was the first time that the Malaysian Parliament had convened since the Perikatan Nasional government, with Muhyiddin Yassin as prime minister, had come into power on March 1, 2020. The Agong opened the parliamentary sitting with a half-hour address. Although a vote of no confidence had been put forward against the newly appointed prime minister, the Speaker of the House of Representatives announced before the session that the motion had been dropped from the agenda.[36]

Citing the COVID-19 pandemic, the government declared that no motions would be allowed during the parliamentary session and that the King's speech would be the only order of business that day.[37] No debates or questions were permitted during the parliamentary sitting. It was a pro forma session held to satisfy – in form only – the constitutional requirement that no more than six months should elapse between parliamentary sittings.[38]

In the months to follow, Prime Minister Muhyiddin Yassin proclaimed a state of emergency due to the coronavirus pandemic and suspended Parliament. For more than half of 2021, Parliament remained shut down. No motion of confidence in the government was permitted or voted on throughout Muhyiddin's tenure.

To be sure, the Malaysian government's move to bypass usual democratic procedures in the name of the COVID-19 pandemic was not exceptional when viewed through a global lens. Throughout the pandemic, national executives across the world exercised expansive powers in response to the health crisis,[39] generating debate over whether the pandemic has accelerated the rise of authoritarianism globally.[40] Much of the discourse on the role of government power during the

[35] See Richard C. Paddock, "Democracy Fades in Malaysia as Old Order Returns to Power," *New York Times* (May 22, 2020), www.nytimes.com/2020/05/22/world/asia/malaysia-politics-najib.html.

[36] See "Malaysian PM Delays Confidence Vote Citing Virus Battle, Mahathir Cries Foul," *Reuters* (May 13, 2020), https://www.reuters.com/article/idUSL4N2CV1WY/.

[37] "May 18 Dewan Rakyat Sitting Only for Royal Address," *New Strait Times* (May 13, 2020), www.nst.com.my/news/nation/2020/05/592216/may-18-dewan-rakyat-sitting-only-royal-address.

[38] Federal Constitution of Malaysia 1957, Article 55(1).

[39] See generally Tom Ginsburg and Mila Versteeg, "The Bound Executive: Emergency Powers during the Pandemic," *International Journal of Constitutional Law* 19: 1–38 (2021).

[40] See, e.g., Selam Gebrekidan, "For Autocrats, and Others, Coronavirus Is a Chance to Grab Even More Power," *New York Times* (April 14, 2020). www.nytimes.com/2020/03/30/world/europe/coronavirus-governments-power.html; Larry Diamond, "Democracy versus the Pandemic," *Foreign Affairs* (June 13, 2020), www.foreignaffairs.com/articles/world/2020-06-13/democracy-versus-pandemic.

COVID-19 pandemic focused on the accrual of power by elected executives worldwide.[41]

The Malaysian experience during the pandemic offers an example of the expansion of power by another executive branch actor: the monarch. As the Muhyiddin administration struggled to respond to the coronavirus pandemic, the King launched a series of interventions.

Consider the use of emergency powers. Prime Minister Muhyiddin Yassin first sought to invoke a national emergency in late October 2020. This push for emergency rule, which came several months after the one-day parliamentary session in May, after which time Parliament had been suspended, was justified by Muhyiddin as necessary to curb the spread of COVID-19 in the country. For many, the proposed emergency was simply another attempt by the premier to avoid a showdown in Parliament that might challenge his precarious position.

Stunningly, the Agong rejected the prime minister's request to declare a state of emergency. This display of royal authority was unprecedented: never before had the constitutional monarch rejected a request made by the prime minister, tendered on the advice of the government – on a matter of national emergency, no less.[42] Nor did the Agong hesitate to make clear his view on the matter, announcing that he saw no need for an emergency declaration and sternly calling on the politicians to end their politicking.[43]

The Agong's move was lauded by the public. At a time when citizens coping with pandemic restrictions were becoming increasingly disillusioned with the infighting among the political elite, the monarch's refusal of Prime Minister Muhyiddin's request boosted popular support for the Agong, who was widely praised for defending democratic values.[44]

Earlier that month, the King had also refused to recognize opposition leader Anwar Ibrahim's claim that he commanded a parliamentary majority such that he could

[41] See, e.g., Symposium, "Power and the COVID-19 Pandemic," *Verfassungblog*, https://verfassungsblog.de/category/debates/power-and-the-covid-19-pandemic-debates/ (accessed April 16, 2022).

[42] Constitutionally, the power to proclaim an emergency lies with the Yang di-pertuan Agong. Federal Constitution of Malaysia 1957, Article 150(1) ("If the Yang di-Pertuan Agong is satisfied that a grave emergency exists whereby the security, or the economic life, or public order in the Federation or any part thereof is threatened, he may issue a Proclamation of Emergency making therein a declaration to that effect.").

[43] See "Malaysia's King Rejects PM's Push for COVID Emergency Rule," *Aljazeera* (October 25, 2020), www.aljazeera.com/news/2020/10/25/malaysias-king-rejects-pms-push-for-coronavirus-emergency.

[44] See, e.g., A. Ananthalakshmi and Rozanna Latiff, "Malaysia's King Wins Plaudits during Political Storm," *Reuters* (October 27, 2020), www.reuters.com/article/us-malaysia-politics-royals/malaysias-king-wins-plaudits-during-political-storm-idUSKBN27C1M3; Serina Rahman, "Commentary: Malaysian King Steers a Country through Rough Waters," *Channel News Asia* (November 20, 2020), www.channelnewsasia.com/commetary/malaysia-king-agong-anwar-muhyiddin-johor-covid-19-mco-678786.

unseat the incumbent Muhyiddin Yassin. Unconvinced by the evidence produced – Anwar had supplied the King with the number of legislators that he claimed supported him, but not their identities – the King had dismissed Anwar's bid for the premiership.

Eventually, however, the Agong acceded to Prime Minister Muhyiddin Yassin's request for a national state of emergency. On January 12, 2021, the King declared a state of emergency, which was set to expire on August 1. With the emergency decree, Muhyiddin Yassin's administration gained broad powers, claimed as necessary to tackle the COVID-19 spread. The emergency also allowed for suspending Parliament and the holding of any elections. It was the first time in more than half a century – since the country's devastating racial riots in 1969 – that a national emergency had been proclaimed.[45]

In January 2021, Parliament was promptly suspended, and the legislature did not sit for more than half of the year. Opposition politicians denounced the declared emergency as a blatant attempt by the government to cling to power. Throughout the months-long state of emergency, there were repeated calls for Parliament to reconvene, including from the Agong, who, on at least three separate occasions, publicly reiterated his call for Parliament to resume proceedings as soon as possible.[46]

Political tensions simmered and eventually reached a tipping point in July 2021. Faced with mounting criticism over the lengthy emergency rule and the government's handling of the pandemic, the government eventually held a special session of Parliament at the end of July. During that session on July 26, Prime Minister Muhyiddin Yassin's administration declared that all emergency ordinances had already been revoked – a sudden announcement that came as a surprise to the legislators, since the issue had not been debated in Parliament.[47]

Almost immediately, the King publicly announced that he had not given his assent to revoke any emergency ordinances, asserting that he had agreed only to the proposal being presented to Parliament. In a rare rebuke to the administration, the Agong expressed his "great disappointment" with the announcement that the government had revoked the emergency ordinances, emphasizing that the statement was "inaccurate and had misled members of the house."[48] The King excoriated Muhyiddin's Cabinet, stating that the misleading statements had not only failed to

[45] On the historical use of emergency powers in Malaysia, see Tew, *Constitutional Statecraft in Asian Courts*, 189–192.

[46] See "Malaysia's King Calls for Early Resumption of Parliament," *Reuters* (June 16, 2021), www.reuters.com/world/asia-pacific/malaysias-king-calls-parliament-resume-earliest-2021-06-16/; Eileen Ng, "Malaysian King Says Parliament Must Resume Despite Emergency," *AP News* (June 16, 2021), https://apnews.com/article/malaysia-coronavirus-pandemic-health-government-and-politics-d115ac90b085760247df9c30be8d5709.

[47] See Shannon Teoh, "Confusion in Malaysia as Govt Refuses to Explain Ending of Covid-19 Emergency law," *Straits Times* (July 27, 2021), www.straitstimes.com/asia/se-asia/confusion-in-malaysia-as-govt-refuses-to-explain-ending-of-covid-19-emergency-laws.

[48] Adib Povera, "YDP Agong Disappointed Emergency Ordinances Revoked without Consent," *New Straits Times* (July 29, 2021), www.nst.com.my/news/nation/2021/07/712776/ydp-agong-disappointed-emergency-ordinances-revoked-without-consent.

uphold the rule of law but also ignored the Agong's functions and powers as the head of state, which included the power to promulgate and revoke emergency ordinances.[49]

The palace's statement made no bones about the King's conception of the role of the constitutional monarch:

> His Majesty is aware of the necessity for His Majesty to act in accordance with the advice of the Cabinet as stated in Article 40(1) of the Federal Constitution. Nevertheless, the King emphasizes that, as the Head of State, His Majesty has the responsibility to advise and reprimand in the event of any unconstitutional action taken by any party.[50]

In the aftermath of the palace's damning rebuke, which fueled public outrage over his government's handling of the emergency, Prime Minister Muhyiddin Yassin resigned on August 16. He conceded that he no longer had majority support in Parliament, ending his tenure after a turbulent seventeen months in power.

When a prime minister resigns, the Federal Constitution of Malaysia provides for the dissolution of Parliament, followed by elections, or for the King to appoint a new prime minister. The Agong ruled out holding a national election because of the COVID-19 pandemic. Instead, the monarch consulted with political party leaders, and the palace issued a call for members of Parliament to indicate their choice of a prime minister – through email, fax, or WhatsApp – to the palace.[51]

Yet again, the King was positioned as kingmaker. Soon after, the King announced that he was satisfied that that Ismail Sabri Yaakob – a leader from the United Malays National Organisation, which had been deposed in the 2018 national elections – had the backing of a (bare) majority of 114 of the 220 parliamentarians.

Five days after Muhyiddin Yassin's resignation, Ismail Sabri was sworn in as Malaysia's new prime minister on August 21, 2021, taking over as leader of the Perikatan Nasional alliance previously headed by Muhyiddin Yassin. It was the second time in less than two years that the leader of the government had assumed the premiership through royal appointment, instead of through an electoral outcome or a parliamentary vote of confidence.[52]

[49] Bernama, "Agong Expresses Utmost Disappointment over Revocation of Emergency Ordinances without Consent – Istana Negara," *Astro Awani* (July 29, 2021), www.astroawani.com/berita-malaysia/agong-expresses-utmost-disappointment-over-revocation-emergency-ordinances-out-consent-istana-negara-311109.

[50] Istana Negara, Facebook (July 29, 2021). www.facebook.com/IstanaNegaraOfficial (translated from Malay by the author).

[51] See Anisah Shukry and Yantoultra Ngui, "Malaysia's New Prime Minister May Be Chosen through WhatsApp," *Bloomberg* (August 16, 2021), www.bloomberg.com/news/articles/2021-08-17/malaysia-s-king-summons-party-leaders-after-pm-quits-kini-says.

[52] See Shad Saleem Faruqi, "Political Instability and Enhanced Monarchy in Malaysia," *ISEAS Perspective* (February 25, 2022), 6, www.iseas.edu.sg/wp-content/uploads/2022/01/ISEAS_Perspective_2022_18.pdf.

13.4 CONCLUDING REFLECTIONS: CONSTITUTIONAL MONARCHY AND CONSTITUTIONAL DEMOCRACY

On August 5, 2017, in a speech at a convention held in the administrative capital city of Putrajaya, Sultan Nazrin Shah, the state Ruler of Perak, put forward his account of the constitutional monarch in striking terms:

> The King is not a rigid decorative ornament – without life – without soul .... It is a mistake to think that the role of a constitutional monarch is the same as that of a President, limited to what is written in the Constitution. The role of the Ruler goes above what is contained in the provisions of the Constitution.[53]

That statement would turn out to be predictive. In the four years after the speech was delivered, the monarch would emerge as a critical actor in the creation and governance of the federal government. When the Pakatan Harapan government collapsed in early 2020, the King intervened into the political dispute by appointing a new prime minister. And, as the new administration sought to maintain its tenuous hold on power while struggling to manage the coronavirus pandemic, the Agong came to play a crucial role in declaring the start, and the end, of emergency rule in the country. These royal interventions at the federal level throughout 2018 to 2021 placed the monarch at the very heart of the nation's constitutional politics.

Does an enhanced role for the monarch serve to protect or undermine constitutional democracy? Answers vary, unsurprisingly, depending on who you ask, and when that question is asked. For some, the constitutional monarch played a crucial part in "stabilizing" political crises and as a "check-and balance to the government in power."[54] Others have decried the royal assertiveness as illegitimate intrusions into the democratic process – indeed, some have called the monarch's actions a "royal coup"[55] – and voiced fears about "overreach by future

[53] Nazrin Shah, Sultan of Perak, Speech, "Institusi Beraja Satukan Negara" (Monarchical Institutions Unite the People), *Utusan Malaysia* (August 5, 2017) (translated from Malay by the author).

[54] Yang Razali Kassim, "Malaysia's Political Crisis: A New Power Twist?," *RSIS Commentary* (December 2, 2020), www.rsis.edu.sg/wp-content/uploads/2020/12/CO20206.pdf; Yang Razali Kassim, "Malaysia's King Becomes Kingmaker," *GIS* (November 13, 2020), www.gisreportsonline.com/r/malaysia-political-crisis/; Serina Rahman, "Commentary: Malaysia King's Role Comes into Sharper Focus as Country Sails through Bleakest COVID-19 Days," *Channel News Asia* (July 20, 2021), www.channelnewsasia.com/commentary/malaysia-king-role-sultans-agong-covid-19-parliament-rulers-2046151; see also A. Ananthalakshmi and Rozanna Latiff, "Malaysia's King Wins Plaudits during Political Storm," *Reuters* (October 27, 2020), www.reuters.com/article/us-malaysia-politics-royals/malaysias-king-wins-plaudits-during-political-storm-idUSKBN27C1M3.

[55] Editorial, "The Guardian View on a Royal Coup: A King Overturns a Historic Election," *The Guardian* (March 3, 2020), www.theguardian.com/commentisfree/2020/mar/03/the-guardian-view-on-a-royal-coup-a-king-overturns-a-historic-election#maincontent (discussing the King's appointment of Muhyiddin Yassin as prime minister in February 2020 and concluding that "a king has overturned a democratic election result that challenged a corrupt old order").

monarchs."[56] What seems undeniable is that the monarch's position and powers have been augmented to an extent not seen since before Malaysia's independence in 1957.

How and why has the monarch come to assume such an empowered position in contemporary constitutional governance?[57] Those viewing the King's enlarged powers as "substantially departing from Westminster-modelled constraints" raise concerns over whether recent interventions have left "a lasting imprint on an 'Eastminster Constitution' with an enhanced monarchy."[58] As Andrew Harding asks: "Do we live in postmodern world of constitutionalism in which even apparently defunct or declining institutions can take on new life, taking their place alongside both the familiar and the innovative?"[59]

The revival of constitutional monarchy in contemporary Malaysia underscores the ways in which constitutionalism and practices of constitutional governance exist beyond the written text. In terms of constitutional design, the Malaysian experience highlights how the drafting of the written constitution and the structure it sought to put in place may produce effects unintended by the framers. When Malaysia's Federal Constitution was created at the Federation's independence from the British, the nation's founding fathers envisaged a Westminster-model constitutional monarchy, with a symbolic role for the Rulers. It was clear, Kobkua Swannathat-Pian notes, that they "were not in favor of a return to a time where the Rulers had socio-political powers"; rather, it was their "ardent desire that the Rulers' role would be limited to simply that of the symbolic kind."[60] The framing of the constitutional text reflected these aspirations, with limited discretionary powers afforded to the King. Unlike Britain, Malaysia's constitutional system accorded supremacy to a written text.[61]

Yet, there can be significant play in the joints when it comes to constitutional text and constitutional practice. Even in countries that accord primacy to the written constitutional document, like the United States, constitutionalism is recognized also to encompass the actual institutional practices of government.[62] For emerging

56 Rozanna Latiff, "Monarchy Reshaped as Malaysia's King Looks to End Political Turmoil," *Reuters* (August 19, 2021), www.reuters.com/world/asia-pacific/monarchy-reshaped-malaysias-king-looks-end-political-turmoil-2021-08-19/ (quoting constitutional lawyer New Sin Yew); see also Joshua Kurlantzick, "Malaysia's Political Crisis Is Dooming Its COVID-19 Response," *Council on Foreign Relations* (July 26, 2021), www.cfr.org/article/malaysias-political-crisis-dooming-its-covid-19-response (stating that "the very fact that [the King] is wielding so much power is itself a blow to the country's democracy").

57 See generally Saleem Faruqi, "Political Instability and Enhanced Monarchy in Malaysia."

58 Ibid., 9.

59 Andrew Harding, "The Rulers and Centrality of Conventions in Malaysia's 'Eastminster' Constitution," in *Viceregalism: The Crown as Head of State in Political Crises in Postwar Commonwealth* ed. H. Kumarasingham. Palgrave Macmillan, 2020, 273.

60 Suwannathat-Pian, *Palace, Political Party, and Power*, 407.

61 *See* Federal Constitution of Malaysia 1957, Article 4(1) ("This Constitution is the supreme law of the Federation.").

62 See generally Samuel Issacharoff and Trevor W. Morrison, "Constitution by Convention," *California Law Review* 108: 1913–1954 (2020).

democracies in Southeast Asia – of which Malaysia is a case in point – institutional practices and constitutional conventions are far from being settled. In a setting in which constitutional norms are still in flux, institutional actors – like the monarch – have greater space to negotiate their role in constitutional governance. That's especially so in times of political turmoil, during which the lack of established constitutional rules and political norms often create a lacuna that allows, or even compels, a monarch to step in.

In times of political or constitutional crisis, a monarch may take on a key role to resolve the conflict.[63] Tom Ginsburg describes the monarch's function in this kind of situation as "crisis insurance."[64] Examples of sovereigns who have acted to provide a "focal point" during times of crisis include King Juan Carlos I denouncing the 1981 Spanish coup d'etat attempt in a televised address, or Thai King Bhumibol summoning the prime minister general and the leader of the anti-government protest movement to the palace in 1992 for a royal audience that was broadcast on television.[65] This account captures part of the story, although Malaysia's constitutional monarch has taken on a role that arguably goes beyond serving as a symbol of unity. The Agong emerged as the critical actor that directly facilitated the government's turnover in early 2020 by deciding who to appoint as prime minister.

Recall the King's unprecedented intervention in interviewing all the legislators individually to determine who commanded majority support during the government crisis in February 2020. "Politically neutral institutions such as the judiciary and monarchy attract attention in such circumstances as potential power-brokers," Harding observes.[66] Of course, many established democracies in the West have also witnessed the breakdown of what have been thought to be well-established political and constitutional norms. In many constitutional systems, the spotlight has been on the rise of the courts as the institution empowered to decide. We see this, for example, in the United Kingdom Supreme Court's invalidation of the Boris Johnson administration's prorogation of Parliament in the lead up to Brexit at the end of 2019.[67]

In a system of fragile (judicial) constitutionalism, as in Malaysia, it is the monarch that stepped into the breach by intervening in the immediate political moment.

63 See Ginsburg, "East Asian Monarchy in Comparative Perspective," 3. See also Michael Vatikiotis, "Monarchy and Modern Politics in Southeast Asia," *Brookings* (September 3, 2015), www.brookings.edu/opinions/monarchy-and-modern-politics-in-southeast-asia/; H. Kumarasingham, ed., *Viceregalism: The Crown as Head of State in Political Crises in the Postwar Commonwealth*. Palgrave Macmillan, 2020; Sonam Tshering, "Bhutan: The Role of the Constitutional Monarch in a Public Health Crisis," in *Covid-19 in Asia: Law and Policy Contexts* ed. Victor V. Ramraj. Oxford University Press, 2020, 279–293.

64 Ginsburg, "East Asian Monarchy in Comparative Perspective," 9.

65 Ibid., 9, 20.

66 Harding, "The Rulers and Centrality of Conventions in Malaysia's 'Eastminster' Constitution."

67 See R (on the application of Miller) v. The Prime Minister, Cherry and others v. Advocate General for Scotland [2019] UKSC 41; see also Yvonne Tew, "Strategic Judicial Empowerment," *American Journal of Comparative Law* 72 (2024), available at: https://doi.org/10.1093/ajcl/avad040.

Turning the lens to other monarchies in Southeast Asia, think of the neighboring state of Thailand. Although described as following "in form" a "Westminster-style constitutional monarchy ... in practice, the monarch [in Thailand] reserves the ultimate extra-constitutional powers to interpret, intervene, reject, or direct a course of action on the affairs of the state."[68] On this account this kind of assertive monarchy reflects a Southeast Asian model of constitutional monarchy.[69] Some have used the term "Eastminster" to describe British postcolonial systems that have developed and deviated from a Westminster model.[70] But cautionary tales exist, and monarch that is not circumspect about guarding their legacy risks damaging its institutional legitimacy and authority. [71]

The rules of democratic and constitutional engagement are not yet to be fully specified in regimes undergoing democratic transition(s),[72] or after a decades-long equilibrium has broken down in a dominant party system, as occurred in Malaysia. In such circumstances, a non-electorally legitimated institution – like the monarch – that draws on its reserve powers to intervene in a stabilizing capacity may well renegotiate its role in the country's governance.

Periods of instability or political transition may present a monarch with the opportunity to play a decisive role in modulating the transition process. A monarch's enhanced function in times of crisis may prove dysfunctional at a later time, however. And in a political system has emerged from an initial period of instability, it may prove challenging to tie the hands of a monarch that has come to wield an expansive part in affecting the democratic character of a regime.

68 Suwannathat-Pian, *Palace, Political Party, and Power*, 408; see also Kobkua Suwannathat-Pian, "The Hard Struggle," in *Kings, Country and Constitutions: Thailand's Political Development 1932–2000*. Routledge, 2003, 145–168.

69 Suwannathat-Pian, *Palace, Political Party, and Power*, 408–409.

70 H. Kumarasingham, "Eastminster – Decolonisation and State-Building in British Asia," in *Constitution-Making in Asia: Decolonisation and State-Building in the Aftermath of the British Empire* ed. H. Kumarasingham. Routledge, 2016, 1–36.

71 See, e.g., Kate Ng, "Coronavirus, Thai King Self-isolates in Alpine Hotel with Harem of 20 Women amid Pandemic," *Independent* (March 29, 2020), www.independent.co.uk/news/world/europe/coronavirus-thailand-king-maha-vajiralongkorn-grand-hotel-sonnebichl-germany-a9431936.html; Pavin Chachavalpongpun, Opinion, "Why Thais Are Losing Faith in Monarchy," *Washington Post* (May 15, 2020), www.washingtonpost.com/opinions/2020/05/15/why-thais-are-losing-faith-monarchy/.

72 See generally Adam Prezeworski, "The Games of Transition," in *Issues in Democratic Consolidation* ed. Scott Mainwaring, Guillermo O'Donnell, and J. Samuel Valenzuela. University of Notre Dame Press, 1992, 105.

Index

www.ingramcontent.com/pod-product-compliance
Lightning Source LLC
Chambersburg PA
CBHW072343140125
20401CB00004B/118